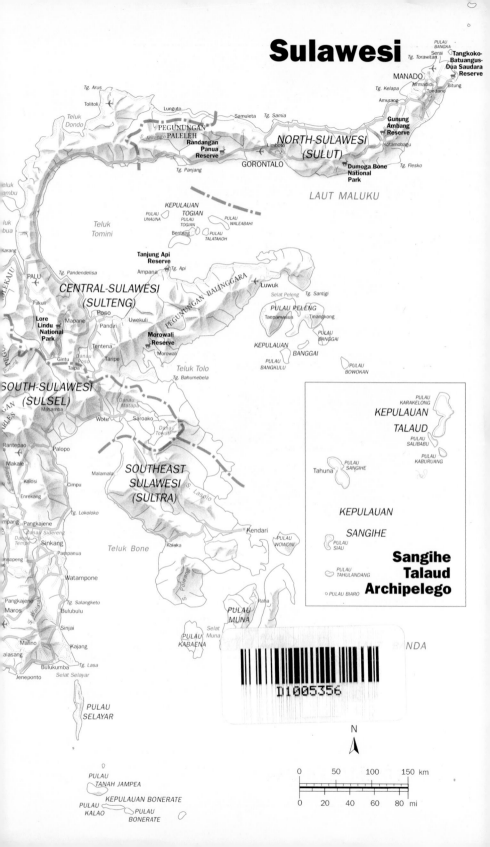

Sulawesi

PULAU
BANGKA
Serai
Tg. Torawitan
Tangkoko-
Batuangus-
Dua Saudara
Reserve
MANADO
Airmadidi
Tondano
Tg. Kelapa
Bitung
Amurang
Gunung
Ambang
Reserve
Kotamobagu

Tg. Arus
Tolitoli
Lunguto
Samuleta
Tg. Samia
Teluk
Dondo
PEGUNUNGAN
PALELEH
S. Milango
NORTH-SULAWESI
(SULUT)
Randangan
Panua
Reserve
Limboto
GORONTALO
Tg. Panjang
Tg. Flesko
Dumoga Bone
National
Park

LAUT MALUKU

Teluk
Tomini
KEPULAUAN
TOGIAN
PULAU
UNAUNA
PULAU
TOGIAN
PULAU
WALEABAHI
Benteng
PULAU
TALATAKOH

luk
ambu
luk
bua
Karang

Tanjung Api
Reserve
Tg. Api
Ampana

PALU
Tg. Pandendelisa
Luwuk
Selat Peleng
Tg. Santigi
CENTRAL-SULAWESI
(SULTENG)
Pakuli
PEGUNUNGAN-BALINGGARA
PULAU PELENG
Taepanasua
Tinandkong
Lore
Lindu
National
Park
Mapane
Poso
Uwekuli
Pandiri
PULAU
BANGGAI
Morowali
Reserve
KEPULAUAN
BANGGAI
Tentena
Morowali
PULAU
BANGKULU
Gintu
Danau
Poso
Taripe
Teluk Tolo
PULAU
BOWOKAN
Taipa
Tg. Bahumebela

SOUTH-SULAWESI
(SULSEL)
Masamba
Danau
Matapa
Wotu
Saroako
Danau
Tokuti
Rantepao
Palopo
Makale
Kalosi
Cimpu
Enrekang
Malamala
Tg. Lokoloko
mpang
Pangkajene
Danau Sidereng
Danau
Tempe
Sinkang
Panpanua
Kolaka
msopeng
Watampone
Teluk Bone
Kendari
PULAU
WOWONI
Pangkajene
Tg. Salangketo
Maros
Bulubulu
Sinjai
Malino
Kajang
alasang
Bulukumba
Tg. Lasa
Jeneponto
Selat Selayar
Raha
PULAU
MUNA
PULAU
KABAENA
Selat
Muna

Sangihe Talaud Archipelego

PULAU
KARAKELONG
KEPULAUAN
TALAUD
PULAU
SALIBABU
PULAU
KABURUANG
Tahuna
PULAU
SANGIHE
KEPULAUAN
SANGIHE
PULAU
SIAU
PULAU
TAHULANDANG
PULAU BIARO

NDA

N

PULAU
SELAYAR

PULAU
TANAH JAMPEA
KEPULAUAN BONERATE
PULAU
KALAO
PULAU
BONERATE

| 0 | 50 | 100 | 150 km |
| 0 | 20 | 40 | 60 | 80 mi |

SULAWESI
THE CELEBES

Edited by

TOBY ALICE VOLKMAN
and
IAN CALDWELL

PERIPLUS
EDITIONS

Sulawesi

South Sulawesi

Tana Toraja

Central Sulawesi

North Sulawesi

Southeast Sulawesi

ISBN 0-945971-10-9

Distributors:
United States of America
Passport Books/NTC, 4255 W. Touhy Avenue
Lincolnwood [Chicago], Illinois 60646
UK/Europe (except Benelux)
McCarta Ltd.
15 Highbury Place London N5 1QP
The Netherlands
Nilsson & Lamm bv
Postbus 195 1380 AD Weesp
Indonesia
C.V. Java Books
P.O. Box 55 JKCP Jakarta 10510
Singapore and Malaysia
Periplus (Singapore) Pte Ltd
Farrer Road P.O. Box 115 Singapore 9128

Publisher: Eric Oey
Designer: Peter Ivey
Cartography: Mary Chia

Cover: A Toraja man, wearing a boar-tooth necklace, takes part in a funeral ceremony. Behind him is the elaborately painted coffin of the deceased. By Kal Muller.
Pages 4-5: Toraja children stand outside the highland village of Paken early in the morning. By Deborah Hill.
Frontispiece: A Toraja noblewoman displays her finest beadwork at a funeral ceremony. By Kal Muller.

Periplus Travel Guides

SUMATRA

JAVA

BALI

KALIMANTAN
Indonesian Borneo

SULAWESI
The Celebes

EAST OF BALI
From Lombok to Timor

MALUKU
The Moluccas

IRIAN JAYA
Indonesian New Guinea

UNDERWATER INDONESIA
A Guide to the World's Best Diving

WEST MALAYSIA
and Singapore

MALAYSIAN BORNEO
Sabah and Sarawak (with Brunei)

The name PERIPLUS, meaning "voyage" or "journey," derives from the Greek. One of the earliest classical texts to mention Southeast Asia was the *Periplus of the Erythrean Sea*, an Alexandrian sailing manual dating from the first century AD. Periplus Editions, founded in 1988 by Eric Oey, specializes in the arts, cultures and natural history of the Malay archipelago—making authoritative information on the region available to a wider audience.

Contents

REQUEST: Much practical information in these travel guides is constantly changing. Addresses and prices change, hotels close their doors or have just opened, bus services are changed, travel bureaus go out of business or take new names. Periplus Editions has people on the road to check and add to our Practicalities sections, but we also welcome suggestions and tips from travelers, which will be printed in future editions. If you have recent information for future editions, please write to: Editorial Department, Periplus (S) Pte Ltd, Farrer Road P.O. Box 115, Singapore 9128, Republic of Singapore.

Periplus Editions
ADDITIONAL PUBLICATIONS

TRAVEL GUIDES

JAVA
ISBN 0-945971-11-7
BALI
ISBN 0-945971-08-7
SPICE ISLANDS (The Moluccas)
ISBN 0-945971-07-9
NEW GUINEA (Indonesian Irian Jaya)
ISBN 0-945971-06-0
BORNEO (Indonesian Kalimantan)
ISBN 0-945971-09-5
EAST OF BALI
ISBN 0-945256-12-5
SUMATRA
ISBN 0-945971-13-3
UNDERWATER INDONESIA
A guide to the world's best diving.
ISBN 0-945971-14-1

ARTS & CULTURE

TEXTILES IN BALI - Urs Ramseyer et al.
160 pages; hardback; ISBN 0-945971-29-X
MONUMENTAL BALI - A.J. Bernet Kempers
200 pages; hardback; ISBN 0-945971-16-8
BALINESE MUSIC - Michael Tenzer
144 pages; hardback; ISBN 0-945971-30-3
BOROBUDUR - J. Miksic and M. Tranchini
160 pages; hardback; ISBN 0-945971-15-x
WOODCARVINGS OF BALI
- Fred and Margaret Eiseman
96 pages; hardback; ISBN 0-945971-00-1
SEKALA & NISKALA I & II
- Fred and Margaret Eiseman
Insight into the unseen Bali: Religion, Ritual, Art, Tradition, Community Life, etc.
384 and 400 pages; ISBN 0-945971-3-6/5-2

NATURE

BIRDS OF BALI - Victor Mason
80 pages; hardback; ISBN 0-945971-04-4
FRUITS/FLOWERS OF BALI
- Fred and Margaret Eiseman
64 pages each; hardback;
ISBN 0-945971-02-8/01-X

HISTORY

BALI: A PARADISE CREATED - Adrian Vickers
The creation of Bali's Paradise-like image.
256 pages; ISBN 0-945971-28-1

PHOTOGRAPH BOOK

INDONESIA IN COLOR
- Kal Muller
147 Splendid photographs; outstanding text.
80 pages; ISBN 0-945971-26-5

PART I

Introducing Sulawesi

Like the petals of a windblown orchid, the unruly peninsulas of Sulawesi reach out into the Celebes, Molucca, Banda, and Flores seas. Within its odd, dancing outlines—the product of the collision of ancient continents—are found extraordinary landscapes. Rugged mist-covered mountains, primal tropical jungle, emerald-green rice terraces and deep, mysterious lakes dominate the interior. Along the coast, dazzling coral reefs encircle dormant volcanoes that jut dramatically out of the sea. Stretches of white sandy beach fringed with coconut trees and scattered fishing villages are flanked by rugged limestone outcroppings that might have stepped out of a Chinese painting.

Sulawesi—once known as the Celebes—is home to an amazing variety of peoples. Fishermen inhabit its coasts, catching flying fish, shark, tuna, mackerel, and squid, as well as scores of fish for which no names exist outside of the area. Sailing and trading peoples, in particular the Bugis, Makassar and Mandar peoples of the south, are renowned for their remarkable wooden sailing crafts and their voyages to destinations as distant as Singapore and Australia. There are lowland-dwelling peoples who farm wet and dry rice, maize and manioc, sago and vegetables, coffee, cacao, and cloves. Numerous small groups of upland peoples practice slash-and-burn agriculture in the interior. Dispersed along the coasts are the boat-dwelling Bajau, many of whom are now settled on land.

Sulawesi is home to Muslims, Christians, Buddhists, Hindus and Confucians, as well as followers of indigenous religions whose names are unknown. There are dancers, singers, and drummers; weavers of silk sarongs and exuberant *ikats*; pounders of bark cloth; forgers of iron; master architects of houses and sailing vessels.

With its tremendous expanse of coastline, Sulawesi has never been isolated from the outside world. For centuries, its skilled seafarers linked the island to extensive trading networks that brought not just goods but also ideas, practices and people from India, China, the Middle East, and Europe.

In the 1970s the colorful ritual life of Sulawesi's Toraja people was "discovered" by foreign tourists. But this remarkable culture constitutes only a part, albeit a stunning part, of the complex, ever-changing tapestry of the island. From the mysterious megaliths of the Bada Valley to the opulent Islamic Sultanate of Buton, the island of Sulawesi offers a visual and cultural feast for the traveler with sufficient time and a sense of adventure.

We have divided this book into five parts. Although Sulawesi consists officially of four provinces, a separate chapter has been devoted to Tana Toraja (part of the province of South Sulawesi), in part because it is the area most frequently visited by travelers to Sulawesi, and in part because of the striking cultural differences between the Toraja and other groups in the south. But while Tana Toraja is the area most frequently visited by travelers to Sulawesi, the other regions of the island are equally as fascinating.

We have sought to provide all the practical information a traveler needs to know, while at the same time offering a view of what the island is about: its history, its people, its social and cultural life, its contemporary struggles. The writers of this book, many of whom are experts in their fields, have attempted to convey their enthusiasm for Sulawesi along with a basic understanding of what has happened—and is still happening—on this remarkable island.

—*Toby Alice Volkman*

Overleaf: *The beautiful Toraja highlands. Photo by Deborah Hill.* **Opposite:** *A Bugis girl dressed in her traditional best. Her transparent outer garment is made of silk. In her hands she carries an old and rare* sirih *set made of Ming porcelain pieces held together by gold. Photo by Kal Muller.*

GEOGRAPHY

Oddly Shaped Island of Contrasts

Quite likely the world's most strangely shaped island, Sulawesi with its gangling appendages evokes the image of a drunken spider, or perhaps a scarecrow in a hurricane. The island is composed of a group of elongate land masses thrust together by geological shifts whose repercussions continue to this day. The island's flora and fauna have been greatly influenced by the island's proximity to the Philippines, the Lesser Sundas and the Moluccas, though not to any marked degree by its closest neighbor, Borneo. Yet its natural history is not totally Asian—its Australian links can be seen in eucalyptus trees and possums or phalangers.

The total land area of Sulawesi and its adjacent islands is 227,000 square kilometers (87,645 mi), a little smaller than England and Scotland combined. The distance from the northernmost island, Miangas (just 90 kilo-meters or 55 miles south of the Philippine island of Mindanao), to the southernmost, Satengar, is equivalent to a trip from Amsterdam to Moscow—nearly 2,000 kilometers (1,200 miles).

Sulawesi is divided into four provinces of unequal size. South and Central Sulawesi are the largest, at 83,000 sq km (32,000 sq mi) and 68,000 sq km (26,000 sq mi), respectively. Southeast Sulawesi is 36,000 sq km (14,000 sq mi). North Sulawesi, while extending over the greatest linear distance, is so narrow that it occupies only 25,000 sq km (10,000 sq mi), or just 13 percent of the island's surface area.

Turbulent beginnings

About 250 million years ago, the earth comprised two great continents: Laurasia (including present-day North America, Europe and much of Asia) and Gondwanaland (present-day South America, Africa, India, Australia, Antarctica and the rest of Asia). Up until the last decade, the widely accepted view of the geological history of Indonesia and surrounding regions was that the Malay Peninsula, Sumatra, Java, Borneo and western Sulawesi had been part of Laurasia, separate until just recently (geologically speaking) from eastern Sulawesi, Timor, Seram and other islands which had been part of more southerly Gondwanaland.

This picture has changed with the results of new geological work. It now appears that

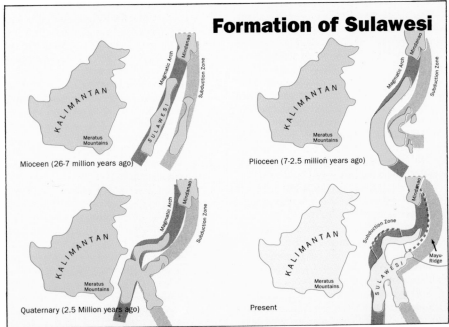

Formation of Sulawesi

Mioceen (26-7 million years ago)

Plioceen (7-2.5 million years ago)

Quaternary (2.5 Million years ago)

Present

southern Tibet, Burma, Thailand, the Malay Peninsula and Sumatra were actually part of Gondwanaland, and that they rifted from the margin of the Australia-New Guinea part of the continent some 200 million years ago. Western Sulawesi, together with Sumatra, Borneo and other islands, is thought to have separated from Gondwanaland about 180 million years ago. Some 90 million years later, eastern Sulawesi, together with New Guinea, the Moluccas and Australia, broke away from Antarctica, and galloped northward at 10 centimeters (4 inches) a year.

About 15 million years ago, what is now eastern Sulawesi separated from New Guinea and collided with land that is now western Sulawesi, hitting it like a spearhead and causing the southwest peninsula to rotate counter-clockwise. The Gulf of Bone was created between South and Southeast Sulawesi, and the north-pointing northern peninsula pivoted about its tip, rotating clockwise 90 degrees (see map).

It has been suggested that three million years ago western Sulawesi collided with eastern Borneo, closing the Makassar Strait. Hard evidence to support this theory is lacking, but along the northern and deeper parts of the strait, the submarine contours of eastern Borneo do fit neatly into western Sulawesi. Thick sediments in the Makassar Strait indicate, however, that the straits have been open for at least 25 million years.

Sea levels have risen and fallen considerably during the last 10 million years in coordination with the waxing and waning of the Ice Ages. During times when the sea level was low, islands surfaced, particularly in the south. When sea levels were 100 meters (330 ft) lower than today, an almost continuous sheet of land would have stretched between southeast Borneo and southwest Sulawesi. When seas were high, Sulawesi would have comprised a number of islands dissected by straits near Gorontalo and Lake Tempe.

The most recent peak in sea level was about 4,000 years ago, when the sea was five to six meters (16 to 19 ft) higher than at present. Sulawesians tell stories of a time when travelers did not have to sail round the southern tip of Sulawesi, but could take a short cut from the Gulf of Bone to the Makassar Strait through the then brackish Lake Tempe.

Still-active fault lines stretch across Sulawesi—near Gorontalo, from Palu south to Koro, through Lake Matana, and near Luwuk. The main island is still undergoing a process of fragmentation, and Sulawesi in the

distant future could become a cluster of islands separated by narrow straits, like the Philippine archipelago today.

Coasts and reefs

With its several long and narrow peninsulas, Sulawesi has more coastline relative to its land area than any other Indonesian island. No point on the mainland is more than 90 km (56 m.) away from the sea, and most are within 50 km (30 mi). In addition, the four provinces include more than 110 offshore islands with land areas in excess of 1.5 sq km (1 sq mi).

Coral reefs occur around most of Sulawesi's shores. The most accessible (and therefore disturbed) are the 16,000 sq km (6,180 sq mi) of reef in the Sangkarang or Spermonde archipelago. The reefs around Bunaken and neighboring islands off Manado in the north are also quite accessible. Less well-known are the coral reefs of the Togian Islands in Tomini Bay. These are unique in Indonesia because all the major reef environments—fringing, barrier and atoll—can be found around their shores. Sulawesi also boasts some very remote and little-disturbed reefs and shoals, such as those at the extreme end of the Tukang Besi Islands in Southeast Sulawesi.

Above: *Morning breaks through the canopy of a North Sulawesi forest .*

ALAIN COMPOST

Volcanoes and rock formations

Sulawesi is largely mountainous. Most of the island lies above 500 meters (1,650 ft), and fully one-fifth lies above the 1,000-meter mark (3,300 ft). The highest peaks are found in Central and northern South Sulawesi; the island's highest point is on Mt. Rantemario, north of Enrekang, at 3,450 meters (11,200 ft). The climb to the summit is strenuous—and very cold—and the mountain can be reached from the south, with two nights spent on the slopes.

In South Sulawesi there are several dead volcanoes whose debris has contributed, as in Java, to the fertility of the surrounding plains. The most prominent of these is Lompobatang ("swollen belly"), southeast of Ujung Pandang.

Northern Sulawesi's volcanoes are far from dead. In 1983 a mighty eruption sent a plume of ash 15 km (9 mi) into the sky, with some falling 900 km (560 mi) away in southeast Kalimantan. The explosion blew apart the small island of Una Una in Tomini Bay: fortunately, the Vulcanology Service had predicted a major eruption and all the island's inhabitants were safely evacuated.

Sulawesi has 11 active volcanoes (Java has 17 and Sumatra 10) and many fumaroles (crevices through which hot vapors issue) and volcanic springs. The majority are in the Minahasa region of North Sulawesi. In the last decade the most troublesome volcanoes

have been Soputan-Aeseput, Lokon-Empung, and Gunung Api Siau on the island of Siau, between the mainland and Sangihe Island. Sangihe Island's volcano, Awu, erupted in 1966, claiming more than 7,300 lives.

These volcanoes are active because the seabed north of Tolitoli and east of Minahasa and the Sangihe arc is moving toward the northern arm of Sulawesi. Instead of piling up in a crumpled heap, the seabed is forced under the island at an angle of some 60 degrees. The enormous forces and friction involved produces earthquakes and heat so intense that the rocks melt. The molten stone generally cools down way beneath the earth's surface. But on occasion it is forced up through a weakness in the crust, and the volcano above it erupts.

Parts of Sulawesi (in the south and southeast) have the greatest extent of ultrabasic rocks in the world. These rocks yield notoriously infertile soils, due to high levels of magnesium and heavy metals. The distribution of ultrabasic rock is marked by the boundary between uncultivated and cultivated land (except where overambitious resettlement or agricultural schemes have tried to cultivate land farmers would never touch).

Mineral wealth

Sulawesi is blessed with considerable mineral deposits. Parts of the north are currently experiencing a gold rush, with individuals and small companies using traditional methods of extracting the metal. At the upper end of the scale, joint ventures between Indonesian and foreign companies conduct detailed surveys and state-of-the-art mining.

Petroleum fields have been discovered, but none has yet been exploited commercially. Oil has been found south of the eastern arm of Sulawesi near Luwuk; this area may become a production field in the not-too-distant future. Large reserves of natural gas exist near Lake Tempe. Buton Island off Southeast Sulawesi holds Asia's largest deposits of natural asphalt.

The island's largest mine, at Soroako on the shores of Lake Matana, is situated on a huge deposit of low-grade nickel. Inco, a Canadian-based company, began to construct

Above: *A cascading waterfall in North Sulawesi. The island has no long rivers, but waterfalls are common in the island's limestone hills.*
Opposite: *Mount Lokon near Tomohon in North Sulawesi. This active volcano recently erupted, evaporating the lake seen here.*

its massive processing facilities here in 1968. The ores in this ultrabasic rock have transformed life in a former village of shifting cultivators, and the once dense green jungle that was their source of livelihood has been razed.

Lakes and rivers

Sulawesi has 13 lakes of more than 5 sq km surface area, including Towuti and Poso, the second and third largest lakes in Indonesia. In the wet season, Lake Tempe rivals Lake Poso in size: surrounded by low-lying land, it can more than treble in area from 10,000 to 35,000 hectares (25,000 to 86,5000 acres). Some lakes, like Tondano and Moat in North Sulawesi, occupy the craters of old volcanoes, while others have been formed by tectonic activity. Some are extremely deep, such as Lake Matana. The bottom of Lake Matana, 540 meters (1,755 ft) from the surface, lies 160 meters (520 ft) below sea level.

The shape of Sulawesi precludes the development of any large rivers such as those found on Sumatra or Kalimantan. The longest river in Sulawesi, the Lariang which flows into the Makassar Strait below Palu, is barely 200 km (120 mi) long.

Climate

Starting in September, cool northwesterly winds pick up moisture while crossing the South China Sea, and arrive in North Sulawesi via the Sulawesi Sea in about November. Similar winds arrive on the west coast of South Sulawesi via the Java Sea in late November or early December. The west coast of central Sulawesi is sheltered from the effects of these winds by the close presence of Borneo, and so is relatively drier.

By April, variable humid southeasterly winds blow toward eastern Sulawesi. Rainfall peaks on the southeast coast occur between then and June, and on the northeast coast sometime later. Southeasterly winds from the now dry and wintery Australian land mass become stronger and drier, influencing Sulawesi's southern tips. Jeneponto in the southwestern peninsula has a long dry season between April and November, while Manado on the northern peninsula experiences a short dry season from August to October.

Areas on the west coast of Sulawesi tend to have their highest rainfall in December, whereas those on the east coast have their wettest month around May. There are areas between these with two dry seasons. Valleys oriented in a north-south direction are in a rain shadow for virtually the whole year. The sheltered nature of the central part of the west coast results in the Palu Valley being one of the driest areas in Indonesia, with yearly rainfall of less than 600 mm (24 in). Here, and on the dry tip of the southwest peninsula, the thriving prickly pear cactus testifies to the severity of the climate.

— *Tony Whitten*

ALAIN COMPOST

FLORA AND FAUNA

Straddling Wallace's Line

The great 19th-century naturalist Alfred Russel Wallace was the first to observe that the Indonesian archipelago is inhabited by two distinct sets of wildlife. "Wallace's Line," as this boundary is still known, is drawn between Bali and Lombok and between Borneo and Sulawesi. The birds and mammals of Borneo and Sulawesi are strikingly different, although the islands are not separated by any significant physical barrier. For botanists, the line is less apparent: Sulawesi's plants appear to be most closely related to those of other dry parts of the archipelago.

What little is known of the island's prehistoric wildlife comes from fossils excavated in river sediments in South Sulawesi. Among the finds are an enormous tortoise with a shell two meters (6.5 ft) long, a pygmy elephant and a giant pig. There are also two stegodonts, similar to modern elephants but with curved tusks growing closely together. It is believed that these animals probably swam north to Sulawesi from the Lesser Sunda Islands.

These beasts became extinct thousands of years ago, but even today Sulawesi is noted for its peculiar fauna. Of 127 native mammal species, 62 percent (79 species) are found only on Sulawesi, a figure which rises to an astounding 98 percent if 62 species of bats are excluded. By comparison, only 18 percent of Borneo's mammalian species are endemic. Sulawesi's birds are a bit less distinctive, but still exceptional: 34 percent of the non-migratory species are found nowhere else, the highest figure in Asia except for the island of New Guinea.

Extraordinary mammals

The largest Sulawesi mammal is the dwarf buffalo, or *anoa*. There are two species: one in the mountains with smooth conical horns, and the rough-horned lowland *anoa*. Captive *anoa* sometimes may be seen in villages, but no attempt should be made to approach them. Although they look like small versions of placid water buffalo, they are unpredictable and aggressive, and sensibly feared by locals. *Anoa* are generally solitary but will share a single water spring. They are sometimes shot (illegally) by hunters who know the spots and wait in nearby blinds.

Perhaps the strangest of Sulawesi's mam-

ALAIN COMPOST

mals is the enigmatic *babirusa,* or "pig deer." The male's upper canine teeth, while initially growing normally, turn upwards so that they pierce the skin and curl around toward (though not quite into) the skull. These tusks appear to be used in fighting, to jab other males. If a *babirusa* can hook his curved upper tusk over an adversary's lower one, the latter is rendered useless and the advantaged male can stab his opponent's throat or face.

Babirusa were kept by early rulers and may have been given as gifts to visiting emissaries. It is likely that some were brought by Bugis traders to Bali, where they may have inspired demonic *raksasa* masks. Interestingly, the *babirusa,* whose hoof is uncloven, is considered *halal* (permitted, or "kosher") by local Muslims.

Tailless monkeys

Sulawesi is home to four species of black or brown tailless macaques, whose ancestors may have arrived from Borneo. All four species live in forests in groups of 15 to 30. They may be seen in great numbers at the splendid Tangkoko-Batuangas Reserve on the northern tip of North Sulawesi.

The tarsier, another local native, is among the world's smallest primates, with head and body length of just 10 cm (4 in), a tail twice as long, enormous eyes, and a weight of just 100 grams. Tarsiers live in family groups consisting of an adult pair and their offspring. Just

before dawn, when they cease their nocturnal perambulations, the entire family sings a complicated territorial call of squeeks and squeals. After the song, the group retires to its nest hole in a tree, a thicket, or in tangles of roots and vines. Tarsiers live in a wide range of habitats including secondary scrub and even urban areas (though humans may not be aware of their presence).

The only other medium-sized mammals in the canopies of Sulawesi's forests are two cuscuses. The slow-moving, dark-brown bear cuscus can be seen during the day feeding on leaves. The dwarf cuscus is nocturnal (hence rarely seen), and feeds on fruit. Both species have a prehensile tail which they use as a fifth limb when climbing from tree to tree.

Dazzling birds

Most remarkable among the 88 bird species found only on Sulawesi are the dark green Purple-bearded Bee-eater, the brightly colored Red-knobbed Hornbill, the Crowned Mynah, the long-tailed White-necked Mynah, the black and white Piping Crow, and the Finch-billed Starling which nests in hundreds of holes pecked out of dead trees. Several bird species are rare, and the Caerulean Paradise Flycatcher of the Sangihe Islands

Opposite: *The bear cuscus, a shy and slow-moving leaf-eater.* **Below:** *The rare* anoa, *a dog-sized buffalo, is unique to Sulawesi.*

may have recently become extinct, its forest habitat having been almost entirely converted to coconut plantations. Sulawesi's most unusual bird is surely the Maleo (see "The Maleo Bird," page 213), which incubates its 250-gram eggs in mounds of soil warmed by sunlight, hot springs, or volcanic vents.

Endangered fish

Some of the most remarkable animals in Sulawesi are the residents of the high lakes, such as Matana, Towuti, Mahalona, and Wawontoa. Of the 60 species of crustaceans, snails, and fish unique to those lakes, only one—a shrimp—is found in all four. Each lake appears to have evolved its own fauna. Two other large lakes, Poso and Lindu, share

ALAIN COMPOST

members of a group of fish unknown outside Sulawesi. Unfortunately, species from elsewhere in Indonesia have been introduced for fisheries without regard to the native animals, and some of the latter have become rare, perhaps even extinct, due to competition or newly introduced parasites.

Cave life

Sulwaesi has large areas of limestone around Bantimurung (near Maros), between Lakes Matana and Towuti, and southeast of Lake Towuti. The majority of these areas are rich in caves, some of them among the longest in Indonesia, and most can be explored for some distance without specialized equipment. Commonly encountered residents of

the grottos are swiftlets (small echo-locating relatives of the common swifts) and a variety of bats; there are also scuttling cockroaches, nightmarish spiders, grotesque whip-scorpions and crickets with huge antennae. A hitherto unknown species of blind shrimp was recently found in one of the Bantimurung caves, indicating that it has been there long enough to adapt to total darknesss.

Coconut crabs and giant turtles

The sandy beaches of Sulawesi are used as nesting sites by four species of sea turtle. The largest of these is the enormous leatherback turtle, or *Dermochelys coriacea,* which has a dark brown, ridged carapace (upper shell) up to 2.5 meters (8 ft) long and can weigh up to a ton. It is one of the curiosities of nature that this species feeds solely on jellyfish. It is a strong swimmer and can maintain a body temperature 18 degrees above sea temperature. Individuals migrate over long distances, and though generally limited to the tropics they have been found as far away as the Arctic Circle.

No description of Sulawesi's exotica would be complete without mentioning the famous coconut crab. Once widely distributed throughout the western Pacific and eastern Indian oceans, in Sulawesi the coconut crab is now restricted to small islands, preferably those unblemished by man. What makes this crab stand out in a crowd is his fabled ingenuity and skill in gathering his food. According to legend, the crab scurries up the trunk of a coconut palm, snips off a juicy pod, then dashes it to the ground to crack it open, after which he rips into it with his powerful pincers. While the crabs do actually use their claws to open coconuts, accounts of the tree-climbing bit are not reliable, usually third-hand or second-hand at best. If you catch one in the act, let us know.

Sulawesi is also the home of the world's largest snake, a 10-meter-long reticulated python. Estuarine crocodiles used to be common around the coasts of Sulawesi, as well as in its rivers and some lakes. Not many decades ago, riverside villages had to be protected by sturdy fences to prevent crocodiles from entering at night. In local lore, crocodiles are often associated with the ancestors and are treated with respect.

— *Tony Whitten*

Above: *The Celebes macaque.* **Opposite:** *The* babirusa *or "pig-deer" in his wallow.*

PREHISTORY

Hunters, Gatherers and Navigators

From the viewpoint of early human history, just as early animal history, the single most important observation about Sulawesi is that it lies within Wallacea, the region of deep water and islands separating the continental shelves of Australasia and Asia. Thus, unlike what was the case for Java, Sumatra, and Borneo, no land bridge connected Sulawesi to the Asian continent during the last ice age

In Java are found remains of Homo erectus as old as around 1,000,000 BC; whereas Australia and New Guinea were not clearly settled until around 40,000 years ago. And although geography suggests that these settlers first came by sea from Asia via Sulawesi and the Lesser Sunda Islands, direct evidence of human occupation in Sulawesi only begins at around 30,000 BC.

This archeological evidence comes from a single cave in the limestone hills near Maros, northeast of Ujung Pandang. Here, some 30,000 years ago, families were collecting riverine shellfish and making fine flakes and blades of chert. Pebble tools and flakes which might be older have been collected from river terraces in the Walanae Valley between Soppeng and Sengkang, together with the bones of extinct giant pigs and elephants, including the important genus *Stegodon*. The age of the Walanae tools is uncertain—the stone tools and animal bones could have been washed together from different sources by river action—and though cruder than those from Maros, they are not necessarily older.

Beginning of the Holocene Period

About 10,000 years ago the present interglacial period—the Holocene—began. In the cave at Ulu Leang in the limestone hills of Maros, deposits dating between 10,000 and 7,000 years have produced thick chunky stone flakes and cores of chert, characteristic of both Indonesia and Australia at this time.

The inhabitants of Ulu Leang lived by hunting and gathering. Few traces of their plant foods have survived, but a mound of shells at Paso, on the shores of Lake Tondano in Minahasa, was built up over several centuries from the shells of edible gastropods from the nearby lake. Both sites have produced the bones of wild pigs, together with smaller numbers of bones of *anoa*, monkeys, rodents, birds, tortoises and snakes. Pigs do not appear to have been domesticated until the beginnings of settled agriculture, perhaps as late as four thousand years ago.

Maros points and microliths

About 8,000 years ago, the stone tool industries of the southwestern peninsula of Sulawesi underwent major changes. Small blade tools and microliths made a sudden appearance in the southwest peninsula, as they did at similar dates in the Philippines, Australia, and parts of Java. It is difficult to explain these changes. At present there is no evidence to suggest settlement by a new population in Sulawesi—neither is there any evidence that such tools were made elsewhere in Sulawesi—though possibly improved techniques of stone tool-making, especially for arrowheads and spearheads, were introduced from some unknown outside region.

The Toalean stone-tool industry of South Sulawesi is the most elaborate of these new industries discovered anywhere in Southeast Asia. (The Swiss Sarasin cousins who discovered it in 1902 supposed the Toale people, who still lived in the forests and caves of Camba, to be the physical descendents of the prehistoric stone toolmakers.) Toalean sites occur in caves, rock shelters, and in open locations on slightly raised alluvial deposits near rivers. The best sequence comes from the higher levels of the shelter of Ulu Leang, where small elongated or trapezoidal-shaped microliths appeared about 8,000 years ago and distinctive hollow-based and serrated projectile points ("Maros points") at about 6,000 years.

Other artefacts found in Toalian levels include flakes with an edge gloss that may have resulted from mat or basket manufacture, bone points, and possible bivalve shell scrapers. Like their predecessors, the Toalians also hunted native Sulawesi mammals—tree-dwelling marsupials, macaque monkeys, civet cats, *anoa*, and pigs (both *Sus*

Opposite: *The exquisitely crafted Dong Son drum of Selayar, probably cast in Viet Nam at the beginning of the first millenium AD.*

celebensis and the unique Sulawesi *babirusa*).

Paintings of pigs and "hand stencils" (outlines of human hands made by blowing red haematite pigment over a hand placed flat onto a surface) are found in some Toalean caves. The hand paintings are paralleled in the rock art of Australia, and while the Maros examples cannot be dated, they could well belong to the pre-agricultural era marked by the Toalian tools.

The Austronesians

The present inhabitants of Sulawesi speak Austronesian languages introduced to the island from the north, via Taiwan and the Philippines, about 4,000 years ago. The modern population of Sulawesi is part of the southern Mongoloid grouping which today occupies most of Southeast Asia. The current explanation for this major period of human expansion, which affected all the islands of Southeast Asia, is that it was linked to population growth and a need to clear new coastal lands for cultivation, though trade may also have been a factor. Early Austronesian-speakers are known to have been adept canoe builders and navigators—many of them settled the far-flung islands of Polynesia.

The hunters and gatherers who occupied Sulawesi until about 4,000 years ago, and whose archaeological remains have just been described, are presumed to have been of generalized Australo-Melanesian physical appearance, according to the rather slight skeletal evidence which has survived in other parts of Indonesia. We will never be able to trace the languages spoken by these groups, even though some of these populations might still have existed as isolated groups until recent centuries. Many of their genes undoubtedly live on today in the modern inland populations of the island.

The early agricultural pioneers of Sulawesi were few in number, and probably restricted to the coastal regions. The equatorial rain forests and wet climates of interior Sulawesi would not have been favorable to stone-using rice cultivators. Settlement of these areas may not have occurred until well within the last 2,000 years, by which time iron tools were widely available, but rice may have arrived in the island as early as 2,000 BC, since it is known to have been grown in Borneo at this time.

The most important Neolithic site discovered to date on Sulawesi lies close to the Karama River at Kalumpang, inland from Mamuju in the west-central part of the island. Kalumpang has produced a remarkable range of stone adzes, slate spearheads, a stone bark cloth beater (bark cloth was used before loom-woven cloth in Indonesia), and fascinating pottery with fine and detailed geometric ornamentation. Although the Kalumpang find is undatable, similar pottery found in Sabah in East Malaysia is as old as

3,000 years. The Kalumpang assemblage as a whole may be related to that carried by the first Austronesian-speaking settlers of the Pacific islands, bearers of the so-called Lapita culture.

The Bronze and Iron Ages

By about 2,000 years ago the peoples of Sulawesi had learned how to cast bronze and smelt iron. By this time, they would have found themselves on the edge of the zone of Indian influence which was to be so important for Bali and Java. Sulawesi was never "Indianized" to any major extent, and even its coastal cultures may be considered fundamentally Austronesian until the spread of Islam in the sixteenth and seventeenth centuries. However glass, carnelian, and agate beads of Indian inspiration, and in some instances even of Indian manufacture, were imported into the island and are found in the majority of Metal Age sites.

Metal Age artifacts and sites are known from many parts of the island, although these do not so far include any specimens of the massive Vietnamese Dong Son bronze drums which were widely distributed across southern Indonesia from about 2,000 years ago. The closest example in geographical terms is the splendid drum from Selayar Island, with its characteristic friezes of birds and feathered warriors (the latter highly schematic, shown around the middle of the mantle), and its more naturalistic and unique elephants and peacocks. It may have been manufactured in Vietnam in about AD 200; elephants and peacock are unlikely to have been introduced into Sulawesi as early as this.

Another famous bronze object, the large "flask" purchased in Ujung Pandang and now on display in the Jakarta Museum, has stylistic features, including a face mask, which relate it to the massive bronze drum from Pejeng in Bali. Both of these items are probably of local Indonesian rather than Vietnamese manufacture, but whether the flask was actually made in Sulawesi we may never know.

During the first millennium AD the inhabitants of Sulawesi appear to have adopted the custom, common at this time in the Philippines and parts of Borneo, of burying the bones of the dead in pottery jars in caves. Several assemblages of this type are known from the Maros caves in the southwest, but the best-documented one comes from a cave called Leang Buidane in the Talaud Islands northeast of Manado. The mortal remains of the Leang Buidane people were placed in large jars and pottery boxes on the cave floor, and were accompanied into the afterlife by small and finely decorated pots, carnelian and agate beads from India, bronze axes and iron tools, and shell and glass bracelets. These artifacts probably date to some time during the first millennium AD. Sites with

KAL MULLER

IAN CALDWELL

almost identical assemblages have been discovered in coastal portions of Borneo and the Philippines around the Sulawesi Sea, attesting to considerable inter-island trade and contact at this time.

Burial jars and statues

Other well-known archaeological features of Sulawesi include the remarkable *kalamba,* stone burial jars with carved lids which are located in the Lore Lindu National Park in the mountains west of Lake Poso, in the central part of the island. Some of the jars near Besoa and Bada recently investigated by Indonesian archaeologists have yielded pottery and items of iron, and the general context suggests a first-millennium AD date. Near the jars, there are a number of large stone statues up to four meters (13 ft) high, with carved features including headbands, carved flat nipples, and clearly delineated genitalia of both sexes. (See "Bada Valley," page 168.)

When this ancient culture first became known to scholars shortly before the First World War, the megaliths were ascribed to an Aryan, Mediterranean people, who had supposedly wandered through the archipelago searching for gold and pearls. This strange hypothetical people was thought to have brought the art of constructing irrigated terraced paddy fields, of carving in stone, of washing gold and working metals. Today the megaliths are recognised as part of the general Austronesian culture which spread across Indonesia and the Pacific starting 5,000 years ago.

Other large stone monuments of Sulawesi—the circles and rows of standing stone memorial pillars which are found throughout the Toraja region around Rantepao, together with the *waruga,* stone burial jars of Minahasa—are most probably of fairly recent date, although none of these monuments have yet been thoroughly investigated by archaeologists. The *waruga* are generally believed to be associated with Chinese pottery, which was probably not imported into Sulawesi until around AD 1400. The so-called "megalithic" tradition that pervades many Sulawesi cultures is not, however, an easy subject for archaeological investigation, mainly because the structures rarely exist in undisputed association with datable artifacts, as they are not usually buried underground. Nonetheless, the use of upright stones, sometimes carved in human form, is so widespread in the Austronesian world that it is undoubtedly a tradition of great antiquity.

—*Peter Bellwood*

Opposite: *A stone figure of unknown origin in the Bada Valley stares across the millennia.*
Above: *"Hand stencils" on cave walls near Maros in Southeast Sulawesi, produced by blowing haematite over a hand, may be very old.*

EARLY HISTORY

Ancient Kingdoms of the South

May my mouth be torn open, may my tongue be torn out, may my head be split open should I cause offense. Now he who was called Simpurusia descended into the world and she who was called Patiajala arose also from the foam of the wave; she married Simpurusia, may I not swell...

Thus begins the Chronicle of Luwu, the oldest, and for several centuries the most powerful kingdom in Sulawesi. Simpurusia's name is a corruption of Sanskrit *sinhapurusa*, "lion-man," while his wife's name—also Sanskrit—means "she who trapped her lord in the snares of a net." But Indian influence was slight: unlike Java or Bali, Sulawesi has no great temples or stone inscriptions, and the Indian epics, the *Ramayana* and *Mahabharata*, are completely unknown.

Simpurusia and Patiajala are probably composite figures, the distant memories of ancient rulers, perhaps dating back to the first millenium AD, for Luwu's origins are shadowy. Most historians place its early capital on the Cerekang River, about halfway between Wotu and the sleepy village of Ussu. Here, according to the epic Bugis poem *I La Galigo*, the gods descended to earth to establish the first kingdom in South Sulawesi. The son of the second ruler, Sawerigading, is a great seafarer, and the places he visited are mentioned: Taranate (Ternate in the Moluccas), Gima (Bima on Sumbawa), Jawa Rilau and Jawa Ritengga (East and Central Java). After many adventures he marries Wé Cudai, a princess of Cina, a prehistoric kingdom recently discovered near the mouth of the Cenrana River. And if we accept Luwu's location in the Wotu-Ussu region, awaiting discovery somewhere along the Cerekang River lies her ruined capital, Ware.

Makassar chronicles

The early history of Sulawesi is, in effect, the history of South Sulawesi. There are no known chronicles from the other three provinces dating back to pre-Islamic times. Bugis, Makassar and (as yet unexamined) Mandarese chronicles form our only real sources before the arrival of Dutch traders in the early 17th century. From these chronicles, we learn that 15th century Luwu dominated the entire east and south coast, and the west coast as far as Makassar. Her economy was based on trade. Valuable resins and alluvial gold—and perhaps also slaves—were brought down the pass leading from Rantepao to Palopo (a much more likely location for Luwu's capital) in exchange for fish, salt and weapons. Nickel and iron ore dug from mines near Malili was exported to Java, where even today, a certain type of laminated nickel in the Javanese *keris* is called *pamor* (damascene) *Luwu*.

The origins of the kingdoms of South Sulawesi can be traced to the 13th-14th centuries. This is the limit of the written sources, as the Bugis-Makassar script (probably based on a South Sumatran script) was invented around the year 1400. A recent archaeological survey of the landlocked kingdom of Soppeng has revealed a large kingdom dominating much of the central Walanae Valley as early as AD 1200. The capital of this kingdom, called West Soppeng, was on a hilltop seven kilometers (4.2 mi) north of Watasoppeng. More than 2,000 pieces of broken Chinese, Vietnamese and Thai stoneware and porcelain sherds were collected from the site, many dating back to the 12th or 13th century. Away from the wooden palaces and warehouses, at the far end of the hill, lay the graves of her 15th- and 16th-century rulers, some still containing pieces of the blue-and-white Ming jars in which their cremated remains were once placed.

Chiefdoms and conflict

What was Sulawesi like before the arrival of Europeans in the 16th and 17th centuries? The southern peninsula was divided into several large kingdoms, occupying roughly the same areas as the modern *kabupaten* (regencies) which today bear their names. These kingdoms consisted of a number of chiefdoms—28 in the case of Soppeng—each with its own ruler and territory, loosely united round a central "king." The king ruled direct-

Opposite: *18th-century representation of a king of Makassar touring his realm by boat. Europeans at this time would have seen a Sulawesi virtually unchanged for several centuries.*

ly only his own chiefdom; the rest of the territory was administered by his chiefs, an arrangement which at times must have severely limited his power.

Islam did not become an official religion until the 17th century. Sulawesians may have worshipped the sun and moon, as early Moslem graves are oriented east-west rather than north-south as is the Islamic custom. The ruler, seen as the source of fertility, took part in elaborate rituals assisted by his transvestite *bissu* priests, who appear to have originally been, or included, women.

Ruling power was limited to a small hereditary elite, believed to belong to the line of the *tomanurung*, heaven-descended founders of the kingdoms. Purity of descent was jealously guarded, and careful records were kept of the royal families and their marriages. Marriage of a woman to a man of lower status was strictly forbidden under pain of death.

Both women and men could rule. The first historical individual about whom we have any real information is a queen of Soppeng who ruled around the year 1400. A powerful monarch (the chronicle of Soppeng states that she "broke the long and split the broad"), her reign is remembered as a time of prosperity and good harvests. She directed the expansion of wet-rice agriculture along the southern edge of Lake Tempe, to which settlers flocked "as ants to sugar."

The 15th century saw an important shift from trade to wet-rice agriculture as the basis of political power. Several rulers are remembered as having "taken an interest in agriculture." Luwu, which had little agricultural land (her staple food was sago) was challenged by Bone, situated on a large and fertile plain. Three times in the 16th century the armies of Luwu and Bone clashed. On the third occasion, Luwu was defeated: her royal umbrella was captured and the ruler of Luwu allowed to flee—on the express orders of the king of Bone—with just 20 of his men.

The rise of Gowa

Bone's great rival was Gowa, 17th-century Sulawesi's most prosperous and powerful kingdom. Gowa's rise was also rapid: in the early 16th century, it was just one of a number of small chiefdoms located on the southwest coastal plain. Through a series of conquests and alliances, by 1600 Gowa (allied with neighboring Tallo) had wrested control of most of the western and southern coasts of the peninsula. A palace coup in 1593 brought Karaeng Matoaya, an ambitious and capable Tallo prince, to the seat of power. Around 1605 he embraced Islam, then proceded to forcefully Islamize the major Bugis kingdoms (with the exception of Luwu, which had accepted Islam in 1603) in a series of battles through which Gowa established itself as the preeminent power on the peninsula.

—*Ian Caldwell*

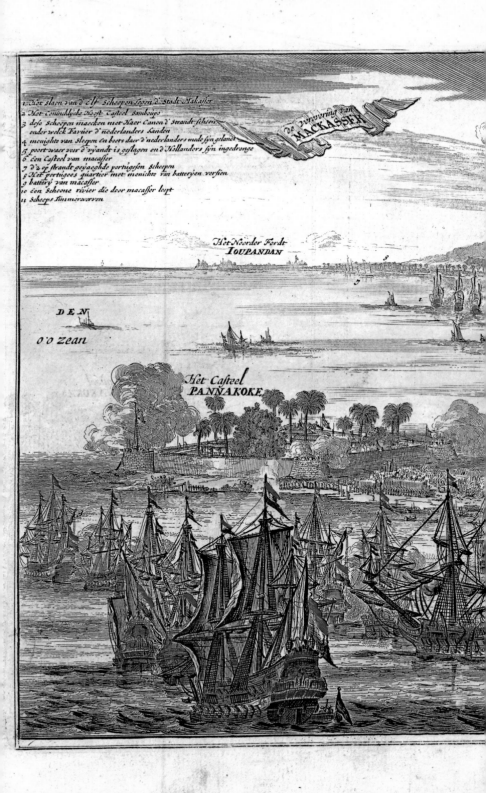

De Verovering van
MACKASSER

1. Het slaen van d'elf Scheepen tegen d'Stadt Makasser
2. Het Coninclijcke Hoost-Casteel Samboupo
3. dese Scheepen maecken met haer Canon d' strandt-scheur
   onder welck Favier d' nederlanders landen
4. menighte van Sloepen en beets daer d' nederlanders mede syn gelandet
5. poort waer voor d' vyandt is geslagen en d' Hollanders syn ingedronge
6. een Casteel van macasser
7. d'2 op strandt gejaeghde portugese Scheepen
8. Het portugees quartier met menichte van batterijen versien
9. batterij van macasser
10. een Schoone rivier die door macasser loopt
11. Scheeps timmerwerven

Het Noorder Fordt
TOUPANDAN

DEN
o'o Zean

Het Casteel
PANÑAKOKE

c. decker. fe.

DUTCH HEGEMONY

The Fall of Mighty Makassar

The Dutch arrived in Asia in 1596 with the aim of seizing Portugal's trade in pepper and spices. Allying themselves with Ternate, the strongest of the spice-island "clove sultanates," the Dutch quickly found themselves leading a predominantly Islamic coalition against both the Portuguese and the Spanish, who had bases in the Philippines.

Within fifty years, this conflict had spread to northern and eastern Sulawesi. In 1617 the Spaniards established a small fort at Manado, which supplied rice to their garrisons in the Moluccas. Attempts to establish the Catholic faith in the populous rice-growing Minahasan area around Lake Tondano met with resistance, and in 1643 local chiefs invited the (Protestant) Dutch to their aid. By 1657 the Dutch had the upper hand in North Sulawesi, as well as in the Moluccas, and had established a permanent base at Manado.

CORNELIS SPEELMAN
Gouverneur Generaal van Nederlands Indien

The Battle of Makassar

In the southern area of the island, Makassar's importance as a trans-shipment point in the international spice trade had been growing steadily throughout the 16th century. Makassar received an added boost when Portuguese Malacca surrendered to the Dutch in 1641. English, Portuguese, Danish and Gujarati factors had headquarters in Makassar, buying and re-shipping the valuable spices that poured into Makassar from the eastern spice islands.

The Dutch East India Company knew it had to break Makassar if it was to make its attempted monopoly of Moluccan cloves and nutmeg effective, but it might never have succeeded in doing so without the help of neighboring Bone, smarting since 1644 from the humiliation of defeat and subjugation by Gowa. Encouraged by the Dutch Admiral Speelman, Aru Palakka, an outstanding Bugis warrior with a particular grievance against Sultan Hasanuddin of Makassar, gathered a large Bugis army, and in 1666 the joint war against Makassar began. Makassar was defeated at Buton, then Bantaeng, and finally at Galesong and Barombong just south of the capital. In November 1667 the Treaty of Bungaya effectively hamstrung Makassar, banning European traders from the city and transferring the fort at Ujung Pandang to the Dutch. In June 1669, fighting broke out again, this time resulting in the total destruction of old Makassar.

The proud aristocracy of Makassar could not reconcile itself to defeat, and time and again attempts were made to reverse it. Many Makassarese fled Sulawesi to fight the Dutch again with the troops of Trunojoyo in East Java or of Banten in the west. Some fled to Siam, where in 1688 they met their demise in the courageous "Revolt of the Makassars" against the growing French colonial presence. In Sulawesi, the first rebel to succeed in uniting the country behind him was Karaeng Bontolangkasa, who seized the throne of Gowa and besieged the Dutch in their fort in 1739. His eventual defeat brought fresh humiliation and destruction. A new rebellion, and a new devastation of the Gowa capital, took place in 1778. This long and bitter series of confrontations not only

Overleaf: The conquest of Makassar by combined Dutch and Bugis forces. **Left**: *Admiral Speelman, commander of the Dutch fleet.* **Opposite**: *19th-century view of Fort Rotterdam in Ujung Pandang.*

destroyed all physical trace of old Makassar, but also served to reinforce the conservative aspects of Makassar society. Having been the most ardent borrowers of Western ideas in Indonesia, they were now obliged to identify such ideas with the enemy.

The Bugis diaspora

Initially it was Bone which profited from the new situation. The Dutch were not interested in ruling South Sulawesi, only in preventing their ejection from their Makassar foothold. Bone, which enjoyed the advantage of distance, dominated South Sulawesi until Aru Palakka's death in 1696, bringing fire and sword to districts such as Wajo and Mandar which had remained loyal to Gowa. Even the Toraja, well protected in the fastness of their mountain domains, remember Aru Palakka as the threat which united their villages into a defensive federation.

The people of Wajo, with perhaps the keenest sense of local autonomy of any in pre-colonial Sulawesi, had become active sailors and traders in the last decades of their alliance with Makassar. When Makassar and then Wajo itself were destroyed, many of these traders left the island to seek their fortune in eastern Kalimantan, Malaya, Sumatra or even further afield. Many royal dynasties, like those of Kutai (Kalimantan), Johor and Selangor (Malaya), and Aceh, originated with these late 17th-century emigrants. The Bugis diaspora also provided the basis for reviving Wajo itself. Arung Sengkang La Ma'dukelleng (1700-65), a Wajo aristocrat who had made himself raja of Kutai in Kalimantan, returned in 1737 to liberate Wajo from the Bone yoke. For a century and a half thereafter Wajo was left in freedom to pursue its extensive trade throughout the archipelago. Many of the Bugis now living in Malaya are descendents of Wajo traders. Wajo also acquired a reputation as having the most democratic institutions in the archipelago.

Minahasa and the Dutch

In 1667, the Bungaya Treaty had designated most of Makassar's South Sulawesi dependencies as Bone territory. Makassar's further-flung and more tenuous tributary states were allotted to another Dutch ally, Ternate. (Banggai and Tobungku in eastern Sulawesi remained nominally under the sovereignty of Ternate until 1900, and sent an annual tribute of their fine steel swords.) In 1693, however, Ternate was forced by the Dutch Company to relinquish its slender claims to North Sulawesi.

To make the Dutch presence effective, Robert Padtbrugge, the Dutch governor of Ternate, traveled throughout North Sulawesi in 1677-79. Fort Amsterdam was established in Manado as the main Dutch base, and the Sangir-Talaud islands were conquered. Gorontalo and its twin-state Limbotto made

an agreement with Padtbrugge in 1677, but had to be chastised by a Dutch-Ternate fleet in 1681 for their independent spirit.

Padtbrugge was more successful with the tiny *walaks* (domains) which would later comprise the Minahasa, persuading 24 of them to sign a treaty with the Dutch Company in 1679. These states were obliged by the agreement to send annual deliveries of foodstuffs to the Dutch posts at Manado and Ternate. These eventually became the basis for the Dutch system of forced coffee cultivation in Indonesia in the 19th century.

The rise of colonial power

In the late 18th century, the sway of the Dutch Company had weakened throughout its colony. In the south, Bone became such a threat that it virtually took over the Noorderdistricten (northern administrative region) of Maros and Pangkajene, which the Dutch had attempted to rule since the Bungaya Treaty. Between 1811 and 1816 the British occupied Makassar, Manado and other Dutch possessions including Selayar, Bantaeng and Bira. The British also took arms against those they had earlier encouraged to rebel against the Dutch (Holland was from 1808 an ally of Napoleonic France), as in the case of Bone in the Maros area.

With the Dutch restoration, stability gradually returned. From 1817 Minahasa was firmly part of the Dutch Indies, and one of the few directly-ruled areas outside Java. Its effective conversion to Protestant Christianity was the work of two German Pietist missionaries, Johan Riedel and Johannes Schwarz. During the 19th century, the Netherlands Missionary Society (NZG) also developed an effective education system in the region, using the Malay language as the medium of instruction.

In the south, Dutch control was less secure even in the areas near Makassar which it ruled directly. Only after Dutch troops attacked Bone itself, in 1824-25, was Bone influence eliminated from the Noorderdistricten around Maros, which provided the rice for Makassar.

During the 19th century, improved communications, along with the spread of Singapore-based trade to small ports, made the Dutch increasingly uneasy about the effective independence enjoyed by Gorontalo, Tolitoli, and all the Bugis states. The British adventurer James Brooke, who established his own *raj*, or kingdom (albeit in distant Sarawak), underscored the weakness of the

Dutch hold. Through the second and third wars against Bone (1858-60) the Dutch established their sovereignty on Sulawesi, though they still actually ruled only its two opposite extremities.

Dutch rule

Not until the first decade of this century did the Dutch resolve to attempt subjugation of the entire island of Sulawesi, and to make contact with the little-known people of the highlands. Under the aggressive military policy of Governor-General van Heutsz, small mobile military units were sent all over the island, pursuing even the remotest chiefs who refused to submit to the new order. By 1906 all the rulers were obliged to sign a Korte Verklaring (Short Declaration) agreeing to accept all instructions from the Netherlands Indies Government. This victory for the Dutch, however, was achieved at the cost of great bloodshed.

Armed opposition had to be overcome in Donggala, Tolitoli, Gorontalo, Kulawi, and Banggai. Much the heaviest fighting, however, was against the proud and populous Bugis and Makassar states. The Dutch expeditionary force first attacked Bone in July 1905, hoping that its defeat would provoke a general submission. The Bone capital was taken after a bitter fight thought to have cost more than 1,000 lives.

After the city's capitulation, the raja, La Pawawoi was pursued and finally captured in four months of guerrilla warfare. On other fronts, the main Dutch force had moved against Gowa in October 1905, forcing the sultan to flee northwards with his closest followers. The sultan of Gowa made his most important resistance efforts at Sawitto (Pinrang), in alliance with the bellicose La Sinrang, son of the raja of Pinrang. Sultan Husen of Gowa died in December 1906, still in flight from Dutch troops.

Subsequent Bugis resistance was short-lived. A number of leading Luwu aristocrats died in a short but desperate stand on the beach at Palopo in 1906. From Palopo, Dutch columns fanned out in several directions, encountering their stiffest resistance in northern Toraja. There Pong Tiku had established an unprecedented degree of power by wresting control of the newly established trade in coffee and slaves—obtaining in exchange rifles, salt, and foreign produce from the Bugis of Palopo and Sidenreng. The Dutch attacked his base at Pangalla in April 1906, but did not finally capture him until a

year of difficult guerrilla warfare later. He was executed in Rantepao in July 1907. In this manner, many of Sulawesi's hitherto impregnable mountain areas which had withstood all previous assaults from outside were eventually brought within the suzerainty of the Netherlands Indies.

Scholars and missionaries

The success of the Dutch "pacification" campaign made it possible for ethnographers such as the Swiss cousins Sarasin to explore the center of the island, and for Christian missionaries to work among peoples who had been scarcely touched by the Islam which dominated the coasts. Dutch Protestant missionaries entered the Poso area in 1892, and began making converts following the Dutch subjugation of the area. In the Sa'dan Toraja area (modern Tana Toraja), more Dutch missionaries began their holy struggle in 1913, though their efforts did not bear fruit for nearly twenty years .

The 35 years of effective Dutch rule were probably the longest period of peace in Sulawesi's history. The population was mobilized to build the present network of roads and irrigation works. A centralized administration was established. The Governor in Makassar presided over Assistant-Residents in Parepare, Palopo, Watampone (Bone), Majene, Bantaeng and Baubau (Buton), while the Resident in Manado was responsi-ble for Gorontalo, Donggala, and Poso.

Among the directly ruled areas of Sulawesi, Minahasa held a special place. Its people were overwhelmingly Christian in number and better educated than other groups in Netherlands India. Hence they were extensively used as teachers and clerks throughout the colony.

In 1919 Minahasa was rewarded with a part-elected representative council—the *Minahasaraad*. Because of their generally advanced social standing, the Minahasans were later also better represented in the nationalist movement than any of the other peoples of Sulawesi.

Most of Sulawesi was, in theory, indirectly governed using Dutch contracts with coastal rajas as the pretext for controlling the interior—even if most hill people had little more than a trading relationship with the coast. Financial control was firmly in the hands of the Dutch, and the two most powerful thrones in Sulawesi, Bone and Gowa, were left empty. Only in 1931 was it deemed safe to place the son of the last Gowa sultan, Andi Mappanyuki, on the Bone throne. Five years later, the Gowa dynasty was restored to a faded grandeur in Sungguminasa.

—*Anthony Reid*

Above: *Dutch soldiers look on as La Pawawoi, the last Bugis ruler of Bone, is carried to the sedan chair which will take him into exile (1905).*

INDEPENDENCE

The Rocky Road to Nationhood

Even if the modern (and largely Western-educated) Indonesian nationalist movement was little developed outside the two major cities of Sulawesi, the spirit of resistance towards Dutch rule remained strong in many areas. When the lightning Japanese advance on Indonesia began in January 1942, Indonesians in several parts of the island pre-empted them by taking action against Dutch authority. In Gorontalo a committee led by Nani Wartabone seized power several weeks before the Japanese arrival, imprisoning the Dutch community in the local jail. Similar events followed in Luwuk, Tolitoli, and Bone. These independence committees, however, were soon swept aside by the Japanese tide, and the red-and-white Indonesian flag they had proudly raised was banned.

A leading Minahasan nationalist intellectual educated in Zurich, Dr. Sam Ratulangie (1890-1949), was brought from Java to head the propaganda organization Sudara and to "advise" the military in Sulawesi. Following the declaration of independence in August 1945, Ratulangie was appointed by Sukarno as the first Republican Governor of Sulawesi.

The return of the Dutch

Australians troops arrived in Makassar to accept the Japanese surrender on September 21, and in Manado on October 2. They were received enthusiastically by Indonesians, including even the fledgling Republican movement. The efforts of young activists were directed primarily against the Dutch presence, and only when the Australians handed control back to Dutch administration in January 1946 did serious fighting begin. Young nationalists attacked the Dutch units in Palopo (South Sulawesi) and held the town for two days, suffering hundreds of casualties against the better-armed Dutch.

Even in Minahasa, where the Dutch had rapidly set about recruiting new soldiers for the colonial army, there was strong resentment against the unexpected return of colonial attitudes with the returning Dutch. Minahasan units of KNIL (the Netherlands Indian Army) revolted in support of independence on February 14, 1946. The rebels held much of the Manado-Minahasa area for a month, though a settlement was eventually arranged peaceably with the Dutch.

In the south there was very little support for the Dutch return except among Christian and other minorities and a few Bugis aristocrats. After a number of skirmishes with patriotic youth forces, the Dutch arrested Ratulangie, his six principal lieutenants, and the rajas of Bone and Luwu in April 1946. Most of the youth resistance then moved to Java, to return at the end of 1946 with better arms and military training. They were able to launch a very effective guerrilla movement, to which the Dutch responded by embarking upon the harshest campaign of terror anywhere in Indonesia. Between December 1946 and March 1947, at least 3,000 people were killed in the province by the notorious Captain "Turk" Westerling's "special troops."

The struggle for power

In an attempt to compete with the popularity of the revolutionary Republic of Indonesia, the Dutch in December 1946 initiated a federal "State of East Indonesia" (NIT), with its capital in Makassar. The state's first prime minister was the ambitious Makassarese Nadjamoeddin, who tried in vain to get a hearing for the state at the United Nations. He was indicted for corruption in September 1947, having fallen foul of his companions.

Faced with increasing popular opposition, the federal state was dissolved into the unitary Republic of Indonesia on August 17, 1950. In addition to finishing off the Dutch as colonial masters in Indonesia, the victory of the Republic also presaged the end for the rajas who had dominated Sulawesi for centuries. They were so powerful in many areas, however, that initially the government could not do without them.

The most serious conflicts of the period from 1950 to 1965 were inside the military itself. The end of the Indonesian revolution saw a struggle for power within the new army by various groups who had fought the Dutch in Java or in the jungles of Sulawesi. The leader of the discontents in South Sulawesi was Kahar Muzakkar, a Bugis teacher who had been prominent in organizing Sulawesi armed youth in Java. In July 1950 he abandoned his position in the

Indonesian army (TNI) and began a rebellion, periodically interrupted by negotiations. Increasingly it took on both an Islamic and a "locals-first" flavor, and eventually it joined the West Java-based *Darul Islam*, nominally fighting for an Islamic state. In South Sulawesi during the 1950s the government had firm control only over the main cities and the districts of Tana Toraja and Selayar.

Rebellion in the north

North Sulawesi's discontent was more economic than political, centering on the flourishing copra trade and the inefficient efforts of the central government to control and regulate it. The whole of Sulawesi shared the general discontents of the period, partly comprised of regionalism, partly of impatience with the weakness of the government in Jakarta, partly of the excessive expectations the revolution had aroused. On March 2, 1957, 50 leading military and civilian figures in Makassar signed the Permesta Proclamation, the name being an acronym for *Piagam Perjuangan Semesta Alam*—Charter of Inclusive Struggle. At the same time, martial law was proclaimed throughout Eastern Indonesia, on the authority of the Minahasan military commander Ventje Sumual. These prominent signatories denied they were rebels, but sought fundamental changes in the way regional affairs were run.

Within three months, Jakarta had undermined military support for the Permesta movement in the south by creating a military command for South and Southeast Sulawesi under Bugis-Makassar control. Lt. Col. Sumual, the last of a succession of North Sulawesi officers who had dominated military affairs in the island, withdrew to Manado in June. Henceforth Permesta's only secure base was in North Sulawesi. In February 1958 it threw in its lot with the more overt rebellion known as the PRRI, based in Sumatra. Their aim was not only to protect regional interests against Jakarta, but even more to reverse what was seen as a drift toward a more authoritarian communist-influenced government under Sukarno's personal control. It sought and obtained clandestine arms and air support from the United States.

The central government responded with full force. Manado was bombed on February 22, but the government thereafter was busy quelling the Sumatra rebels until May. The TNI invaded North Sulawesi, taking Manado on June 26, though failing to capture the rebel headquarters at Kotamobagu until

more than a year later, in September 1959. Resistance did not finally end until 1961.

In the south, the restoration of government authority was largely the work of Colonel Andi Mohammad Jusuf, a Bugis soldier who had received professional training first at Bandung and then at Fort Benning in the U.S. Appointed local commander in 1959, he made the army both more disciplined and more local in composition. He became a cabinet minister in 1965, and later Minister of Defense. The other factor in the defeat of Kahar Muzakkar was the Siliwangi Division, brought from Java in 1963 to pursue the rebels. Kahar was finally killed in 1965.

Only after peace was restored could the work of development go ahead. Sulawesi got off to a slow start in restoring communications, rebuilding the national infrastructure, and opening the country up to tourism and investment. The development-oriented New Order government of President Suharto, which began in 1966, coincided with the first period of peace in Sulawesi since 1941. Progress in Sulawesi has been rapid since 1970, as evidenced by the new roads and buildings which are being built across the island.

—*Anthony Reid*

Above: *Captain Raymond "Turk" Westerling, whose notorious "special troops" brought terror to the villages of South Sulawesi. His campaign was part of the Dutch "pacification" program.*

ECONOMY

Fisheries, Farms and Forests

Most of the inhabitants of Sulawesi derive their living from the land, the forests, and the sea. Within the region, however, there is much variation in patterns of livelihood, depending to a great extent on geography. North and South Sulawesi are more fertile and wealthier than the Central and Southeast provinces, due to their rich volcanic soils.

Agriculture

The cultivation of food crops—rice, corn, cassava, vegetables and fruits—probably employs more people in Sulawesi than any other occupation. Rice is grown mainly in paddies (rain-fed or irrigated fields), though in some areas dry rice is grown. Rice cultivation is concentrated in the fertile, irrigated southern peninsula, whence a large surplus is exported to other parts of Indonesia.

North Sulawesi also grows much of its own food, but its major agricultural wealth derives from tree crops, in particular coconuts and cloves, but also nutmeg. Veritable fortunes continue to be made from cloves, used largely to flavor Indonesian *kretek* cigarettes, especially in Minahasa. North Sulawesi accounts for some 30 percent of Indonesian clove production, but "clove fever" has been spreading throughout Sulawesi over the last two decades, as even a few trees in one's backyard can provide substantial cash .

Commercial crops, such as coffee in South Sulawesi and cacao in western Southeast Sulawesi, are becoming increasingly important, along with secondary food crops such as soybeans.

Agricultural production in Sulawesi is small-scale, and commercial estates are rare. Most farming is done by individual smallholders on family-owned plots, growing a variety of crops. Livestock is important—South Sulawesi is the third largest cattle-producing province in the country—but breeding and rearing are also small-scale, with only one or two ranch-style operations.

Fishing and forests

Fishing provides a livelihood for a large number of Sulawesi's inhabitants. Much of the coastal fishing is carried out using "traditional" boats and techniques, but modern fisheries and processing facilities are also being established. The most dramatic developments have been the establishment or expansion of coastal (brackish-water) fish and shrimp ponds, particularly in the south. Large fortunes are to be made in freezing shrimp for export to Japan.

Other important natural resources are forestry and mining. With its valuable hardwoods, Central Sulawesi derives important revenues from forestry, while Southeast Sulawesi is a producer of teak. Rattan is another a valuable source of revenue. In the past, logs and rattan were exported unprocessed, but recent government regulations have banned the export of logs and other unprocessed forest products.

Mining is dominated by the Inco nickel mines at Soroako in South Sulawesi, where low-grade ore is partially processed for export; only recently has the operation managed to break even. Nickel ore is also mined at Pomalaa in Southeast Sulawesi, and asphalt on the island of Buton. In recent years, gold fever has swept Indonesia and has encouraged a small-scale search for gold, notably in the Bolaang-Mongondow district of North Sulawesi. Deposits of copper in North Sulawesi and a few other minerals offer future prospects of developments.

Limited manufacturing

Despite the area's wealth of important natural resources, manufacturing has contributed only in limited ways to economic development. Small-scale processing of agricultural products and manufacture of foodstuffs is fairly widespread. A large flour mill (using imported wheat) operates in Ujung Pandang, while several factories turning out coconut products—in particular cooking oil—are found in North Sulawesi. Several cement factories and limestone quarries in South Sulawesi take advantage of widespread demand, while a paper mill is found in Gowa to the south of Ujung Pandang. Sugar mills

Opposite: *P.T. Inco's nickel smelting plant at Soroako near Malili on the Gulf of Bone. The Canadian-run mine is one of the world's largest producers of low-grade nickel.*

have recently been constructed in the district of Bone in South Sulawesi.

Sulawesi in general, however, suffers because of its distance from important domestic markets. It has a small local population and high labor costs compared with densely populated Java, the site of most Indonesian manufacturing .

Service industries such as transportation and tourism are becoming more important. With improvements and expansion in the road system, land transport is now light-years ahead of its status in the early 1960s. Air services linking provincial capitals and some of the smaller centers are also well developed.

For centuries Sulawesi has been famous for its sea transport, and the armada of South and Southeast Sulawesi sailboats, many now motorized, still accounts for a substantial proportion of inter-island and local shipping. Tourism is a much more recent industry, for which the government has high hopes. To date, however, tourism has had an impact only in South, and to a lesser extent in North Sulawesi, the only two provinces with any real tourism infrastructure.

The economic future

What does the economic future hold for Sulawesi? To a great extent this will be determined by world commodity prices, as well as by government policy and practice. In the past, the government's role was extremely influential, and development seemed to be synonymous with government initiative.

After a long period of stagnation during the regional rebellions of the 1950s and 1960s, initial emphasis was placed on infrastructure, in particular roads and irrigation systems. Rice cultivation received much attention, since Indonesia was determined to regain, and maintain, self-sufficiency in rice and other food crops. Only since the early 1980s, however, has much attention been given to secondary food crops (cassava, corn, pulses), which are far more suitable than rice in many areas of Sulawesi.

As Sulawesi continues on the fifth of Indonesia's five-year plans, people throughout the country, as well as the government, are beginning to pay greater attention to environmental conservation and sustainable development. Increased global consciousness is playing a role here, but equally important are the obvious long-term consequences of greedy or technologically inappropriate exploitation. Declining revenue from oil exports means that the prominence of government in economic development will decline, while the private sector—small and medium-sized firms, but mainly the hundreds of thousands of small-holder families—will play a leading role.

—Tim Babcock

PEOPLE

An Island of Great Ethnic Diversity

The extraordinary variety of Sulawesi's landscapes is matched only by the island's great ethnic, cultural and religious diversity. Over half of the 11.5 million Sulawesians counted in the 1985 census inhabit the fertile plains and valleys of the south, while another million cluster around Manado and the adjacent Minahasa district on the island's northeastern tip. Ujung Pandang, the largest city in Sulawesi, is a polyglot of peoples and cultures.

Best known are the coastal and lowland peoples of the south: the Bugis (3.5 million), the Makassarese (half a million), the Mandarese (also half a million), and the highland Toraja (330,000). There are scores of lesser-known groups: the Wana, Mori, Kaili, Taijo, Pendau, Lauje, Kahumamoan, and others of the rugged center; and the Tolaki of the Southeast. In the north, the Minahasans are a large and well-known group, but there

are also the Sangirese, the Bolaang Mongondow, and the Gorontalo peoples.

Names alone do not convey the richness and complexity of the island's cultural life. While each of these groups have both shared and distinctive social forms and expressive arts, there is also great variation. Take language, for example. The Minahasans of the north, who number nearly a million, have a strong sense of ethnic identity, and yet speak half a dozen different (though related) languages. The Mandarese, who live primarily from fishing and trade, and who are often casually grouped with their Bugis neighbors to the south, actually speak several languages (primarily Mandarese and Campalagian). The term "Toraja" (from the Bugis *to riaja*, "highland people") was formerly applied to most non-Islamic peoples of the highlands. But the southern (Sa'dan) Toraja speak a language closer to their Mandarese and Bugis neighbors than to the either the eastern or western Torajan languages. While the Luwurese speak a language closely related to those of their Torajan neighbors, they are considered "Bugis" because of their shared Islamic culture. The "Toraja," for their part, have stressed their Toraja identity in recent years both as a way of countering Islam, and as a means of enhancing their attractiveness for the tourist market.

Outside of urban and official contexts, where *Bahasa Indonesia* is spoken, the traveler is more likely to hear the lively local languages of the island. Many people speak several local languages as well as Indonesian. And if they are ritual specialists, they may even speak some of their "high" poetic forms, rich in metaphor and allusion.

Many of these ancient literary and ritual forms, however, are fast disappearing. Within the last ten years, transcriptions and translations (into Indonesian) of poetic forms of speech have appeared in small books published in Sulawesi (and in a number of anthropology dissertations). Similarly waning is the ability to read the old manuscripts, on which the histories of kingdoms in the south were chronicled in the indigenous script.

A great crossroads

Like so much of Southeast Asia, island Sulawesi has always been open to new ideas

KAL MULLER

Overleaf: *A Toraja noble displays his aristocratic dress and a proud demeanor at a death feast.*
Left: *Young Bugis girl at a wedding, wearing distinctive traditional clothing.*

Language Groups

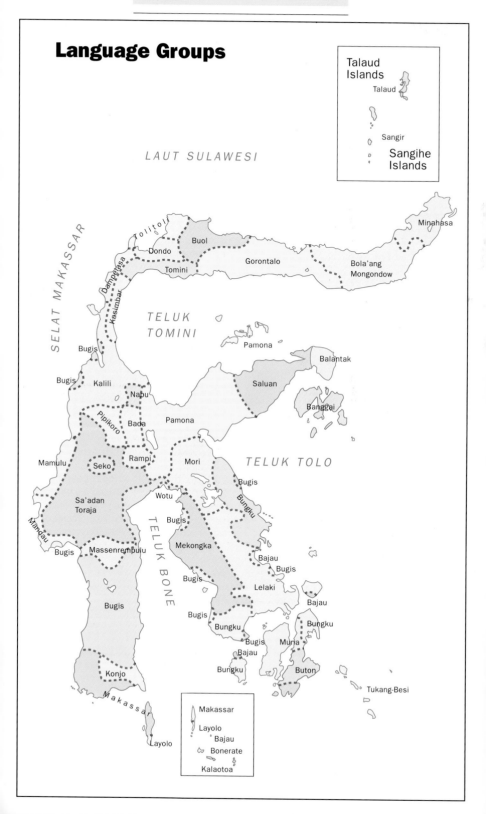

Talaud Islands
Talaud
Sangir
Sangihe Islands

LAUT SULAWESI

Tolitoli
Dampelasa
Kasimbar
Buol
Dondo
Tomini
Gorontalo
Minahasa
Bola'ang Mongondow

SELAT MAKASSAR

TELUK TOMINI
Pamona
Balantak
Saluan
Banggai

Bugis
Bugis
Kalili
Napu
Pipikoro
Bada
Pamona
Mamulu
Seko
Rampi
Mori
TELUK TOLO
Bugis
Bungku

Mandau
Sa'adan Toraja
Wotu
Bugis
Bugis
Massenrempulu
Mekongka
Bajau
Bugis
Lelaki
Bajau
Bugis
Bugis
Bungku
Bajau
Bungku
Muna
Bugis
Bajau
Konjo
Bungku
Buton
Tukang-Besi

TELUK BONE

Makassar
Layolo

Makassar
Layolo
Bajau
Bonerate
Kalaotoa

from distant worlds across the sea. This has been true from the time of the ancient Austronesian-speaking agriculturalists and navigators who arrived perhaps as early as 4,000 years ago from the north via Taiwan and the Philippines. In the great age of commerce, the *Pabicara Butta* (prime minister) of Makassar, Karaeng Matoaya, kept a library of European books and studied the latest developments in mathematics and optics. Outside influences were strongest on or near the coasts, and in urban ports and centers, penetrating less directly into the deep forests and high mountains where so many Sulawesian peoples have maintained their distinctive character even unto the present.

As elsewhere in Indonesia, the Chinese in

Sulawesi live mostly in the major cities. There have been Chinese resident in Makassar and Manado since the 17th century, and today about one percent of the population is Chinese. Although most are now Indonesian citizens, 43,000 were still registered as Chinese nationals (or as stateless) in 1980. Many are Christians, though there are substantial numbers of Buddhists and Confucians as well.

In recent years Sulawesi has also become home to Javanese and Balinese transmigrants, people moved by the government from their overcrowded islands to more sparsely populated and (it is hoped) potentially productive land. Balinese have been migrating to certain parts of Sulawesi since

the early 20th century, and probably account for most of the 47,000 Hindus recorded in the 1980 census. Nearly 54,000 Javanese have settled on the island since 1962.

One large and particulary successful community of Javanese is in Wonomulyo, along the western coast north of Parepare. Some Javanese ply their trades in non-Javanese communities: in Mandar, women sellers of *jamu* (herbal remedies) do a brisk business providing drinks to the fishwives who line the shore each morning, awaiting the day's catch from incoming ships.

Islam, Christianity and *adat*

Although today the majority of Sulawesi's population is Muslim, in the 16th century Portuguese and Spanish spice traders—and their Catholic priests—had extensive dealings with states on the west coast and in the north. In the second half of that century, a number of local rulers in Siang (on the west coast of South Sulawesi), Siau, Manado, and Kaidipan were baptised along with thousands of their followers. In most areas, such conversions were short-lived, particularly after the Portuguese captain of Ternate (in the neighboring Moluccas) murdered the sultan there in 1570. The anti-Portuguese crusade launched by the sultan's son led Gorontalo, Buton, Banggai, and other parts of Sulawesi to convert to Islam.

According to legend, Islam was first brought to South Sulawesi in 1603 by three holy men from the Minangkabau area of Sumatra. They went first to Luwu, then to Makassar (the twin state of Gowa and Tallo). Having converted the ruling elite, they continued on to the southern Bugis kingdoms, including Bone. By 1611 they had persuaded rulers throughout the whole of South Sulawesi, except for the Toraja highlands, to accept Islam.

In fact, Islam (as well as Christianity) had been known in the south long before these dramatic conversions. Malay Muslim traders lived in the south as early as the 15th century, though by the mid-16th century South Sulawesi was one of few important nodes on the inter-island trading network where Islam had *not* yet been officially embraced.

The Islamic conversions of the early 17th century were sweeping but not always smooth. One account describes the inauguration of the first royal mosque in South Sulawesi: On the eve of the Friday prayer (the holiest time of the week), a prince of Gowa slaughtered pigs inside the mosque and smeared their blood across its walls. This act of desecration—the ultimate befoulment in Islamic terms—was ironically carried out by drawing on pre-Islamic sacralization rites of touching pig's blood to persons and places. In Bone and Soppeng there was strong opposition to the new religion from the nobility, and Islam finally entered Gowa only on the edge of a sword.

Today Islam is embraced by 80 percent of the population of Sulawesi. It is Islam of the Sunni tradition with some Shi'ite vestiges, such as festivities to celebrate Maulud, the Prophet's birthday. Throughout the Bugis, Makassarese and Mandarese areas of the south, Kaili, Donggala, Palu, and Tolitoli on the west coast, Gorontalo in the north and Buton in the southeast, the domes of mosques are visible in town and countryside, and the droning call to prayer (now taped and sounded over loudspeakers even in remote villages) awakens villager and visitor alike before dawn each day.

Islam in Sulawesi has been, and continues to be, remarkably flexible. This is not to say that it is not extremely serious, or that its followers are not devout: even the rebellion which began in the 1950s was later cast in ardently Islamic terms. But Sulawesi's Muslims have long found ways of joining their Islamic devotion with local practices associated with ancestors and with spirits of earth, rice and sea. One sees such conjunctions in all kinds of acts: from boat-blessings or healing rites to the esoteric chants of transvestite *bissu* priests; from the magical potency of Thursday night (*malam jum'at*) for spells and charms, to the practice of requesting favors at graves of Muslim saints or ancestors.

Church spires

A visitor to Sulawesi will see not only mosque minarets but church spires. The island's substantial Christian population (17 percent Protestant, 2 percent Catholic) is concentrated in the north (Minahasa and the Sangir-Talaud islands), in the Poso district of the center, and in the southern highlands of Tana Toraja, where a rapid process of conversion has taken place just since Indonesian independence. There are Christian minorities as well in most towns and cities.

In the north, where European presence has a long history—the Portuguese arrived from Ternate in the mid-1500s with priest, and the Spanish followed—the area came under full Dutch control only after 1800, when massive conversions to Protestant

Christianity took place. This conversion was enhanced by the spread of schools: by the turn of the century, there was one school for every 1,000 people in Minahasa, compared to one per 50,000 people in Java. Though the Protestant Church (descended, as in Toraja, from the Dutch Reformed Church) is dominant, scores of other sects and churches are found today. But not all the north is Christian: the Gorontalo and Mongondow people are almost entirely Muslim, the latter having accepted Islam only in the 19th century.

Missionaries of many sorts, including institutions ranging from the Dutch Reformed Church to the Salvation Army, have been active in Central Sulawesi since the late 19th century. Christianity came

slightly later to Tana Toraja, where the first Dutch Reformed missionary was killed in 1917 (his successors took a more conciliatory attitude toward traditional ritual). Today, while ritual continues to flourish and draw the public eye, Protestant, Catholic and Pentecostal churches in Toraja still engage in sometimes tense debates about their relationship to local belief and practices.

Nomads of the sea

One of Sulawesi's most interesting groups

Opposite: *A Toraja man wearing a boar's-tusk necklace, a mark of elevated social status.*
Above: *A woman from the Bada Valley in Central Sulawesi.*

are the Bajau, formerly known as "Sea Gypsies," who for centuries have followed a nomadic way of life aboard their small, broad-beamed boats. The Bajau are actually one of several related groups who have established themselves across the Riau and Lingga archipelagos, around coastal Borneo, and on the east coast of Sumatra.

The provenance of this seaborne people remains conjectural. Since the times of recorded history in Sulawesi, the Bajau have been peripherally connected to Makassarese and Bugis centers of power. The name of the Bajau (pronounced "Bojo" in the Bugis tongue) most likely derives from Wajo, one of the semi-independent Bugis states around bone and Luwu.

Expert sailors and skilled collectors of marine products—notably trepang and tortoise shells—the Bajau supplied much of Sulawesi's export material for the China trade, through Makassarese and Bugis middlemen. They traditionally spent their entire lives upon their boats, disdaining the settled existence of the shorebound peoples with whom they traded to obtain foodstuffs, cloth and a few other basic necessities.

As with most of the world's formerly nomadic peoples, the Bajau have today been tamed by governmental policies, competition from big industry, and international fishing laws. Most of them have been absorbed into the land populations, though a small number,

a thousand or so, remain moored off of the islands outside of Kendari Bay in Southeast Sulawesi. Fishing and gathering are still the source of life for these last semi-nomadic Bajau families. Their handsome craft ride just offshore, ready to weigh anchor for a *trepang* hunt on east Timor or the north coast of Australia (where they risk arrest).

Ritual and the spirit world

Sulawesi is probably best known for the tiny percentage of its population which does not count itself as part of a "world" (or officially sanctioned) religion, but continues to practice some form of "animism," a term coined by 19th-century anthropologists. In animist beliefs, the universe is considered to be suffused with and animated by a kind of cosmic energy or life-force.

This energy or potency pervades the world, but it often has nodes in specific places in the landscape—rocks, trees, mountaintops, streams or rainbows—or in the realm of human technology—house rafters, boat navels, ancestral cloths or swords. Power and well-being depend on tapping this energy, drawing it to both the community and individuals through various means including trance-possession, spirit and healing cults, meditation, and a great many other ritual practices, large and small.

Ritual in Sulawesi, as elsewhere in the archipelago, is not only a rich component of a

KAL MULLER

complex social fabric, but also the means by which health, wealth, and fertility are called forth, assured and displayed. It is also the arena for struggles over power—in the family, the kin group, the community; in the kingdom (now the state) and in the cosmos.

The best-known rituals of Sulawesi are the death rites of the Toraja. These, however, represent just a fraction of Sulawesi's abundant ceremonial life. A ritual may be as simple as an offering bowl of rice and incense placed by a Mandarese fisherman's wife at the house "navel" post, when her husband goes to sea. It may be as dramatic as the launching of a flying-fish boat in the same village, with a profusion of offerings, Islamic prayers, raucous children, and the night-time torching of the *prahu* on the beach. Throughout the island, there is great variation: lavish Bugis, Makassarese, and Mandarese weddings and circumcisions sparkle in brilliantly colored silks; neither of these occasions, however, is ritually elaborated in Toraja.

Rituals in Sulawesi are partly about establishing status. The Toraja funeral is perhaps the most dramatic example, as participants compete to bring the most splendid water buffalo, or to host the greatest number of followers from afar. But status and links with spiritual potency are actually inseparable. The Toraja *maro* ritual, for example, simultaneously demonstrates a family's rank and creates an open field for trance and spirit possession. Even the drummings and summonings of a Wana shaman in the hills of Central Sulawesi are intended not merely to call a spirit and heal a patient but also to create an audience, and thereby enhance the authority of a shaman.

Witnessing traditional rituals

One of the great pleasures of traveling in Sulawesi is the opportunity to be present at rituals—though one of the perpetual frustrations is not understanding what is going on. Nonetheless, just being at a ceremony conducted as an integral, essential part of social life, is a privilege which few Westerners are able to enjoy in their own society. We cannot simply join in a stranger's, or even a neighbor's, wedding on the streets of Manhattan, Paris or London.

Beyond the fascination of access to a world defined by the West as private, the rituals of Sulawesi seem to offer a glimpse of a social world more whole than our own, a world in which rituals do have meaning, in which there is a community larger than the

individuals who comprise it, and in which the sacred is not lost but is heightened.

While in a way all this is true, travelers should remember that too romantic a view of "otherness" may cause one to forget that Sulawesians, like everyone else on this planet, live in the late 20th century. They too are caught up in the crises of this era, in questioning and contesting the meaning of their rituals, the rifts within their communities, the nature of spiritual potency and political power. A Toraja funeral is not simply an unchanged ancestral act—it may well be a hotly debated demonstration of a particular family's claim to status, or a drama highlighting tensions between animists and Christians, or a great performance that will find its way to television screens in Europe and America, and in the process assert the significance of Toraja identity in a vast multi-cultural state.

A traveler's experience in Sulawesi will be considerably enriched by understanding that one is witnessing, maybe even participating in, not endless replays of unchanging perfect rituals, but contemporary dramas which are both personal and political, in which the outcome may be uncertain.

—*Toby Alice Volkman and Kal Muller*

Opposite: *A Konjo horseman equipped with a lariat for catching deer.* **Above:** *Women preparing to pray at a mosque in South Sulawesi.*

LANGUAGE & LITERATURE

A Wealth of Idiom and Ideology

Linguistically, Sulawesi is very complex compared with other parts of Indonesia. No less than 80 separate languages are spoken; Java, by contrast, has just five. Sulawesi's languages all belong to the huge Austronesian language family which stretches in a great island arc more than halfway round the world, from Madagascar on the African coast, to Easter Island in the remote Pacific.

The largest language groups are found in the most densely populated province, South Sulawesi. Five related but distinct languages are spoken here: Makassarese (with 1.5 million speakers in the South, on the island of Selayar and on several smaller islands), Mandarese (300,000 speakers in the northeast region), Sa'dan Toraja (spoken by half a million people in the Toraja highlands), Massenrempulu (200,000 speakers between the Mandar and Sa'dan area) and Bugis,

whose 3.5 million speakers make it the largest linguistic group in Sulawesi.

As in other parts of Indonesia, these local languages are gradually being displaced by *Bahasa Indonesia*, the national language of modern Indonesia. Most inhabitants of Sulawesi have at least some knowledge of Indonesian, while a growing number of young people—due to a strict language policy in favor of Indonesian carried out at all levels of education—have Indonesian as their mother tongue. Malay—the ancestor of modern Indonesian—for centuries played a major role in Sulawesi as the language of trade, commerce and religion. Important Malay dialects, including Manado Malay and Makassar Malay, are still spoken in Manado and Ujung Pandang.

The literature of Sulawesi

Written traditions exist only in South Sulawesi and on the southeast island of Buton. Little is known of the latter, written in the Wolio language and consisting mainly of poetry and religious works. Makassarese and Bugis literature (and to some extent Mandarese) have been studied more extensively.

All three reveal a rich literary heritage, written in a syllable-based script which derives from an Indic system. Similar scripts, called *ka-ga-nga*, after their first three characters, were once used as far away as Sumatra and the Philippines, but Bugis, Makassarese

GREG ACCIAIOLI

and Mandarese used the script long after other peoples had switched to Arabic or Roman writing systems. The syllabary, has 23 letters, representing consonants with the inherent vowel *a*, altered by adding dots or dashes. Manuscripts written in this script were originally on leaves of the *lontara'* (papyrus or fan) palm; surviving texts today are mostly on paper.

Writing appears to have developed around 1400, probably based on a South Sumatran script. At least two scripts—the ancestor of the modern South Sulawesi script and the Old Makassarese script—were in use up to the late 17th century.

The first use to which writing was put appears to have been the recording of genealogies. Entries were made in a single line of text on a continuous strip of palm leaf; the strips were then glued or stitched together and rolled into spools which were set in simple wooden frames.

Because of unfavorable climatic conditions, manuscripts of more than one century old are rare. Fire and rats also took their toll. Most of the surviving older manuscripts are preserved in European libraries and the majority of these are copies made for European scholars from borrowed originals. One Scottish administrator, however, who was posted to Makassar in 1810, appears to have made off with a borrowed manuscript of the Bugis romance *I La Padoma*: both the copy he had commissioned and the original were sold to the British Museum in 1846.

Forms of Bugis literature

Makassar and Bugis literature is extremely varied, but can be divided into two basic categories: metric and non-metric. Metric texts include long heroic poems (*tolo'*) in meters of eight syllables. Non-metric texts include myths, histories, king lists, law books, tracts, diaries, genealogies, and wise sayings. There are also a number of prose translations and adaptations from Malay and Arabic literature, and many Islamic legends and tracts.

Both the Makassarese and the Bugis are well known for their tradition of history writing. Every kingdom, big or small, had its own state history, which related the origin of the state, its successive rulers and the events of their reign. These histories are chronologically ordered and unusually reliable. Most of them date from the 17th century, but are based on earlier sources. Supernatural events are rare and reasoned explanations prevail. In the History of Wajo, for example, the

chronicler carefully distances himself from an account of the sale of a tortoise said to excrete gold, and relates with wry humor the disappointment of the buyer who did not get what he expected. Also unusual are the state diaries, daily registers kept by a high official and sometimes by the king himself. In these registers all matters of importance are scrupulously noted down, with the dates often given in both the Muslim lunar and the Julian calendars.

I La Galigo

Few are aware that probably the longest literary work in the world is found in South Sulawesi. This is a vast epic cycle written in Bugis, known as *I La Galigo*. Its size is estimated at approximately 6,000 folio-pages. Set in a meter of five and occasionally four syllables, it relates events from pre-Islamic, 14th century Luwu, the cradle of Bugis culture.

Consisting of dozens of different episodes, each with its own protagonists, and covering several generations, using a wide range of literary conventions such as flashback and foreshadowing, the epic tells the story of the arrival on earth of the gods and the adventures of their descendants. The main protagonist of the story is Sawerigading, the great Bugis culture hero, who travels to remote places and falls deeply in love with his twin sister. This incestuous love is strictly prohibited and Sawerigading ultimately marries another woman. In the end the whole divine family gathers in Luwu and all the gods depart from the earth, having lived there for seven generations.

—*Roger Tol*

Opposite: *Man reciting prayers near Lore Lindu. He is probably requesting help for a healing or recovery of a lost article, or offering thanks for a the resolution of such a problem.* **Above:** *A 19th-century copy of the* Tragedy of La Padoma, *a Bugis romance, somewhat rat-worn.*

ARCHITECTURE

Pile Dwellings and Saddle Roofs

Traditional styles of architecture in Sulawesi share some ancient features found in other parts of the archipelago. Pile buildings with saddle-shaped roofs and outward-sloping gable ends, and gable finials in the shape of crossed horns, are widespread throughout island Southeast Asia. The dramatic forms of the Toraja house, for example, with their impressive bamboo roofs sweeping up to high, arching points, are clearly related to the structures of the Toba Batak and the Minangkabau of Sumatra.

Engravings on bronze-age Dong Son drums (ca. 500 BC—AD 100), made on the Southeast Asian mainland and in Indonesia, show similar pile dwellings with saddle roofs. These are the earliest-known representations of such buildings to have survived, but the style is probably much older. The Dong Son drums were mostly made in what is now Vietnam, and were traded far afield throughout the Indonesian islands. But the influence of Dong Son culture, formerly made much of by archaeologists, was probably too fragmentary and diffuse to account for the spread of a style of architectural construction.

The same style of building can be found even farther away in Micronesia, an area not touched by Dong Son Bronze Age influences. In New Guinea, too, the saddle roof has undergone some amazing elaborations in the forms of men's ceremonial houses. All this points to the conclusion that this unique style of house construction originated with the early Austronesian settlers, whose migrations through the Indonesia and Pacific islands from somewhere on the Southeast Asian mainland began at least 6,000 years ago.

Pile dwellings

Pile building is to be found almost everywhere in Indonesia: carvings from 8th-century Borobudur show houses on piles, although in Java and Bali a shortage of wood in subsequent centuries led to houses being built directly on the ground. In Sulawesi, however, it remains the favored form of building, though Javanese-style brick houses are beginning to appear.

Pile dwellings are remarkably cool, having excellent under-floor ventilation, and offer protection from heavy rains and mud. But a second type of foundation structure, made of heavy logs crossing each other at the corners (much like a log cabin) was typical of Central Sulawesi, as well as in an older and now almost vanished style of Sa'dan Toraja house. This style also appears to be ancient: it is depicted on a bronze age drum from South China, which shows people storing grain in two crossed-log granaries.

The Bugis house

Little survives of older Bugis architectural styles, largely because of the destruction of houses during the troubled 1950s, when older buildings were often linked by Muslim fundamentalists with pagan ways. Formerly, there were at least three house styles, each with a different type of roof line: straight, convex, or saddle-shaped. Today, the typical Bugis house has a straight ridge line, often ending in gable horns at each end. These may be simple extensions of the rafters, or sometimes are more elaborately carved.

Like most traditional houses of Indonesia, the house is symbolically divided into three levels: the undercroft, where animals are sometimes tethered and waste is thrown down from the kitchen; the floor level, inhabited by humans; and the roof space, the most sacred part where heirlooms are stored. These correspond to the underworld, the earth, and the upperworld of traditional Austronesian cosmologies.

Houses are treated as if they were in some sense living entities; the "spirit" of the house is attached at the central pillar, the *posi' bola* ("navel of the house"). It is sometimes spoken of as an abstract force, and sometimes as a personified guardian spirit. Such ideas fit within an indigenous pre-Islamic world view in which everything is considered to be imbued with its own share of a cosmic vital force.

Communal houses of the north

Numerous peoples of Sulawesi formerly lived in enormous houses accomodating several nuclear families. These were built on massive

Opposite: *An old-style pile-built Toraja house with thatched roof.*

piles seven to nine feet high, and had steep roofs to facilitate the run-off of rain water.

Typically, the communal house consisted of a large central room with anywhere from two to five apartments giving off each side. As many as ten nuclear households could occupy one structure, each maintaining its own hearth and rice bins. This type of house has long vanished, however, and the style which is today regarded as "traditional" in Minahasa is actually one which developed in the 19th century.

The Toraja house

In highland South Sulawesi, some of the peoples living north of Tana Toraja also built multi-family houses. Today the To Maki still do. In Central Sulawesi in the early decades of this century, several styles existed, mostly featuring very steeply pitched shingled roofs with carved gable horns.

In the region east of Poso, various types of temple (*lobo*) associated with the traditional religion were formerly to be found. Great changes have been wrought in this area since the turn of the century by Salvation Army missionaries, however, and none of these structures survive.

The most vigorous and spectacular architectural tradition still flourishing in Sulawesi is undoubtably that of the Sa'dan Toraja, whose nobility continue to construct their magnificent saddle-roofed houses, covered with carved and painted panels in red, black, yellow, and white Some stylistic changes can be noticed in newer houses, namely a preference for ever greater extension of the ridgeline, the eaves ending in a sharper point. This style, now general, was formerly typical only of the Rantepao area, and is actually a recent development.

Surviving older houses have much blunter, shorter eaves than their predecessors, and only a slight curve to the roof; the older houses also tended to be much smaller. Today, house carpenters have increasingly become centralized in Rantepao, and this has also led to some standardization in the execution of the carved patterns which decorate the wall panels.

Economic growth in Tana Toraja since the late 1960s seems to have reversed a trend towards the extinction of these buildings, which today are still regarded as an important index of a family's social standing, and as essential sites for the performance of ceremonies. New wealth has begun to erode traditional social hierarchies, and people who in the past would have been prohibited from building large, carved houses may now, in defiance of the old rules, build themselves much grander houses. Much of the money for rebuilding houses comes from successful migrants who use this as a means of enhancing their family's prestige.

—*Roxana Waterson*

DEBORAH HILL

SHIPS

Sulawesi's Archipelagic Fleet

Perhaps the world's most impressive fleet of sailing wooden trade vessels are the Bugis *prahus* of Indonesia. Today there are an estimated 800 of these craft engaged in the timber trade from Kalimantan to Java, ranging in size from 120 to 200 or more tons. As many as 200 large *pinisi* may be seen in the port of Sunda Kelapa in Jakarta, while Ujung Pandang's Paotere harbor is lined with smaller boats: copra-carrying *lambo* cutters of Buton; single-masted *pinisi* unloading Kalimantan timber; motor boats from nearby islands laden with passengers and vegetables; and lateen-rigged boats from islands far off in the straits, carrying dried fish which will be exchanged for household wares and daily articles.

Gone are the days when large sailing schooners carried trade throughout the Indonesian archipelago, visiting even the small ports in remote islands. Most of today's large *pinisi* ply the waterways between Kalimantan and Java, carrying timber. It is still possible to see a few of them, though, trading among the outer islands, carrying kerosine, cement and household pots and pans. All but a few are motorized: the last of the true *prahu pinisi* of Surabaya, driven by sails alone, sank in 1987.

The age of trade

When Western explorers and traders first came into contact with the archipelago in the 16th century, *prahus* from South Sulawesi were sailing as far as Malacca on the coast of West Malaysia. The Portuguese apothecary Tome Pires, writing during a voyage in Malacca in 1515, recorded that Bugis-Makassar traders "come in their large well-built pangajavas [*pajalas*] with merchandise. They bring many foodstuffs: very white rice; they bring some gold. They take [home] cloths from Cambay and black benzoin in great quantities, and incense."

Local 18th and 19th-century sea charts show routes reaching to the coasts of Indochina and Burma. Sailing regulations and maritime laws of various South Sulawesi kingdoms dating from the early 18th century give fixed costs and schedules for cargo and passengers carried to Malaka in the west, Cambodia in the north, and as far east as Papua New Guinea.

In 1792, the English country-trader Captain Forest stated: "I have seen, 25 years ago, 15 Prows at a time at Bencoolen [on the west coast of Sumatra], loaded with a mixt cargo of spices, wax, cassia, sandle wood … and the cloths of Celebes called cambays." Early European settlers on the north coast of Australia were astonished to find Bugis and Makassarese *prahus* collecting trepang (sea cucumber, an expensive ingredient in Chinese cuisine) around the coasts of Australia, usually with the help of hardy Bajau "Sea Gypsies." The goods were then sold to Chinese traders in Makassar. Even today, every year some 30 vessels are caught in Australian waters, fishing without licenses, their crews asserting a centuries-old tradition of working the seas on Australia's coastal shelf.

In the 19th century a fleet of 800 *prahu padewakeng* sailed from as far east as Dobu in the Aru Islands to Singapore, bringing back a wealth of goods including cotton cloths, gold dust, birds' nests, tortoise shells, bird-of-paradise feathers, *trepang*, sandalwood, coffee and rice. In his journals, the future rajah of Sarawak, James Brooke, noted: "It is on the return cargo that the Bugis usually make their profits; it consists chiefly of arms, gunpowder, opium and cotton."

The trade routes of past centuries were fixed by the monsoons. With the end of the rainy season in March, ships used the slackening westerlies to sail to the eastern islands of the archipelago, where they collected local products. When the east monsoon started up in April, these goods were exchanged for other commodities along the coasts of Java, Kalimantan, and Sumatra. With the return of the west monsoon in September, sailors returned homeward to dock and refit their vessels during the stormy months of December and January.

Motorization and change

Today's elegant three-masted, eight-sailed Bugis *pinisi* is modeled on the 19th-century

Opposite: *Schooner docked at Paotere Harbor in Ujung Pandang.*

European schooner, which had a carrying capacity of 100-200 tons. If the winds were good, it could sail from Ujung Pandang to Surabaya in three days. Today, they are outfitted with diesel engines.

Motorization has brought considerable changes to the *prahu pinisi*: modern hulls are stronger and much larger, sometimes of up to 500 tons carrying capacity, and the mizzen mast and bowsprits have been shortened. Purists lament the passing of the earlier vessels, which were unquestionably more elegant than the huge "timber tankers" which have replaced them.

Motorization has also brought great changes to the dozen or so traditional centers of trade and shipbuilding in Sulawesi: Bira on the southern coast has been a village of sailors and shipowners for centuries. During the 1930s, some 4,000 men were employed on 300 Bira schooners. Today the harbor is virtually empty, with only a handful of small vessels docking at its shores. Many of today's *pinisi* crews are either Javanese or Madurese, or perhaps Bugis living in the port cities of Surabaya and Jakarta.

The last of the real sailors

The decline of sailing has meant a decline in seamanship, as engines strong enough to hold a fixed course with less fear of the hazards of wind and sea have replaced much of the knowledge formerly indispensable for long voyages. Knowledge of weather and winds, splicing and working ropes, and the maintenance of rigging and sails is no longer taught to youngsters who in former times followed their fathers out to sea as cooks and deckhands at the age of twelve. The ship's course, once set by knowledge of stars, sights, waves, and clouds, is today fixed by compass and chart.

There are still a small number of sailors who follow their trade in real sailing ships. Perhaps one thousand small vessels still go as far abroad as Singapore, where they may exchange birds from Irian Jaya and the Moluccas for consumer goods. Their crews still sail over the whole of Indonesia with two charts only—one for the western part, one for the east—and still rely more upon the stars than upon the small compasses they carry for navigation.

This dying breed of "real" sailors in Sulawesi still retain the traditional knowledge of uncharted reefs off forgotten islands, or of currents between dangerous straits far from the regular trading routes. On board the ships, one experiences the unchanging essence of a millennia-old way of life—lying becalmed on an oily sea before a storm, running with a good wind to an island never visited by anything other than these sailing boats, and gliding with a rising evening breeze into a sunset on the open sea.

—Horst H. Liebner

ARTS AND CRAFTS

Silk, Iron, Bamboo and Gold

From huge wooden boats evocative of Noah's ark, to tiny filigree earrings found on Makassar's street of gold; from boldly patterned *ikat* cloths of Kalumpang to the simple plaiting of a reed rice pouch in Toraja—Sulawesi's arts are almost entirely creations of the hand. As elsewhere in Indonesia, cloth, metal, wood and bamboo are the main resources.

Sulawesi is famous for two dramatically different types of cloth: the delicate checked silks of the south—some so fine that you can draw them through a gold ring—and the magnificent, massive, zig-zag *ikats* of Rongkong and Kalumpang.

Silk has been woven into sarongs by women of South Sulawesi for centuries. Today Soppeng is the center of Sulawesian sericulture, thanks to a project initiated in the mid-1970s with Japanese assistance. Much of the finest silk thread used by Sulawesi's weavers, however, is still imported.

The brilliant colors of modern Bugis silks at once catch the eye: startling juxtapositions (mostly in plaids) of multiple shades of magentas, blues, greens, purples, yellows, indeed every imaginable (and some unimaginable) color combination. Occasionally one finds an exceptionally subtle silk: ivory-colored squares laced, for example, with thin stripes of violet and silver.

In Mandar, home of the most refined silks in the archipelago, typical patterns are small checks, and colors tend to be more somber than the work of the Bugis: dark reds, browns, and indigos. As among the Bugis, natural dyes have been replaced by aniline colors, which are far simpler to prepare.

In both Bugis and Mandar society, silk sarongs are not merely treasured garments for both men and women, but are signs of wealth and status. In the past, certain patterns were restricted to the nobility. This is no longer true, but people still remember pattern-names and ranks.

Silk is not the stuff of everyday life, and silk sarongs are usually worn only at weddings, on Islamic holidays, and sometimes for Friday mosque prayers. It is not unusual in South Sulawesi to see a well-dressed couple zooming by on motorcycle, clad in stunning silks that somehow seem impervious to the dusty road.

All cloth in Sulawesi is made by women, using a backstrap or body-tension loom. The process is complex (spinning, dying, threading the warp, and eventually weaving), and the work is laborious. On the other hand, weaving can be carried out at home, and, if necessary may be stopped at any moment, the loom quickly rolled up and stored.

Traveling through South Sulawesi, it is not uncommon to see women weaving in the shade beneath their house, or on the front porch. In parts of Mandar, every woman wove both silk and cotton a century ago. Now weaving is becoming increasingly rare: other work (fish-trading, for example) is more lucrative. And, as throughout Indonesia, ready-made clothing is now easily available and more popular.

Exuberant *ikats*

Unlike silk, which was and still is produced primarily for clothing, the cotton *ikat* textiles of Central Sulawesi were woven not as garments, but as ceremonial hangings and shrouds. *Ikat*, "to tie," entails tying the pattern into the threads before they are dyed. The knotted sections are covered with a fiber that resists the dye, the design emerging in the woven cloth.

The magnificent *ikats* from the Rongkong and Kalumpang river valleys were originally funeral shrouds. They were also traded to other parts of Sulawesi, and in southern Toraja, they were used as funeral banners.

Both Rongkong and Kalumpang were destroyed in the guerrilla war that raged from 1951-64, but many of the cloths produced there survived in other areas. Today such cloths appear in shops in Rantepao and Ujung Pandang, as local people, encouraged by high prices, sell once-precious family heirlooms. A few spectacular examples of 19th-century cloths survive: these textiles "radiate power" through their monumental vision, precise execution, and their "warm orange glow, like embers in a forge."

Right: *Weavings in the remote Rongkong Valley in Tana Toraja. In the background are handsome Toraja rice barns.*

Metalwork

A pairing of cloth and metal is often found in Indonesian ritual, the cloth associated with female, metal with male. In the past, brass and copper ornaments, amulets, and small statues were produced in Central Sulawesi by the "lost wax" (*cire perdue*) casting method. Today this art is no longer known, but metalworking survives in Tana Toraja where a number of iron-forgers still practice the trade using the traditional "Malay bellows."

A unit of paired bamboo pipes is fired from below; the forger sitting above and pumping the bellows with a pair of pistons tipped with chicken feathers. On an anvil, long knives are fashioned from automobile springs and other scrap iron, to be used for purposes both sacred and mundane. Iron has a tremendous historical significance in this region: it is likely that the source of nickel-rich iron ore in Malili was a basis for the greatness of the ancient kingdom of Luwu.

Elegant 18th and 19th-century silver *sirih* (betel nut) sets and the delicate silver *caping* worn by young girls can still be purchased in silver and gold shops along Jl. Somba Opu in Ujung Pandang. The workmanship is exquisite: bold, flower-shaped spittoons, delicately beaten *sirih* servers and silver bowls with embossed floral patterns compete for the eye.

Of all metals, gold is the most highly prized, and in poetry is referred to as the highest good. Village women keep and wear gold if at all possible; in the past only the nobility could do so. In earlier times the gold was often mixed with silver in equal proportions. Modern silver filigree-work from Kendari is also sold along Jl. Somba Opu. Delicately fashioned earrings and pendants, hair pins and bracelets can be purchased either in silver or gold. In some shops, the goldsmiths are working in the back, and you may ask to watch.

Bamboo and basket-weaving

Bamboo containers are used everywhere for transport and storage. These range from a freshly cut green bamboo stem full of frothing *tuak* to a smoke-blackened tobacco container, decorated with fine plaited bamboo strips and a carved wooden lid.

Baskets are woven throughout the island, but the finest examples come from Tana Toraja. The classic Toraja basket, the bamboo *baka,* is carried by a woven tump line across a woman's forehead, the basket supported on her back.

Another classic item which has changed only slightly from earlier times is the conical bamboo hat worn by Toraja women. These hats have an extraordinarily delicate weave. Often sold to tourists, they are still an indispensable possession for every village woman.

—*Toby Alice Volkman*

FOOD

Spicy Rat and Buffalo Cheese

Chances are the visitor will arrive in Sulawesi at Ujung Pandang, the capital of South Sulawesi and a city renowned all over Indonesia for its seafood. Crabs, shrimp, squid, and lobster are prepared here by roasting over charcoal, then served with rice and fresh chili sauce. *Bandeng* (milkfish) or *baronang*—popular with foreigners because it has relatively few bones—freshly grilled and dipped in a piquant-sweet sauce, is a truly memorable dish. Poached fish, called *pallumara* in Makassarese, is another tasty method of preparing seafood.

Ujung Pandang is also famous for a dish called *coto Mankasara*—a spicy stew of chopped buffalo innards flavored with a dash of fresh lime and chili sauce. It is normally served in the morning with rice cakes steamed in woven leaf containers.

A unique specialty of the Duri-speaking area of the Enrekang district is *dangke,* a cheese made from buffalo milk, which is sometimes eaten fried. East and Southeast Asian cultures in general traditionally make little use of milk or dairy products; the buffalo-milk cheese of this part of South Sulawesi is a rare exception.

Chili rat

The largely Christian Minahasans of north Sulawesi seem to consider almost no dish to be palatable without a generous addition of *cabe* or chili peppers. Any dish with the words *rica-rica* in its name is likely to be plastered with a *sambal* mixture of hot peppers, tomatoes, onions, garlic and ginger. A further local distinction is a predilection for unkosher dishes including wild rats, bats, and of course pork. *RW* (pronounced "airway," and meaning "fine-haired") is a euphemism for dog.

But fear not: there is food too for the faint of heart. Try delicious charcoal-grilled Manadonese pork *sate*, or fried carp (*ikan mas*), eaten with a hot chili, onion, tomato and lime dip known locally as *dabu-dabu*. Even better (though strangely uncommon in restaurants) is local smoked tuna (*cakalang fufu*) fried or cooked in coconut milk.

Another popular Manadonese dish is *tinutuan* or *bubur Manado,* a thick savory rice porridge mixed with various greens and eaten with bits of fried salt fish. *Milu,* a won-

KAL MULLER

derfully clear, slightly sour soup made with kernels of young corn, small shrimp, chilis, lime, and other seasoning, is native to the Gorontalo district in western Manado.

An Eden of tropical fruit

Bananas come in all shapes and sizes in Sulawesi, ranging from the tiny *pisang lilin* (candle banana) to the huge *pisang tanduk* (horn banana). Eat them raw, fried in batter, cooked in a sweet, coconut cream stew (*kolak*), or fried in little chips.

Citrus fruits here are also of an abundance unknown in the West: sweet *jeruk siompu* from Buton in Southeast Sulawesi and *limung cina* from Manado are excellent. Mixed with boiling water and plenty of sugar, *jeruk panas* (variously called *air jeruk*, *jeruk peres*, or *jeruk nipis*) is a marvelous drink, even on a hot day. *Markisa* or passion fruit juice—available in bottles—is great with gin.

Other local specialties include the reddish-purple mangosteen (*manggis*) the huge rough-skinned jackfruit (*nangka*), and the hairy red-skinned *rambutan* (related to the lychee). Exotic creatures like the palmyra fruit (*lontar*), the *salak* or snakefruit, along with papayas, mangos, starfruits, guavas and soursop, round out this cornucopia of tropical delicacies. And then there is the durian.

If you are fortunate enough to be in Sulawesi during April—the peak of the durian season—you will see stalls piled high with the huge spiky fruit set up along the sides of roads. The smell and the appearance are unmistakable. Approach the durian with an open mind and persist beyond the first attempt at friendship; it is, as they say, "an acquired taste."

Drinks and sweet confections

Sulawesi produces some of the finest *arabica* coffee in the world, but little of it reaches the local market. The coffee drunk in Sulawesi is of the common *robusta* variety, frequently "cut" with maize, and prepared by simply pouring boiling water over fresh grounds and a teaspoonful of sugar in a glass. Or drink it with a dollop of sweetened condensed milk as an after-dinner treat. Plain tea (*teh tawar*) is served everywhere with meals.

No account of food would be complete without mention of *tuak*, or palm wine. *Tuak* is tapped from a variety of palms—the best comes from the flower of the sugar palm (*Arenga saccharifera*). The liquid of the *lontar* palm of the drier regions of South Sulawesi is also quite good, while the sap of the coastal-dwelling *nipah* palm is considered inferior. Good *tuak* is a superb drink, slightly sweet but becoming more potent and acidic as the day progresses. The quality varies considerably—if you are not enchanted the first time, don't hesitate to try again.

Manioc (tapioca) roasted or deep-fried is also a popular snack. There are various kinds of meat-and-vegetable turnovers, called *jalan kote* in the South and *panada* in the North. Numerous *kue*, or cakes, come with an assortment of fillings. Not to be missed are roasted cashew nuts, a major product of the islands of Southeast Sulawesi but also grown in parts of South Sulawesi as well.

In the North, one should look for *halwa kenari*, a candy made of the *kenari* nut coated with local brown sugar, and various other confections such as *bagea*. Other treats are confections of brown palm sugar mixed with coconut or peanuts (*wajik*) wrapped in individual leaf containers. *Eskrim goreng* (fried ice cream) is another Manadanese specialty which should definitely not be overlooked on a gastronomic tour of the region.

The etiquette of eating

To eat in Sulawesi, as in most parts of Asia, means to eat rice. Indeed, in many of the languages of Sulawesi, the word for "rice" is identical to the word "eat."

Food is an important part of hospitality in Sulawesi. Even a very poor family will offer you at least a glass of boiled water, or send someone up a tree to cut a few coconuts. You should ignore what you are offered until your host has invited you to eat and drink—apart from perhaps making a polite suggestion that your host or hostess should not go to any trouble on your account.

It would be impolite to refuse a host's offering, but then again don't polish off everything put in front of you—you could be eating your way through tomorrow's provisions. Food and drink on such social occasions are a way of initiating friendship and goodwill, and probably not an attempt to appease the appetites of ravenous travelers.

When in Sulawesi, you may be surprised to see someone seated in a restaurant look around the room and gesture for all present to join him in his meal. The invitation isn't meant to be taken literally—it indicates generosity as well as the social nature of eating in this culture.

—*Tim Babcock*

Opposite: *Hanging fish out to dry.*

PART II

South Sulawesi

Covering 82,768 square kilometers (51,730 sq mi), an area the size of England, the province of Sulawesi Selatan or South Sulawesi (often referred to as Sulsel), is geographically and culturally diverse. Sulsel possesses a fertile lowland rice bowl—the most densely populated region of Indonesia outside of Java and Bali—as well as towering mountains, an arid southern zone, and an unusually long coastline dotted with fishing villages, where thousands of boats and ingeniously designed traps of rattan and bamboo line the shore.

Southern Sulawesi is home to four major ethnic groups and several minor ones. In the northern reaches of the peninsula, fecund plains and rolling hills give way to 3,000-meter mountains, a region inhabited by some 550,000 people collectively designated as "Toraja," and known locally by a host of other names. The best known of these peoples, the Sa'dan Toraja, derive their name from the great brown river that courses through the mountains. (See Part III: "Tana Toraja.")

Nearly three million Bugis live along South Sulawesi's extensive coastal areas and throughout much of the fertile central lowlands. One and a half million Makassarese are concentrated in the southern part of the province and around the port of Ujung Pandang, which is the largest city in eastern Indonesia. Along the peninsula's northwestern coastal strip live half a million Mandarese, said to be the finest sailors in all of Sulawesi. These three peoples are renowned throughout the archipelago for their skill and fearlessness as seafarers and (in the case of the Bugis) as colonizers of distant coasts.

The people of South Sulawesi draw their life from the land as well as the sea. Rice abounds in the well-irrigated paddies of the lowland plains, while the province's gently rolling hills yield important crops, including maize, cassava, sesame, pepper, cloves, nutmeg, coffee, cacao, coconuts and bananas. Silk weaving, lake fishing and trade provide additional cash income for many inland farming families.

Rulers in the lowland kingdoms first embraced Islam in the early 17th century, and the people of South Sulawesi are known today for their devotion. In villages one awakens to the hum of small boys and girls chanting the Koran. The chants are repeated daily for years until properly memorized.

Islam in Sulawesi, while important, is generally quite tolerant, and people have found ingenious ways of incorporating elements of older beliefs and practices into their daily lives. There is no contradiction in offering a prayer to Allah and a bunch of bananas to the spirits of the sea.

In the former kingdoms and petty states of Sulawesi, rank and status were paramount concerns, and were carefully demarcated. While the kingdoms no longer exist, the hierarchy of status is still important in the upper levels of society. Language, dress, how and where one sits, the utensils with which one is served, and numerous other cues serve to indicate one's social position.

Weddings, circumcisions, childbirth, and other life-cycle events are celebrated with style in South Sulawesi. Every family attempts to hold the largest, most splendid ceremony it can afford. A large gathering will include crowds of men smoking and drinking coffee under awnings erected outside the house. The women are inside, arranging platters of sticky rice cakes and bananas, or gossiping in the front room, clad in their best silk sarongs, fanning themselves to stay alert in the overpowering heat. The highest compliment that can be paid to a ritual is the word *ramai*, meaning crowded, noisy, and filled with energy and life.

—*Toby Alice Volkman*

Overleaf: *Bugis schooners unloading at Paotere Harbor, Ujung Pandang. Photo: Kal Muller.* **Left:** *A fisherman, the same harbor. Photo: J.-L. Dugast..*

PEOPLES OF THE SOUTH

Seafarers, Traders and Christians

South Sulawesi is home to four major ethnic groups: the Bugis, the Makassarese, the Toraja and the Mandarese. Each of these groups speaks a related but mutually unintelligible language. The Bugis and Toraja languages are quite similar, sharing many common terms, while Mandarese and Makassarese are more distantly related. Each language has numerous dialects, many of which are associated with the kingdoms into which Sulawesi was formerly divided.

Major groups

The Bugis, numbering about 3,200,000, are the most populous of the four peoples of Sulsel. Most Bugis occupy the central area of the peninsula, including the broad, fertile plain between Pinrang and Watampone. Although counted among the most staunchly Islamic populations in Indonesia, the great majority of Bugis, like their Makassarese and Mandarese Muslim neighbors, continue to observe some older, pre-Islamic customs.

The Makassarese, who number about 1,500,000, share close cultural ties with the Bugis. The lands they occupy are generally less fertile (with the exception of very productive land in the vicinity of Maros) and they depend to a greater extent than do the Bugis on the sea for their livelihood.

The Mandarese are also culturally close to the Bugis. About 400,000 Mandarese occupy the less hospitable northwestern part of the peninsula, as far north as Mamuju. Unlike the more prosperous Bugis and Makassarese people, who occupy better land, the Mandarese never developed extensive and centralized kingdoms, but lived in loosely-united and relatively autonomous villages.

The Toraja occupy the northern part of the peninsula, where they are distributed over a large and difficult terrain. They are divided into a number of sub-groups, including the Sa'dan, Rongkong, Seko, Mamasa and Mangki. About 330,000 Toraja live in the central highlands known today as Tana Toraja, while another 200,000 live in the lowland towns and cities of South Sulawesi. Because they inhabit a mountainous area, the Toraja have insufficent wet-rice land to feed their population, and many make a living by growing coffee, rice and sago.

Social hierarchies

Bugis and Makassarese social life is characterized by a highly formalized class structure. Pre-colonial society was divided into nobles, commoners and slaves. While the nobility tried to maintain the divisions, capable young men could be "recruited" by marriage to a higher-status family.

The most desirable occupation today for a

JILL GOCHER

Bugis is a high-level job as a government employee (*pegawai negeri*). But unlike the Javanese, the Bugis do not consider trade and business inherently low-status occupations. For centuries the Bugis have been known throughout the Indonesian archipelago as traders, pirates and settlers. Crawfurd, an early governor of Singapore, described the Bugis as being among "the most advanced people ... and the most enterprising of all the native tribes of the archipelago." Marsden, in his *History of Sumatra*, mentions their reputation for courage. Today, the Bugis are still regarded as one of the most enterprising and forthright peoples in Indonesia.

The Toraja share few cultural affinities with the Bugis, Makassarese and Mandarese.

Living in the remote mountainous interior, the Toraja were isolated from contacts with the European traders and Islamic teachers who influenced the lowlands and coasts. Not until the 19th century did Dutch missionaries make contact with the Toraja. Since then, some 60 percent have become Christians and 7.5 percent Muslims. The others, especially the older people, have remained adherents of *aluk to dolo*, the traditional religion.

Family

Most people in Sulsel live in small villages. Kinship and marriage is similar to Western patterns: individuals belong equally to their mother's and father's families, and a married couple lives in their own house.

The relationship between father and son is rather formal: it is considered improper for a son to contradict his father. Brothers—having equal status—are often great rivals. In the Chronicle of Tanete, a small west coast kingdom, constant quarrels between brothers cause their father to seek a successor to the throne from neighboring Segiri.

Mothers and daughters enjoy a closer relationship, but the most affectionate relationship is that between brother and sister. According to the Bugis and Makassarese, a brother is the protector and guardian of his sister. This is an important theme in the Bugis epic poem *I La Galigo*, which narrates the separation of Sawerigading and his twin sister Wé Tenriabéng, and their efforts to find one other.

A girl is the symbol of her family's honor. In earlier times, even an accidental meeting between an unmarried girl and a young man could have serious consequences, as custom required that the girl's brother seek vengeance by killing the offender with a dagger. In the tragic poem *I La Padoma*, the hero La Padoma is killed by his lover's brother, who catches them alone in her bedroom. Even today, a male visitor will sometimes cough before entering a house in order to give young women the opportunity to withdraw.

Between the ages of three and seven, most Makassarese and Bugis girls are submitted to clitoridectomy and ear-piercing. Boys are circumcised at ten to fifteen years of age. The feast accompanying the operation is often very elaborate, especially among the higher classes. Filing of the upper incisors and subsequent blackening with varnish, a practice dating back hundreds of years, once took place around the age of puberty for both sexes, but is no longer practiced.

Most marriages are arranged by the parents of the couple, usually with the help of a respected elder. There is a strong preference for marriage with one's relatives; the ideal marriage is between first cousins, but second- and third-cousin marriages are more common. In the competetive, status-conscious societies of South Sulawesi, an ambitious young man with an aggressive personality is a the ideal partner. A girl is supposed to have the complementary personality: obedient and timid. But today many more young people are choosing their own partners, often classmates from their school or university. If a couple cannot obtain their parents' blessing for marriage, they may elope.

Inter-ethnic rivalry is common. For

instance, the Bugis—still the dominant group in South Sulawesi—are quick to point out that Tana Toraja used to be a source of slaves and that today many Toraja work as domestic servants in Ujung Pandang. Their acceptance of such jobs, and their ignominious past as slaves, indicate that the Toraja are of a low rank. According also to Bugis wisdom, the Makassarese are hot headed, inferior farmers, and dubious Muslims. The inhabitants of Jeneponto, a dry and poor area in the extreme south, are the butt of numerous jokes.

—*Ian Caldwell*

Opposite and above: *Bugis children. Numbering over three million, the devoutly Muslim Bugis are the largest of Sulawesi's numerous ethnic groups.*

C.W.M. van de Velde.

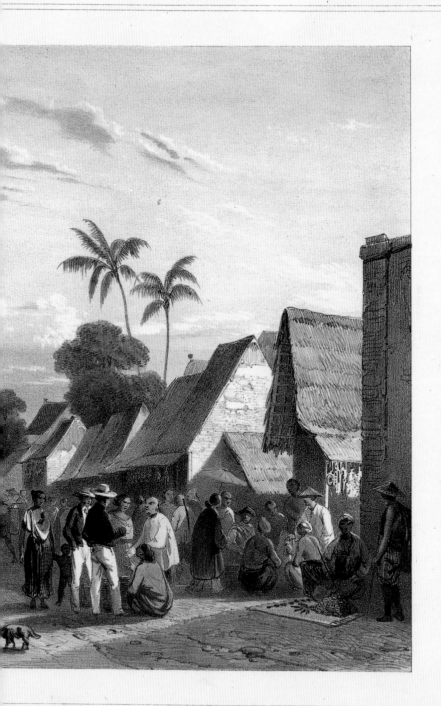

F. Lacona

OLD MAKASSAR

Cosmopolitan Kingdom by the Sea

Generations of travelers have come to Ujung Pandang by sea, and this is still the best way to approach this charming city. The only Indonesian city which actually embraces the sea, Ujung Pandang curls along a narrow strip of beach ridges facing westward to the Makassar Straits. For Joseph Conrad it was "the prettiest, and perhaps the cleanest-looking, of all the towns in the islands."

One feels the sea most strongly on Jalan Penghibur, sipping a drink in one of the kiosks facing the sea, watching the odd fishing boat pass on its way to the islands; in the bustle of the *prahu* harbor at Paotere; or in one of the fish markets. The great mass of Fort Rotterdam dominates the central waterfront, and it is not difficult from its battlements to visualize a Makassarese galley, a Dutch East Indiaman, or Joseph Conrad himself on the bridge of his British trading ship, calling at these same shores.

The modern city stretches ever further inland, the road to the airport now taking the place of the waterfront as the gateway to Makassar. While the modern buildings of the central government and the regional House of Assembly lead the way in urban expansion away from the waterfront, most of the life of the city still remains in its historic heart—the commercial center stretching north of the fort where architectural relics dating back more than 300 years can be seen. Here one feels the pulse of a great Asian city—where Chinese, Indians, Europeans, Japanese, and every manner of Indonesian jostle each other in the streets and shops.

Traders and sea nomads

The city's original name, Makassar (or Mangkasara), is at least as old as the 14th century. In the 16th century it had become Sulawesi's major port and political power, due to the rising influence of the Gowa and Tallo kingdoms, as well as the maritime might of the Bajau "sea nomads."

Malay traders made their home in the city in the 1550s, and the first mosque was reportedly built for them two decades later. The city grew rapidly between 1600 and 1630, by which time it was one of the great trade entrepôts of Southeast Asia.

Tallo and Gowa had their own original centers, where kings were crowned and buried. The trading city and kingdom of Makassar developed between these two semi-sacred centers, and was defended by a series of forts and a long sea wall stretching along the coast. The most important fort was Sombaopu ("homage to the lord") at the mouth of the Jeneberang, which has now been partially restored. Sombaopu contained the elevated wooden palaces of the king and leading nobles, a round mosque, and various warehouses and living quarters. Just to the north of Sombaopu were the Portuguese and Gujerati quarters; to the south of the fort were the market, a large residential area including Ternatan and Makassarese *kampungs*, and the major port area.

After defeats by a combined Dutch/Bugis military force, Makassar was forced in 1667 to surrender the fort of Ujung Pandang, about seven kilometers north of Sombaopu. The Dutch renamed it Fort Rotterdam and made it the base of their operations against the Makassarese. In 1669 Sombaopu was razed, and the Sultan of Gowa was forced to live on the outskirts of the new Dutch town where he could be controlled.

The new Dutch city was a small one, dominated by the imposing figure of Fort Rotterdam. In 1730 the population was only 5,000, half of which were slaves. Company officials and soldiers were lodged in the fort, while the remaining Europeans, Chinese and Christians lived within the small walled city of Vlaardingen. This was bounded by present-day Jalan Nusantara and Jalan Jampea, and stretched north of the fort as far as Jalan Lembeh. At night it was kept locked and guarded. This area is the oldest part of the city, with many surviving 18th-century buildings. Its origins are remembered in the names *Kampung Belanda* ("Dutch village") and *Pintu Dua* ("two gates"), which locals still apply to the area.

Some of the Malay trading community of old Makassar eventually returned to live in Kampung Melayu, just to the north of the walls of Vlaardingen, at the end of the 17th century. A little farther north was Kampung Wajo, where the Bugis traders lived. The Vlaardingen area, gradually becoming more

Chinese in composition, was to remain the commercial center of Makassar until after Indonesian independence in 1945.

During the 19th century the economy of Makassar changed from one based largely on the fort and the slave trade, back to its previous role as a collecting point for all the produce of eastern Indonesia—pearls, sea-slugs, rattan, sandalwood, copra, and the famous "Makassar" oil from the nuts of the *bado* tree, which Western gentlemen of the time used to pomade their hair.

With its increasingly dynamic economy, Makassar grew rapidly. Estimated at around 15,000 in the early 19th century, Makassar's population reached 84,855 in 1930, and shot up to 708,465 by 1980. In 1938 Makassar had become the capital of a new Dutch superprovince called "The Great East," embracing all of eastern Indonesia. The governor's mansion built on Jalan Sudirman was of a palatial opulence appropriate for the ruler of such an extensive territory. During the Second World War the mansion was occupied by the Japanese official responsible for an even larger chunk of Indonesian real estate, which also included Kalimantan. From 1947 to 1950 it was the residence of the president of the state of East Indonesia.

The rapid growth of Makassar in the 1950s, swelled by multitudes of refugees from fighting in the interior of the province, brought about many physical changes in the city. The former moat and parkland behind the fort was filled in to make room for a post office and other public buildings. The swamps and salt-pans which had bounded the city to the northeast were drained to provide a site for Hasanuddin University, officially founded in 1956. The eastward expansion of the urban *kampungs* continued. In the early 1970s many streets in the oldest part of the city were widened, sacrificing the traditional old storefronts to the freer movement of traffic. A vast Chinese and Christian cemetery was moved out of the city and replaced by the present Central Market and the commercial area around it.

Daeng Patompo, the city's mayor during this period of tremendous growth, also increased the area of Makassar by legislation in 1971. Makassar's growth, however, was the loss of neighboring regions like Maros and Gowa. As a concession, perhaps, the name of the city was changed to Ujung Pandang, the name customarily used by the Bugis and Makassarese of the interior. The name Makassar lives on, however, in local titles and organizations, and in the mythic presence of the city's exciting past.

—*Anthony Reid*

Overleaf and above: *Artists' impressions of the "Malay market" in Makassar. The Turkish flavor of the one above suggests that the artist never made it anywhere near the archipelago.*

UJUNG PANDANG

Gateway to the Eastern Isles

Ujung Pandang is the largest city and communications center east of Surabaya. It is the focal point not only for the populous province of South Sulawesi, but for the thousands of islands and hundreds of ethnic groups which make up the social fabric of eastern Indonesia. From these islands, people come to Ujung Pandang to trade, study, work, buy supplies, or simply to escape the constraints of village life and to step into a wider world.

At one level Ujung Pandang is a typical Indonesian city, with its government offices, Chinese and Indonesian shops and markets, Muslim and Christian places of worship, and a public life conducted in *Bahasa Indonesia*. You will soon discover, however, that Ujung Pandang is also a microcosm of the eastern seas, and that dozens of languages are spoken in its surrounding *kampungs*. The official government census reveals only the larger language groups in the city. At latest count, in addition to the large proportions of Indonesian, Makassarese, and Bugis speakers, there were 2000 speakers of Javanese, 300 of Sundanese, 380 of Batak, 130 of Minangkabau, and 100 of Banjarese, but tens of thousands in the "others" category which comprises most of eastern Indonesia's myriad languages.

The temples of the Chinese and Balinese are the most obvious signs of Ujung Pandang's cultural diversity; but there are also churches for the Ambonese, Minahasan, Torajan, Batak and Sangirese communities, and mosques favored by Gorontalese, Javanese, Madurese, or Ambonese. Clusters of people from the islands of Selayar, Buton, Tanimbar, Kei, Alor, Bonerate, and Banda live in *kampungs* near the city. In the tourist shops of Jalan Sombaopu you will find carvings from Irian Jaya and eastern Kalimantan, masks from Tanimbar and Bali, bronze drums from Alor, *ikat* weavings from Flores, wooden canes from central Sulawesi, clove ships from Ambon, betel-sets and metalware from the Bugis-Makassar area, Chinese ceramics, and old Dutch, British and·Spanish coins brought in from all over the archipelago. Ask the seamen at Paotere where they hail from, and you will understand how the life-blood of the eastern seas continues to pulse through this great city.

Fort Rotterdam

The massive walls of the waterfront Dutch fortress formerly known as Fort Rotterdam guard fine buildings of the 17th to 18th centuries. Now a museum and cultural center, the so-called "Benteng" now houses offices of the Indonesian Archaeological Service.

The name Ujung Pandang first appears as one of several forts protecting the heart of the Makassar kingdom. The first fort on this site, with earth walls, was built about 1550 under King Tunipallangga of Gowa. This fort was rebuilt in brick in 1634 by Sultan Alauddin to protect the northern suburbs of the city as it then was.

In 1667, it was specified in the Treaty of Bungaya that all the Makassar forts were to be destroyed except two. The king could remain at Sombaopu, though this was also destroyed two years later. The northern fort, Jumpandang, was to become the Dutch headquarters. It was described by the Dutch commander, Admiral Cornelis Speelman as "a strong fortress with a supply of good drinking water and situated in a healthy locality, possessing moreover a suitable harbor where our ships can shelter from almost any wind, so that it might well be termed a bastion of the valuable Easterly Districts."

Under Admiral Speelman the name was changed to Fort Rotterdam (his birthplace) and plans were made to transform it into a well-fortified castle, a center for administration as well as defence. A complete reconstruction in stone was begun in 1673, with a thousand workmen taking several years to complete the walls alone. Stone was brought from Maros, wood from Bantaeng and Tanete, lime from Selayar. The fortifications were completed well before their greatest test in 1739, when the forces of Karaeng Bontolangkasa launched several unsuccessful assaults against them.

Most of the buildings inside the fort were constructed in the late 17th or early 18th century to house the Dutch garrison and the offices of the Governor of Celebes. The Dutch traveler Stavorinus noted in 1775 that the lofty church in the center had been "neatly rebuilt a few years ago, and has room for

Ujung Pandang

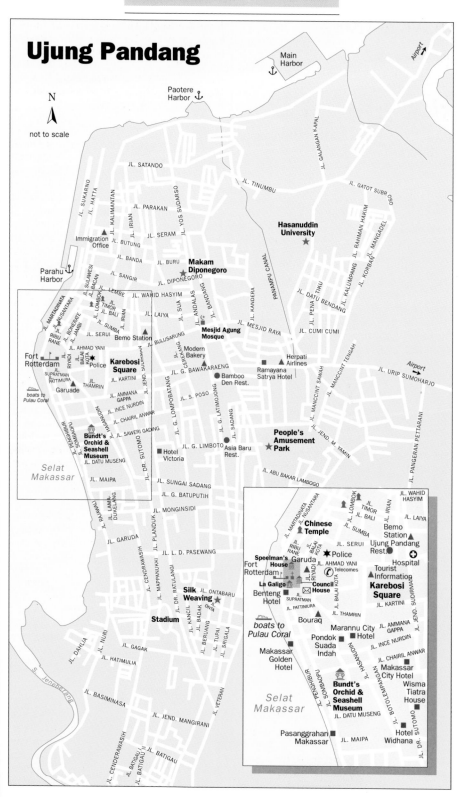

N

not to scale

Main Harbor

Airport

Paotere Harbor

JL. SATANDO

JL. SUKARNO

JL. HATTA

JL. KALIMANTAN

JL. PARAKAN

JL. IRIAN

JL. BUTUNG

JL. SERAM

JL. YOS SUDARSO

JL. TINUMBU

JL. GALANGAN K-APAL

JL. GATOT SUBR OSO

JL. RAHMAN HAKIM

JL. KALUMPANG

JL. KORBAN-MANGADEL

Hasanuddin University

Immigration Office

JL. BANDA

JL. BURU

Parahu Harbor

Makam Diponegoro

JL. SANGIR

JL. DIPONEGORO

JL. SULAWESI

JL. BACAN

JL. LEMBE

JL. WAHID HASYIM

JL. LAIYA

JL. SUA

JL. ANDALAS

JL. BANDANG

JL. MESJID RAYA

JL. KANDERA

PANAMPU CANAL

JL. DATU BENDANG

JL. PENA TIMU

JL. CUMI CUMI

JL. MARTADINATA

JL. NUSANTARA

JL. LOMBOK

JL. TIMOR

JL. BALI

JL. SUMBA

JL. IRIAN

JL. SERUI

JL. BONERATE

JL. JAMBI

JL. RIBU RANE

JL. AHMAD YANI

JL. RIYADI

JL. BALAI KOTA

JL. JEND. SUDIRMAN

JL. BULUSARUNG

JL. CEREKANG

JL. G. BAWAKARAENG

Modern Bakery

Mesjid Agung Mosque

Bemo Station

Fort Rotterdam

Police

Karebosi Square

JL. SUPRATMAN

JL. PATTIMURA

Garuade

JL. THAMRIN

JL. KARTINI

JL. AMMANA GAPPA

JL. INCE NURDIN

JL. CHAIRIL ANWAR

JL. SAWERI GADING

JL. HASANUDDIN

JL. DR. SUTOMO

JL. G. LOMPOBATANG

JL. S. POSO

JL. G. LATIMOJONG

JL. SADANG

Bamboo Den Rest.

Herpati Airlines

Ramayana Satrya Hotel

JL. MANCINT SAWAH

JL. MANCINT TENGAH

Airport

JL. URIP SUMOHARJO

JL. JEND. M. YAMIN

JL. PANGERAN PETTARANI

boats to Pulau Coral

Bundt's Orchid & Seashell Museum

JL. DATU MUSENG

Hotel Victoria

JL. G. LIMBOTO

Asia Baru Rest.

People's Amusement Park

JL. ABU BAKAR LAMBOGO

JL. PENGHIBUR

JL. SOMBAOPU

JL. LAMR-DUKELANG

JL. MAIPA

JL. SUNGAI SADANG

JL. G. BATUPUTIH

JL. MONGINSIDI

JL. GARUDA

JL. CENDRAWASIH

JL. MAPPANUKKI

JL. PLANDUK

JL. L. D. PASEWANG

JL. RAJAWALI

JL. DR. RATULANGI

Silk Weaving

JL. ONTABARU

JL. ONTA

Stadium

JL. KANCIL

JL. BADAK

JL. BERUANG

JL. TUPAI

JL. SRIGALA

JL. VETERAN

JL. DAHLIA

JL. NURI

JL. GAGAK

JL. HATIMULIA

S. Jeneberang

JL. BASIMINASA

JL. JEND. MANGIRANI

JL. CENDERAWASIH

JL. BATGAU II

JL. BATIGAU

JL. BATIGAU

Selat Makassar

Inset

JL. WAHID HASYIM

JL. MARTADINATA

JL. NUSANTARA

JL. LOMBOK

JL. TIMOR

JL. BALI

JL. IRIAN

JL. LAIYA

Chinese Temple

JL. SUMBA

Bemo Station

JL. SERUI

Ujung Pandang Rest.

JL. RIBU RANE

JL. BALAI KOTA

Police

Speelman's House

Garuda

Hospital

Fort Rotterdam

JL. AHMAD YANI

Telecomes

Tourist Information

La Galigo

Council House

Karebosi Square

Benteng Hotel

JL. SUPRATMAN

JL. BALAI KOTA

JL. RIYADI

JL. KARTINI

JL. PATTIMURA

Bouraq

JL. THAMRIN

JL. AMMANA GAPPA

boats to Pulau Coral

Marannu City Hotel

JL. HASANDIN

JL. INCE NURDIN

Pondok Suada Indah

JL. CHAIRIL ANWAR

Makassar Golden Hotel

Makassar City Hotel

JL. BOTOLEMPANGAN

Wisma Tiatra House

JL. DR. SUTOMO

Selat Makassar

Bundt's Orchid & Seashell Museum

JL. DATU MUSENG

Pasanggrahan Makassar

JL. MAIPA

Hotel Widhana

two hundred persons. The seat of the governor is wholly gilt, and is under a canopy, opposite the pulpit."

During the Napoleonic period, when the English under Raffles took over Dutch claims in the Indies, a British detachment was sent to occupy the fort. A contemporary Malay diary recorded that on 26 February 1812 the Dutch commander solemnly surrendered the keys of the fort to commandant Roy Phillips. The (English) ships discharged their guns, all the ships' cannon firing, after which the guns around the fort fired. The (Dutch) Company's flag was lowered and the English flag hoisted on the flagstaff.

Within a few years the Dutch returned, and the range of their power was gradually extended. By the middle of the 19th century, the governor was able to move out of Fort Rotterdam into a more spacious abode (now the police office in Jl. A. Yani, just east of the Grand Hotel). Yet it was not until 1937 that Fort Rotterdam ceased to serve as a military installation, when it was handed over to the Fort Rotterdam Foundation for cultural uses. At the same time, it was listed as a historical monument in the register of the Archaeological Service.

During the Japanese occupation of World War II, the fort was used as a center of scientific research in agriculture and linguistics. After the war an attempt was again made to develop it as a cultural center, but the trou-

bles of South Sulawesi were far from over. The fort was pressed into service as emergency housing for nearly twenty years, making proper maintenance impossible and causing extensive damage. The present restoration began in 1970 when the whole area was again available for cultural purposes.

The fort's original name, Ujung Pandang, can be variously translated as "the furthest visible point" (as seen from the south) or as "Screwpine Cape," from the screwpine or pandanus palm which grew at this point, and was used in making mats. It was also known as Benteng Panyu (turtle) because it looked like a huge turtle crawling to the sea. This creature was seen as a symbol of the Makassarese, who are based on the land but make their living at sea; moreover, the fort protected the people of Makassar, as the turtle's hard shell protects its body.

Construction of the fort

The walls of the fort are about two meters wide and seven meters high, forming a square with protruding bastions at each corner, and a fifth in the middle of the seaward wall, beside the main gate. Each of these bastions is traditionally named after a district or island in eastern Indonesia. The walls and bastions still stand intact except for the southern wall (behind the La Galigo Museum), which was demolished after World War II. At the same time the moat around the fort

was filled in and the two bridges, one to the main gate and the other to the postern gate on the east, were removed. A circuit of the present walls is best made by climbing the stone stairway in the barracks building (now a library) on the eastern side, then turning northwards and continuing around until reaching the seaward side. It is possible to descend in any of the three front bastions.

"Speelman's House," an imposing structure on the left as you enter, is the oldest of the present buildings in the fort, dating from 1686. Speelman himself had left Makassar by then—he became Governor-General of the Dutch East India Company in Batavia in 1681 and died in 1684—but the house did serve as governor's residence for nearly two centuries. The fine floors and doorways are particularly notable.

Unmistakably Dutch in style, the central chapel dates from well into the 18th century. Excavations on the eastern side of the building have revealed the foundations of an earlier building on the site. The present restoration of the chapel has been assisted by financial support from the Netherlands. The peculiar windows in the room on the south end of the building had to be completely rebuilt. It is now used for meetings.

To the east of "Speelman's House" and set at the same angle are the officers' quarters, while the troops lived in the building along the eastern wall—now a library. Before the war, this house contained the library and offices of the Matthes Foundation, now the Cultural Foundation of South and Southeast Celebes. At present it houses a collection of ceramics found in burial sites in South Sulawesi. The buildings between it and the troops' barracks date from the Japanese occupation of the fort.

Farther south along the eastern wall is the council house or main administrative building for the Dutch Company's local affairs. The arcaded porch is particularly elegant. The ground floor of the building served as a prison. Today the offices of the National Archaeological Service are located here.

The long south range of buildings, with its beautiful veranda, is an eloquent reminder that the primary purpose of the Dutch Company was trade. The great halls where the cargoes piled up ready for transshipment to Batavia and thence to Europe now make excellent exhibition areas for the new La Galigo Museum. Among the exhibits are a model of the fort, ethnographic displays, musical instruments, heraldry, reconstruc-

tions of archaeological sites, numismatics, and art objects. An excellent view of the fort is obtained from the dormer windows in the top loft at the eastern end of the building.

Behind the ground floor facade of the building in the southwest corner of the fort is a long, low dungeon sunk deep into the bastion behind and lighted only by a grill giving onto the small anteroom. This is reputed to have been the prison in which the famous Javanese rebel prince, Diponegoro, was held for several years until his death in 1855.

Visiting hours are 8:00-13:30 daily except for Mondays, when the fort is closed. Entry is free on Sundays.

The ports and esplanade

The Makassarese, the Bugis, and the Mandar are the great seafaring peoples of Indonesia. Their craft are remarkable for their sturdiness and grace, as well as for the exceptional skill of the ship-builders who still today fashion heavy ships purely from wood. The many different styles of fishing and sailing boats which ply the seafront in the harbor of Ujung Pandang give the town a unique charm and ambience. From the broad esplanade (Pantai Losari) a great variety of traditional sailing

Opposite: *Fort Rotterdam from the air.* **Above:** *The esplanade at Ujung Pandang, where townspeople regularly come to eat. Every evening foodstalls line the strand for over a kilometer.*

vessels can be seen making their way towards the port.

Among the many types of vessel to be found here are the *prahu pinisi*, the elegant ketch-rigged schooner which has become the symbol of South Sulawesi; the *pantorani*, which has two rectangular sails slung obliquely and is used to capture flying fish; the *lambo*, a stubby, single-masted cargo vessel; the *balolang* and many varieties of *lepa lepa*, sailing boats with outriggers.

There are three *prahu* ports in Ujung Pandang, all accessible only by *becak* or private transport. The busiest and most colorful of these is Paotere, to the north of the town along rough narrow streets. The maze of masts, rigging and brightly-painted *prahus* is picturesque, particularly at dawn or sunset. The scene is particularly lively with fishermen unloading their catch in the early mornings and mid-afternoon. Fish caught in bamboo fishtraps (*bagang*) far out at sea are collected each day in the early hours of the morning and brought into the city markets.

Some of the fishing boats sail with their catch to the fish market (Pasar Ikan, or Palelangan Ikan) on Jl. Rajawali. Here the fish is auctioned, usually about 6.00-7.00 am and 3.00 pm. It is worth a visit to appreciate the variety of fish which are spread out in heaps on the concrete floors of the market. They range in size from large swordfish, tuna, octopus, and rays to small prawns and tiny fish like whitebait.

The biggest *prahus* moor in the harbor which lies between the ports of Hatta and Sukarno, off Jl. Martadinata. They carry goods to ports such as Donggala (Central Sulawesi), Ambon, Banjarmasin, Samarinda, Surabaya, and Jakarta. Some will take passengers, but facilities are basic, and passengers and crew often remain on deck for the duration of the trip. The best time for sailing off Ujung Pandang is during the east monsoon, between May and October.

Chinese temples

There are four public temples in Ujung Pandang. The most important is Tian Hou Gong, or "Temple of the Heavenly Queen," on the corner of Jl. Sulawesi and Jl. Serui. It was probably built in the early 18th century, and was restored in 1738, 1803 and 1867.

The statue of the "Heavenly Queen," Tian Hou, to whom it is dedicated, stands at the back of the main altar, behind a wooden partition. Patroness of sailors, she is also associat-

ed with fertility. There are a number of side altars. The first on the left is dedicated to the "Golden Mothers of the Golden Immortals;" the second to Xuan Tian Shang Di, venerated in Indonesia for his medical powers; the third to the Patroness of Fertility. The altars in the courtyard behind are dedicated to various Buddhist divinities, including Guan Yin, the Goddess of Mercy.

The Long Xian Gong, or "Temple of the Apparition of the Dragon," at Jl. Sulawesi and Jl. Bali, was built in 1868. The central altar is dedicated to Xian Mu, "Mother of the Immortals;" that on the right to Mi Lo Fo, patron of jewelers; that on the left to Tu Di Gong, god of the soil and of wealth.

The Temple of the Association of Merchants of Guangdong, near the Long Xian Gong, was damaged when the road was recently aligned. It is dedicated to Guan Di, who is the patron of the Guangdong associations. The Chinese used to come here to swear oaths before testifying in court. On the left of Guan Di stand a horse and rider to whom mothers prayed that their children would be obedient.

The fourth temple, located on Jl. Lombok, is relatively new. It was built after 1953 to replace an older one on Jl. Sulawesi which

Above, left: *Stall selling chicken soup on the esplanade.* **Above, right:** *Detail of a becak pedicab.* **Opposite:** *Boat at Ujung Pandang.*

had been destroyed during the Japanese occupation of the island.

Orchids and sea shells

Mr. C.L. Bundt began to grow orchids as a hobby, but has gradually built up a business of world renown. His experiments in cross-fertilizing and breeding have produced some unique blooms which are registered in Sander's List in London. He has cultivated many rare specimens, as well as the common orchids of South Sulawesi which can be purchased at his home on Jl. Mochtar Lufti 15. There is also a large collection of seashells and coral on display.

To visit his three-hectare (7.5-acre) orchid garden outside the city, make a sharp right (not the adjacent oblique right) just before the electricity generating station 7.5 km (4.5 mi) out of Ujung Pandang on the main road north. At successive T-junctions turn left, then right, then right again, to find the garden tucked away at the end of the road, about 0.6 km from the main road. Remember that this is a private garden, and that you must seek permission before entering.

Diponegoro's tomb

Prince Diponegoro was born in 1785, son of Sultan Hamengkubuwono III of Yogyakarta. He led the last great Javanese resistance against the Dutch, in the "Java War" of 1825-30. He was captured through treachery and deported to Manado and then to Makassar, where he died in 1855. He has been declared a national hero. His tomb, built in the Javanese style, is in a small but well-kept cemetery on Jl. Diponegoro. The family tree displayed on the wall of the tomb indicates that his descendants remained in Ujung Pandang. The custodian, his great-grandson, lives at Jl. Irian No. 83.

Silk weaving

Silk spun from cocoons grown near Soppeng is dyed and woven at Tenunan Sutera Alam on Jl. Ontah. The raw fiber is boiled for six and a half hours, when it becomes soft and glossy. It is then dyed in brilliant colors somewhat like the dyes for Thai silks, and then hung out to dry.

The skeins when dry are taken to a nearby room to be wound onto spools ready for weaving. In other rooms, on a number of large frames, silks in a variety of gorgeous colors are interwoven and blended—rich blues and purples; yellows, golds, greens, pinks, and reds. Some are woven in intricate designs; for others, the attraction lies in pure color and fine texture.

The factory management has opened a shop on the premises where silk is sold by the meter as well as in *sarung* lengths. Shoes may be ordered covered in the same fabric, with bags and hats to match.

—*Anthony Reid*

JEAN-LÉO DUGAST

SIDETRIPS FROM U.P.

Coral Islands, Caves and Waterfalls

Just off the coast of Ujung Pandang lies one of the world's loveliest coral reefs. Magnificent coral formations and brilliantly-colored tropical fish combine to produce a superb underwater garden. Mushroom and fire corals vie for attention with rainbow-hued parrot fish, while blue-spotted stingray dart rapidly away if approached, leaving behind a fine cloud of sand. Grouper and silvery barracuda glide past, while curious blue- and white-tip sharks circle at a cautious distance.

The endangered reef

Sadly, in the last couple of decades the coral reefs around the scattered islands off Ujung Pandang have been seriously damaged, partly by explosives used to kill the fish, and partly because of depredation by thoughtless coral and sea-shell collectors. *Tridacna gigas*, the giant clam which serves as a baptismal font in many Dutch churches, is now extinct. The populations of corals and reef-dwelling creatures in this area, which was once one of the world's richest in numbers of different species, have declined sharply. It is still possible that the reef may be saved: dynamite has been banned (though the ban is not fully effective) and coral and shell collecting are discouraged.

Nevertheless, the area remains a delightful place to visit, offering much better swimming than the nearby mainland beaches. Some islands are uninhabited, or nearly so; others support large fishing or trading villages. Most offer shelter in the form of coconut, breadfruit and other trees. As you travel further out into the waters, the corals, seaweeds and coraline algae change with the physical features of the underwater realm: the first zone is all but dead, but from 6 to 60 km out (4 to 40 mi), where the underwater shelf plunges 2,000 meters (6,500 ft) down into the ocean's depths, the reef is still vibrant with life.

Islands and sand bars

One of the region's most pleasant spots for swimming and snorkeling is Samalona, an island of white sand beaches with plenty of shade and some coral. In the pre-independence days of Dutch colonial rule, the island was accessible only to members of the Makassar Yacht Club and the "De Harmonie"

society. Now, however, anyone who can afford to hire a boat is welcome.

Other nearby coral islands include Barang Lompo, Barang Caddi, and Kudingareng Lompo, all of which are populated. Barang Lompo, which has a population of some 3,000, supplies fresh drinking water for surrounding islands; a small *warung* there offers simple but good fish meals. Barang Lompo, Pandang Lae-Lae and Kayangan do not offer very good swimming. Further out you will reach Bone Tambung, a small island surrounded by a big reef.

Another very pleasant place to snorkle or dive is Kudingarang Keke, an uninhabited sand-bar which provides no shade other than a single wooden house. The sand here is white and dazzling, and the coral largely undamaged. Strikingly beautiful fish and the occasional barracuda glide by. The reef is large and falls off at its edge to a sandy bottom 35 meters (115 ft) down. Bring plenty of water and food. The journey out from the harbor takes about an hour.

The deep

Experienced divers with a sense of adventure (and a feeling of security around sharks) can venture out to the edge of the continental shelf. The reef at Kapopasang fortunately offers some protection from the fearsome hammerhead shark. The common blue- and white-tip reef shark is inquisitive but rarely

known to attack, while the hammerhead's reputation is justified. This is deep water: within less than 10 meters (33 ft) the reef plunges to a breathtaking 800 meters (2,600 ft)—a truly awesome sight. Giant manta rays glide past dense schools of sparkling fish (which you may later encounter as charcoal-grilled delicacies in the seafood restaurants of Ujung Pandang).

The islands of Lanjukang and Langkai offer no protection from sharks: at the end of a 100-meter (330 ft) shelf, a sharp drop of some 600 meters (1950 ft) takes you into the heart of hammerhead territory. The diving here, certainly a stimulating experience, is not recommended for the faint-hearted.

Getting there

To reach the islands, hire a motorized *prahu* from Jl. Pasar Ikan, or from the pier between the sea police office and the place where boats leave for Kayangan Island, opposite the entrance to the fort. There is a regular ferry to Kayangan, a town consisting of a somewhat neglected former hotel with a number of ramshackle chalets, changing sheds, a bar, restaurant and a discotheque which operates only on weekends. Snorkeling gear can be purchased from sports stores on Jl. Somba-

Opposite: *One of many idyllic tropical islands near Ujung Pandang.* **Bottom:** *An example of the islands' spectacular underwater coral gardens.*

KAL MULLER

JEAN-LÉO DUGAST

opu and Jl. Nusantara and around the central market. Scuba diving gear is difficult to hire. Perhaps the best person to talk to is Wempy Dahong (Jl. Gunung Merapi 203, tel. 24925), a member of the local diving club. It may be possible to rent and to fill tanks at the compressor dealer on Jl. Sunai Cerekang. A travel agent, Pt. Ceria Nugraha Tours and Travel Service on Jl. Usman Jafar 9, plans to start island tours in the near future.

When walking on the reef, always wear rubber-soled track shoes, or at the very least a pair of stout flip-flops. The only possible danger within the reef is the stone fish; you will not see these, but you do not want to step on one—an injection from their poisonous dorsal spines means almost certain death. And above all, please do not remove any coral or shell. The reef is a fragile environment and deserves our respect and protection.

Rich scenery, prehistoric caves

A short distance to the north of Ujung Pandang lie the extraordinary limestone formations of the cordillera which stretches between Maros and Pangkajene. This is an area of great natural beauty, with rushing waterfalls and brightly bedizened butterflies. The limestone hills are also famous for their prehistoric caves, in which the remains of neolithic man have been found. Some of these caves are open to visitors, and a visit to the caves can be combined with a trip to the

waterfalls at Bantimurung.

To get to the caves and the waterfalls at Bantimurung, you must first take a *bemo* to Maros, an hour north of Ujung Pandang, and then a second *bemo* east towards Bone. *Bemo*s for Maros leave from the central *bemo* terminal in Ujung Pandang; the journey takes an hour and costs Rp 500. As you leave the city, you may see men pushing two-wheeled carts laden with long bamboos, and cyclists carrying nipah palm leaves from the swampy areas to the northeast of the town. For centuries these have been the basic roofing materials of the area. Note on the left the new building of the provincial assembly, which makes use of a five-layered structure in the roof eaves, a feature which was once the exclusive prerogative of Bugis and Makassar sovereigns.

About 5 km (3 mi) outside the city, the road passes the site of a vast Chinese cemetery covering an area of about 12 hectares (30 acres). The oldest graves, at the rear of the site, have been there for over a century; most of the others were moved here in about 1970, after their removal from the old cemetery on the site of the present-day Central Market. All these graves were relocated yet again to make way for further government buildings. Another kilometer down the road are the Hero's Cemetery on the right, predominantly for the military, and a Christian cemetery on the left.

Past the cemeteries, a sharp right just before the large power station leads to Mr. Bundt's orchid park. Continuing along the main road, cross the Tallo River, and a few km later you will see the new campus of Hasanuddin University on the left. The campus was built with assistance from the Asian Development Bank, and opened in September 1980.

Farther along the road, just before a military compound and half-hidden from the road (on the right), is a Balinese temple, Pura Giri Natha. Its syncretism is nicely displayed by the matching statues of Krishna and Buddha at the entrance. The first road on the left after entering *kabupaten* (region) Maros leads to the mosque headquarters of the Khalwatiah mystical order.

After crossing the Maros River you enter the town's new administrative center. Here you take a *bemo* to Bantimurung for Rp 250. The road leads east towards Bone and Bantimurung, through the older part of Maros town. About 10 km (6 mi) later, a left turn leads to the Archaeological Park (Taman

Purbakala Leang-Leang). The caves in this area are the most accessible to the public among all those in the region, and have prehistoric paintings dating back as much as 5,000 years. There are 55 such caves in South Sulawesi, where the limestone cliffs of the central ranges are tunnelled with fissures. The caves are a valuable source of information about the prehistory not only of Sulawesi but of Southeast Asia in general, and archaeologists are anxious to extend their knowledge of the area. Unfortunately their work is impeded by plunderers who destroy the sites in search of antique porcelain, as well as by farmers taking soil to replenish their exhausted terrain.

The caves at Ulu Leang appear to have been occupied between 8,000 and 3,000 B.C. The two caves which are sign-posted are Ulu Leang I, or Gua Pette, and Ulu Leang II, Gua Pettakere. A clear mountain stream which flows near the mouth of these caves is pleasant for swimming. To see the caves, follow signs to a ticket-office at the gate. A path leads to Gua Pettae, which measures about 15 by 20 meters (49 by 65 ft), and has stencils of human hands in a cavity on the wall..

Ulu Leang II (Gua Pettakere) opens from the south wall of the cliff, about 20 meters (65 ft) above the floor of Ulu Leang I, and has other small passages leading to the cliff-face. It was probably used as a burial site, as it was found to contain a number of human bones.

On the cliff above the opening is a painting of a *babirusa* which has unfortunately been badly defaced. If you carry a flashlight you can explore other parts of the cave, where there is another painting of a *babirusa*.

Farther along the road on the left are other caves, less clearly signposted but open to the public. These are the Leang Jarie, Leang Saripa and Leang Karrasa. They also have stencils of human hands.

Waterfalls and butterflies

From the caves you must return to the highway and hail a passing *bemo* to continue on to Bantimurung. You cannot miss the entrance to the park: the road leads beneath the legs of a concrete monkey standing 6 meters (20 ft) high. This area, with its spectacular waterfalls, cliff and chasms, and its butterflies and birds, has always attracted visitors. In 1856-57 the British naturalist Alfred Russel Wallace spent "some of the most pleasurable moments of [his] life" here, catching many rare specimens of insects, birds and butterflies, including the *Papilio androcles*, one of the largest and rarest swallow-tailed butterflies. Wallace wrote, "Such gorges, chasms

Opposite: *Clamming on the beach near Ujung Pandang.* **Above:** *Bamboo being floated down the Tallo River in bunches. Bamboo is a basic and versatile material, providing tools, building materials, containers, and even food.*

and precipices as here abound, I have nowhere seen in the Archipelago ..." His detailed descriptions have attracted numbers of archaeologists, prehistorians, and lepidopterists, including Vladimir Nabokov, who wrote a scientific article on the butterflies he discovered here.

Today Bantimurung has been proclaimed a protected area, as many species of its wildlife are threatened by overenthusiastic collectors. Nevertheless, visitors will find themselves beseiged by children with boxes of brilliantly-colored butterflies. The best time to see the butterflies in the living state is when the sun comes out after a rain, as they flutter over the water and around the vegetation nearby.

In the dry season the waterfall is a sheet of clear, surging water which falls about 12 meters (40 ft) from a rounded mass of rock into a deep pool below. Steep steps lead up beside the falls to the river above. From here, unless the torrent is too strong (as is common in the rainy season) you can wade along the edge of the stream to a bank 50 meters away on the left, whence a shady patch leads through the bush to a second waterfall. This fall is smaller but broad, and cascades into a pool of conflicting currents and eddies—the pool is stimulating but at times slightly dangerous to swim in, as it forms whirlpools. Nearby there is a cave which you will need a flashlight to explore. This is a popular picnic spot, especially on Sundays, and a delightful place for walking, swimming, or just enjoying the scenery. The recent addition of large cement frogs has, unfortunately, robbed the waterfall of much of its charm. Walk up behind the falls to the river and the dark rocky gorge through which it flows.

Malino

Two hours and 70 km (42 mi) to the east of Ujung Pandang lies the refreshingly cool market town of Malino. It is a delightful place to visit if you have the time. Malino lies on the lower slopes of Mount Bawa Karaeng, and coaches and mini-buses leave for here regularly from the main bus terminal in Ujung Pandang. The road leads south through Sungguminasa, and you can stop here and visit the ruins and the old palace before continuing on by mini-bus to Malino. (See "Historical Sights," page 84.)

After the Gowa palace, the road to Malino continues straight ahead at the main crossroads (the road to the right leads to Jeneponto and the south coast). Soon afterwards, you pass the Pabrik Kertas Gowa, the largest paper factory in Indonesia at the time of its establishment in 1962. It was seen as a sign of hope for a province long held back by political turmoil. Built with Japanese help, it uses

Above: *Bantimurung waterfall.* **Opposite:** *Children playing in a stream near Ujung Pandang.*

about 80 percent bamboo for its pulp, with smaller amounts of acacia, mangrove and pine.

Opposite the factory lies Lake Mawang, once a favored location for boating among the prolific lotus blooms. The lotus have disappeared, along with the boats, but one can still picnic beneath the trees.

Continuing out of Ujung Pandang toward Malino, 29 km (18 mi) further down the road, on the left, is the entrance to the natural silk project. Since 1974, with Japanese technical assistance, Japanese and Chinese varieties of silk worms have been bred here to provide South Sulawesi farmers with eggs which they raise to the cocoon stage.

The road to Malino was completed in 1927, after which the town was developed as the hill resort of the Makassar area. In the colonial period, this was a hill station where Dutch officials and their families could escape from the heat of the plains. Market-day in Malino is Sunday morning, and this is when the quiet town comes alive. The area is famous for its fruits and vegetables, tree-tomatoes (tamarillos), passion fruit (*mark-isa*), and avocados, which are a bargain. Orchids, birds, and woven baskets are among the wares to be found here. Its greatest moment came in July 1946, when the "Malino Conference" laid the foundation for the ill-fated Dutch strategy of federalism for post-war Indonesia.

Twice a year, in May and November, Malino is ablaze with flowers from the tall red tulip trees which border the roads and parks. The cool mountain air is conducive to long walks among the pine forests and surrounding hills.

Hikes

There are lots of delightful walks through the area's pine forests and rice fields, surrounded by mountains, river valleys and cascading waterfalls. Two spectacular waterfalls can be reached from a winding road south of Malino, just past the Takapola bridge in Desa Buluttana. To the right of the road, the Balan-iparang waterfall plunges 50 meters down a sheer cliff face. A little farther on, a smaller waterfall to the left of the road is better for swimming: take a footpath about 500 meters (0.3 mi) alongside the river to where the cascade sprays out into a deep basin.

Mount Bawa Karaeng can be climbed in about 3-4 hours from the village of Ngangre Apiang, at the highest point on the road beyond Malino. It is best to arrange for guides and to spend the night before your climb at Malino, so as to be able to set out early and avoid the likelihood of afternoon rain. Only from July to September can you be sure of wholly dry weather. It is a lovely walk among towering forest trees with lichen, orchids and numerous species of birds.

—*Anthony Reid*

KAL MULLER

Ujung Pandang

City code 0411. All prices in US$. S=Single; D=Double. AC=air-conditioned.

Most visitors to South Sulawesi simply pass through Ujung Pandang on their way to Tana Toraja, perhaps staying overnight in order to catch the morning bus or plane. But the city has much to offer the interested visitor. For almost five hundred years Ujung Pandang—or Makassar—has been the gateway to the fabled "spice islands" of the eastern archipelago. In the fifteenth and sixteenth centuries, nutmeg, pepper, clove and mace—spices whose value was reflected in the gold dust used to pay for them—poured by the boat-load into her warehouses.

Today, Ujung Pandang is the administrative center for the province of South Sulawesi, a city where development experts and international bankers gather to plan the island's future. Yet the city still maintains a relaxed, unhurried atmosphere. Many of the large grassy areas have been preserved from the Dutch period, and the city is spacious and pleasant.

GETTING THERE

Ujung Pandang is the center of communications for eastern Indonesia, and is well connected with other parts of the archipelago. (See "Getting There" in Travel Advisory.)

The airport is 25 km (16 mi) north of town on the road to Malino, half an hour's drive. The information counter at the airport has a list of hotels and telephone numbers, but you will have to ask for this. Certain hotels are strongly promoted. The Makassar Golden Hotel and the Marannu City Hotel have offices at the airport. There is a telegraph and telephone office (open from 08:00 to 18:00) and a coin-operated phone booth, as well as a money changer, restaurant and snack bar. Pay at the airport for an irresponsibly fast half-hour taxi ride into town ($6 or $8 AC), or walk 500 meters (0.3 mi) to the main road and catch a *bemo* for $1 including luggage.

Airline offices - Ujung Pandang

Bouraq, Jl. Veteran Selatan 1.Tel: 83039, 851906
Garuda, Jl. Slamat Riyadi 6. Tel: 315405, 315719
Merpati, Jl. Bawakaraeng 109. Tel: 24114, 24155

TRANSPORTATION

Self-drive cars and Toyota Land Cruisers are difficult and expensive to hire. Taxis can be hired through most hotels for about $40 per day. The best way to get around is by *bemo* (*pete-pete* in the local slang). The drivers are usually helpful and will tell you which *bemo* to stop and where to get off. It helps to have a few words of Indonesian. The fare in town is Rp 150 for any distance. The **Bemo station** is on Jl. Cokroaminoto.

For Rp 500-1000, you can travel by *becak* to almost any part of the city. Ignore the coaches and lorries bearing down on you as your driver executes a sudden right turn across a two-lane highway; the best policy is not to look. Be sure to arrange the price before you set off, and check that the driver knows where you want to go to, which is hardly ever the case. Many of the drivers are from the impoverished south and their knowledge of Ujung Pandang is hazy.

ACCOMMODATION

Lodging in Ujung Pandang is expensive by Indonesian standards. At the lower end of the scale there are many cheap lodging houses around the port area, but these are not recommended. Most of the larger hotels add 21% service and tax; smaller ones may add 10%. Telephone numbers should be checked: the telephone system is being upgraded and new numbers are being issued. Location is important: Ujung Pandang can be a pain to get around if you have to walk long distances in the heat or bargain constantly with non-English-speaking *becak* drivers.

Luxury ($50 and upwards)

There are two international-standard hotels in Ujung Pandang. The **Makassar Golden** is well located, but the **Victoria** is quieter and offers excellent service.

Makassar Golden Hotel, Jl. Pasar Ikan 52. Tel. 314408. Telex 71290 MGHUP IA. Fax: 317999. $60-85 S, $75-100 D, $135-350 suite. Spectacularly situated on the waterfront in the center of town, with views of the small offshore islands. Coffee shop, bar and restaurants, swimming pool. Magnificent sunsets from the Toraja-style terrace restaurant. Free transport to the airport; (from with reservation). Major credit cards.

Victoria Panghegar Hotel, Jl. Jendral Sudirman 24. Tel. 311553, 311556. Fax: 312468. 70 rooms, $50-80 S, $70-90 D. Bar and restaurant, coffee shop, swimming pool. This luxurious, privately owned hotel offers a wide range of services, from safety deposit boxes to chauffeur-driven cars. Free transport from airport and seaport upon request. Major credit cards.

Marannu City Hotel, Jl. Sultan Hasanuddin 3-5. Tel. 315087, 311010, Telex: 71303 MARANU IA. Fax: 21821. Total of 410 rooms, including adjacent Marannu Tower Hotel. $50-70 S, $55-80 D, $110-500 suite. Major credit cards. Coffee shop, bars and three restaurants serving Western and Chinese-Indonesian food: set lunch $9.50, dinner $12. Small swimming pool. Centrally located, just ten minutes' walk from the harbor, fort and main Post Office. Airport transfers free of charge; taxis and car rentals available. Discotheque and billiard room. Non-residents may use the pool for $2 including towels.

Marannu Tower Hotel, Jl. Kajaolalido 16. Tel. 28051, 28050. Telex: 71303 MARANU IA. Fax: 319934, 21821. Room rates and meals same as Marannu City Hotel, adjacent and sharing facilities - total of 410 rooms.

Hotel Kenari, Jl. Yosef Latumahina 30. Tel: 84250, 852353-4. Fax: 82126. $52 S, $65 D, $125 Suite. Set lunch $8, set dinner $10.

Intermediate ($20-50)

Makassar City Hotel, Jl. Chairil Anwar 28. Tel. 317055, Telex: 71526 MCH U.P.I.A.. Fax: 311818. 65 rooms, $34 S, $38 D. $45-50 suite. Coffee shop, bar and restaurant. A cozy hotel located in the commercial center of Ujung Pandang offering a useful range of services, including a drug store. Pleasant staff.

Pondok Suada Indah, Jl. Sultan Hasanuddin 12. Tel. 317179. 312856. $20-25 S, $25-30 D, AC. A cavernous hotel, centrally located but overpriced. Breakfast is included; service is decidedly unimpressive. The Hotel Marannu City is directly opposite.

Pasanggrahan Makassar, Jl. Somba Opu 297, Tel. 852616, 854218. 25 rooms, fully AC, $45. A real seaside hotel, with a restaurant serving Chinese-Indonesian food. Breezy and clean, with pleasant and helpful staff.

Hotel Widhana, Jl. Botolempangan 53, Tel. 21393. 25 rooms, fully AC. $15-25 S, $20-30 D. Bar and restaurant, Western, Chinese and Indonesian menu. A modern, clean and dark hotel ten minutes south of the city center.

Budget (below $20)

Hotel Apiat, Jl. Bandar Udara Hasanuddin 1. Tel. Mandai (108) 25. 20 rooms, $6-10 S, $10-15 D, AC. Restaurant, Chinese-Indonesian menu. Right at the entrance of the airport on the road to Ujung Pandang: a convenient and reasonably priced hotel from which to make forays into town.

Wisma Tiatra House, Jl. Dr. Sutomo 25, $12-15 S, $15-20 D. A pleasant little hotel just ten minutes from the center of town on a quiet street.

Pondok Delta, Jl. Hasanuddin 25, Tel. 312655. A popular place to stay among long-term expats; pleasant staff and good accomodations. $12 S, $15 D, including breakfast.

Ramayana Satrya Hotel, Jl. Bawakareng 121, Tel. 24153, Fax: 22165. 65 rooms, $6-14 S, $ 10-16 D, some rooms AC. The hotel has a direct bus service to the **Wisma Maria** in Rantepao. Diagonally opposite the Ramayana is the slightly cheaper **Hotel Marlin**.

Hotel Virgo, Jl. Sumba 109. Tel. 21451, 22244. 40 rooms, $10-15 S, $12-16 D. Fairly centrally located. No restaurant, but you can eat at the budget-style **Samalona** or **Lumayan** restaurants close by on Jl. Samalona.

FOOD

The main attraction of eating out in Ujung Pandang is the seafood: huge shrimps and lobsters, dark-skinned fish with delicate white flesh, and giant, juicy crabs. The best cooking is usually the simplest. The true local specialty is *ikan bakar*, fresh fish lightly cooked over a charcoal brazier. The fresh-water crab and the local fish are a bargain. Strangely, tea and coffee are usually quite awful: although some of the best coffee in the world is grown in the mountains behind Palopo, little ever reaches Ujung Pandang. Really cold beer (ask to feel the bottle) is the perfect accompaniment to seafood: Bir Bintang is streets ahead of its cheaper rivals Anker and San Miguel. Or try refreshing *jeruk nipis*, freshly squeezed lime juice with sugar and ice. (Note: It is generally best not to take ice with your drinks in Indonesia, unless you are certain that it is made from boiled water—seldom the case.)

Seafood

Surya Super Crab, Jl. Nusakambangan 16, is the best-known crab restaurant in Ujung Pandang. The Surya Super Crab ($4) comes in a gluey sweet sauce but the fresh-water crab is delicious, and one serving is enough for two people. The *cumi-cumi mentega* (squid in margarine) is enough to induce diabetes. Refuse the bottled *sambal* and ask for some freshly chopped chili in soy-sauce. Try the garlic shrimps ($4), the shark's-fin and crab soup ($10) and the squid in batter ($3); the *kangkong* (a Chinese vegetable) is delicious.

Restaurant Ujung Pandang, Jl. Irian 42. Live singing. Expatriate residents rate the *saus kepiting* (fresh-water crab in sauce) even more highly than Surya's. Prices are similar: $10 per head including drinks.

Rumah Makan Labbakang, Jl. Chairil Anwar, serves delicious *udang kukus* (steamed shrimps with lime) for just $3. Also worth trying are the *ikan barongan* ($3) and the *ikan bandeng* ($4). Strongly recommended.

Asia Baru, Jl. Salahutu, serves charcoal-grilled prawns and fish, as does **Rumah Makan Empah** on Jl. Siau. Both are popular travelers' restaurants; price and quantity are the main attractions.

Bamboo Den, on Jl. Gunung Latimojong, serves the coldest beer in town; ask for a bottle from the green refrigerator: the jacket of ice melts while you drink. Wide range of saccharine-sweet seafood dishes in a dark, air-conditioned room, accompanied by loud music and the occasional *karaoke* singer. Expensive at $20-30 for two. Better to sit outside with your drink and choose from a range of ice creams.

Pleasant and efficient service.

Aroma Mattoangin, Jl. Gunung Latimojong offers a standard Indonesian menu of chicken and *ikan bakar* at reasonable prices. There are several similar restaurants on Jl. Gunung Latimojong, popular with budget travelers.

The Kantin Baik Dan Murah ("The Good and Cheap Canteen") above the Gelael Supermarket on Jl. Sultan Hasanuddin, serves tasty Indonesian food at very reasonable prices.

Western food

Modern Bakery (formerly Holland Modern Bakery), on the corner of Jl. Bawakaraeng and Jl. Gunung Latimojong, serves a breakfast of sweet rolls with raisins and chocolate rice topping, with bad tea and coffee. $2-3.

Donald Bakery and Ice Cream on Jl. Karunrun (at the southern end of Jl. Sutomo) has a wider range of rolls and cakes and good tea and coffee. The perfect place for breakfast if you are staying at the nearby Wisma Tiatra House.

Kentucky Fried Chicken has a large AC restaurant over the Gelayal Supermarket on Jl. Sultan Hasanuddin, close to the Marannu Hotel. Rival **California Fried Chicken** is on Jl. Pasar Ikan, close to the Golden Makassar Hotel.

Golden Ice Cream and Pastry Shop, in front of the Golden Makassar Hotel, sells a variety of delicious ice cream at 60 cents a cone, insipid apple pie and good, sticky Danish pastries.

Local food

At night the food stalls on the waterfront along Jl. Penghibur stretch for more than a kilometer. This is where the ordinary people of Ujung Pandang eat: *bakso, mi goreng, mi kuah, gado-gado* and freshly-grilled *ikan bakar*, served with the minimum of fuss and eaten sitting cross-legged along the sea front wall. Most famous is *coto Makassar*, a spicy soup made from the left-over bits of the buffalo: lungs, intestines, liver and tripe. Devotees go a long way for the most renowned stalls. For dessert, try delicious *pisang epe*, grilled honeyed banana, an Ujung Pandang specialty, or saunter up to the ice cream and cake shop outside the Golden Makassar Hotel for real ice cream at just 60 cents a cone. Flavors include *durian, salak* and lychee as well as the more familiar mocha, chocolate and strawberry. Good *murtabak*, a delicious Indian folded omlette with vegetables, can be found near the mosque

Alternatively, you could eat in one of the inexpensive restaurants facing the food stalls in the other side of Jl. Penghibur.

NIGHTLIFE

Nightlife in Ujung Pandang is surprisingly good. Apart from the usual leisure establishments for sailors, there are many respectable bars and places of entertainment. Many feature "beer girls" who will fetch and pour your beer, making sure to keep your glass full. These girls are not hostesses, but are employed by the beer companies and receive a small commission from every bottle sold. Unlike the ordinary staff, these girls know where the coldest bottles are. Just ask for the girl selling your favorite brand.

An excellent place to begin a night tour of Ujung Pandang is the **Kiosk Semarang** on Jl. Penghibur, a favorite watering hole for the Western expat community. Go to the top floor for the best view of the sea and the mile-long row of foodstalls below, or try the quieter **Kiosk Makassar** next door.

After dinner at a good seafood restaurant, stroll along the stalls along the seafront, or play a game of billiards with the locals in the **Marannu City Hotel**, or **Blue Ocean**, Jl. Nusantara. There are several discos; the best is probably the **Marannu's**. The **Makassar Golden Hotel** has live music on the terrace.

Film fans will enjoy the newly opened **Studio 21** complex on Jl. Ratulangi, which has several theaters and shows Western and Asian Films for $3. Bring a sweater: the air-conditioning is powerful. The soft padded chairs will leave you looking like a Javanese *keris* handle for a week, and the reels which compose the film may not be in the order you remember, but none of this seems to bother the locals.

But the real Ujung Pandang action is in the *karaoke* lounges. If you have never sung in public before, this is the place to start. The largely Japanese expatriate audience will applaud your most hesitant performance and even pay for your songs (a small charge is levied); if you completely funk it, your beer girl will hum the tune. Top of the *karaoke* spots is the **Irani** (5th floor) at the south end of Jl. Somba Opu. Definitely something to be experienced.

SHOPPING

Gaudy silks from Soppeng, old cotton weavings from the remote mountains of Rongkong, smoke-blackened Toraja bamboo *tuak* containers (some perhaps a century old), decorated black earthenware pots from Barombong, fake Dutch and Spanish *real* silver coins (dozens bearing the date 1759), elaborately carved wooden Toraja trays and engraved bamboo containers, antique porcelain and 14th-century *celadon* stoneware—looted by grave robbers and prohibited from export—are just some of the things you will find in the shops along Jl. Pasar Ikan and Jl. Somba Opu.

Somba Opu is the street of the gold and silver workers; the delicate filigree jewelry is called Kendari silver, although today it is mostly made in Ujung Pandang. Filigree silver haircombs sell for $15 and elegant earrings for $5. The silver is about 80% pure and will darken over time, but the work is exquisite. Antique silver can still be picked up in some of the shops; if you are fortunate, you may find an antique silver *cache-sexe*; all that the young daughters of the Makassar nobility wore until puberty.

MEDICAL

Dr. **Santa Jota** on Jl. Baumasepe is a Dutch-trained cardiologist and internist. His hours are 16:00-19:00 daily. Dr. **Setatwijaya** who works at the Rumah Sakit Stella Maris is an ear, nose and throat specialist (ear infections are a fairly common affliction among visitors to South Sulawesi). Should you require emergency treatment, Dr. **Louis Rajawali** at the Rumah Sakit Akademis is a highly-regarded surgeon. The **Rumah Sakit Akademis** and the **Rumah Sakit Stella Maris** are the best hospitals in Ujung Pandang; hospitals outside the capital offer only basic medical attention.

Kimia Firma on Jl. Ahmad Yani is the largest pharmacy in Ujung Pandang. Open 24 hours; generally a prescription is not required.

MISCELLANEOUS

Visitors with kids might like to try the **Jumbo Roller Disco** on Jl. Timur, a roller skating disco with western music. Skates can be hired, European sizes up to 44. Afternoons only; in the evenings it turns into a normal disco.

The money changer **Haji La Tunrung** on Jl. Monginsidi 42, just north of the fort, offers a similar rate to the banks, no service charge.

Jameson's Supermarket and Restaurant, Jl. Irian 147-9 and **Gelael Supermarket** in Jl. Sultan Hasanuddin stock a wide range of Western products and food. Jameson's restaurant on the second floor serves Western and dishes; it also has a salad bar.

The **Tourist Information Office** is inconveniently located on Jl. Panggeran Petta Rani. Unless you stop in on your way in from the airport it is hardly worth the journey to collect the odd hotel brochure and inaccurate street map of Ujung Pandang.

The **General Post office** is at Jl. Slamet Riyadi 10. The **Telephone** and **Telex** are at Jl. Balaikota 2 and Jl. Jend. Sudirman.

VISITING SOMBAOPU

The excavations at Sombaopu can be visited in half a day from Ujung Pandang. From Sentral, take a *bemo* to Cendrawasih, alighting after 7 km (4.5 mi) at Tanggul Patompo. Here you take a *sampan* across the Jeneberang River for 25 cents (Rp 200). Walk 100 meters down the clearly marked trail to a fork in the path. Take the left-hand fork and continue on for 500 meters until you reach the excavations.

LEAVING UJUNG PANDANG

There are daily bus services to all the major towns in South Sulawesi. Getting out of Ujung Pandang, however, can be a hassle. Coaches and minibuses to other towns leave from terminal Panaikan. Allow at least a half hour for the journey. First take a *bemo* (Rp 150) or *becak* (Rp 500-1000) to Sentral (the central *bemo* terminus) and from there a second *bemo* to Panaikan. From here buses leave regularly throughout the day for major towns in South Sulawesi, departing as late as 19:00. If you want a good seat on a comfortable coach, it is better to book tickets at the bus companies' offices in town, but if you simply turn up at Panaikan you are almost certain to get a seat. Minibuses are faster but cramped. Fares are very reasonable: to Soppeng and Bone just $2, to Singkang $2.50. The journeys take four and five hours respectively. Buses for Toraja leave at 07:00, 13:00 and 17:00: the fare is $4 and the journey takes 8 hours. **Liman Express**, Jl. Laiya 25, and **Litha & Co.** on Jl Gunung Merapi 160 are two of the better bus companies.

Merpati flies to 27 destinations, including Tana Toraja (see "Toraja Practicalities"), Kendari, Luwuk, Palu and Poso. There is a daily flight to Denpasar. **Garuda** flies to Kendari and Palu and major Indonesian cities. **Garuda Indonesian Airlines** has an office on Jl. Selamat Riyadi 6, Tel. 315405, 315719; **Merpati Nusantara Airlines**, Tel. 24114, 24155, is on Jl. Bawakareng, close to the Hotel Ramayana. Opening hours are 08:00-17:00 weekdays, 08:00-15:00 on weekends. **Bouraq**, Tel. 83039, 851906, is at Jl. Veteran Selatan 1. **Mandala**, Tel. 22253 is at Jl. Cokrominoto 7.

From the Sukarno-Hatta harbor in the center of Ujung Pandang it is possible to get ships to many parts of Indonesia, as well as to Singapore, Europe and Japan. The luxury liner **Rinjai** calls once a month on its way to Surabaya and Jakarta: a first-class cabin is cheaper than flying. Check at **Pelni's** offices at Jl. Martadinata 38. If you speak Indonesian, it is possible to catch a *perahu* to just about anywhere in Indonesia. Travel is slow: most of your time will be spent waiting for the boat to leave.

—*Ian Caldwell*

HISTORICAL SITES

Reminders of a Royal Past

The royal tombs, ruins, and sacred sites of Gowa and Tallo are today the only reminders of the vanished greatness of 17th-century Makassar. The two small kingdoms united in the 16th century to form the powerful Makassar kingdom which dominated much of the peninsula before its defeat by the Dutch and Bugis in 1669.

Gowa and Tallo each had their own centers of spiritual power, where kings were both crowned and buried, and where a large wooden palace on stilts housed members of the royal family. The royal ground of the kingdom of Gowa was the area now known as "Kale Gowa," situated on slightly elevated ground alongside the Jeneberang River, to the south of the city. The royal ground of Tallo was at the western side of the Tallo River, where the royal graves and coronation stone may still be seen.

Old Gowa

The royal tombs, graves, palace and treasures of Gowa can be visited by catching a *bemo* from the central terminal (fare: Rp250). Just before the portals of *kabupaten* Gowa, 8 km (5 mi) out of the city, a road leads off to the left to a complex of graves in the center of the old Gowa Kingdom (Kale Gowa).

The first tomb complex which you will see, on the left, is the most venerated grave in the Makassar area. Syech Yusuf (1626-94) was Makassar's foremost religious scholar. On his return in 1644 from a pilgrimage to Mecca, he taught the mystical Khalwatiah doctrine in Banten (West Java), married the daughter of Sultan Ageng there, and became the soul of the resistance effort against the Dutch, who attacked Banten in 1682. He was captured in 1684 and exiled, first to Ceylon, and in 1693 to the Cape of Good Hope. Both in Ceylon and South Africa he is credited with a major role in inspiring their small Islamic communities.

Despite opposition from purist Muslims, the tomb is constantly visited by those seeking some favor—by pouring oil, scattering flowers, and lighting candles around the tomb. Although Yusuf is venerated as Tuanta Salamaka ("Our lord who grants us blessings"), it is not his tomb which receives the most attention, but that of his wife, who is said to be helpful to women wanting a child.

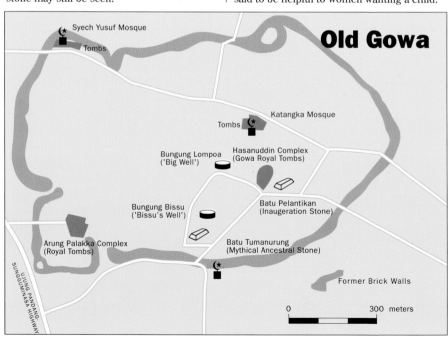

Ancient mosque and domed graves

A little farther along the road to the east, a sign at the entrance to Katangka Mosque announces that it is the oldest in South Sulawesi, built in 1605—the date when the kings of Gowa and Tallo accepted Islam. There is little evidence for this, although the solidity of the walls and the four central pillars suggest that parts of the present building date from the 18th century or earlier. The mosque is surrounded by the graves of the Gowa royal family of the 18th and 19th centuries, each dome containing the grave of a ruler and his close relatives.

From the mosque, continue eastward along the road for a few hundred meters, then take a sharp right turn onto a rough road leading up to the higher ground of Tamalate, the sacred center of Gowa and site of a 16th or 17th-century palace. On the highest point is the stone on which rulers of Gowa were inaugurated. The coronation established the new ruler's link with the sacred stone as well as to the heavenly nymph Tumanurunga, who on this spot married the mortal Karaeng Bayo and founded the Gowa dynasty.

Inside the modern enclosure are one of the domed graves like those of Katangka, and nine large stone graves shaped in the manner of many Islamic graves elsewhere, but on such an enlarged scale that one can move about inside an inner room containing the real tomb. No serious study has been made of the unique tomb structures of South Sulawesi, even though they provide important physical information on the early kingdoms. Since the dome-like structures require difficult arching, and most of them can be shown to date from the 18th century, it is assumed that this is a later form. This would mean that the one domed tomb in the Tamalate complex, that of King Tunibatta who ruled for only a month in 1565 before being killed in a war with Bone, was in fact built long after his death. It is nevertheless intriguing why this single pre-Islamic tomb should be here.

In general it appears that before Islam's arrival, rulers were buried only in earth mounds, perhaps with a wooden house-like structure above such as one still occasionally sees in Toraja. It is significant that Kale Gowa, more particularly the area around Syech Yusuf's tomb, is also referred to as "Lakiung," a variant of the Toraja term for the high house in which an aristocratic corpse is

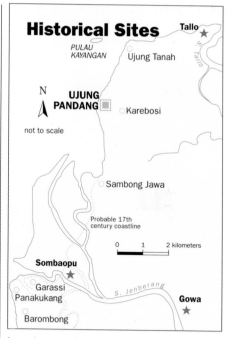

Historical Sites

Tallo
PULAU KAYANGAN
Ujung Tanah
N
UJUNG PANDANG
Karebosi
not to scale

Sambong Jawa

Probable 17th century coastline

0   1   2 kilometers

Sombaopu
Garassi
Panakukang
S. Jenberang
Gowa
Barombong

kept during a death-feast.

A little farther to the west, but also approachable from the main Ujung Pandang-Sungguminasa road, is another group of tombs dominated by that of Aru Palakka, the great war leader who rallied the Bugis and allied with the Dutch to defeat Makassar. When he died in 1696 he was the most powerful man in South Sulawesi, but he chose to be buried in this heartland of the Gowa he had conquered rather than in Bone, where he had been proclaimed king. Although regarded by many Bugis as a great liberator, he was understandably resented by Makassarese, and his tomb fell into great disrepair until the Dutch took it in hand in the 1930s. It may be significant that he also chose a burial spot close to the tomb of Karaeng Pattingalloang (d. 1654), the learned chancellor of Makassar who is said to have been a patron of the young Aru Palakka. Pattingalloang's tomb is a little to the east.

The Sungguminasa palace

Further up the main road at Sungguminasa is the royal palace of Gowa. The palace was built in 1936, in traditional style on stilts, with an imposing roofed flight of steps leading up to a large reception room. The rank of the occupant is shown by the maximum five wooden panels in the gable of the roof. Other than the architecture, the main points of interest are the treasure and royal regalia

KAL MULLER

(*pusaka*) kept locked in a room on the left. (Apply first at the *bupati's* office across the green for permission to see the royal treasure.) The regalia was considered crucial for the validity and magical power of the rulers at coronations and other important ceremonies of state.

The treasure room is set up as if for a ceremony to honor the regalia, with incense, candles, offerings of betel, food, and various requisite herbs. The oldest parts of the regalia are closely connected with the mythological origins of the Gowa dynasty. The first female ruler, Tumanurunga, is held to have descended from heaven already equipped with the magnificent gold crown. The latter is displayed in a central showcase together with four gold bracelets made in the form of coiled serpents (*naga*) with realistic heads and gaping jaws. One of the snakes has two heads, and all have precious stones for eyes. Another important object claimed to have come from heaven with the first princess was a gold chain, I Tanisamanga, which was ritually weighed each year in the presence of the raja's council. If its weight had increased during the past year, this was taken as a good omen for the kingdom; if it had decreased, as a bad omen. Unfortunately, this chain has disappeared.

Of the three royal swords, the most sacred is the black one, Sudanga, said to have been brought by Lakipadada. According to the Gowa tradition he was the brother of the prince Karaeng Bayo, who married Tumanurunga to begin the Gowa royal line.

The spectacular *keris* studded with precious stones, its gold handle a *wayang* (shadow-puppet) figure, is Javanese and associated with the Islamic sultanate of Demak. It may have been a gift from the ruler of Demak or Mataram, in Java, in the late 16th or 17th century. In the same display case are spearheads; a delicate *keris* ornamented in gold; two sets of gold cymbals; and three gold medallions, two presented by the Dutch king in 1818 and 1829 respectively, the third by the British in 1814 to "Krain Lemban Parang, Rajah of Gowa, as a token of friendship and esteem and in testimony of his attachment and faithful services [in fighting Bone]."

In the opposite showcase the gold jewelery on display includes a chain necklace said to have come from Manila (*rante* Manila); eight heavy ornamental gold earrings; twelve rings, made mainly of gold with precious stones; and six braided gold epaulettes for ceremonial uniform.

Other exhibits include various musical instruments, ceremonial regalia such as a large parasol, brooms used for ritual sweeping after the harvest, and bamboo clappers to announce the birth of a royal child.

Old Tallo

The Tallo dynasty reportedly began with Karaeng Loe, a 15th-century prince of Gowa who sought to establish a new kingdom at the strategic point of land formed between the sea and the Tallo River. In the early 16th century this dynasty formed an alliance with the expanding power of Gowa, to make the Makassar state "one people with two kings." Although Gowa provided the senior monarch, Tallo frequently provided the court chancellor (*pabicara butta*) who exercised day-to-day control of the affairs of state.

This dualism was especially marked during the heyday of Makassar between 1590 and 1654. The greatest king of Tallo, Karaeng Matoaya or Sultan Awal-ul-Islam (r. 1593-1636), as Chancellor of Makassar was largely responsible for the Islamization of South Sulawesi. The first official Friday prayer for

Above: The grave of a Makassarese noble at Kale Gowa. **Opposite:** The palace at Sungguminasa in 1888, before it was rebuilt. The five gables denote royalty; non-ruling nobles were allowed three, commoners only one. The section between the steps and the house is an audience hall.

the newly-Islamized court of Makassar was held in Tallo in 1605. True to its seaside location, Tallo appears to have been consistently more open to external and commercial influences. With the Dutch conquest of Makassar in 1669, however, the Tallo dynasty gradually lost any real significance.

Tallo lies on the old road north, 3 km (1.8 mi) from the city center, on the far side of the Tallo River, where the low-lying fish-ponds (*empang*) make old Tallo almost an island. Since 1977 the royal graves have been gradually restored. The two tallest stone graves are from the 17th century. The one in the northwest corner is locally claimed to be that of the great Karaeng Matoaya, reverently known as "the white tiger of Tallo." His grave is more reliably located in Gowa: these two stone graves are probably those of the two subsequent rulers of Tallo.

Along the seashore you can see the stone foundations of the great sea wall of Tallo, built under Portuguese supervision in the early 17th century. The wall is 2.5 meters (8 ft) thick, and can be traced along the coast westwards for about 500 meters (0.3 mi), with some remaining mounds still 2 meters (6.5 ft) high. The total length of the wall was over 2 km (1.2 mi), enclosing almost all of the semi-island at the river's mouth. Like the other forts of Makassar, it was destroyed on Dutch orders in the 1660s.

A sacred coronation stone and well are also to be found within the old walled area. Occupants of the radio communications complex (Stasion Radio Pantai) will show you the round coronation stone, now almost swallowed up by a great *waringin* tree. Farther to the southwest is an ancient well alongside what may be the ruins of a royal bath.

The grave of Khatib Tunggal Datu ri Bandang can be seen in Kampung Kaluku Badoa, 300 meters to the left down a dirt road off Jl. Tinumbu, shortly before a prawn factory and Jl. Gatot Subroto. Datu ri Bandang was the Sumatran apostle who instructed Karaeng Matoaya in Islam, and is revered in many parts of South Sulawesi as the herald of the new religion. (Bantaeng and Selayar also claim his grave, though less plausibly.) The grave itself is unimpressive, though it is much visited as a *kramat* (miracle-working) site through which spiritual and material favors can be obtained.

Sombaopu

Sombaopu ("homage to the lord"), 7 km (4 mi) south of Ujung Pandang, was the mightiest of eleven great fortresses that once lined the coast of Makassar as far north as Tallo. It was the royal fortress, lying at the mouth of the Jeneberang River, serving as the personal residence of the ruler and the heart of the sprawling trading port which extended to the north and south. A Dutch map of the early 17th century shows houses on the east and

northern sides of the fort, and two enormous palaces, storehouses and a mosque in the southwest. Outside the walls lay the southern and northern markets, the houses of the commoners and, stretching north along the coast, the Portuguese and Indian quarters.

The origin of Sombaopu appears to lie in a Malay settlement just south of the Jeneberang. Here in the mid-16th century, a small group of Malay traders were encouraged to settle by Tunipalangga, the 10th ruler of Gowa. The Chronicle of Gowa relates how Tunipalangga promised not to enter the Malays' compounds, and to exempt them from seizure of property under Makassarese law. Tunipalangga is also remembered for standardizing weights and measures, and for building the brick walls of Sombaopu.

The Malay community grew steadily as Makassar began to make itself a major collecting point for spices from the eastern isles. The expansion in trade was accompanied by expansion in political control over the south coast, with military expeditions against Jeneponto, Bantaeng and Selayar. This coast was the first step on the route to the Moluccan spice islands, while Bira and Bulukumba were important ship-building areas. Together with Selayar, they also produced Makassar's major manufactured export, the checkered "Makassar cloth" which was in great demand throughout the archipelago.

By the 17th century, Makassar had emerged as the richest and most powerful kingdom in the eastern archipelago. The growing importance of the city as a source of spices also attracted Europeans. By 1625, as many as 22 Portuguese frigates visited the port every year. The English established a factory in Makassar in 1613, the Danes in 1618; Spanish and Chinese traders began to appear in 1615. The foreign "factories" were located north of Sombaopu, on the opposite bank of the Jenebereng River. Makassar was renowned for being a kingdom "kind to strangers." Despite the fact that it was an Islamic state, there were places of Christian worship and the city was home to a number of prominent refugees.

In June 1669, after months of bitter fighting between Makassarese and Bugis-Dutch forces, Dutch soldiers managed to mine and blow a 20-meter (65 ft) gap in the 3-meter-thick walls of Sombaopu, where the Makassarese had made their stand. The following day, fighting was so heavy, with Dutch musketeers firing 30,000 bullets, that "old soldiers have perhaps never heard its like in Europe itself." Dutch and Bugis troops, many sick with dysentery and tropical diseases, found themselves confronting reinforced dwellings which had to be taken in hand-to-hand street fighting. Not until nine days after the assault began and the sacred cannon *anak Makassar* had been captured, was Sombaopu firmly in

Dutch hands. The mighty kingdom of Makassar lay in ruins. Surveying its burnt-out villages and settlements the following year, Speelman wrote: "And then comes Sombaopu, now razed and thrown into chaos."

After his victory in 1699, Speelman ordered the complete destruction of Sombaopu. In subsequent years, the main channel of the Jeneberang shifted south-wards, and a delta began to build up around Sombaopu, isolating it from the sea. The new

colonial city grew up 7 km (4.5 mi) to the north, and the remains of Sombaopu were totally neglected. Over the following centuries the remaining bricks were used for Dutch buildings, or by locals for making wells and house foundations. By the 1980s, little was left. Here and there a rise in the soil indicates the remains of a defense wall, but there is little to suggest Sombaopu's former importance.

Since July 1989 a team of Indonesian archaeologists has been working to preserve and protect this historic site. The restoration has been guided by two maps. One is a Dutch map of Makassar dated 1638, discovered recently in a European library. The other is an 18th century palm-leaf map written in the Makassarese script by an unknown author, showing the layout of the city and plans of the royal palace.

The excavations have produced many surprises, including strange hollow spaces built into the walls at 8-10 meter (26-33 ft) intervals. The reason for these spaces, which must have seriously reduced the defensive strength of the wall, is unclear. Many of them have produced evidence of cooking, suggesting occupation by troops. Other finds include stone cannon balls, bricks with pictures of boats and strange geometric designs etched on them. Others have the deep imprints of cats and dog's paws, indicating that animals were sacrificed as part of the building pro-

cess. Perhaps the most intriguing find is a brick showing an unknown script, possibly an earlier version of the Old Makassarese script formerly used in the royal courts before the 18th century.

The palaces and houses of Sombaopu were protected by a single brick wall, except on the north side, which in the 17th century bordered the main channel of the Jeneberang River. Here the wall was of triple thickness: a strong central wall made of large bricks and two lighter outer walls. In between, the walls were packed with earth, a sound defense against cannon fire. The bricks of this northern wall were also cemented. Iron slag and a bellows' mouthpiece show that iron forging, probably for weapons and cannon balls, took place within the fort.

Future plans include the excavation of the ruler's palace and warehouses. Many questions are expected to be answered, and many new ones raised. Large sections of the walls, however, will be left intact for future scholars to examine. It is planned to open Sombaopu to visitors, with a museum to house the objects found during excavations. (See "Ujung Pandang Practicalities" for directions on how to get there.)

Alongside Sombaopu, four cultural villages are being built. They will be living villages, aimed at preserving the traditional way of life and customs of South Sulawesi's four main ethnic groups: Bugis, Makassarese, Toraja and Mandarese. It is hoped these cultures will be able to maintain their identity in the face of today's rapidly changing world.

—Anthony Reid and Ian Caldwell

Opposite: *Crown of the former rulers of Gowa, now in Sungguminasa, probably dating from the 17th to 18th century. Note the spaces where the larger jewels have been pried out.* **Above, left:** *Brick with unknown inscription. Many bricks of this design have been found at Sombaopu.* **Above, right:** *An empty space in the wall at Sombaopu.*

WEST COAST

The Road North to Parepare

The journey north from Ujung Pandang takes you along a narrow, fertile coastline dominated by spectacular limestone ranges and shady, cool lagoons and inlets. Most visitors to Sulwesi will head along this road as far as Parepare, then inland towards the mountains. The west coast is home to some of the earliest-known kingdoms of South Sulawesi and some of its oldest traditions. Segeri, halfway between Ujung Pandang and Parepare, is famous for its sacred plough rituals and its "college" of transvestite priests.

Leaving Ujung Pandang, the road heads north through ricefields dominated by the spectacular limestone range, with its extraordinary honeycomb maze of steep outcrops festooned with tropical growth. These are said to be the remains of a coral reef dating from the Tertiary period. Their intricacy is best appreciated from the air.

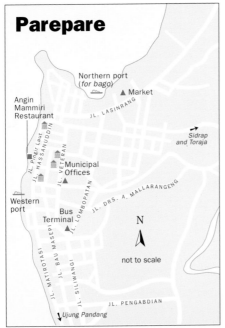

Pangkajene, 53 km (33 mi) up the coast, lies on the border between the Bugis and the Makassarese regions. This area was part of the earlier kingdom of Siang, which before the 16th century and the development of Makassar was one of the liveliest commercial centers on the coast. Many ancient Chinese ceramics have been found in this district, as well as a few gold objects. Some of these are on display at the cultural office (*kantor kebudayaan*), together with musical instruments, arms, coats of mail, models of boats, etc. Ask to see the golden mask which is kept locked away. Probably a funerary mask, it is of a type not found elsewhere in Indonesia. Dating from the 14th to 16th century, it was found in 1967 in a tomb with other gold objects which have since been lost.

Several kilometers past Pangkajene are the Bungaro natural springs, on the right. A pool has been formed from a source in the limestone cliffs, but it is not very inviting. There are caves in the cliff face which the local people will guide you through with flashlights. Just past Bungaro (on the right) is the scenic road to the Tonasa II Cement Factory, which leads past limestone cliffs honey-combed with caves. Stalactites and stalagmites beneath the luxuriant vegetation give an air of unreality to the area, which is worth exploring on foot.

Segeri, 74 km (46 mi) down the road leading to the north, is a town of quaint but dilapidated painted houses, the former eminence of which is now reflected only in the remaining college of *bissu*, the transvestite priests in charge of the sacred *arajang* (regalia) of each Bugis kingdom. Segeri is the northernmost center of the region brought under the direct control of the sultans of Makassar (Gowa) in the early 17th century, and then conquered and annexed by the Dutch in 1667 as the Noorderdistricten (northern districts) of Makassar. Just as the Dutch conquered this rich rice-growing area between Segeri and Maros on their way to Makassar, so too did Bone at the end of the 18th century, and the region was not under firm colonial control until 1824.

The prominence of the *bissu* in Segeri dates from 1776, when a prince of Luwu settled there and was accepted as ruler. He brought with him a number of *bissu*, who were otherwise limited to the more powerful

Opposite: *Stilt fishing tower near Parepare. The fisherman seated on the tower hold the ropes leading to nets, which he pulls up occasionally.*

courts of Bone, Wajo and Luwu itself. They conducted the palace rituals, and looked after the *arajang*—in the case of Segeri a magical plough which had to be used during the *mapalili'* ceremony in late November to begin the ploughing season. *Bissu* were shamans, able to communicate directly with the gods and speak in their special language, the *basa bissu*. In trance they are able to stab themselves without pain. Since the fall of the rajahs the *bissu* have lost most of their functions, and it is a sign of the times that their leader, the *puang matoa*, has become a Muslim haji. Only in the *mapilili'* ceremony is the *bissus* role still believed essential.

At Balusu, 119 km (74 mi) along the road, a detour just after the bridge leads one kilometer along an unpaved road to one of the few remaining examples of aristocratic architecture, dating from the late 19th century.

Shortly after Balusu, the road returns to the coast, as the foothills of the central range advance further into the plain. The remainder of the journey is a beautiful drive along the seashore, with good swimming at beaches about 12 km (7 mi) before Parepare. About 2 km (1.3 mi) before Parepare, the village of Bangange houses an "ethnology museum" run by Haji Hamzah, who is related by marriage to the former *arung* (ruler) of Bacukiki. He has a collection of traditional costumes and gold ornaments used for royal ceremonies, as well as ceramics, brassware, musical instruments and traditional tools of various sorts.

The town of Parepare

Parepare (population 86,000) has a relatively short history. It was formerly part of the kingdom of Suppa, which played an important role in the history of the area. The Portuguese claimed that the raja of Suppa and some of his nobles were converted to Christianity in 1543, more than 60 years before Makassar became Muslim.

Parepare, the second largest port in South Sulawesi after Ujung Padang, is now known chiefly as an important trade center, and a stopping-place for travelers between Ujung Pandang and Toraja. The main animal export harbor in the province, it has a regular boat service (not renowned for its safety) to Donggala, Kalimantan and Surabaya. Passengers travel above, and cattle below. There is also a freight service, mainly for cattle, to Singapore and Hong Kong. Boats are built and repaired in the port.

There are views of the town and the bay from the hills to the north (turn right at the stadium and take the main road toward Pangkajene and Toraja). The bay can also be appreciated from the waterfront. There are magnificent sunsets and a lively night market here. At the harbor you can see the *bago*, a local type of *prahu*.

—Anthony Reid

MANDAR

Ship Builders of the Northwest

Mandar, a little-known ans seldom-visited region of fishermen, sailors and boat-builders, awaits the intrepid traveler who braves the bumps, grinds and dust of the coastal road leading north and west from Parepare. Stands of kapok and coconut trees, dusty villages, occasional sun-blinding glimpses of the Makassar Strait, and pastel-colored Buginese-style houses grace the journey north.

Mandarese culture is a complex amalgam of seaborne influences, particularly that of Islam, which arrived in the 17th century. The local ritual life reflects a rich diversity of cosmological conceptions, and a fervent belief in Islam is joined with ancient Indic practices (forehead, hands and navel are daubed with mixtures of herbs and rice flour at curing, birth and boat-launching ceremonies) and indigenous beliefs concerning local guardians, ghosts, and the spirits of flying fish.

Life in Mandar focuses on the Makassar Strait and its abundance of fish—silvery scads, long yellowfin and skipjack tuna, swordfish, shrimp and flying fish—as well as the produce of the land, such as bananas, papayas, pineapples and jackfruit. Hand-pressed, high-quality coconut oil and woven silk sarongs are also produced.

Until the 1930s, wind-powered Mandarese cargo vessels departed from Luaor village, near Majene (the district capital) and sailed to distant islands in the eastern archipelago—Morotai, Ternate, Tidore—doing a brisk trade in manufactured goods obtained in Makassar (from Indian and Chinese merchants), including plates, tobacco and hand-woven Mandarese rope. Six months later, moving west with the monsoon, they returned with fragrant cloves, cinnamon and nutmeg, as well as turtle meat and shells, copra and live plumage birds.

To many older fishermen, the ocean is a kingdom ruled by spirits who control the currents, whirlpools, waves, winds and weather. These spirit guardians also control man's fate at sea—determing whether fishermen will return from their journeys and whether fish will be captured. The flying fish is traditionally regarded as a divine creature endowed with the power to oversee everything that happens.

Foreign markets are driving the Mandarese to reevaluate their ideas of the marine world, its regulation and resources. Demands for seafood products have stimulated new industries in shrimp fry, shark meat and fins, red snapper, agar agar and tuna.

Visiting Majene

Majene, the capital of *kabupaten* Mandar, is a small and pleasant town on a wonderful half-moon-shaped bay. But, like the rest of Mandar, it is not well-equipped to handle tourists. Do not try to stay in the nearby villages overnight, as this creates problems with local police. In Majene itself, there are several rudimentary and rather depressing guesthouses (*penginapan*). Bring along plenty of mosquito coils.

A more attractive alternative is to stay at the pleasant and strategically located harbor home of Ibu Darmi Mas'ud at Jalan Amanna Wewang No. 12. The *warung* on Jl. Syukun Rahin is the best place in town to eat lunch; the fare is both savory and inexpensive (see "South Practicalities").

In the morning, walk along the Majene sea wall—the scene of bustling activity as tuna and scad boats return to land. By 8 am the sea wall is thronged with the wives, sisters, aunts and nieces of fishermen, who receive the fish, sort and price them—and amidst a cacophonous commercial roar—sell them to housewives and traders arriving on foot, by *becak*, and on motorcycles.

In the afternoon, walk north following the sea wall and turn left down the paved street leading past the green-and-white mosque of Pangali-Ali. This is a densely settled village of raft-fishing families and civil servants.

Walk through Pangali-Ali past the last house on your left, and follow a path that winds up the craggy, wind-blown promontory. Behind you and to the south stretches Majene harbor, while to the east east lies the deep-blue Makassar Strait. Continue north (the only way to go) through a rock wall until you reach Cilallang fishing village, its mosque's bulbous tin minaret shimmering in the sun. Tall *prahu sande* with twin outriggers and white sails squat like graceful water-spiders a few hundred yards offshore.

Past Cilallang, turn right and continue on

CHARLES ZERNER

to the old graveyard at Ondongan—a site which is now being restored by the government office of historic remains and antiquities. On this high promontory you can walk among more than 600 graves, some antedating the arrival of Islam in the 17th century. Many are adorned with intricately carved, weather-worn markers in the shape of a female torso with hands on her hips, bird forms or cylindrical phallic shapes. At the southernmost edge of the graveyard you have a panoramic view of Majene town and harbor with the *bago* fleet lying at anchor; of the hills and mountains of Toraja-Mamasa; and of the expansive Makassar Strait. Find shade under a sacred tree (look for the signs of former offerings), relax and take shelter from the sun.

If you are inclined to hike to other, possibly older gravesites, ask for walking directions to Salabose. Here, in the hills above Majene, you may examine a ring of worn, black gravestones that suggest the memorial menhirs (*simbuang batu*) of Toraja. This worn ring of black stones, on a sacred headland overlooking the sea, stands as testimony of Mandar's pre-Islamic past and its links with the indigenous religions of the interior.

Salabose also has a smaller, more cluttered graveyard than the one at Ondongan. Here too are old, finely carved stone graves, as well as recent ones covered in pink and yellow tile. Unlike Ondongan, this site is still in use. It is a pretty place, filled with flowering frangipani trees. A building houses the tomb of Syekh Abdul Manan, said to have first brought Islam to Mandar from Mecca. Families visit his tomb to request blessings or favors, or to honor vows.

Back in Majene, shop around the market for some fresh fish, delicious fruits and a profusion of checkered silks. Although Mandarese silk-weaving is in decline, you may still wish to view and purchase some of the locally produced, finely woven silk sarungs, available in patterns of squares and checks, as well as in eccentric, eclectic, flamboyant Bugis-influenced patterns. Large flowers in shades of peach, electric green, and brilliant blues are shot through with sinuous lines of metallic silver and gold thread. Women weavers continue to work in Luaor and especially in Pambusuang (*kabupaten* Polmas). In Polmas, you may also visit the market at Tinambung, which is the center of the silk *sarung* production and trade.

The trip north to Mamuju is recommended if you enjoy torpid, slow-moving, unbearably hot Southeast Asian coastal towns. Muddy roads, less than indifferent food, and a decaying fishing pier await you under the glaring eye of an equatorial sun.

—*Charles Zerner*

Above: *Mandarese boat-builder. No nails are used; the ribs are attached with wooden pegs.*

SOUTH COAST

Maritime Makassarese Homeland

The southern coast of the peninsula is the Makassarese heartland. Boat-building and many other traditional crafts can best be seen here. There are excellent beaches, fine scenery, and a good main road. Modest hotels and restaurants are found at Bantaeng, Sinjai and Benteng (on Selayar Island).

By road, the trip from Ujung Pandang all around the south coast to Sinjai through Takalar, Jeneponto, Bulukumba and Kajang is 221 km (138 mi) long. The return journey can be made either by passing over the hills via Malino, or farther north via Watampone (Bone). Although a sidetrip to the boat-building center of Bira may involve a poor road, there are now places to eat and stay there before taking the ferry to Selayar.

Boats, pottery and flying fish

Coaches and minibuses leave regularly for Jeneponto and Takalar from the main bus terminal in Ujung Pandang. A direct coach to Bira leaves daily at 7.00 am and connects with the afternoon ferry to Selayar. Travel along the south coast is easy, and it is possible to stop off and explore the countryside along the way. From Jeneponto and Takalar, minibuses and *bemos* take you on to Sinjai and Bone. The distances given below are measured from Ujung Pandang.

Leaving Ujung Pandang, the road turns right to cross the Jeneberang River past Sungguminasa. At Limbung, 22 km (13 mi) from the city, a turn off to the right leads to Galesong (9 kms on a semi-paved road), through rice fields all the way to the coast. Galesong has always been one of the important Makassarese ports and political centers, but the progress of the city has scarcely touched it. The beach is a forest of small sailing craft, particularly in May and June, with hundreds of flying fish boats (*patorani*) drawn up on the sand. The people of Galesong are famous as experts with two-masted, tilted, rectangular rigs. They are also known for what is said to be the most spectacular boat ritual in Sulawesi—a feast and a race to a small island held on the day the fishermen leave in search of flying fish.

From Galesong a return can be made to Ujung Pandang by a poor but attractive coastal road north to Barombong, site of a new school for sailors and of the nearest

JEAN-LÉO DUGAST

beach to the city, thence back by a short sealed road to the main southern highway. Or continue south from Limbung, past a region of brick kilns and monuments to heroes of the revolution. The Polambangkeng region of Takalar in particular played a big part in the fight for independence.

Takalar (34 km) is a new administrative center on the main road. To the right, 5 km (3 mi) away, lies Takalar Lama, the colonial capital of the district, with an old Dutch jail as the principal monument to those times. Takalar is famous for its pottery, and a little north of Takalar Lama women can be seen at work beneath their houses making clay pots for storing rice and water, burning incense, and cooking. Much of the pottery is sent out by sailing craft to distant ports in Kalimantan or Sulawesi. The gray clay of the rice fields is the basic material, with a reddish earth from the mountains adding the decoration.

Some 10 km (6 mi) past Takalar, you enter Jeneponto district, the driest, poorest, and in some respects most traditional region of South Sulawesi. The land gets progressively drier as you advance, with rice tending to give way to maize (a staple in Jeneponto), oranges, kapok, and the lontara palm. This palm thrives in dry conditions and provides the owners with leaves for fine baskets and mat-making; sugar; palm-wine (*tuak*), and the fruit itself (*buah lontara*), a refreshing jelly-like substance sold in beautiful little baskets along the roadside. Don't eat the skins.

Horses are prominent everywhere in South Sulawesi (except Toraja), especially in hauling goods and people to market in little carts (*bendi* or *dokar*). Only in Jeneponto, however, do they rival the water buffalo as a symbol of wealth and strength. Horse meat is still often served at weddings and other feasts as a special honor to the guests.

One Jeneponto village researched in 1980 had a per capita annual income of only US $30. Many of Jeneponto's young men are forced to seek a living in Ujung Pandang as *becak* drivers, or in the Bone sugar factory or elsewhere. Unlike the Bugis however, they do not migrate permanently, but retain their roots in this stubbornly beautiful area. Jeneponto people have the reputation of being prouder than other Makassarese, more conscious of their *siri*, and ready to kill even close relatives when this appears to be required for the honor of the family.

At 57 km (38 mi) a very rough road to the right leads to the village of Cikuang, governed by a kind of theocracy of descendents of the original Arab *sayyid* who reputedly Islamized the village three and a half centuries ago. Its distinctive religious tradition is best seen in its colorful Maudu Lompoa festival in the Islamic month of *maulud*. There is a government resthouse on stilts here.

Opposite: *Fishing boats at Galesong harbor.*

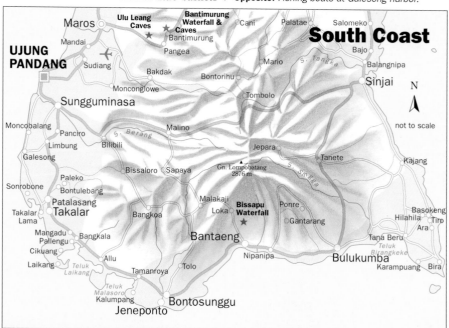

At 63 km (39 mi) a fine view of the sea and the hills is offered as you approach Bangkala. To visit the former boat-building center of Pallengu, pass the mosque, cross a bridge, and follow the main road as it curves right. Immediately before a line of small shops there is a bumpy road to the right, leading 2 km (1.8 mi) down to the small village of Pallengu on a narrow estuary.

This was the former center of the fiefdom of Bangkala, the leading aristocratic families of which had a long history of shipping ventures. Most of the male population of Pallengu are seafarers, and their operations cover the whole archipelago. The largest shipowner is Karaeng Getah (Haji Akbar), whose shipping company is now centered in Jakarta. All the boats were built in his home village, however, using the master-craftsmen of Ara as well as some local labor. The dry season was the time for building.

In the early 1980s, the waterside still looked as though several Noahs had all decided to build their arks at once. Now, all boat construction has moved to Tana Beru. The broad motorized vessels (up to 1000 cu. meters) are less elegant than the *prahu pinisi* which predominated a few years back, but the miracle of construction entirely by hand is even more impressive as the size of the ships grows larger.

Hereafter the road is closer to the coast, offering a good view of salt pans in the dry season, which are converted to fish ponds (*empang*) during the rains. As the salt water dries the salt is raked up and sold by the roadside at pathetically low prices, in baskets made of *lontara* leaves. The fish ponds are more profitable, using the brackish water of the rainy season to grow the spawn of the *ikan bolu* as well as prawns.

Farther east there is an important subsidiary income to be had from scooping up the spawn of the *bolu* at the sea's edge (as this fish can only spawn in salt water) and selling it to the *empang* owners. Other than this, Jeneponto is not a fishing area, despite its long coast.

Continuing along the road, you will pass the Tirta Ria swimming resort (*pemandian*) on the right (74 km). The spot is generously endowed with bamboo groves and breadfruit trees which provide plenty of shade. There are sheds where you can change clothing before using a mediocre beach. More popular with local visitors on Sundays are two pools filled with spring water.

At 77 km, a road to the left leads upward 4 km to the royal graves of Bontoramba. Human and animal figures are carved on several of the graves of the Binamu dynasty, which was centered here before moving to Jeneponto Lama in the 19th century.

At 90 km, turn right for Jeneponto Lama, the pre-war capital and seat of the Karaeng Binamu. This has the predictable old colonial jail and *controleur's* house, and many fine aristocratic Makassar houses. If this road is followed past Jeneponto Lama, it skirts the coast closely enough to give access to a number of fine beaches. Just after Jeneponto, a poor road to the left leads up to the former Dutch hill station of Malakaji, which was fashionable before Malino opened in 1922.

As the road descends onto the coastal plain (108 km), there is a sweeping view of the valley, surrounding foothills and the sea. After this point the road runs along the coast for 20 km, past traditional villages and colorful *prahus* with their fishing nets hung out to dry. At various times of the year villagers can be seen working in groups netting eggs from the sea for their fish ponds, or taking fish from their traps.

Bantaeng

Bantaeng (123 km) was ceded to the Dutch under the terms of the Treaty of Bungaya (1667). It was originally occupied by Aru Palakka's Bugis, but later became a Dutch post. It became the capital of the southeast-

JEAN-LÉO DUGAST

ern region in the colonial period, but is now only slightly ahead of the other south coast capitals as an urban center. Bantaeng region is the best irrigated on the south coast, and provides rice and vegetables for Ujung Pandang.

For a spectacular waterfall (*air terjun Bisappu*) turn left towards Bissapu before Bantaeng. The waterfall, about 4 km north of Bissapu along a rough road, is about 100 meters (325 ft) high. In 1840 James Brooke, the raja of Sarawak, admired its "undisturbed solitude and complete seclusion," and on a weekday it still enjoys this claim. Brooke went on to climb Mount Lompobatang, or Bantaeng Peak, highest point in the southern cordillera; it took him three days to reach the summit from Bantaeng. Between Bantaeng and Bulukumba the road follows the coast, giving access to some good beaches.

Bantaeng

Kabupaten Bulukumba (146 km) occupies the rocky southeast corner of the province. As the road is rough and stony, the going is slow. After skirting the coast for a short time it turns inland, along a rocky terrain suitable only for forest and grazing. Cattle, buffalo, goats and horses are seen here. Further towards the coast there are *empang*, which attract flocks of white ibis.

Along the beach at Tana Beru (174 km, homestay available), you may observe tradi-

tional boat-building, noting the sign: "Lokasi Konstruksi Pinisi." At 178 km the road turning inland to Ara and Bira is well marked, the last signs you will see. At 181 km turn left at a fork in the road. At 188 km a T-junction: Ara to the left, Bira to the right. At 195 km begin a very steep, rocky descent to Bira (5 km): the center, as for centuries past, of the South Sulawesi boat-building industry.

There are three harbors in the little town of Bira, two for *prahus* and one for the vehicular ferry. The water is delightfully clear for swimming, and the white sand beaches shady and pleasant, especially near the ferry wharf. In the past, *prahus* gathered here to set sail for the Moluccas and Irian, when Bira was still a center for sailors and boat-owners. There are several hotels and eating places in Bira and nearby Tanateng. (See page 110.)

You may sail from Bira to Selayar by ferry; there is bus or private transport on the island. At least one night is necessary in Benteng on Selayar. It pays to arrive a little early, especially on the return trip. The crossing may be rough, as there are some treacherous currents in this area. However, it is generally calm, with crystal-clear water and lots of fish. The rocky coast and sandy beaches near both terminals are very inviting. (See "Selayar Island," page 100.)

Opposite: *A young Bugis girl at Tana Beru.*
Above: *A farmer on horseback at Jeneponto.*

JEAN-LEO DUGAST

Ara and Kajang

Returning from Selayar to Bira, continue back to the turnoff (a 5-km ascent) towards Ara, which lies about 13 km away. There are glimpses of the sea through the trees. Ara, a prosperous village, is famous for its ship-builders, who travel all over Indonesia. The village has in fact no easy access to the sea (2 km away) nor to timber supplies. Still, 80 percent of the working males (about 1,000 in all) are employed in ship-building in various parts of Indonesia, always returning to their families in this village.

The signpost for the Ara caves (Gowa Purbakala Ara) on the main road gives the distance as 0.5 km. However, the way to the caves is through heavy brush and undergrowth and the caves themselves are disappointing; fairly open, with scattered remains of broken porcelain, coffins and bones.

Continue on the coastal road to Kajang to Tiro, a few km north of Ara. Here is the grave of Dato Tiro, Khatib Bungsu, one of the three Muslim holy men from Minangkabau who brought Islam to South Sulawesi in the 17th century Tiro also has a pre-Muslim cliff grave similar to contemporary Toraja graves, in a cave overlooking the sea.

On the road east to Kajang there is a big government rubber plantation (formerly Dutch), the only one in South Sulawesi.

Kajang (266 km) is situated on a deep, pleasant bay. Travelers can stay overnight in Pondok Sisihorong, 10 km north.

Members of the Tanatoa religious sect centered west of Kajang wear black and have a formidable reputation for magic which has helped to protect their pre-Islamic culture.

Sinjai

The road to Sinjai is a pleasant, hilly drive around the slopes of Mount Lompobatang (2871 meters/9330 ft), an extinct volcano which according to local tradition was one of the first areas to emerge from the primordial sea. There is a mixture of crops on the terraced hills: cloves, some rice, corn, and fruits. The corn is hung out to dry in woven palm-leaf sheaths under the houses. As you reach Sinjai there is a fine view of the town and the coast.

Sinjai (221 km) is separated from *kabupaten* Bone by the river Tangka. The port lies in the adjoining town of Balangnipa, where there is a former Dutch fort, built in the 1860s. It is now used as a police office. From here, you can take a boat to Pulau Sembilan (Nine Islands), picturesque mountainous islands covered in jungle.

The road from here to Malino has recently been paved, and offers an alternate route back to Ujung Pandang. If you take this road for 1.5 km there are hot springs at Uwae. The sacred grave at this spot, which is looked after by a holy man (*sanro*), is frequently visited by the local people who come to pray and bring offerings. North of Sinjai, but difficult of access, are the caves, Gua Karampuang and Gua Bappajeng, and nearer Sinjai is a traditional aristocratic house.

The road to Bone travels along a flat plain cultivated in rice, with some grazing land. To the west of Marek, 30 km from Bone, are the hills where according to legend Prince La Darapung took refuge when exiled from Luwu because of leprosy. Having no other company but his dog, he had two children from this animal, humans with white skin and blue eyes. The horrified inhabitants of the area banished the family, who went off to populate Europe.

There is a sugar factory on the right as you continue, with 5,000 hectares (12,350 acres) of cane. The factory, the biggest outside Java, began production in 1975. Much of its labor force is seasonal, drawn especially from the poorer areas to the south.

—*Anthony Reid*

Above: *Women bathing in Sinjai.* **Opposite:** *A Kajang horseman carries his saddle on his head.*

SELAYAR ISLAND

Beaches and an Ancient Drum

Selayar's position as a long, narrow barrier on the trade routes to the Moluccas has thrust it into history despite the stubborn rockiness of its soil. Currents frequently wash wreckage up onto its 100-kilometer-long (60 mi) west coast, which perhaps accounts for the presence of a 2,000-year-old Vietnamese Dong Son drum. Yet Selayar must have been a trading center in its own right by at least the 14th century, when it is mentioned in the Javanese *Nagarakertagama* poem. An unusual abundance of Chinese and Sawankhalok (Thai) ceramics of about the same period has also been dug from grave sites on the island.

Islam appears to have come to Selayar in the 16th century from the eastern islands of Ternate and Buton. But it was Makassar which first imposed its political dominance over the island's many feuding principalities. Selayar was a valuable prize not only through its location, but because its coarse blue-and-white cotton "Selayar cloth" was in demand all over the archipelago. At least from the 16th to the 19th centuries, cotton was the major crop and export product of the island, and tribute had to be paid to its successive masters in this cloth.

Ternate (in the Moluccas) claimed Selayar in the Treaty of Bungaya, which carved up much of the Makassar empire (1667), but the Dutch wrested it back in the early 18th century. Thereafter the fourteen autonomous "regents" of Selayar had to bring their homage and their cloth to Fort Rotterdam. In the last 150 years Selayar cloth has declined to nothing in the face of factory production. The economy is now perilously dependent on coconut harvesting and whatever can be earned by other trade. The island's population has grown very little in the last century, as its earlier favorable location has given way to isolation.

This isolation (both internal and external) has sustained a surprising variety in Selayar, including the linguistic peculiarity of a Buton language surviving in the south. The southern village of Binanga Benteng was also the center of the Mahdi Akbar movement, a quasi-Islamic messianic movement centered around the mystical teachings of Abdul Sani ("Tuang Opu"), who died there in 1922. In the 1930s some of its adherents were led into the fold of Christianity and after 1966, when the Mahdi Akbar moverment was banned by the local Moslem body, others took refuge under the umbrella of Hinduism.

The ferry to Selayar leaves daily from Bira at 14:00 and arrives at 16:15. A direct bus which connects up with the ferry leaves from Panaikan bus terminal in Ujung Pandang at 07:00. It pays to be a little early, especially on the return trip.

The inviting beaches to the north of the ferry are as good as most on the island. From Pamatata ferry, minibuses drive west across a barren, rocky terrain where the white coralitic rock is used for neat stone walls. Water is very scarce in this area, yet it has a prosperous and well-kept air despite the poverty of the soils. Along the west coast the road is asphalted but bumpy, fringed with rows of towering coconut palms. At sunset it is a picturesque drive down the coast past fishing villages to the main town of Benteng, where there is a clean new hotel.

In Benteng, the residence of the former *controleur,* which dates from the 1890s, overlooks the central green (*alun-alun*). On the

north side of the *alun-alun* is a very solid-looking Dutch jail, which also dates from the 1890s. To the west, a sculptured figure with a *keris* lunges out to sea to repel invaders.

The *nekara*—the famous Dong Son drum of Selayar—is kept at Bontobangun, 3 km (1.8 mi) south of Benteng, in a wooden shed near the palace of the former raja of the area, Andi Arman, whose son now lives there. It was excavated around the 17th century at Papalohia (the center of a pre-Islamic kingdom). The drum is a magnificent specimen, measuring 95 cm high and 115 cm across (38 x 45 in), with four stylized frogs arranged on the sides of the top surface around a central raised star with 16 points. (One of the frogs was cut off but fortunately recovered.) Around this star there is an intricate pattern forming sixteen concentric circles.

On the sides, which are triple-tiered, are four handles, arranged in pairs. The pattern varies from tier to tier, with elephant motifs, birds and coconut trees around the base, abstract motifs in the middle section, and peacocks in the top section.

With the drum are kept three beautifully carved pieces of a wooden *prahu* wrecked at Metalallong and kept by the raja of Bontobangun as a magical craft in which he sailed to Gowa. These consist of the head of a *naga*, about 110 cm (43 in) high, with ornate wings, head and teeth; the tail, about 1.5 meters long, in a style reminiscent of Majapahit; and

an *anjungan*, the place where the captain sat to give orders to the boatmen. Inscribed in Arabic are the words "Sultan Abdul Malik, Tuban," suggesting that it dates from the 16th century, when Tuban was still a great East Javan port.

From a little below the microwave station overlooking Benteng you can walk east along a jungle track to the hilltop fort of Gantarang. One of the strongest pre-Islamic states in the region, Gantarang had links with Buton and Luwu. The village of about forty houses (it is said that formerly there were 700) lies on top of a hill reached only by three paths. The settlement is protected by nine-meter-high walls surmounting the natural stronghold.

The mosque in Gantarang is said to have been built in the 16th century at the behest of Datu ri Bandang, who spread Islamic teaching in the Makassar area. The old layered roof is supported on an ancient wooden frame on four pillars, with a short central pillar suspended from cross-beams. There is also a very old *mimbar* (pulpit), and two ancient *khotbah* (sermons) written in Arabic on sewn paper.

According to local legend a mark in the rock close to the mosque is the left footprint of the Bugus hero Sawerigading; the right is said to be in Mecca.

—*Anthony Reid*

Below: *The splendid Dong Son drum of Selayar.*

BONE AND SOPPENG

Vanished Bugis Kingdoms

The capitals of three former Bugis kingdoms, located in the central and eastern parts of the peninsula, can be reached in just a few hours by bus from Ujung Pandang. Each has a distinctive character. Watansoppeng (Soppeng) is set among rolling foothills; Watampone (Bone) has old Dutch houses and spacious squares; while Singkang is a bustling market town overlooking Lake Tempe.

From Ujung Pandang, the road to Bone and Soppeng leads north, turning off to the right at Maros. After this turnoff, the road starts to climb over the limestone ranges. Soaring cliffs hung with tropical creepers are interspersed with the dense jungle of the National Forest. The crumbling rock lends itself to fantastic formations, caves and stalactites, with occasional waterfalls and glimpses of rivers far below. The area is rich in prehistoric remains. Camba, at 67 km (42 mi) from Ujung Pandang, guards a pass in the southern range, dominated by Maros Peak, Bulu Saraung (1360 meters/4420 ft).

The road runs along a grassy plain with signs of severe erosion in the surrounding hills. At Lepangun (123 km), just after passing two *warungs* on the right, the road forks. The right fork leads to Bone, left to Soppeng. A little way up the road to Soppeng is Lamuru, a strategically important mountain kingdom on the pass between Bone and Soppeng. The tombs of the rajahs of Lamuru, Kompleks Makam Kuno, lie on the right just off the road about 10 km later. The guard on the left has a key and there is an information center on the left inside the gate.

Powerful kingdom of Bone

Capital of the most populous *kabupaten* in South Sulawesi, Bone was formerly the strongest of all Bugis states. The recorded list of Bone rulers goes back to the 14th century, when the original *tomunurung* came down from heaven, married a mortal, and began a dynasty. By the 16th century Bone dominated the region, linked with Wajo and Soppeng in the Tallumpocco alliance (1582) against the rising power of Makassar. In 1610-11 Bone accepted Islam and the loose hegemony of Makassar (Gowa) after being defeated on the battlefield. Renewed defiance brought a much more bitter defeat in 1640 and again in 1644, after which Bone was

ruled as a conquered province. This led to the rebellion under Aru Palakka in the 1660s, and the alliance with the Dutch which ultimately destroyed Makassar in 1669.

Aru Palakka ruled in Bone from 1672 until his death in 1696. His victorious alliance with the Dutch added Bantaeng, Lamuru and parts of Bulukumba and Soppeng to his fiefdom, while in 1670 he conquered the vital Walanae (Cenrana) River outlet of Wajo to the sea. Bone continued through the 18th century to be the strongest Bugis power, supported by the Dutch until it began to threaten Makassar itself at the end of the century. The messianic Gowa rebel Sankilang held the most sacred Gowa regalia—the Sudanga sword—during his long resistance in the hills, but on his deathbed in the 1790s he passed it to the Bone ruler. This encouraged Bone's claims on Gowa itself, and from 1794 Bone attacked and dominated the Maros area to the north of Makassar. This forced the occupants of Fort Rotterdam to move against Bone—first the British (1816) and later the returning Dutch, who in 1824 briefly occupied and destroyed Watampone itself.

Nevertheless, Bone remained a substantial power. James Brooke found in 1840 he could achieve little among the Bugis without the Bone ruler, and when he finally gained audience in 1840 the scene was impressive:

"A body of 3000 or 4000 were ranged within and without the courtyard, dressed precisely alike, in skull-caps and blue sarongs over the kris. A dead silence was preserved as we passed through them, and afforded a striking contrast to the inexpressible tumult of our reception at Tesora [Wajo]. Eight or ten spearmen, clad in coats of bright chain armor, guarded the entrance, and presented the only display of arms we saw.

... Behind the monarch were half a dozen handsome boys, his own relations; and two rows of young rajahs were seated cross-legged on his right hand. Like those without,

they were naked to the waist, wearing only skull caps and sarongs, and preserving a profound silence."

After repeated difficulties, the Dutch sent another expedition against Bone in February 1859. The doughty female ruler retreated to the hills, but the Dutch expedition was a disaster and had to withdraw with its commander dead. A bigger force landed more cautiously in Sinjai in November 1859, taking Watampone in December and Pampanua in January. In 1931, after a long interregnum,

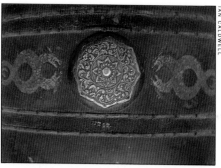

Andi Mappanyuki was placed on the throne, which continued to be the most influential one in South Sulawesi until the monarchy was abolished in 1955.

Visiting Watampone

The devastations of numerous invasions of the capital, Watampone, have unfortunately not left a great deal of historic interest, except for one colorful wall of the *kabupaten* office, part of the 19th-century Bone palace which was taken to Makassar after the 1905 defeat and returned in 1931 to form part of the new palace. The royal grave complex, with 17th-century tombs similar in style to those of Gowa, is at Bukaka on the road leading north towards Singkang.

About 4 km (2.5 mi) east of the city is the port of Bajoe, which takes its name from the Bajau boat people who at one time inhabited the waterways throughout much of the archipelago. Many of them now live in houses over the water at the port. Legend links the origin of the Bajau with Luwu, where the

Opposite: *Palace of the ruler of Bone, built by the Dutch following his restoration to the throne in the 1930s.* **Above, left:** *Grave of Collipujie, an 18th-century ruler of Lamuru, said to have invented the letters of the Bugis alphabet.* **Above, right:** *the shield of the raja of Bone, kept in the Bone Museum. "Rose-style" brass studs represent the nine cardinal directions of Hindu mythology.*

Bugis hero Sawerigading felled a giant tree, forming an island, causing a flood, and washing the Bajau out to sea. The yolk from the broken birds' eggs which fell from the tree is supposed to have stained the Bajaus' hair a yellowish color (this was more likely due to a vitamin deficiency). On the strength of this legend, eggs are considered taboo among the Bajau. From Bajoe a ferry leaves nightly at 11 pm for Kolaka on the Southeast peninsula, arriving at about 6 am, whence there is a well-paved road to Kendari.

Limestone caves and a lost kingdom

The largest and most spectacular series of limestone caves in South Sulawesi, Gua Mampu, are 34 km (21 mi) north of Watampone. These comprise two upper caves lit by collapsed roofs, and two lower ones for which artificial light is needed. Take the road to Singkang, turning left at the village of Ulae. Guides and flashlights are available in abundance. This cave has been celebrated for centuries not only for its natural shapes, but for the legends associating it with the lost kingdom of Mampu. The members of the Mampu court are said to have been turned to stone, as the result of a curse delivered when a princess, Apung Mangenre, dropped her spool, and being too lazy to pick it up herself, asked her dog to do the job for her. There are varying versions of the legend, but all seek to explain particular strange shapes. James Brooke was so excited by the stories of a Mampu kingdom that he made enormous efforts to reach the cave in 1840 in the hope of discovering some vanished civilization. While his hopes were unfulfilled Brooke conceded the remarkable beauty of the cave.

Watansoppeng (Soppeng)

One of the prettiest towns in the province, Soppeng has won prizes for its gardens. Sprays of moon orchids frequently festoon the verandahs of Soppeng's buildings. One of the most remarkable features of the town is the vast numbers of bats which swarm in the tall trees of the town center, around the mosque and the office of the *bupati*. Local mythology has it that if the bats leave Soppeng, the town would collapse. Since they seem careful to only eat the fruit of non-Soppengers, they are never disturbed, but hang squeaking in their thousands, to take off in swarms at dusk and dawn.

The graves of the rajas, Taman Purbakala Kompleks Makam Kuno, Jena Lomoe, are located 800 meters from the town center, to

the left of the road to Ompo. Note the unique house-like structure of these stone graves. Continue on the road to Ompo and turn right upon reaching Ompo, heading for the springs and pool (*Pemandian Ompo*). Many villagers go directly to the springs behind the swimming pool to wash and bathe; but the pool is refilled every Friday with fresh spring water, and is very spacious, with pagodas along the sides to sit under. There is another natural pool at Lawo, nearby. Megaliths, some probably very old, are also to be seen in abundance in the village of Lawo, where the villagers use many of them for house supports.

Silk is now cultivated here as a home industry. Women take about a month to produce a piece two meters (6.5 ft) long. Visitors can stop to watch and to buy. Spinning can also be seen in small shops in the town. The main area for cultivating the silkworms is north of Soppeng, on the road to Pangkajene where mulberry trees are abundant.

Vanishing lakes

The road north to Singkang runs through a flat plain with *sawah* and tobacco production visible along the roadside. The tobacco leaves are dried, shredded and baked in bamboo tubes about two feet long in drying houses for two to three days. The cylinders are

Above: *Moslem children going to the mosque at Singkang.* **Opposite:** *Fish traps in Lake Tempe.*

then simply sliced open for sale. Cabenge is the main marketing center of the tobacco-growing district, and is especially lively on market day, when the villagers arrive in brightly painted and decorated pony carts.

The road crosses the Walanae River, the only marine outlet for the Wajo people, who are nevertheless great seafarers. The river flows into Lake Tempe, which is gradually drying up because of heavy silting brought about by erosion. This has speeded a slow natural process of change, dating from the Pleistocene period, whereby large tracts of land have gradually emerged from the sea. Lake Tempe is the largest remnant of an inland sea which is thought to have originally divided the peninsula in two.

Nowadays the lake is hardly much more than two meters (6.5 ft) deep, and in the dry season vast areas dry up completely. In 1972 you could cross from Tempe to the other side in a horse and cart. Although Lake Tempe still provides fish for export, production is dropping. One specialty of the area is small shrimp (*lawa*), which are served seasoned and flavored with lemon juice.

At times the lake floods. People then move around by boat, and there are even floating shops. The birds in this area are particularly prolific. Boat races, which used to have a ritual significance, have been reintroduced for the celebration of Independence Day, the 17th of August.

Singkang: Bugis silks and dances

Capital of the *kabupaten* of Wajo, Singkang, along with its twin town of Tempe on the lakeside of Lake Tempe, retains a traditional character. From the government resthouse (*Baruga We Cudai*) situated on top of the hill across the square from the mosque, there is an excellent view over the two towns, each of which has a large mosque built in the Middle-Eastern architectural style. In the background glimmers Lake Tempe.

Singkang is renowned for its silk weaving. An energetic princess of Wajo named Andi Bau Muddaria, who takes particular interest in her people's traditions and culture, was the first to set up a local workshop modelled on Thai silk production, in a large house near the mosque. Other workshops have since followed suit. Sarongs and meter lengths of silk may be purchased at the silk factory on Jl. Sentosa Baru.

Andi Bau Muddaria is reviving a number of cultural traditions, such as a colorful Bugis wedding in the ancient style, reenacted in Singkang in 1981. Wajo dance groups are often asked to represent the aristocratic traditions of the Bugis people. There is an excellent dance group composed of local aristocratic ladies here, and a traditional orchestra including flutes, violins and *kecapi* (a kind of two-stringed lute).

—*Anthony Reid*

JEAN-LÉO DUGAST

LUWU

Land Where the Gods Descended

The sign as you enter *kabupaten* Luwu from Siwa announces that this is "the land of Sawerigading." According to Bugis chronicles, it was in the vicinity of the Cerekang River, between the present towns of Wotu and Malili, that the gods first descended, and that their descendent, Sawerigading, performed his legendary deeds. The first Bugis kingdom may have been located here, perhaps in the 13th and 14th centuries, and may provide the historical basis for the tale.

In the centuries that followed, Luwu's main asset was always its cachet as the oldest kingdom with the most potent *bissu*. In reality the Bugis population of Luwu was always very small and its military and economic significance negligible, yet the sultanate managed to draw tribute from a host of diverse people from Tana Toraja to Poso and even Kolaka. The Dutch colonial regime after 1904

initially reinforced this shadowy authority, and it was not until the late 1940s that Toraja and Kolaka were separated from Luwu.

In 1937, however, Luwu began a new era as the open frontier of South Sulawesi, with new immigrants opening rice fields, where for centuries the main food crop had been the sago trees which grow wild in its vast forests. The Dutch sponsored the first Javanese "colonists" to the area of Bonebone and Wotu, though these had to undergo terrible hardships in the turbulent years that followed. When these years finally came to an end in the late 1960s with the crushing of the Darul Islam rebellion, both official "transmigration" of Javanese and Balinese and spontaneous migration of Toraja and others has been far more intensive, doubling the population of Luwu in the last ten years (1980 population 503,700). An ambitious irrigation and road-building project, "Project Luwu," has been under way since 1975 to provide the infrastructure for these migrants. In addition, one of the world's biggest nickel mines is now operating at the eastern fringe of Luwu.

Visiting Luwu

Buses from Ujung Pandang to Luwu leave in the early morning from the main bus terminal. The journey takes you north to Parepare (see "West Coast"), then inland to Pangkajene, capital of *kabupaten* Sidrap. The most prosperous rice-growing district in South

JEAN-LÉO DUGAST

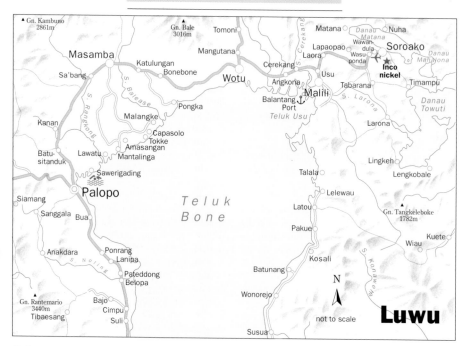

Luwu

Sulawesi, Sidrap owes its fertility to the Sa'dan irrigation system set up by the Dutch in the 1930s, which has recently been upgraded. Double-cropping is thus normal here, and the commercialization and mechanization of agriculture has proceeded further than elsewhere.

Note the handsome old aristocratic house, brought intact from Wajo, which is now an annex to the government resthouse behind the *bupati*'s office.

From Anabanua, the road continues east through Siwa, a picturesque town on the river Tuguerange. The land is dry and barren at first, with coconut palms and some *sawah*.

Shortly after Pandangsappa the road draws near the coast, then moves a few kilometers inland again because of mangrove swamps. This is a scenic drive, with the mountains of Central Sulawesi looming mistily on the northern horizon. The approach to Palopo offers magnificent views of the bay, though even more so if you approach from Rantepao.

Palopo: gateway to the iron hills

To appreciate the setting of Palopo, the major town of Luwu, drive out onto the long pier which runs for 1.5 km (1 mi) alongside the river and out into the bay. This area is a scene of great activity, with various types of *prahu*, junks and *bagang* (fish-traps), and ferries to Luwuk and remote islands. From the end of

the pier there is a lookout tower, offering a magnificent panorama of the bay.

The Mosque opposite the post office, Mesjid Kuno Batupassi, is probably the oldest in South Sulawesi. Built around 1603 when the area was Islamized it is oriented to the west instead of the northwest as it should be. People now pray there facing the northwest corner. The stone walls are about one meter thick.

Said to have been built by the same artisan who built the mosque, the royal graves (*Makam raja-raja*) are in the single-domed pyramidal tomb (*lokkoh*) to the right. The caretaker next door has a key, but does not usually let tourists enter this holy tomb. It possibly replaces a wooden *lokkoh* such as the Toraja use if there is no cave available.

Other sites include the small Batara Guru museum in the house of the former rajas. There is a swimming pool at Latuppa, and beaches at Sawerigading (northeast of the town), Songka, and Plywood Beach. It is pleasant to take a boat out to the small island of Lebukan.

From Palopo to Malili

This 188-km (118-mi) journey takes about six hours, thanks to a very good asphalt road developed as part of "Project Luwu." The large dam 21 km (13 km) from Palopo is part

Opposite: *Palopo harbor.*

of an extensive irrigation project for the area. To the north lies the central mountain range, dominated by Mt. Kambuno (2,950 m/9600 ft) and to the southeast Mt. Bale (3016 m/9800 ft). Hardy travelers interested in walking could visit the traditional weaving centers of Rongkong, Seko, and Makki north of Sabbang. Each village has a different style of weaving. The aboriginal people of this area, the Toala, wear a distinctive form of dress. They are more approachable here than around Poso, where they are suspicious of foreigners.

To get there, it is possible to walk from Sabbang to Rongkong in 1.5 days, to Seko (3 days), then to Makki (2 days). It is then a difficult six-day tramp from Kalumpang to Rantepao; or you could walk from Kalumpang to Tamlea, where you can take a river boat to Mamuju. This trip is only for the most adventurous, who must carry provisions and medical supplies.

From Masamba (61 km), the adventurous can hike northward to Lake Poso. After Masamba, the swampy coastal plain to the south of the road is a major transmigration area. 20 km (12 mi) past Masamba is Katulungan, one of the area's oldest settlements.

The center of the transmigration and irrigation projects of the region is at Bonebone (101 km). There is a fascinating mixture of peoples and cultures in this area. Toraja ricebarns and wooden churches exist side by side with mosques, Javanese bungalow cottages, and Balinese temples. Javanese *wayang kulit* or *gamelan* performances can be seen in some transmigration villages on special occasions.

At 139 km is Wotu, a small town with a *losmen*. The *prahu* port on the river to the east is worth a visit (not the harbor, which is 3 km away). This could be a scene from a Conrad novel, with houses on stilts built over the water, fishing boats and small industries such as sawmills on the water's edge.

From Wotu begins South Sulawesi's only road link to Central Sulawesi, the road north to Poso. It is often impassable for jeeps, though motorbikes keep up a regular service as far as Lake Poso, whence you can take a boat to Tentena, then a minibus on to Poso. The lake area is beautiful, but still very difficult of access.

Cerekang, 175 km, is believed to have been the center of the old kingdom of Luwu. The Cerekang River is navigable for 15 km north towards Lake Matana, which can then be reached on foot. This area was in the past a source of iron for making knives (*badik*). The sacred graves upriver can only be visited with permission from the *kepala kampung* in Cerekang. According to tradition the god Batara Guru descended to earth here, and Sawerigading bathed in a small river in the hills nearby. Usu (184 km) reveals little trace of its prominent role in the *La Galigo* epic, though it long retained a magical significance for Luwu's kings.

Malili and Soroako

Formerly a picturesque riverside town near the bay of Usu, the town of Malili was destroyed by the rebellion during the 1950s, and was completely rebuilt as the port for the Soroako project. There are good swimming and boating from the sandy beaches of the island of Bulopeway, off the coast from Malili. According to legend, this island was formed when Sawerigading felled a huge *wailendring* tree, which shattered the land and sent the Bajau people out to sea.

In 1968 P.T. Inco began its operations in this area, when the Indonesian Government signed contracts with the Canadian-based company for the design and construction of nickel-processing facilities in the area of Soroako. All equipment and supplies for the plant passed through the port of Balantang at Malili. At first the headquarters were at Malili, but were later moved to Soroako, leaving only a small settlement at the port. Except for the port area the company seems to have hardly made a mark on the town, though a school and hospital were established there.

There is, however, a good road to Soroako which follows the spectacular Larona River gorge through the mountains for about 30 km, when the road leaves the river valley for the undulating valley which stretches to Lake Matana. The village of Wasuponda is the first satellite town of Soroako; a few kilometers farther on there is a turnoff to the second, Wawandula, where the river is dammed for a new electricity station. Schools have been constructed in all three towns, as well as a health center in Wasuponda and a hospital in Soroako for Inco employees.

The dense green jungle around Soroako has been razed for the massive mine complex, which transformed this area almost overnight from a village of shifting cultivators to a site of international importance, with the latest technological equipment. Airplanes and helicopters fly daily into an area previously

ALAIN COMPOST

only accessible by long journeys on foot; motorboats and water-skis disturb the centuries-old silence on the lake; and the former ricefields are now a golf course and an air-conditioned village for workers. Besides the Inco guesthouse, which is expensive and intended for guests of the company, there is a *losmen* in the town; there are several restaurants, as well as the lavish Inco canteen.

The plant is well worth a visit. One of the world's major nickel-producing plants, its massive machinery dominates the landscape. The westernized lifestyle of the predominantly Indonesian workers offers an extraordinary contrast with their environment. The plant has attracted workers from all over Indonesia, though Bugis and Toraja predominate. Naturally this has caused problems in the original village, which has grown beyond the limits of its facilities, and has also lost its original agricultural land. However there are compensations in the increased pay-packets brought in by those employed by Inco, the side-benefits of improved communications, schooling, health, electricity and water supply. The company appears anxious to restore the damage done to the environment by mining, and to avoid pollution of the lake, one of the great natural attractions of Sulawesi.

Lakes Matana and Towuti

One of the deepest lakes in the world, Matana has but few fish: an oddly shaped transparent fish called *botinu*; the *opudi,* and the *kolami,* a small crayfish. There are burial caves in the cliff edge around the lake, which is clear, cool and delightful for boating and swimming. At the head of the lake is Matana village, where there is a spring popularly believed to be the lake's source. "Matana" means literally "this eye."

The largest lake in Sulawesi, Lake Towuti is 48 km (30 mi) wide and stunningly beautiful. There is a bus from Malili to Wawondula and then to Timampu on the shores of the lake, but no tourist facilities.

This area at the northeastern tip of South Sulawesi encapsulates the attractions, the problems and the promise of future expansion for the province. Less than 15 years ago, Soroako was an isolated village. Today it has an up-to-date nickel plant, with two airstrips and a good highway to the sea.

Since the province opened to tourists several years ago, the number of visitors has rapidly escalated. Improved communications are rapidly breaking down the isolation which helped maintain its unique character. Whether the natural beauty admired in the 19th century by Wallace, Brooke and others will remain unimpaired by material progress is another question.

—*Anthony Reid*

Above: *600-meter-deep (2000 ft) Lake Matana near Soroako in South Sulawesi.*

South Practicalities

Includes Parepare, Mandar, Selayar, Bone, Soppeng, Sinkang, Pinrang, Palopo. Telephone code 0421. All prices in US$. S=Single, D=Double. AC=air-conditioned.

Outside Ujung Pandang and Toraja, tourist facilities are limited. There are clean and comfortable hotels in Parepare, Watansoppeng (Soppeng), Pinrang, Watampone (Bone) and Palopo, though food is sometimes a problem. A basic command of Indonesian is of course useful, but someone who speaks a few words of English can usually be found. Bring a *sarung* for sleeping in, as well as a pair of rubber flip-flops and your own toilet paper. Mosquito repellant is a must.

Travel in South Sulawesi is remarkably easy. Coaches and minibuses cover the entire province, leaving throughout the day from terminals in every major town. It is not necessary to book (except for Toraja in the peak season), though you should be prepared to wait an hour or two until there are enough passengers.

The major roads are now well paved and maintained. Vestiges of the old colonial roads are the gracious tamarind trees on both sides, and stone markers every kilometer showing the distance from "Makassar" and the nearest *kabupaten* capital. Self-drive vehicles are difficult and expensive to rent—a Toyota Land Cruiser costs $100 a day—but chauffeur-driven cars can be hired in Ujung Pandang from $30.

One way of visiting the extremities of the province would be to take a **Merpati** flight to Soroako or Mamuju from Ujung Pandang and a bus back. The reverse procedure involves risks of being stranded, since local flights do not always run according to the timetable.

Taxis and minibuses with an English-speaking driver/guide can be hired at good hotels in Ujung Pandang. Rates are about $3 per hour (two hours minimum) or $30-40 per day, a bit more for air-conditioning, newer vehicles and longer journeys. Families or small groups can charter a private mini-bus with driver at about $25 per day plus fuel. Stopovers and side trips can be planned, and this is an ideal way to see South Sulawesi.

Parepare

Parepare was formerly part of the kingdom of Suppa and an important coastal port for the inland kingdoms of Sidenreng and Rappang, near the central lakes. Today it is a busy port and a stopover spot between Ujung Pandang and Toraja.

The most interesting place to stay is the **Hotel Gandaria** at Jl. Bau Masepe 171 (rooms w/bathroom $6). Haji Zainuddin, the proprietor, has a valuable collection of ritual objects, ornaments, and wedding costumes which were once used by royal families, some of which he rents out for marriages. He is happy to show these to his guests. **Restaurant Sempurna**, also Jl. Bau Masepe, serves reasonably priced seafood. The newer **Restaurant Asia** serves decent Chinese-Indonesian food in clean surroundings, while **Angin Mammiri** on Jl. Pingir Laut has reasonable food, good snacks and a superb view across the bay.

Majene (Mandar)

Majene, like the rest of Mandar, is not equipped for tourists. The most attractive alternative is to stay at the pleasant, centrally located harbor home of **Ibu Darmi Masud** at Jl. Amanna Wewang 12. Inquiries must first be made in Ujung Pandang with Dr. Darmawan Masud at Jl. Usman Jafarno 9, Tel. 22482. Nice rooms with delicious meals at reasonable prices. For breakfast, as you watch the *bago* fleet return from the Strait, you can drink rich Mandar coffee, fried sweet bananas, and sticky rice with dark palm sugar and grated fresh coconut. Dinner may be freshly caught silver scad, or sauteed tuna steak prepared in sun-dried green mango sauce, rivaling California nouvelle cuisine. The tuna is right off the *bago* boat.

Walk around the corner to the *warung* on Jl. Syukur Rahim, for an excellent lunch of *soto ayam* (chicken soup), crisp fried chicken, fried rice, or stir-fried vegetables.

Bulukumba

Accommodation in Bulukumba is very basic. Try **Penginapan Sinar Jaya**, Jl. Sawerigading 4. Tel. 129. 4 rooms with toilet/mandi and fan, $4.50. Dormitory upstairs $1.50. Grubby.

Tana Beru

One can stay at **Homestay Anda** in this traditional boat-building town for $2.50 single per night.

Bira

Bira is a pleasant village with lovely shady, white sand beaches.

ACCOMMODATION

Yaya Homestay (6 rooms) In the village, a couple of kms from the beach. Two mandi/toilets. $5 including 3 meals.
Anda Bungalows opened May 1991. 7 bungalows with private shower and toilet and veranda, 100 m from the beach. Restaurant. $5 D, $4 S, including breakfast.
Bira Beach Hotel (16 bungalows) was built at the beach in the summer, 1991. $13.
Riswan Guest House (10 rooms), in Tanateng near the beach. $4, including tea, coffee and 3 meals.

Shared mandi/toilet.

FOOD

There is the restaurant at Anda Bungalows and an eating stall near the vehicular ferry.

Selayar

The ferry from Bira (southeasternmost tip of South Sulawesi) to Pamatata harbor on Selayar leaves daily at 14:00. There is a direct bus from Ujung Pandang's Panaikan terminal at 07:00 which connects up with the ferry. There are two hotels in Benteng: **Hotel Berlian** is the newer ($4 S, $6 D). The return ferry leaves at 10:00 the following day.

Watampone (Bone)

A sleepy, spacious town with several old wooden buildings from the Dutch period set in grassy, overgrown gardens. The main attractions here are the museum and the great wooden palace built in the 1930s to house the reinstated Raja of Bone. Alongside is the *rumah adat*, where the *hadat* (council of seven) used to meet.

The museum is on the corner of the main square. Its knowledgeable and enthusiastic director is named Andi Mappassissi. Among the sacred objects in the museum, held essential for the validity of a Bone ruler, are a Javanese *keris* called *La Makawa*, with a massive golden handle, finely carved; and a similarly lavish sword named *La Teariduni*, which owes its name to the legend that it refused to be buried with its original owner, the ruler of Alitta (a small kingdom near Parepare), leaving the tomb of its own volition. The ruler's gold necklace, given to him by the Dutch in recognition of his military services, also forms part of the regalia.

The museum contains ceremonial umbrellas, traditional clothing, and the ritual apparatus used by the *bissu* (transvestite ritual priests) for court ceremonies.

Watampone is small enough to cover on foot. *Bemos* will take you any distance for Rp 150, and *becaks* can be hired for Rp 2,500.

ACCOMMODATION

There is a good range of small, reasonably priced hotels in Watampone; the price generally includes a simple breakfast of bread, eggs and tea or coffee.

Wisma Watampone, Jl. Biru 14, Tel. 362. $15-30 S, $20-40 D, is the best hotel in Bone. All rooms AC; coffee shop, drugstore and swimming pool. Modern, clean, good service, but somewhat characterless. 21% tax and service.

Wisma Bola Ridie, Jl. Merdeka 6, Tel. 412, 5 minutes from the town center. A rambling Dutch building straight out of the 1930s; the cool, spacious rooms have 4-meter-high ceilings and decorated tile floors. The name translates as "the yellow house": yellow was the color of South Sulawesi

nobility and the hotel is owned by a descendant of the last Rajah of Bone. There are 6 rooms, ranging from $4-8 including tea and a simple breakfast.

Wisma Rio Rita, Jl. Kawerang 4, Tel. 53, is a small, pleasant hotel with white tiled walls and floors and a cool, open lounge. It is set on a quiet street. 10 rooms, some AC, each with bathroom, $9-14 with a simple breakfast.

Mario Pulama Hotel at no. 16 on the same street is less attractive: rooms here range from $6-9 S, $9-15 D, some rooms AC. Breakfast.

Wisma Amarah, Jl. Jendral Ahmad Yani 2A, Tel. 569, is small but clean with 7 rooms at $6. Set on the main road near the center of town, it might be a little noisy. Breakfast.

Wisma Cempaka, Jl. Biru 36, Tel. 414 has 18 rooms from $4-10, including breakfast.

Penginapan Ramayana is a *losmen*-style hotel in the center of town above a car-repair shop. 18 rooms from $4-6.

Losmen National, Jl. Mesjid 86 is more spacious; rooms $3.

FOOD

Not one of Bone's major attractions. There are several restaurants along Jalan Mesjid. The **Rumah Makan Ramayana** is a clean restaurant serving Chinese-Indonesian food. But their *gado-gado* is a cold, coagulated mess of soggy rice cakes covered by a thick gray paste reeking of palm oil. Nor do the **Rumah Makan Padang Raya** and the **Rumah Makan Victoria's** flyblown window displays of Sumatran-style fried chicken wings inspire confidence. Much better to eat delicious, freshly-fried *murtabak* from the roadside stalls outside for 30 cents (Rp 250) a portion.

The only decent place to eat in Bone is the **Restaurant Pondok Selera**, Jl. Biru 28. This spacious, clean restaurant serves a good range of Chinese and Indonesian dishes and seafood. Service is prompt; the food is fresh and tasty. A half-serving of steamed shrimps, *cap cai*, rice and fresh lime juice will set you back $3. The grilled squid is a little overcooked but the delicious fried potatoes should be ordered by the plateful. At the back of the restaurant is a little rock garden and pool.

SHOPPING

Local crafts include spinning and weaving in silk, gold-threaded *songkok* (Moslem hats) of fine white straw, and mats. These are in the *pasar* (market) and at **Usaha Rakyat Bone** (Handicrafts of Bone) at Jl. Makmur 37.

LEAVING BONE

Coaches and minibuses to Ujung Pandang, Sengkang, Sinjai and as far away as Palopo depart from the central terminal. The fare to Ujung Pandang is $2.

To visit the caves at Mampu, take a mini-bus north to Uloe (35 km/22 mi), then a *bemo* or minibus to Gua Mampu. Travelers to Southeast Sulawesi (Sultra) can catch a *bemo* to the port at

Bajoe, 6 km (3.5 mi) east of Bone. The fare is 30 cents (Rp500). Here you can buy a ticket on the daily ferry, departing at 23:00 and arriving at Kolaka at dawn. The first-class fare is $5 with AC and comfortable, fully reclining seats. Alternatively, pay a little less for second class and sleep out under the stars on a mat on the bow of the ship: on a clear night you can see the Milky Way with breathtaking clarity and watch meteorites streak across the sky.

Watansoppeng (Soppeng)

This is a small town set amid rolling hills on the western edge of the fertile Walanae Valley, which runs northwards from the southern mountains to the marshy edge of Lake Tempe. *Kabupaten* Soppeng (pop. 240,000), of which Watansoppeng is the capital, is primarily a rice-producing area.

Watansoppeng is known for its silkworm factories which produce the raw silk used by weavers in Enrekang, Rappang and Singkang, while on the eastern hills farmers grow *kemiri* (candle nuts), palm sugar, peanuts and tobacco. The tobacco is cured with palm sugar in bamboo tubes and exported as far as Sumatra, where it is smoked by Bugis settlers and traders. Cocoa—you will see the beans being dried at the sides of the road—is a recent crop which flourishes in the powdery soil.

Bemos are Rp100 for any distance: small horse-drawn carts called *dokar* can be hired for Rp.2-300.

ACCOMMODATION

Wisma Munasko, Jl. Kemakmuran 12, has spartan but reasonably clean rooms for $4 with bathroom and $3 without. The more up-market **Hotel Makmur** at Jl. Kemakmuran 104 has rooms from $4 to $8 with bathroom. Breakfast, lunch and dinner can be ordered in advance. The **Hotel Aman**, near the royal graves at Jera Lomopoe, is an old Dutch house with large, cool rooms.

The government rest house, **Villa Julianna**, is an extraordinary neo-Gothic house built in 1911. It was formerly the residence of the Dutch *Controleur* or Commissioner.

FOOD

There are very few eating places in Soppeng. **Rumah Makan Ompo** and **Rumah Makan Sedap** at 27 and 33 Jl. Attang Benteng serve grilled squid, *ikan bakar* and fried chicken, plus the usual Chinese-Indonesian dishes. Be sure to ask for the small, tasty bananas called *pisang berangen*, which are grown only in Bone and Soppeng. If the restaurant has none, ask the staff to fetch some from the market. There is little else to buy in Soppeng.

Singkang

Singkang is a pleasant, medium-sized town nestling in the foothills overlooking Lake Tempe. In recent years, tourists have started to visit the town, which offers good accommodation and small but presentable restaurants. There are many attractive walks in the region and good views of the lake, which is only 2 meters (6.5 ft) deep and varies in size according to the season. Silk *sarungs* and *kain* (1-20 meter lengths of cloth) are woven in town and in outlying villages. Singkang is a town for early risers: the extraordinarily powerful loudspeaker system in the large central mosque is guaranteed to wake the soundest sleeper. The call to prayer is broadcast five times a day for more than thirty minutes, starting at 4:20 am.

Bemos are Rp100 for any distance; *becaks* can be hired for Rp500 for anywhere in town.

ACCOMMODATION

Singkang offers a wide range of medium to cheap accommodations. The **Hotel Apada** on Jl. Durian has clean, comfortable rooms with green and pleasant surroundings for $8-11. This is *the* place to stay for most visitors, though some might find the cultural atmosphere a little overpowering. The hotel owner is a local aristocrat who is keen to recreate Bugis civilization for her visitors. Eating here is expensive. In the evenings, a traditional Bugis meal is served to guests sitting cross-legged on mats, waited on by girls dressed in traditional costumes. There is a 10% tax along with a service charge.

For a hotel with a view you could try contacting the Regional Office (*Kantor Daerah*) next to the central mosque, for permission to stay at the government-owned **Pasanggrahan Hirawati**, atop a hill overlooking Lake Tempe. Alternatively, the **Wisma Bukit Nusa Indah** on Jl. Lamungkace Toaddamang, halfway up the hill, has quiet rooms (with bathroom) for $4. The **Wisma Pondok Eka** on Jl. Maluku is a traditional raised wooden house owned by a friendly Bugis family on a quiet street, close to the center of town. At the budget end, **Wisma Ayuni** on Jl. Puang Ri Maggalatung is an old Dutch house with huge, high-ceilinged rooms for $2 a person. The rooms are clean, with shower and toilet.

FOOD

There are a number of very presentable little restaurants in Singkang, and the food is surprisingly good. The **Restaurant Tomudi** on Jl. Andi Oddang offers a wide range of chicken dishes; portions are small but satisfying. **Rumah Makan Melati**, Jl. Kartini 54, serves ten sticks of good beef satay, rice and soup for under $1. The cool and breezy **Rumah Makan Romantis** on Jl. A.P. Petta Rani 2 looks decidedly up-market, but prices here are extremely reasonable. The *nasi campur* is good, as are the chicken dishes, and the beer is cold. *Ayam kampung* (farmyard chicken) is widely served in Singkang; it is leaner than *ayam belanda* ("Dutch" or factory-raised chicken) but delicious enough to convert a vegetarian. A restaurant specializing in *ayam kampung* is the **Warung Singkang** on Jl. Mesjid Raya: next door is the **Rumah Makan Mini Indah**, which serves *ikan* *bakar.*

SHOPPING

Singkang is an excellent place to buy traditional silk *sarungs* and woven silk cloth, though it is getting harder and harder to find high-quality handmade pieces. (The best place to find them is along the road south of Rappang.) Factory-produced cloth is attractive, if not of the same quality as comparable Thai factory silk. A 10-15 meter piece takes about a week to complete. Quality and prices are fairly standard, except on the home-woven pieces. Patterned lengths from 1-20 meters sell for $12-14 per meter; plain lengths for $10-12. Heavier plain cloth for jackets goes for $17-20, and 2 meter *sarung* and *selendang* sets (*sarung* plus shoulder scarves) sell for around $30. Traditional *sarungs* in check patterns sell for $20-50, depending on the quality of the materials and weave. When sewn in a tube, the *sarongs* measure 110 x 200 cm (45 x 80 in).

The best place to start is the **Mustaquiem** factory, on Jl. A. Panggaru I, southwest of the market. Here you can see the thread being processed and dyed before being woven into 10-15 meter *kain* lengths. An exhibition in the foyer explains the processes involved.

A small range of silk *sarung* and *kain* are sold in **Toko Akbar**, Jl. Kartini 16B. **Griya Sutera** on Jl. Hasanuddin 5, on the outskirts of town, has a decent selection of modern and traditional pieces, as well as a loom which you can inspect.

LEAVING SINGKANG

Coaches and mini-buses leave regularly from the terminal in the center of town. Fares to Palopo $1.50, Ujung Pandang $2, Cabenge 30 cents (Rp 500) and Bone $1. From here you can also catch a bemo to Tosora, on the edge of Lake Tempe, for Rp 500. Allow half a day for the return journey.

Pinrang

A pleasant town along a tree-lined street, in the heart of the rice-growing district of Pinrang-Sidrap. The region is watered by the Pengairan Sadan, the largest irrigation project in eastern Indonesia.

Accommodation is basic: the **Penginapan Sinapati** on Jl. Jend. Sudirman is clean and pleasant. The **Penginapan Purnama** on Jl. Sultan Hasanuddin is cheaper and more spartan: the adjoining restaurant serves decent Chinese-Indonesian food.

Palopo

This slow-moving town is dominated by the cloud-covered mountain ranges which tower imperiously behind it. The journey down to Palopo from Tana Toraja is worth it for the ride alone. This spectacular pass was for centuries the major east-coast trade exit. Down the pass came gold from the highland river torrents, resins and rare woods from

deep in the forest, fine *arabica* coffee and slaves captured in battle. Up went iron swords and weapons forged in Luwu's coastal armories, salt and dried fish. In the 19th century, guns and gunpowder helped warring Toraja lords to expand their domains.

The **Museum Barara Guru**, Jl. Andi Jemma diagonally opposite the old mosque, is well worth a visit. The former palace of the ruler of Luwu, the old Dutch-style house contains a collection of Chinese and Southeast Asian ceramics, ritual *bissu* equipment and other strange objects. Admission $1.

*Becak*s will take you any distance in town for Rp 2-300.

ACCOMMODATION

The **Wisma Kumda Indah** on Jl. Opu Tosapaille, opposite the police station, is by far the best hotel to stay in. Spotlessly clean. The lounge has tropical fish tanks and a friendly, talkative parrot to entertain you. Non-AC rooms are $6-9, AC rooms $9-11. The **Palopo Hotel** opposite the bus terminal has large, grimy rooms for $3-9. (The AC does not work.) The **Hotel Buana** on Jl. K.H. Ahmad Dahlan is cleaner, with rooms from $4 non-AC and $11 AC. **Pondok Risma** on Jl. A. Jemma is clean but the rooms are small and box-like.

The **Restaurant Victoria** on Jl. Diponogoro, near the Apollo Theatre, is a large, clean Chinese restaurant serving decent shrimp and crab dishes for $3, as well as the usual Chinese-Indonesian menu. (The *bistik* is *not* recommended.) Most visitors to Palopo eat here. The **Pondok Mantili** opposite serves Javanese-style *nasi campur*, as does the **Kios Mimi-Indah** a few doors down. Long-term residents eat at the **Restaurant Segar** on Jl. Sawerigading for a change from the Victoria.

LEAVING PALOPO

Buses bound for major destinations in South Sulawesi depart from the main terminal. Ujung Pandang is 8 hours away ($4); Rantepao is 3 hours ($2). Eastwards, Malili can be reached in 4 hours by minibus ($2.50). For the route north to Pendolo, Tentena and Poso, see "Central Sulawesi Practicalities."

There are ferries leaving nightly for Malili from the pier. There are also boats to Kolaka (see "Leaving Bone").

East of Palopo

Accommodation east of Palopo is basic. Malili is the next big town: **Setia II** is marginally preferable to **Setia I**; neither are recommended. There is an expensive guest house owned by P.T. Inco at Soroako, a *losmen* and several restaurants.

—Ian Caldwell

PART III

Introducing Tana Toraja

The long highway heading north from Ujung Pandang, after some 130 km (78 mi) of hugging the coastline of South Sulawesi, begins its fantastic, winding ascent to the mountains. Passing the "gateway" arch of Tana Toraja, the road leads through the small market village of Mebali. The traveler is now drawn into a majestic landscape of rugged grey granite outcrops and distant blue mountains. These form a sharp contrast with the vivid greens of fertile rain-fed rice terraces and the rusty reds of tropical lateritic soils.

This is Tana Toraja—unquestionably one of the most beautiful regions of Indonesia. On hillocks in the midst of rice paddies, the curved roofs of houses pierce the thickets of bamboo and coconut palms. Children sit astride grazing water buffaloes. In the distance, a jagged ridge of mountains stretches north to distant, isolated valleys.

There are about 330,000 inhabitants of *kabupaten* (regency) Tana Toraja, also known as "Torajaland." Large numbers of Toraja have also emigrated in search of work outside the area. In spite of the splendid landscapes and the rice-field studded mountains, the region is actually land-poor.

Among the aristocrats there are some large landowners, but most people do not own enough land to provide them with rice year-round, and must supplement their diet with cassava, maize, and vegetables grown in small gardens. Rice, however, remains the preferred food in Toraja, and those who can afford it will buy the extra rice they need rather than eat cassava.

Rice is grown in rain-fed hill terraces, many of which must be dug by hand, as they are too narrow to allow the use of buffalo-drawn ploughs. Traditional strains are slow-growing and provide only one crop a year, but in many areas new high-yield varieties are cultivated with the aid of fertilizers and pesticides, permitting two crops a year or even five in two years.

Formerly, groups of villages forming one ritual community would coordinate their work and plant at the same time, each stage of the cycle accompanied by rituals. Death ceremonies would be delayed until the harvest was completed, so as not to mix the rites of death with those of life. Today, people tend to follow their own schedules, and the ritual aspects of cultivation are in decline.

Most Toraja are Christians. The 1980 census lists 64 percent of the population as Protestants and 12 percent as Catholics. People in remote areas still tend to follow the traditional religion (now called *aluk to dolo*, or "ways of the ancestors").

For much of the population of Tana Toraja, life follows the familiar patterns of the past. After a simple breakfast of boiled rice or cassava, villagers head toward their rice fields or hillside vegetable gardens. Children go to the spring to fetch water in bamboo tubes.

In many areas there are no shops other than tiny path-side shacks selling necessities like salt, soap, matches, and paraffin for lamps. People must sell surplus rice, or a pig, to purchase what they cannot produce themselves, or in order to raise money for children's tuition at the local school.

In the evenings, a few men may gather under the tree of a local palm-wine tapper for a drink and gossip, or a game of dominoes may be played by lamp-light at home while dinner is cooking. In the absence of television, children provide the main form of entertainment at home, and most people go to bed early. When ritual activity breaks into the daily routine, people travel for miles and happily stay up all night eating, drinking, talking, and taking turns to join dancers who circle slowly, chanting songs in honor of the dead.

—*Roxana Waterson*

Overleaf: *A water buffalo about to be sacrificed at a Toraja death feast. Photo by Kal Muller.*
Opposite: *A Toraja noblewoman.*

HISTORY

Establishing a New Ethnic Identity

Islam came to to South Sulawesi's lowlands at the beginning of the 17th century. Before that, the culture and religious practices of the Toraja and Bugis peoples appear to have had much in common. The name "Toraja" probably derives from the Bugis *to ri aja*, or "people of the mountains." The Dutch adopted the term in the 19th century and applied it to many of the peoples of Central Sulawesi, as well as the South Sulawesi highlands. Central Sulawesi groups rejected the label, but the people of the Sa'dan region adopted it enthusiastically as a new sense of ethnic identity began to develop in relation to the outside world. The present boundaries of Tana Toraja more or less reflect the district boundaries set up by the Dutch; formerly the Toraja highlands had had no boundaries, or any political unity. No centralized state ever formed here, although in the south the three districts of Makale, Sangalla and Mengkendek had formed a federation and nobles there exercised more autocratic power than elsewhere.

Most people, however, owed their allegiance to petty chiefs or "big men" who held sway over individual villages or small groups of villages. The population was divided into ranks of nobles, commoners and slaves. Many of the Toraja nobility intermarried with the rulers of the small kingdoms of South Sulawesi, and some even sent their sons to stay at these courts. Traditionally some parts of Toraja stood in a tributary relationship to the kingdom of Luwu, though the gifts they sent were apparently more a sign of respect than of submission.

A degree of interdependence is reflected in myths which relate that the ruling families of the kingdoms of Gowa, Bone and Luwu are all descended from a common Toraja ancestor named Laki Padada. Up to the abolition of the kingdoms in the 1950s, a Toraja noble participated in the inauguration ceremonies of a new ruler in Luwu, and the ruling families of the old South Sulawesi kingdoms still send representatives to Toraja to take part in rituals celebrated by the house from which Laki Padada is supposed to have descended.

By the 19th century, however, Luwu was an economic backwater, and the more important contacts were with the southerly Bugis and Makassar kingdoms. Relations became troubled in the 1880s and 1890s when the kingdoms of Bone, Luwu, and Sidenreng sent their forces into Toraja to wrest control of the valuable coffee trade.

Guns and cloth were the main items offered in exchange for Toraja's high-quality *arabica* coffee. In slack periods, the coffee trade was augmented by slave-trading. The Bugis and Makassarese kingdoms desperately needed labor for rice cultivation, and slave-trading reached dramatic proportions in some areas of Toraja in the late 19th century. Toraja nobles with expansionist ambitions allied with Bugis mercenaries to raid remote districts for slaves. Some of these nobles had seized large amounts of land and were consolidating their new political power when the process was halted by Dutch intervention. Dutch troops entered the highlands in 1905, and in spite of the fierce resistance of several Toraja chiefs, who held out in natural rock fortresses in the mountains, Dutch control was imposed throughout the area by 1906. Pong Tiku, the Toraja warlord who defended the Pangala area with cannons and chili pepper squirters, was taken prisoner and later shot in Rantepao, purportedly while trying to escape. Today he is remembered as one of Indonesia's national heroes.

Functionaries and missionaries

The new colonial administration fixed boundaries, imposed taxes, established schools (initially reserved for the children of the nobility, who, distrustful of Dutch intentions, sometimes sent children of their slaves along as substitutes), and introduced Christianity. The Dutch Reformed Church sent its first missionary to the region in 1913. According to colonial policy, different churches were allotted specific regions of activity to prevent direct competition, so it was not until 1946 that the Roman Catholic church established a presence in Makale.

The Dutch also brought an end to the turbulence of the coffee and slave wars, and travel on the island became easier. For the

Opposite: *The traditional method of washing being applied to a new form of conveyence.*

first time, some Toraja began to leave the highlands to pursue education or to work. This widening of horizons in the 1920s and 1930s stimulated a new sense of ethnic identity among the Toraja (as they now called themselves).

The Reformed Church mission made uneven progress at first, and there were very few conversions, as the nobility suspected that Christianity would undermine their traditional authority. In the 1930s there was a small spate of conversions, brought about partly by the effects of education of the children of the aristocracy. When noble children converted, parents, relatives, and followers sometimes followed. But numbers fell away again with the depression years of the late 1930s, when local communities blamed the hard times on violation of traditional customs by the converted. The apostasy was aggravated by World War II and the Japanese occupation, when all the necessities of life were in very short supply.

After independence in 1950, primary and secondary education began to spread rapidly in Tana Toraja. But there were few opportunities within the region, with its subsistence-farming economy, to use one's education. Due to the area's poor infrastructure, travel beyond the highlands was difficult. Guerilla warfare, which raged throughout the region between Islamic rebels and the newly-established government during the 1950s, also made travel and expansion dangerous.

The population continued to grow, however, putting ever more pressure on already limited (and not especially fertile) village rice lands. Education had begun to open young peoples' eyes, and to awaken their curiosity about the world beyond the mountains. So it was no surprise that when peace returned to Sulawesi in the mid-1960s, thousands of young Toraja, motivated by scarcity of jobs and land at home, and intrigued by tales of urban wealth, began to leave.

The possibility of seeking work outside the highlands was furthered by Jakarta's new policy of opening up Indonesia's doors to foreign investors. In this period a large number of multinational companies established operations in neighboring Kalimantan, Irian Jaya, and elsewhere to tap the country's rich resources of oil, timber and minerals. Many young Toraja began to travel far from home to seek employment. Young men found jobs as laborers or mechanics, young women as household servants. The stream of migrants became a flood, as stories of success and the cash to prove it flowed home.

The flood continues unabated today. There may be over 200,000 Toraja migrants living outside of Tana Toraja. The impact of such movement is most dramatic in the villages, where grandparents and their grandchildren are often in the majority. In a society where family continuity and closeness is still

intensely valued, the absence of a whole generation may be quite devastating. The devastation is not just symbolic—old people are left without sources of support and everyday assistance, and everywhere people lament a labor shortage in the fields.

To leave the highlands in search of work or education is not, however, to abandon entirely one's social and cultural ties. Almost all Toraja migrants become Christians, since *aluk* or traditional religion is virtually unpracticeable away from a community of priests and practitioners. However, their experiences away from home in multi-ethnic settings often serve to heighten their sense of Toraja identity. And while they have left their kinship networks temporarily, paradoxically they have done so partly in order to provide for their ancestors (and more immediate family) at times of death. Virtually all migrants return to the highlands for a parent's funeral, to which they contribute great portions of their wealth earned abroad. It is this new wealth or "flying money" that has helped increase (some would say inflate) the amount of ritual activity seen in Tana Toraja during the last twenty years.

Shaking the social order

Traditionally, Toraja society was divided into three classes: nobles, commoners and slaves. What these categories actually meant varied regionally, but everywhere it was the case that one's rank determined the level of ritual performance to which one could aspire. A combination of heredity, marriage, political skill, and luck determined where one ended up in the social hierarchy. The Dutch began to undermine the foundations of this structure when they abolished slavery early in this century, and later when Christian missionaries began to preach the equality of man. The introduction of universal education for nobles and slaves alike further eroded the system, as did new sources of wealth and status. Perhaps the most radical shifts have been made possible by migration, as previously undreamed-of riches can now be earned by former slaves in distant lands where no one is aware of their status.

Even among low-status emigrant Toraja, however, ties to the highlands are incredibly strong, and most return for funerals and other important rituals. It is especially at these occasions that new wealth is poured into performances formerly discouraged by the colonial authorities, or restricted to a small, high-status elite. And it is in part because of such rituals that Toraja ritual has become somewhat controversial even within the region. Is it wasteful and extravagant, or a successful form of distributing wealth? Is it fostering new forms of status competition, undermining the old social order? Or is it a vital link to Toraja tradition, an affirmation of a rich and distinctive culture once looked down upon as pagan and remote?

Whatever the answers, the rituals are a cultural institution of great interest—both in their practice and in debates about their meaning—for the Toraja as well as for the thousands of travelers drawn to the region.

A ritual renaissance

When Dutch missionaries began work in the highlands of South Sulawesi in the early part of this century, they outlawed most local rituals associated with life. "Smoke-rising" rites, for example, with their explicit supplication of the spirits, seemed irredeemably pagan to the Dutch. Ceremonies associated with death were viewed with more ambivalence. For one thing, it became clear that Christianity would make no headway if the rituals were banned entirely. Furthermore, the Dutch Protestants more or less had to admit that death should be accompanied by some sort of ritual.

The peculiar result of this colonial schizophrenia was that *aluk* (roughly, the elements of ritual life which Westerners would call "religious") became separated from *adat* (custom). The balance in the ritual cycle thus shifted, and funerals assumed increasing prominence as the Christian mission (and in later years the Toraja church) won converts. A Christian ritual could be edited, so that only the "customary" parts remained. Today, when the great majority of Toraja are Christians, funerals continue to flourish, while smoke-rising rituals are relatively rare.

Ironically, Christianity seems to have brought about a rise in ritual activity, for while the original tenets of Toraja *aluk* restrict participation in ritual according to a person's social position, Christianity does not recognize the traditional hierarchy. All Toraja Christians, therefore, may now perform even the highest, most elaborate rituals; thus the Toraja have continued to sustain a lively ritual tradition. With this has come a heightened sense of pride and prestige, as well as an increasing sense of Toraja identity in a multi-ethnic Indonesian state.

—*Roxana Waterson and Toby Alice Volkman*

Opposite: *Repainting a rice barn in Tana Toraja*

TONGKONAN

Elaborate 'Houses of Origin'

Toraja houses provide more than shelter, they are extremely important nodes in the kinship network—the points of reference through which one traces familial ties. People may be vague about genealogical links with distant relations, but they can invariably name the houses where their parents and grandparents were born, and are usually able to cite those of more distant ancestors. In a very real sense, they consider themselves linked to others *through* a particular house. The names of houses are often remembered in cases where the individuals have been forgotten, and in talking about kinship, a "house" idiom predominates. People say that their "houses join," or that they are "brothers and sisters within such-and-such a house," as a way of expressing their relationships.

Tracing relationships

There are two words for "house." Houses in general are called *banua*, while houses of origin are called *tongkonan*. The word *tongkonan* derives from *tongkon*, meaning "to sit." *Tongkonan* refers to the place where family members meet to discuss important affairs (marriage, inheritance), to arrange for the upkeep of the house, or to attend ceremonies. Any house where one's mother, father, grandparents, or other ancestors were born may be regarded as an origin-house.

Like many societies of western Indonesia, the Toraja trace descent bilaterally, through both mother and father. Instead of belonging to a single house, people, therefore, belong to several, though they may not necessarily live in any of them. It is almost impossible to trace the outlines of any group of house members, who only act together on rare occasions. This is also why it is possible to maintain membership in many houses. Only when a division of inheritance is imminent, or plans are afoot to rebuild a house or stage a ceremony, is membership activated.

If a house is being rebuilt, its descendants are expected to maintain claims to membership by contributing to the costs; if they are very poor, even a tiny token offering will do. Some say a single grain of rice suffices, embedded in a joint between posts and beams. Similarly, one may maintain membership claims by bringing a sacrificial pig to a ceremony. Sometimes a person may by this means attempt to assert a false claim to *tongkonan* membership. If the pig is refused, this amounts to a rejection of the claim, which, if recognized, might lead to later claims upon *tongkonan* property as well.

If one were to count back only eight generations, all the houses where parents, grandparents, great-grandparents, and so on were born would yield a total 256 houses. In theory, therefore, one could be related to hundreds of houses, and some aristocrats can name an apparently endless string of *tongkonan* to which they have ties. In practice, however, most people maintain relations only with their parents' and grandparents' houses, and after marriage, with the houses of their spouse. At first, these new ties are weak, but they become stronger after the birth of children—who themselves will have membership (and inheritance rights) in houses on both sides of the family.

Husband and wife are expected to pool their resources and help each other to meet the expense of participating in rituals held by either side. At the very least, this involves bringing a pig for sacrifice. Contributions to the family ceremonies on both sides should ideally be kept roughly in balance. This, then, is what effectively limits people's membership claims. It would simply be too expensive to keep up the ritual obligations of belonging to too many houses.

A *tongkonan* has its own stone grave (*liang*), and membership in the house gives one the right to burial there. The grave is spoken of in ritual poetry as "the house without smoke, (the) village where no fire is lit." Since people belong to so many houses, it follows that they also have considerable range of choice when it comes to selecting a final resting place.

House and rank

Not all houses are origin-houses, or qualify for the title of *tongkonan*. In some parts of Tana Toraja, relatively insignificant family origin-houses may be referred to as *tongkonan*,

Opposite: *Facing rows of houses in a traditional Toraja village, Nanggala.*

and it is said that "even the birds have their *tongkonan*," meaning that even those of low rank trace their ties through houses. But in areas such as Saluputti, the term *tongkonan* is reserved exclusively for origin-houses of the nobility. Only the nobility were allowed to have carved and painted houses; most people lived in plain bamboo shacks.

Tongkonan may simply be origin-houses, regarded as important only by a particular family, not by society in general. In the case of major aristocratic *tongkonan*, genealogies are long and carefully memorized, even going back so far as to include the names of famous mythical personages.

Traditionally, the houses of aristocratic chiefs were the visible embodiments of the nobles' wealth, power and ritual superiority. People of lesser rank were prohibited from imitating them and special ornaments could be added to the house façade only when certain expensive rituals had been held. The celebration of rituals was seen as an act of thanksgiving to the deities, and in itself drew supernatural benefits: fertility, prosperity, and general well-being. Since strict rules of social rank determined what rites one could hold, the ritual system served to enhance the prestige of ruling nobles and their houses.

Building and rebuilding

All over Tana Toraja one is likely to come across houses being built or rebuilt. The money for these new houses or restorations of existing houses often comes from successful migrant family members who have done well in distant cities.

The Toraja do not renew their houses just because they are in need of physical repair; often a perfectly good house will be pulled down and rebuilt, re-using some of the same timbers. Rebuilding in itself confers prestige on a house. A house built in one generation and renewed in the next already begins to be viewed as an origin-house; with susequent rebuildings, its claim over other houses grows stronger.

This process may coincide with the emergence of a person of particular energy and verbal skills, who becomes recognized as the spokesperson for the family. Such a person can persuade relatives to contribute to rebuilding a house in which they themselves will not be living, for the sake of enhancing the family's prestige.

All *tongkonan* have a pair of founders, a husband and wife. However, the original owners of the land may often be remembered and named as the founder. The famous *tongkonan* of Nonongan in the Kesu' district is regarded as having been founded by a woman, Manaek, because the house was built on her ancestral land. Since men most often go to live with their wives at marriage, a man often puts his energies into rebuilding a house that belongs to his wife. But should they divorce,

KAL MULLER

he is the one who must leave, though he may receive the rice barn as compensation.

Rice barns are easily dismantled and can be re-erected on another site, but houses should not be moved. When a child is born, the father buries the placenta in a woven reed bag on the east side of the house, the direction which the Toraja associate with life and the rising sun. Perhaps the strongest reason for which a house should never be moved is that numerous placentae are buried there. However far a Toraja may roam, it is said that

he or she will eventually return to the house, drawn by the placenta which is regarded as a sort of twin.

House ceremonies

Rituals traditionally accompany every stage of housebuilding, from the first felling of timber in the forest to the final placement of the bamboo roof tiles. With the scarcity brought about by present deforestation, however, most house timbers today are bought from lumber yards in Palopo. Throughout the building process, carpenters have to be supplied with food, coffee and cigarettes by the home-owners—an expensive proposition. Sometimes money runs out for a while, and the house remains half-built while the owners seek more funds.

The offerings made and the size of the final inaugural feast depend on social rank. At the inaugural ceremony, called *mangrara banua* (*banua* means "house," *rara* "blood") the poorest people might offer chickens, while those of middle rank sacrifice pigs. The largest aristocratic ceremony lasts three days and is called *ditallu rarai*, "three kinds of blood." This refers to the ritual sacrifice of chickens, pigs and dogs.

A huge house ceremony was held in 1983 for a *tongkonan* known as Nonongan in Kesu' district south of Rantepao. This *tongkonan* is one to which many noble families trace a link, and over 100 branches of the house descen-

dants attended, all bringing enormous pigs. The mythical ancestor Laki Padada, whose children are said to have founded the Bugis and Makassarese kingdoms of Goa, Bone and Luwu, features in Nonongan's genealogy. All these kingdoms sent representatives from their royal families to take part in the ceremony. Although themselves Muslim, the Luwu contingent brought a large pig. The house was magnificently decorated, resplendent with precious heirlooms hung from the façade: *ikat* textiles, ancestral swords, gold *keris* and ornaments, and beadwork ornaments or *kandaure*. The women of the house were also dressed in *kandaure* (whose patterns are identical to some house-carving motifs) as they greeted guests. On such occasions, even the most distant descendants of a house demonstrate their ties to the ancestral origin-site.

New wealth, new styles

While the traditional saddle-roofed *tongkonan* are enormously impressive from the outside, their interior space is actually quite small, dark and cramped. Many people today want to live in roomier, lighter houses with more room for furniture. A ground-built concrete bungalow has the cachet of modernity. Cheaper, but still offering some of these advantages, is a Bugis-style timber house, pile-built with large doors and windows. In the last decade, carpenters have also developed what might be termed a transitional style, cunningly combining the advantages of modern living with the prestige attaching to the *tongkonan* shape. This is a two-story house, the lower story square in plan, in the Bugis style, and above that a second floor built in true *tongkonan* style and decorated with traditional carvings.

When asked about the meanings of their house carvings, Toraja respond with a variety of explanations, sometimes the inspiration of the moment. Although very seldom does one hear an explanation relating to the carvings as an integral whole, a few general themes can be discerned.

On the weight-bearing wall studs, the buffalo-head (*pa'tedong*), is said by some to represent hope for wealth in the form of buffaloes, while others claim it represents the nobility who hold society together, just as wall studs hold the thinner in-fill planks which are grooved into them. On these planks many of the interwoven spirals are plant motifs. The plants represented are mostly humble ones: water weeds that grow in rice paddies, or perhaps pumpkin tendrils. Trailing plants indicate hope that house descendants, although forming numerous branches, will stay together just as spreading vines remain attached to the parent stem.

A number of other Toraja house motifs also have a water theme: tadpoles, crabs, or water-boatmen. The association with water suggests life, fertility, and flourishing ricefields, while tadpoles and water-weeds, which multiply rapidly, are also said to represent hope for many descendants. Some designs also represent ritually important species, including the banyan tree (*pa'barana'*), cordyline shoots (*pa'lolo tabang*), or betel leaves (*pa'daun bolu*).

The latter are always used in offerings, and they are typically found near the top of the house façade, beneath the design of cocks and sunbursts (*pa'barre allo*) at the top of the gable triangle. This part may be taken to represent the heavens, and some Toraja interpret the placement of the designs on the whole façade as representing, from bottom up, the gathering of the house descendants to make offerings to the deities.

The cock figures aptly as a mediator between earth and heaven, for when the cock crows, the sun rises. In several myths, the cock has the power to crow the dead hero back to life and to fulfil wishes. The cock also appears as a constellation in Toraja cosmology. Some people identify the cock on house facades as the cock of Tulang Didi' or Lapandek, two of the protagonists of Toraja mythology.

Still other designs represent objects, such as the hilt of a *keris* (*pa'pollo' gayang*), or the lid of a basket in which house heirlooms are stored (*pa'kapu' baka*). The latter, an eight-pointed design, as well as the cross-shaped *pa'doti* motif, both appear to have derived originally from Indian textiles which were long ago traded in the Toraja highlands and have since become valuable heirlooms.

The façades of the most important aristocratic *tongkonan* often have a realistically carved buffalo head with real horns attached, called a *kabongo'*. These are usually surmounted by a strange long-necked bird with a crest or protruberance on top of its head, called a *katik*.

Toraja offer various explanations for the appearance of this creature; some say that these carvings signify the greatness of the nobility, but a more convincing account is that each represents a particular type of ritual. The *kabongo'* buffalo head can only be added to the façade after the performance of one of the highest levels of funeral rites, while the *katik* means that the house has sponsored the celebration of the great fertility-enhancing *ma'bua'* rite, highest of the "rites of the east."

The *katik* is often described as a cock or a mythical bird of the forests, though some believe that it is really a hornbill, whose use as a motif is widespread and important in many of the islands of Southeast Asia. Together, the *katik* and *kabongo'* represent the totality of the Toraja ritual cycle.

—*Roxana Waterson*

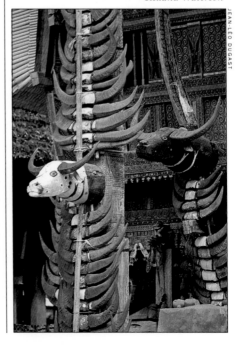

Opposite, left: *Painted decoration on a Toraja rice barn—the motifs are often quite playful.* **Opposite, right:** *An elaborate façade.* **Right:** *A buffalo head carving adorning the main pillar of a tongkonan, with buffalo horns from past sacrifices.*

RELIGION

Aluk—the Way of the Ancestors

Before the Dutch conquest of the highlands in the early 20th century, there was no word in the Toraja language for "religion" and no conception among the Toraja of a separate domain of thought and action directed toward the spirit world. Instead, there was *aluk*—a word which refers to the way in which both rituals and daily life are to be conducted—how houses are to be built, rice cooked (or avoided), children or village heads addressed. *Aluk* contains the rules for the number of buffalo to be sacrificed at funerals as well as the position of the stars when planting should begin. One of its basic tenets is that a constant exchange of gifts, blessings and even curses must occur between the living and the spirits of their ancestors.

Missionaries who followed on the heels of the first Dutch Colonial administrators on Sulawesi in 1906 could not help but notice that the Toraja inhabited a world populated by spirits and ancestors who required feeding and frequent sacrifice. In fact many Toraja today still refer to their religion as "feeding the ancestors," *pa'kandean nene'*.

The first representative of the Dutch Reformed Church was a certain A.A. van de Loosdrecht, who tried to win over converts but ultimately failed in his attempts to put a stop to the elaborate Toraja death feasts. He observed correctly that many people pawned and lost their land as a result of ritual obligations, but in 1917 his intrusion upon Toraja traditions culminated in an outburst of violence, during which van de Loosdrecht died of a stab wound to the chest.

The Dutch Reformed Church eventually refined its tactics and carved out a workable separation between "custom" (*adat*) and "religion" (*aluk,* or *agama* in Indonesian). To sacrifice a water buffalo was acceptable, provided that the meat was distributed to the living—a customary, social act—and not offered to the spirits. It was definitely unacceptable, however, to carve pagan images of the dead.

Thus, it might be said that ritual practices were allowed to continue, while the system of beliefs in which they were embedded gradually withered. Still, Christian conversions only reached 10 percent of the Toraja population during Dutch times. After independence, however, with Islamic rebellion creating tur-

moil and fear throughout the island, conversions increased dramatically, and by 1965 about 40 percent of the population were officially registered as Christians. Today, that figure is much higher and includes Protestants and Catholics together with a number of smaller denominations.

The national government declared in 1969 that the traditional religion of the Toraja, now labeled *aluk to dolo*, "the *aluk* of the ancestors," was officially recognised as a branch of Hinduism. This interesting development came at a time when Tana Toraja was being promoted as an alternative tourist attraction to Bali; and a Protestant Torajaland would appeal less to tourists than a "pagan" one.

But the governmental revival of *aluk* has not succeeded. Although some middle-aged intellectuals still count themselves as *aluk* adherents, most *aluk* people in Toraja are remote villagers, ritual priests (*to minaa*), the very old and the very young (not yet baptized or in school). Clearly, *aluk* will die out, particularly as the younger generation migrates in search of work beyond the highlands. But if *aluk* as an all-embracing way of life and thought is on the wane, as an *idea* it has been revived, and has given the Toraja a firm sense of identity.

Smoke rising, smoke descending

In 1972, a *National Geographic* team described its encounter with "a people so genial

... that even their funerals are more joyous than somber." While there is no question that Toraja funerals are remarkable, what is often overlooked is that funerals form only part of a ritual cycle that extends throughout the year. The article mentions a cycle of "smoke descending" rituals associated with death (*rambu solo*), and "smoke rising" rituals associated with life (*rambu tuka'*). In fact, this opposition does not do justice to the richness of the ritual cycle, which is profoundly linked to agricultural cycles of death and rebirth—to planting, nurturing and harvesting rice. Although such a cycle has no real beginning and end, we can take as a starting point the first soaking of the new year's seed.

Me'datu: rice of the new year

In many parts of Tana Toraja, the season of death and mortuary ritual is brought to a close in September by a rite known as *me'datu*. In the past, *me'datu* also referred to the time when some Toraja brought tributes of gold and chickens to the ruler, or *datu*, of Luwu, in exchange for blessings on the rice seed. Today *aluk* families prepare seed and offer tiny chicks, along with prayers, to the spirits responsible for the fertility of the fields and grain. A visitor is not likely to see

Opposite: *Chanting the* ma'badong—*a lament in memory of the deceased.* **Below:** *A buffalo-fight held as part of an elaborate funeral ceremony.*

this furtive ritual, which is performed quietly in house-yards, fields, and springs—wherever the spirits, or *deata*, reside.

Following the mini-sacrifices, tidbits of chicken are given to children and others who may be present, while the ritual priest or *to minaa* receives the head. The rice seed is taken from the granary, pounded (not, as is usual, by hand, but in this ritual instance by foot, as women loosen their hair and tread upon the grain). It is then sifted in winnowing trays and transferred to baskets (*baka*) which are brought to flooded fields where they will be immersed for several days.

Rice seed is scattered in nursery beds to sprout. The timing varies from village to village, but if you are lucky enough to be visiting in November or December, you will see a patchwork landscape of lush green seedbeds, interspersed with newly cleared rice fields whose flooded surfaces reflect the sky.

When the seedlings are four or five inches tall, it is time to perform the *maro*, a ritual associated with the fertility of the fields and with the fulfillment of desires for wealth, for progeny, and for the greatness of the ancestral house. If the seed has grown well, and if a family has sufficient resources (and, formerly, high status), the *maro* may be held before transplanting.

The *maro* blessing

The *maro* involves the construction of a tall cloth-and-bamboo tower (*bate*), which visually represents the transformation from death to life. At a funeral, a similar tower is erected, the bamboo's tip thrust into the earth. At the *maro*, the bamboo points toward the sky, the direction of growth.

Like many Toraja rituals, the *maro* includes many days of barely visible activity, much of which consists of speech. Toraja priests use a special form of "high language," rich in metaphor, allusion, and repetition. Such speech is considered potent. Its audience consists of spirits, and many people say they do not understand the words. Still, it is essential for the efficacy of the ritual, and men who have mastered its intricacies and memorized hours and hours of such talk are highly respected. At the *maro*, six nights of ritual speech precede the more dramatic and public activities.

Inside a small house, its central room lit only by a hissing pressure lamp, a dozen men sit on woven mats on the wooden floor. Small boys sprawl over older men's legs, others lie in dark corners of the room, asleep. Women, gossiping, are busy at the hearth, preparing rice, boiling water for coffee to keep chanters awake throughout the night. The men, all of whom are *to minaa*, chant in unison, following the cues of their leader, the "mother of the chant," a man with a melliflous voice and an authoritative air. The men chant, sometimes robustly, sometimes soporifically,

KAL MULLER

KAL MULLER

between outbursts of laughter and even argument. The theme of the chant is the *bate*'s quest for riches. The *bate*, they say, bends like a tree to places as near as the next village, as distant as America or "the edge of heaven." The riches it finds will bring blessings to the assembled family.

At dawn on the seventh day, one or more *bate* are assembled in a public arena and given offerings. Each *bate* is carried in boisterous procession to a field where, under the noon sun, to the accompaniment of the chanting *to minaa*, all kinds of spirits are enticed to descend, to draw near, and to enter the bodies of those now dancing and entranced. Men and women whirl about, loosen their hair, jump on drums, stamp on sharp upturned blades, and cut themselves with swords (but draw no blood). Possession by the spirits may last several hours. The spirits' power prevents maiming. By late afternoon, the spirits depart and exhausted trancers go home. The *to minaa* bless the *bate* and take it apart.

Funerary rites

The funeral rite is so important in Toraja that it is held even when a person dies at sea or in a distant land. In an *aluk* rite known as "capturing the wind," family members and a *to minaa* climb to a mountaintop, where they call the wind to fill a sarong. When it billows out, the sarong is closed for a moment, then released. A length of bamboo representing the corpse is then brought home and given a proper funeral.

All funerals in Toraja, however grand or simple, are intended to transport the soul safely to the next world, whether to the *aluk* Puya or to a Christian heaven. All funerals are also intended to free survivors from their attachments to the deceased, and to reintegrate them into the world of the living through some form of sacrifice. For poor people, a symbolic sacrifice will do: a chicken egg, or even just the striking of a chicken basket or a pig pen. But although a symbolic sacrifice may satisfy the spirits, genuine animal sacrifice is at the heart of a socially acceptable ceremony in Toraja.

Aluk requires a strict separation of life and death. When the last rice is harvested from the fields, the mortuary season begins. (In many areas, this happens to coincide with the tourist season, from July through September.) The seasonality of such ritual is made possible by the fact that the Toraja do not immediately bury their dead. When a person dies, the body is wrapped in layers of cloth and kept in the house for months, sometimes even for years, while preparations are made

Opposite: *Teams of young men engage in the sport of kick-fighting at a funeral.* **Above:** *Cuts of ritually slaughtered meat are distributed according to the rank and status of the funeral participants.*

KAL MULLER

for the complicated mortuary rites. Dispersed family members must be brought home and tremendous resources—money, livestock, followers and friends—are mobilized for the event.

Funerals vary according to the region and the status of the deceased: from simple rituals accorded to former slaves or children, to extravaganzas that receive national or even international media attention. The latter may entail the slaughter of hundreds of pigs and water buffalo, and the reception of thousands of guests in specially constructed temporary bamboo shelters. A visitor to Tana Toraja is likely to see something in between.

Behind the scenes

An *aluk* death ceremony begins in earnest after its timing has been agreed upon among family members and village leaders. It must be coordinated with other rituals and with the phases of the moon. The onset of socially acknowledged death is marked by sound and sacrifice: the striking of a gong and a distinctive, death-announcing drum beat echo throughout surrounding villages.

Relatives who have probably been sipping coffee or chewing betel nut out in the yard now enter the house to witness the transition of the corpse from "hot" to "dead," a change which is effected by the sacrifice of a chicken and, later in the day, a pig and one or two young water buffalo. The surviving spouse is wrapped in a large cloth, and for several days will be allowed to partake of no food which has been cooked.

On the next day, the *to mebalun* ("the one who wraps") encloses the corpse in many layers of cloth. During the next few days, there are small sacrifices as relatives and friends appear, helping with the preparations and spending the night chanting *ma'badong*, a lament in memory of the deceased. Men, clad in sarongs stand in a circle in the yard, hands joined, swaying rhythmically and stamping their bare feet in unison. A fire burns in the center, where a pig is later cut, singed, and divided among all present. *Ma'badong* tells the story of the deceased's life in high ritual speech, while women, sitting on the sidelines, sing another form of mourning chant, *ma'londe*, simultaneously. It is said that the voices should sound as though they are "one breath."

Ritual activity continues to build in the house-yard for several more days, as more animals are sacrificed and chants intoned. An effigy of cloth and bamboo is constructed, and mourners, effigy, and corpse all eventually make their way to a special field (*rante*) ringed with a circle of stone boulders which are monuments to important ancestors. This is the site of the climax of the ceremony, the long-awaited moment which either spells glory or shame for the sponsors of the ritual and their guests. This is also the part of the ceremony which is most likely to be viewed by outsiders.

Guests and debts

On the day before the burial, guests arrive in formal processions, or *rombongan*, leading water buffalo and carrying pigs, rice baskets (at a Christian funeral), and huge vats of palm wine (or perhaps cases of beer and whiskey). Next follow men in single file. They are ranked in approximate order by age, status, and even size. Women, ranked in the same way, follow. Before the *rombongan* enters there is a great flurry of activity as the line is reorganized, sarongs straightened, scarves folded.

A gong is sounded to announce the group's arrival, and the procession slowly walks around the ritual field, which is lined with temporary shelters housing guests who cluck approval at the girth of a buffalo, the number of pigs, or the composure and fine attire of the visitors. They may also (and often do) mutter disapproval if the animals are scrawny or the guests in disarray.

Following a ceremonial greeting and betel offering to the leaders of the *rombongan*, its members retire to shelters where they are offered coffee and cookies by the hosts. Later they will be served rice. Much of the success of a ritual depends upon the smooth operation of the kitchen, which is managed by the women of the sponsoring family. For a

funeral involving hundreds or even thousands of guests, meticulous coordination and timing are required.

As the day wears on, the ground is strewn with squealing pigs, and buffalo accumulate on the sidelines. The great attention paid to these animals is not simply in anticipation of meat. In fact, each animal represents a debt, and therefore a social tie. The history of a pig is a complex story that stretches back many generations of pig-exchange between the hosts (normally the children of the deceased) and relatives. If a pig represents the payment of a debt, everyone will know that "the pig has eaten the vegetables," the debt is clean.

Water buffalo also represent debts. One may bring an entirely new buffalo to a funeral in a particular person's name, thereby initiating a new debt relationship. Any Toraja has intricate networks of such debts, acquired by inheritance, adoption, loyalty, or other peculiarities of personal history.

All debts are carefully noted in writing (in the past they were simply remembered). The government also sends a representative to collect a slaughter tax.

The slaughter

The slaughter of the buffalo, when done correctly, is very quick: a single blow to the jugular vein with the long-bladed *la'bo* knife. As the animal collapses, small boys with bamboo tubes rush forward to collect the steaming blood (used in cooking). The meat is hacked up and either distributed from the center of the yard, or thrown down from a tall bamboo platform. With each throw "the divider" (*to mentaa*) shouts the name of someone in the crowd below. As the meat thuds to the ground everyone seems to know exactly who is called, and (in spite of what appears to an outsider as chaos) to see exactly what size and cut of meat is thrown.

It is not at all unusual for tourists to be given a share of meat on such occasions, sometimes a prime cut, dangling from a thin rattan string. This is a sign of honored guest status, and should be graciously accepted. The presence of foreign guests is welcomed, as they help transform the ritual field, if only for a moment, into what it ideally is: the center of the social universe, drawing prestigious visitors from afar.

—*Toby Alice Volkman*

Left: *Clothing a* tau tau *or wooden effigy for the spirit of the deceased.* **Opposite:** *Installing the coffin in its final resting place—a cliffside grave.*

TAU TAU EFFIGIES

Receptacles for the Spirit

The death of an *aluk* noble occasions the creation of an effigy, or *tau tau* (meaning "small person" or "person-like"). Such effigies are of two kinds: *tau tau nangka*, carved of the durable gold-toned wood of the jackfruit (*nangka*) tree, and *tau tau lampa*, ephemeral effigies of bamboo and cloth.

The *tau tau* are thought to be the receptacle of the ghost (*bombo*) of the deceased. Males are clad in a fine batik sarong with a European-style shirt and and oversized sport jacket. Around his neck are hung tubes of incised gold and invulnerabity charms fashioned of boars' teeth. For the headdress, rows of old silver coins are threaded between buffalo horns and crowned with clusters of red-and-yellow parakeet feathers or a bird-of-paradise plume.

Females are more modestly attired in a sarong with lacy blouse or *kebaya*, a betel pouch, a wide cummerbund of silver coins, gold and shell beads and bracelets, and a black cloth tied behind the head to form a bun. On the head is placed a tiny white porcelain plate, reminder of her connection to the kitchen. The faces of both male and female effigies are wrapped in vivid red cloth to which are added white paper or wooden eyes.

When the effigy is complete, the *to mebalun* (who is also responsible for wrapping the corpse) kneels before it and spins the figure around to "awaken" it. He presents it with an offering of pork and rice, and a tiny tube of palm wine. Relatives offer betel and tobacco, requesting blessings and a ripe old age. Later, women mourners embrace the *tau tau*, press their faces to its blood-red face, and utter long, stylized wails. Together with the corpse, the effigy is then carried to the ritual field. At the end of the funeral, when the corpse is brought to the grave, the *tau tau* is stripped of its ornaments and clothing. All that remains on the ritual field is a green bamboo skeleton: the body has gone to its "house without smoke," the ghost has gone south to Puya, and the living have gone home.

In wealthier, more stratified areas, a permanent wooden effigy is carved in addition to the ephemeral *tau tau lampa*. These are the statues that stand in ledges cut high into the limestone cliffs or in volcanic boulders all around the landscape. Like the temporary

tau tau they too are considered receptacles for the spirit; their role, however, is both to guard the tombs which are chiseled into the rock behind them, and to provide blessings to descendants.

These effigies are expensive and time-consuming to produce, and their carving is fraught with many taboos. Although infrequently made these days, both because of the expense and the decline in *aluk*, such figures are still treated by the Toraja—*aluk* and Christian alike—with reverence. But only *aluk* Toraja may participate in a ceremony held every few years to honor the ancestors. At this ceremony ancestral graves are reopened and the *tau tau* reclothed and repaired. Offerings of betel, tobacco, cigarettes, rice, pork, and wine are presented in exhange for continued blessings imparted to the living.

The presence of carved wooden effigies installed in sheer limestone cliffs overlooking the rice fields captured the imagination of the first Europeans to visit Tana Toraja early in this century. Today they still fascinate—their austere, geometric, yet startlingly lifelike faces and wide, staring eyes gaze hauntingly over the lush landscapes; while their soft, faded cotton shirts, caps, sarongs, and betel bags belie their place in the ritual system of their society. *Tau tau* "galleries" are natural outdoor cliffs, not stuffy museums—combining death, art and ritual into one.

Although Dutch missionaries banned their creation early in this century, in recent years *tau tau* have been fashioned for some prominent Christians. This has led to great debate, as some Christians argue that Toraja culture must be maintained and even revitalized at all cost, and that besides the effigies are merely representations. Like photographs, it is said, they have no power.

Defined as "art" by the international market, hundreds of *tau tau* were stolen from their graves during the 1980s. Today the figures have found (and continue to find) their way into museums, galleries and living rooms in Jakarta, Europe and America. The Toraja, Christian and *aluk* alike, have reacted with shock, anger, bitterness and dismay. In desperation, many families have reclaimed their ancestors' effigies and hid them in caves and other secret places.

In 1989 the government commissioned local artists to create "replacements." The crudely carved statues that fill the niches at Lemo are modern substitutes. Elsewhere, locks and barbed wire now shield the once powerful ancestral protectors from the depredations of the living.

—*Toby Alice Volkman*

Opposite: *Cliffside graves guarded by* tau tau *effigies. Note the empty spaces—the result of thefts instigated by international "art" dealers.* **Below:** *A close-up of striking* tau tau *figures.*

KAL MULLER

ROAD TO RANTEPAO

Ascent to the Highlands

Out of Parepare, the road to Rantepao turns inland and begins to wind steeply upwards into the rolling hills above the town. From time to time one glimpses entrancing views of the town below, with its glittering, tin-roofed mosques. In the distance beyond sparkles the sea with its rocky outcrops. Houses are replaced by grassland as the road pushes upwards over a low range of hills, past picturesque villages and scattered rice and corn fields and tapioca. Bananas, papaya and jackfruit grow in luxuriant profusion. Wooden and bamboo stalls piled with fruit and vegetables line the road, where travelers stop to buy treats for the families they are going to visit. Then, almost without warning, a magnificent view to the east signals the brief descent to the plain below.

Shortly after it reaches the plain at the village of Lawada, the road forks: the road to the left leads across an open expanse of rice fields—the major source of South Sulawesi's rice surplus—and into the market town of Rappang. A right-hand fork leads to Sidrap and Palopo (see "Luwu," page 106). Rugged peaks beckon on the horizon. Along the side of the road, women sit in the shade beneath wooden houses, weaving colorful silks on backstrap looms.

Rappang is an attractive little town with winding, tree-lined streets. Wooden shops with overhanging jettys sell rattan furniture. On market day the town comes to life, as cart-loads of produce and wide-horned cattle negotiate the narrow streets. As you leave Rappang, you might even spot a Bugis wedding, identifiable by the awnings set up in front of the household and crowds of people in their best silk sarongs, with loudspeaker systems amplifying music and speeches.

More rice fields. On warm evenings, thunderheads gather as you head for the forested mountains. The road narrows as it enters the foothills, where bamboo groves alternate with little cultivated valleys, and the occasional house nestles between the trees. Near Kabere you catch your first glimpse of the Sa'dan River, now wide and brown after its long journey through the mountains.

The next town is picturesque Enrekang, where the Sa'dan and Mata Allo Rivers meet. It is a predominantly Muslim town—impressive mosques and *pesantren* (Islamic reli-

ERIC OEY

gious schools) line the roads. Enrekang is also famous for *danke*, a cheese-like delicacy made from fried buffalo milk, which is often available in the town's largest *losmen*, overlooking the river and bridge.

Leaving Enrekang, the road narrows and begins its steep, winding climb into the mountains. Roadside engineers and wet-season landslides fight for possession of the sandy soil; in recent years fast-growing casuarina pine trees have been planted along the road to combat the erosion caused by deforestation. This section of the journey offers breathtaking, panoramic views of rugged mountains and valleys, with villages clinging to the steep slopes. Perhaps you will stop at Kotu, where you can buy *baje'*, a favourite local sweet made from glutinous rice and palm sugar wrapped in rice husks.

This region is known as Bamba Puang, after the spectacular mountain which dominates it. The area is rich with mythic and historical significance. Toraja and Duri legends hold that the first human beings descended here from the heavens by means of a celestial ladder. The gods subseqently hurled the ladder to earth in a fit of anger, shattering it into pieces. Older Duri and Toraja folk will point out the fragmented remains of the ladder, now metamorphosed into rocky terrain. In the early years of the 20th century, the mountains were the backdrop for battles with Dutch forces attempting to annex the region.

Some 20 km (13 mi) past Enrekang, Butu Kabobong ("erotic mountain") can be spotted across the western ravine. The terrain on the slopes of the mountain is said to resemble male and female genitalia. Local legends recall how an incestuous couple was punished by being turned into stone and made to lie side by side, eternally separated by the river that runs between them.

A few kilometers beyond Butu Kabobong you reach Puncak Lakawan, where a cluster of unpretentious restaurants offers expansive views of now badly-denuded canyons and mountain ranges. Strong Sulawesi coffee and surprisingly tasty local cooking revive you for the remaining three-hour drive to Rantepao. In the limestone hills across the river below are old burial cliffs with hollowed-out niches containing ancient wooden coffins. For a closer inspection, drive 4 km to Cakke, then turn right onto the road to Barakka. Keep going another 3 km until you encounter the burial cliffs on your left.

Leaving the restaurant, the road continues upwards, past mulberry fields where silk-

worms are raised, to Salubarani. This is the gateway to Tana Toraja. Here the road passes under a large cement arch topped with a miniature *tongkonan*. From the top of the arch you can look down over the river and town. Here you are 1000 meters (3,300 ft) up in the south-central mountains. The inhabitants of this area hold more closely to their traditions than the Toraja of other regions, as ideas, like other commodities, travel less quickly through the area. The Toraja are predominantly Christian, but this southern region has a higher percentage of Muslims and *aluk to dolo* adherents.

Eventually the road opens out onto a hilly plateau, passing clove plantations, pine forests, and pockets of lush rice fields. Then the road begins its gradual, 200-meter (660-ft) descent into the Makale and Rantepao valleys. From Makale the road climbs up into the narrow, winding valley which the deceptively tranquil Sa'dan river has carved out of the limestone mountains. The early morning mists hang over tranquil villages nestled between verdant rice fields and swift-flowing streams. As the road nears Rantepao, ornately carved *tongkonan* complete the magical picture. Here at last is Tana Toraja.

—*Ian Caldwell and Kathleen Adams*

Opposite: *Two boys and a friend play in the Sa'dan River.* **Above:** *A miniature* tongkonan *welcomes visitors to Tana Toraja.*

MAKALE AND RANTEPAO

'Big-City' Life in Tana Toraja

The steep hills of Makale, the administrative capital of Tana Toraja, 17 km (16.5 mi) south of Rantepao, are crowned with church spires, while the valley floor is dominated by large new government buildings, many of which have borrowed themes from traditional Toraja architecture. For many years Makale has been expanding northward along the road to Rantepao. In the last two years alone, several new government offices, a new hospital and new hotels have sprung up along this road. Fearing that tourists would be frightened off by all of this development, the *bupati* (head of the regency) issued a decree that all new buildings along the main road should be embellished with Toraja motifs. The result is a hodge-podge of styles that has stimulated comment by anthropologists and architects alike.

Few tourists stay in Makale, though there is now a large new Marannu hotel just out of town. The town is a good base for visiting west Toraja and nearby Tondon, Suaya and Sangalla. There are several good walks in the region, and the town is clean and pleasant.

On market day the town becomes a hub of activity, as people from distant villages arrive with produce, livestock, hand-crafted mats, baskets and knives. If you follow the road running up the hill directly behind the market, look to your left for a trail leading to some very old limestone burial cliffs. Although many of these graves have been desecrated by thieves in recent years, there are still a few old bones and skulls and the odd coffin to be seen.

Rantepao

Rantepao is a dusty, bustling town that initially conjures up images of the American Wild West, with its long, wide streets and drifting tumbleweed plastic bags. Mountain villagers carrying bamboo tubes of foaming *tuak* lope into town, while *bemo*s packed with plastic buckets, sacks of rice and kerosene bounce in the opposite direction along the pot-holed road.

The main intersection of the town is distinguished by a miniature *tongkonan* set on what appears to be a pink champagne glass, but which is in fact a ceremonial serving dish. (Real antique wood ones can be purchased in the antique shops close to the mini-*tongkonan*.) From here, coaches and mini-buses set out for the long, gruelling ride to Palopo, Soroako, Poso and Palu. On market day this intersection is particularly lively, as passenger-filled trucks, *becaks*, jeeps, tourist vans and motorcycles cruise through town and out towards the market. A money changer, bank, the Post Office and Rantepao's largest general store cluster round this intersection.

Market day. *Bemos* laden with pigs, sacks of coffee beans, corn, rice and sago bounce unsteadily along Rantepao's pot-holed roads. Women carry fruits and vegetables on their backs in baskets, men balance long bamboo tubes filled with frothy palm wine, or carry bundles of carvings and hand-forged knives. Stacks of finely-plaited hats (most of them made at the leper colony just out of town) sit precariously on the heads of small, wiry village women, while men swing bamboo carriers containing squealing piglets or cradle roosters in their arms. Fishmongers transport their goods on bicycles equipped with deep basket saddlebags, while men from distant villages lead large buffalo to the market on foot, stopping for a bath in the river before putting the animals up for sale.

The entrance to the market is a large muddy field crowded with men and buffalo. On market day, hundreds of buffalos can be seen tethered in the field. *Bemos* bounce and sway across the dirt track cutting through the field and through the market, dropping off and picking up passengers and goods. The market is a loose arrangement of different sections. The pig department is a place of great interest: specimens ranging from day-old piglets to large sows and boars lie trussed up, flanks heaving, in neatly arranged rows. Prospective buyers step gingerly between them, discussing their respective merits. When a purchase is made, porters hoist the hogtied merchandise onto a stout bamboo pole and heave it into a passing *bemo*; smaller swine are carried off like handbags. Packed meals to take home—rice, vegetables, eels from the ricefields and pork—are sold for those too tired to cook after their big day at the market.

—*Kathleen Adams and Nancy Caldwell*

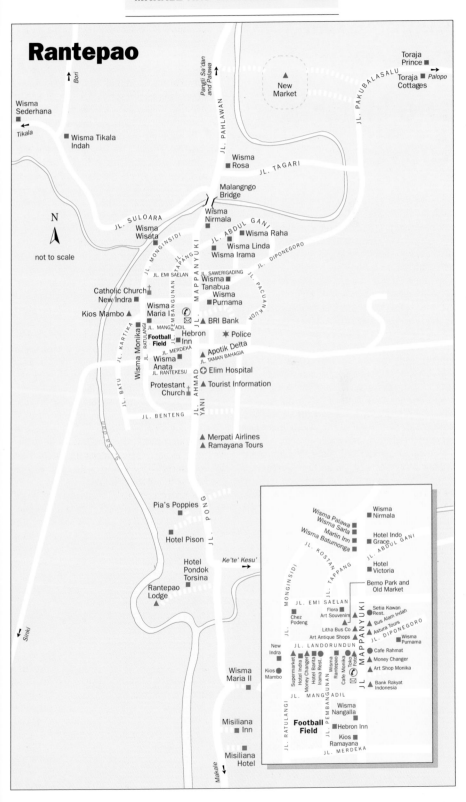

Rantepao

↑ Bori

Wisma Sederhana

↓ Tikala

■ Wisma Tikala Indah

↑ Pangli Sa'dan and Palawa

JL. PAHLAWAN

New Market

▲

JL. PAKUBALASALU

Toraja Prince

Toraja Cottages

→ Palopo →

Wisma ■ Rosa

JL. TAGARI

Malangngo Bridge

N

↑

not to scale

JL. SULOARA

Wisma Wisata

JL. MONGINSIDI

JL. TAPANG

JL. MAPPANYUKI

Wisma Nirmala

JL. ABDUL GANI

■ Wisma Raha

Wisma Linda ■
Wisma Irama ■

JL. DIPONEGORO

JL. EMI SAELAN

JL. SAWERIGADING

■ Wisma Tanabua
■ Wisma Purnama

JL. PACUAN KUDA

Catholic Church
New Indra

Kios Mambo ▲

Wisma Maria I

JL. MBANGUNAN

JL. MANGE ADIL

✉

⚑ BRI Bank

✦ Police

Wisma Monika

JL. KARTIKA

Hebron Inn

Football Field

JL. MERDEKA

Wisma Anata

JL. RANTEKESU

▲ Apotik Delta

JL. TAMAN BAHAGIA

JL. BATU

JL. AHMAD YANI

✚ Elim Hospital

Protestant Church

▲ Tourist Information

JL. BENTENG

▲ Merpati Airlines
▲ Ramayana Tours

JL. SESEAN

Pia's Poppies ■

JL. PONG

Hotel Pison ■

Hotel Pondok Torsina

Ke'te' Kesu' →

Rantepao Lodge ▲

↓ Sinki

Wisma Maria II ■

↓ Makale

Misiliana Inn ■

Misiliana Hotel ■

Wisma Palawa ■
Wisma Sarla ■
Marlin Inn ■
Wisma Batumonga ■

Wisma ■ Nirmala

Hotel Indo ■ Grace

JL. KOSTAN TAPPANG

Hotel Victoria ■

JL. ABDUL GANI

JL. MONGINSIDI

JL. EMI SAELAN

Flora ■
Art Souvenirs

Chez ■ Podeng

Litha Bus Co ▲

Art Antique Shops ▲

JL. LANDORUNDUN

JL. TAPPANG

Bemo Park and Old Market

Setia Kawan ■ Rest.
▲ Bus Alam Indah
▲ Astura Tours

JL. MAPPANYUKI

JL. DIPONEGORO

Wisma ■ Purnama

New ▲ Indra

Supermarket ■
Money Changer ■
Hotel Indra ■
Hotel Barita ■
Irama Rest. ■

JL. MBANGUNAN

Wisma Rantepao ■

Cafe Monika ■

Toko Foto ■

✉ ✆

Cafe Rahmat ■
Money Changer ■
Art Shop Monika ■

Kios ● Mambo

JL. MANGADIL

JL. PEMBANGUNAN

▲ Bank Rakyat Indonesia

JL. RATULANGI

Wisma Nangalla ■

Football Field

Hebron Inn ■

Kios ■ Ramayana

JL. MERDEKA

VISITING TORAJA

Lush Valleys and Hillside Graves

Most of Rantepao's attractions lie within half an hour's drive by car or public *bemo*, providing delightful walks through the surrounding countryside. Many places of interest are close to one another, which means you can visit several in a day. It is best to set off for the more distant villages in the early morning, while it is still cool and the light is good for photography, returning to Rantepao for lunch. If you are not too tired, nearby villages can then be visited in the afternoon.

Most *obyek wisata* (official "tourist sites") charge an admission fee, usually around $1, with additional charges for such things as "offerings" of flower petals ($0.50—a custom imported recently from Bali), a guide ($1), the rental of a storm lantern for caves ($1), and so on. At several of the sites there is an admission fee for cameras (another $1). At the more popular sites, such as Londa and Lemo, you will be lucky to get change back from your Rp 10.000 note.

During the tourist season, you will be pestered continuously by children (and occasionally adults) asking for money and sweets. Children will pose for photographs (at $1 per head), and try to sell you handicrafts from Flores and Bali. Several villages are building walls to keep out visitors who find it all too expensive and insist on looking without paying. There is no point in getting offended by all of this—after all, you've paid a lot of money to airlines and travel agents to get you here, and there is no reason that the local residents should not receive something too.

Visiting sites during the off season is a completely different experience. Often the villages are deserted and you are on your way to the next place by the time the admission book has been located. People have time to chat in between sales, and even the children are reasonably behaved.

Food is not generally available at these sites, though small *warungs* and restaurants are starting to appear. You will usually have to return to Rantepao for lunch, or take food with you. Most of the sites in the area around Rantepao can be visited in about four days, provided you have the stamina.

Karasik and Londa

Karasik is the first village south of Rantepao on the road to Makale. As you reach the edge

KAL MULLER

of town, watch for the Karasik marker indicating a trail up the hillside to the left of the road. Karasik consists of a number of colorfully painted bamboo houses fringing a large ritual field (*rante*) with several stone menhirs. The houses were originally constructed as temporary pavilions for a large funeral ritual held about a decade ago. Normally, such constructions would be dismantled after the funeral, but these houses were reinforced and used for subsequent funerals. Several of these houses have been made into permanent homes, but in 1986 a violent storm destroyed a number of structures, and today Karasik has the feel of an abandoned ghost town.

Another 5 km (3 mi) down the main road is **Londa**, one of the most frequently visited cave burial sites in Tana Toraja. Catch a *bemo* headed for Makale and ask to be let off at the entrance to Londa, then walk one kilometer east; the road is clearly signposted.

Adjacent to the caves is a balcony filled with *tau tau* gazing out over a lush rice field. Traditionally, only certain nobles were allowed to have *tau tau*. Today, Christian religious officials are ambivalent about this practice and some ministers from the Toraja Church have been known to refuse to officiate at funeral ceremonies where *tau tau* are present. The Catholic Church, however, has proven itself much more tolerant as regards the use of *tau tau*.

After a number of the Londa effigies were stolen for resale on the international art market in the 1980s, villagers installed a sliding metal grate, and the few remaining *tau tau* are locked into their balcony each night. (Much to the local people's disgust, some of the stolen *tau tau* are due to appear in an exhibition at the Smithsonian Institute in 1991.) It is sadly ironic that effigies that were once supposed to protect the living must now be protected from the living.

The sheer limestone cliff-face above these effigies is the burial site for numerous aristocrats. Those Toraja who could afford to have the most elaborate funeral rituals are buried farthest up the cliff.

The two burial caves are said to stretch on for a couple of kilometers. Although only the mouths of the caves can be easily viewed, they stretch deep into the hill in a network of caverns. The caves are filled with coffins and bones of both Christian and *aluk to dolo* adherents, with skulls and bones artistically arranged for visitors.

Kerosene lanterns for cave exploring can be rented from the ticket booth at the entrance to Londa for $1 with a guide. If you want to see it by yourself, make sure you bring a powerful flashlight. Drinks and sou-

Opposite: *Rantepao seen from the hills above the town.* **Below:** *The* tuak *(palm wine) commerce at a market in Rantepao.*

JEAN-LÉO DUGAST

venirs are also available here.

A trail to the east of Londa brings you to **Pabaisenan** (Liang Pia). Here you will find a hearty old tree where infants who died before teething are laid to rest. The corpses are placed in cavities cut into the trunk, and these are then sealed so that the tree eventually grows around the infants' remains.

Returning to the main road, a further 3 km (1.8 mi) will bring you to the turnoff for the pool at **Tilanga'**. Turn left at the signpost and follow a somewhat bumpy road for another 5 km (3 mi) to this clear natural swimming hole lodged in a bamboo forest. The water is cool and refreshing, although the pool is to be avoided on Sundays when the local crowds come out in full force. From here you can head on south 2.5 km (1.4 mi) to Lemo, a nice walk through rice fields.

Lemo and Ke'te' Kesu'

Lemo, 12 km (7 mi) south of Rantepao, is one of the most impressive cliffside grave sites in the entire region. To get here, turn left at the marked signpost and head east a few hundred meters.

Dozens of effigies stand solemnly in niches overlooking the valley below. Adjacent to them are carved wooden doors which seal the remains of the deceased in tombs hewn out of the cliff. Sadly, most of the original *tau tau* here were also stolen in the 1980s—only the few effigies in the upper rows are original. The rest are replacements provided by the government in 1988. This site is heavily visited by tourists, and the viewing platforms, souvenir stands and parking lot are reminiscent of sites in Bali. Still, the limestone burial cliffs are dramatic and there are lovely views of the surrounding countryside. For the best photographs, go early in the morning.

Two kilometers (1.25 mi) south of Rantepao on the road to Makale is a left turn which leads into a parallel valley with many interesting villages and ritual sites. The turnoff is clearly marked "To Ke'te' Kesu'."

Buntupune, one kilometer (0.6 mi) from the junction, has two turn-of-the-century traditional houses and six rice barns. The *tongkonan* on the western side was erected by Pong Maramba, a nobleman who was the first district head during Dutch colonial times. When his plan to revolt against the Dutch was discovered, he was exiled to Ambon. After his death his body was carried back to Tana Toraja and buried in the mountain just north of Buntupune.

Another 2 km brings you to **Ke'te' Kesu'**, one of the region's oldest and most-visited "traditional villages," idyllically situated in a virtual sea of rice fields.

On the little hill at the turn-off to the village, you can watch carvers at work. The village itself has four well-kept *tongkonan* and a long row of rice barns. The residents of the village sell handicrafts on the porches of these traditional houses, and the bottom floor of Tongkonan Kesu' (in the middle) has been converted into a small museum.

The path at the far end of the village leads to several mossy menhirs, reminders of the funerals of important aristocrats. To see the village's ancestral burial cliffs, take the trail behind the museum. The large cement tomb adorned with a strikingly realistic *tau tau* belongs to F.K. Sarungallo, a charismatic *tongkonan* leader, church figure and politician who died in 1986.

Just beyond Sarungallo's tomb are hanging graves and burial cliffs with elaborately-carved coffins and bones. There were once 27 *tau tau* here, but 13 of them were stolen one night in 1984 while the entire village was away attending a funeral ritual. The villagers removed the remaining effigies for safe-keeping, and today remain doubtful that they will ever be able to return them to their rightful place in the burial cliffs.

No one lives here anymore. During the summer months it is not unusual for 50-100 tourists to visit this village in a single day.

Tickets must be purchased at the entrance and when tour groups arrive local children will race to hold tourists' hands and sing French songs which end with requests for "bon bons." Despite its commercialism, Ke'te' Kesu' merits a visit.

Just a little further on from Ke'te' Kesu', off the side of the main road, is the village of **Sullukang**. Here there are several large menhirs installed on the *rante*. A group of *tau tau* were once housed under the overgrown shack on the rocky platform, but they have now also been removed for safekeeping.

Palatokke (also known as Mengke'pe') is a seldom-visited village and grave site which can be reached via an idyllic path from Sullukang. As the path wanders through terraced rice fields and quiet villages, you will need to ask directions (you can also hire a guide for $1).

In addition to magnificent scenery, at Palatokke you will find an imposing cliff with stone and hanging graves. Some Toraja maintain that "Palatokke" is a reference to people who are as adept as geckos at clinging to sheer cliffs, and who mounted the *erongs*, or hanging graves, on the cliff-face without the benefit of ladders.

Metalworkers and hot springs

The metalworking village of **La'bo** can be reached by continuing southeast from Palatokke, or by returning to the main road

from Sullukang and continuing on for 3 km (2 mi). Listen for the sound of metal-pounding coming from a small cluster of houses on the right side of the road. Here you will find blacksmiths forging scrap iron into fine knives (*parang*). Their impressive bellows are made from hollowed logs with feather-lined air pumps. The name of the area, La'bo, is a Torajan term meaning "large knife."

Leaving La'bo, the road splits, with the right fork leading to another blacksmith's village called **Randanbatu**. Another 12 km (7.2 mi) down the road lies **Sanggalla**, the site of a bamboo palace constructed on top of a levelled-off hill and a few graves.

You might want to catch a *bemo* from Rantepao to Sanggalla (22 km/13 mi for 30 to 60 cents), and then walk northeast through some delightful countryside for about two hours to Buntao, where you can get a minibus back to town.

A shorter alternative would be to walk southwest from Sanggalla to Suaya, then go 4 or 5 km (2.5 to 3 mi) along a good trail to the Makale-Rantepao highway. (Suaya can also be visited in a morning from Makale.) The trail to Suaya is on the right, leading up the hillside, starting 1.5 km (around a mile) south of Sangalla.

Opposite: *Cave graves at Londa.* **Above:** *A "tree grave" for deceased infants.* **Left:** *A decayed wooden coffin with skulls in Ke'te' Kesu'.*

Follow the trail for approximately 2 km (1.2 mi), where you will reach **Buntukalando**. The town has a small museum run by local aristocracy. Although modest in size, the museum houses some interesting royal paraphenalia and household objects. Another kilometer brings you to **Suaya**, one of the best places to see *tau tau*: more than 40 are crammed into three galleries. There is a lovely church here too.

Go 3 km (1.8 mi) south from the turnoff to Suaya to get to the hot springs at **Makula**. There is an old government rest house here; the rooms have large tubs for running spring water. In front is a small concrete swimming pool fed by the hot springs behind the house. Although the water is not always clear, it's a wonderful place to soak after a long hike. Both the private rooms and swimming pool can be used for a nominal fee. It is sometimes possible to spend the night here.

A left-hand fork at La'bo leads to **Buntao'**, an interesting village to visit on market day. Ask at Rantepao which day of the week the market falls on. Buntao' has a *patane* (house grave) and there are some old graves on the hill above the village, which is 15 km (9 mi) from Rantepao. **Tembamba**, 2 km further down the road, is a mountain pass village with old graves and a magnificent panorama.

Sites east of Rantepao

Marante and Nanggala are the two important ritual sites on the main road east of Rantepao. **Marante**, approximately 6 km (3.5 mi) east of Rantepao, has several large *tongkonans* and rice barns. If you walk along the dirt road just beyond Marante, there is a large cliff with stone and hanging graves. As with other Toraja burial sites, many of these graves have been ravaged by antique hunters. Some coffins, skulls and a cave remain as reminders of what once was.

Nanggala is a traditional Toraja village 15 km (9 mi) east of Rantepao. Turn right off of the main road onto a small dirt road leading to the village. Here you will find a sweeping row of 14 magnificent rice barns with interesting carvings blending old and new themes.

North and northeast of Rantepao

Some of the most attractive and least visited places of interest in this area are north of Rantepao. The easiest way to visit these sites is to take a *bemo* 6 km (3.6 mi) north to the turnoff for Deri. The road quicky deteriorates into a pot-holed, single-lane track which winds alongside the east bank of the Sa'dan River. On the far side lie rice fields and the occasional outcrop dominated by a glittering tin-roofed *tongkonan*.

The first village of interest is **Pangli**, 8 km

Above: *A man feeds a water buffalo which is about to be sacrificed at a funeral.* **Opposite:** *Fertile fields line the valleys around Rantepao.*

(4.8 mi) from Rantepao, where you can see the house grave of a noted Toraja, Pong Massangka, who fought against the first Dutch missionaries but who was later converted to Christianity. The house-grave is 200 meters uphill, just above the new church on the right. In front is a strikingly realistic stone likeness of Pong Massangka.

You can reach Pangli on foot from Rantepao along a parallel trail. Take the road running north out of town, and after crossing the bridge veer left, then turn right at the next fork in the road. A pleasant, leisurely 7 km (4 mi) walk brings you to **Parinding**, a traditional village with impressive *tongkonan* houses and rice barns. **Bori**, another kilometer down the road, has a large *rante*. A short walk will bring you to a T-junction, where you turn right for Pangli (1 km).

From Pangli, the trail continues north along the Sa'dan River to **Palawa**, on the left. A rice barn and a few bogus *tau tau* welcome visitors to the village, where rather splendid *tongkonans* double as kiosks selling souvenir items from all over Indonesia. Children ask for the inevitable money and sweets.

Another 4 km (2.5 mi) down the track, a left-hand fork 500 meters before a bridge leads uphill to **Sa'dan Sangkombang**, a relaxed, friendly village. Here women can be seen weaving traditional textiles beneath their houses. Continuing along the main road 400 meters, a left turn just before the bridge brings you into **Sa'dan To'barana**. At the back of the village are four rice barns set on a manicured lawn; alongside them are some kiosks selling textiles. The village is worth visiting for the spendid views of terraced rice fields and distant mountains to the west.

To the southwest

A pleasant walk southwest of Rantepao along the western bank of the Sa'dan river leads to **Singki'**, set on a hill overlooking the town. The summit of the hill offers an excellent view of the surrounding countryside. From the center of Rantepao go south on the road that parallels the river, then go right over the bridge (there is a Singki' signpost here). Some 50 meters up the road take the trail leading off to the right. Although it's a short walk from here to the peak, the trail is overgrown and slippery in the wet season. You can often ask directions from the neighborhood children—in fact, they will probably follow you up the peak with the hope of being rewarded with a treat.

The road to Singki' continues on to **Siguntu'**, a traditional village 5 km (3 mi) southwest of Rantepao. To get to Siguntu', go beyond Singki' village and follow the road until you spot a road branching off to the right up the hill. Siguntu' offers three elaborately carved *tongkonans*, rice barns and pleasant sunset views of the valley.

—*Kathleen Adams*

TREKS

Hidden Hamlets of Toraja

In this area you may travel on primitive trails through some of the last virgin forests of South and Central Sulawesi. Except on the more remote trails, it is usually possible to stay in the villages. Food is basic here—rice, eggs, vegetables, cassava and fish, and occasionally *papiong ayam* or *babi*, washed down with copious draughts of freshly-tapped *tuak*, available in every village. All water should be boiled or sterilised, even from the cleanest-looking stream.

Useful gifts to bring for the villagers with whom you will stay include soap, sugar, salt and *kretek* cigarettes; small packets of each can be bought in Rantepao.

Day treks

Nanggala to Buntao' (4 to 5 hours). Take a *bemo* northeast out of Rantepao to Nanggala then climb upwards to Pedamaran through a coffee plantation. Walk down to Panikki and cross the ridge to Buntao'. Here you can catch a bemo back to Rantepao.

Deri to Tikala (one-day trek without guide). Take a *bemo* from Rantepao to Deri (start out early). Just before entering Deri, you will see rock graves set into the hill to your left. A leisurely one-and-a-half-hour walk will bring you to the outskirts of Lempo. Continue upwards (a short-cut forks sharply upwards to the left) to Lempo, where there is a Catholic church and a *warung*. Carry on for another hour and a half until you come to Batumongga. Here there are a couple of homestays and small restaurants.

From Batumongga, a clearly-defined track continues on to Lo'ko'mata. Just before you get to Lo'ko'mata there is an enormous boulder with dozens of rock graves hewn into its side. To return to Rantepao, walk back 3 km (1.8 mi) to a turn-off to the right, which leads down to Pana where there are also rock graves. After Pana, a further hour's walk down a small trail up a bank to the left, 300 m before the school, will bring you to Tikala,

where you can catch the *bemo* back to Rantepao.

Tengan to Sangalla (one-day trek with a guide). From Makale, take a *bemo* to Tengan, then walk uphill along a well-defined path through rice fields to Palipu. Continue on to Suaya, where you will find some *tau tau* and graves, then walk one kilometer to Tampangallo, where there are some rarely-visited hanging graves. From Tampangallo, continue to the ceremonial field at Rantelobe, then on to Kambira where there is a tree in which bodies of infants who died before teething were formerly placed. From Sangalla catch a *bemo* back to Makale.

Rembon to Bera (one-day trek with guide). Take a *bemo* to Rembon, on the road to Bittuang. Climb up to Nonok and view the *tongkonan* houses, then continue up to Batusura' for good views of the valleys. Then strike southeast along a ridge to Pangleon with valleys on both side. From Pangleon walk down through the rice fields, then turn north past a waterfall and walk 2 km (1.2 mi) further up to cross the Sa'dan River by boat. Between here and Bera you can pick up a *bemo* back to Rantepao.

Longer treks

Parodo to Rembong (4-day trek with guide). Catch the *bemo* from Makale to Parodo, on the road to Bittuang. Follow the trail to Se'seng, Bittuang and Pali. Stop overnight in Pali. Next day walk through the forest to Sasak, where you can bathe in the river while lunch is prepared; after lunch walk down to Bau, an easy three-hour stroll. Spend the night in a *tongkonan*. Next day go on to Battayan, then up to Balepe and stay overnight in a Bugis-style house. Carry on to Pasapa, then through the forest to Sanik and To'lamba. From To'lamba go to Tobone, Malimbong and Rembong, where you can catch a *bemo* back to Makale.

Tengan to Nanggala (4 days). Take a *bemo* 8 km south of Makale to Tengan and walk to Marinding, then on to Dulang and spend the night in one of the 100 or so *tongkonan*. Next morning, continue down to Malimongan and To'duri, then on to Buntulengke. Leave your packs in a *tongkonan* and walk down to a hot spring one km below the village to bathe. The next day continue on to Tanetebone and spend the night. Next morning you will pass another "baby-tree" on your way to Nanggala, where you may stay the night, returning to Rantepao the following day.

—*Nancy Caldwell*

Tana Toraja

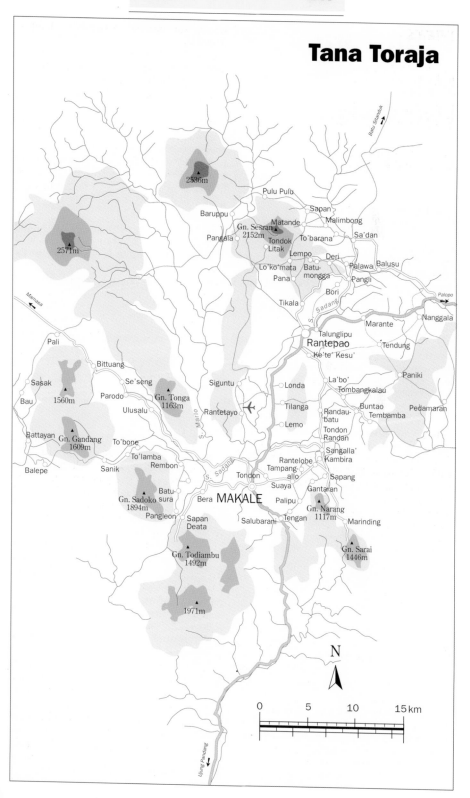

Tana Toraja Practicalities

Includes Rantepao and Trekking in Toraja. All prices are in US$. Telephone code 0411. S=Single; D=Double. AC=air-conditioned.

Rantepao

Rantepao is an unprepossessing, dusty little town of four main roads which converge at a mini-*tongkonan* set on a road island. The town is developing fast; the number of visitors is increasing rapidly, and new hotels and restaurants are opening monthly. Street names are in a state of confusion; many have been renamed but residents have yet to learn what the names are. This is the center of Tana Toraja: most journeys into the surrounding countryside begin and end at Rantepao.

Prices given below are a guide to what you might expect to pay in May or June. Prices in the international-standard hotels are fixed, but those in the smaller hotels and *wisma*s are extremely flexible. Between peak season (July-August) and low season (January-February) hotel rates can vary by as much as 300%. The same is true of car rentals and practically everything else except food. When traveling off-season, it pays to bargain, especially if you will be staying a few days.

GETTING THERE

Merpati flies daily from Ujung Pandang to the airport at Rantetayo near Makale, 24 km (14 mi) south of Rantepao. Planes leave Ujung Pandang at 9:00 and arrive at 9:45. Return flights from Rantetayo depart at 10:15 and arrive at Ujung Pandang at 11:15. Due to the short runway at Rantetayo, flights in carry 22 passengers, but only 14 on the flight out. Flights are sometimes cancelled without notice due to lack of passengers or low-lying fog. During the tourist season flights are heavily booked. Fare one way is $30. **Merpati** also runs a bus service into Rantepao for $4.

Coaches to Rantepao leave daily from Ujung Pandang; **Litha** coaches depart at 7:00, 13:00 and 19:00. The journey takes 8 hours and includes a meal stop. Tickets should be bought in town (see "Ujung Pandang Practicalities") but coaches actually leave from Panaikan bus terminal, 20 minutes out of town by *bemo*.

TRANSPORTATION

Bemos into town terminate in the field behind the old market. *Bemos* to any place out of Rantepao can be picked up around the traffic island in the center of town; passing ones can be flagged down along any road. Fares start at Rp.100. *Kijang* (minijeeps) and minibuses can be hired at the better hotels from $30/day including driver. Another place to rent vehicles is the **Perhimpunan**

Pramuwisata Indonesia, Jl. Mappanyuki 41. Toyota Land Crusers are more expensive at $50/day. An international driving license is required. *Bemo* drivers can be persuaded to take you to almost any destination for $4/hour.

INFORMATION

The staff at the **Tourist Information Center**, 62 Jl. Ahmad Yani are pleasant and helpful, but have little useful information. Sketch maps of the area can be obtained here or from most hotels. Finding out where death feasts and other ceremonies are being held can be difficult, unless you are willing to hire a guide. Keep asking: if you've heard the same story several times it is probably correct. Avoid asking a question that can be answered in the affirmative. When asking about distances, it is better to ask "how long" (*berapa jam?*, *berapa lama?*) rather than "how far." Most people have only a hazy idea about distances, but know how long it takes to walk or drive.

ACCOMMODATION

Prices vary according to demand. From July to September most hotels are full and advance booking is advisable. The rest of the year hotels are often empty and prices fall sharply. All hotels in the luxury and intermediate classes have private bathrooms with hot showers. The better hotels add 8% government tax and 8% service charge. The climate is cool and pleasant and only the luxury hotels have AC.

Luxury ($40-150)

The two luxury hotels are at opposite ends of the town. Standards of service and comfort are similar, but **Toraja Cottages** is the more attractive, with bungalows spread out on the side of a landscaped hill. Its bar is also the focus of nightlife in Rantepao. **Toraja Cottages** is conveniently close to the market (held on Wednesdays) northeast of the town center.

Misiliana Hotel and **Misiliana Inn**. 3 km (1.8 mi) south of Rantepao. Tel. 21234, Fax. 21212. Reservations can be made in Ujung Pandang at Jl. Lembu No. 2, Tel. 84225. 120 rooms, a newish hotel with Toraja decor. All rooms have refrigerator and television. $28-35 S, $35-40 D a night for a standard room. Executive cottages $100, Toraja suite $150. Bar and restaurant, Western and Chinese-Indonesian menu. Swimming pool.

Toraja Cottages, Jalan Pakubalasalu, 4 km (2.4 mi) northeast of town. Tel. 21089, Fax. 21369. 62 rooms $37 S, $42 D. Suite $125. Bar and two restaurants, Western and Chinese-Indonesian menu. Swimming pool. An attractive complex of chalets set in lush tropical greenery.

Toraja Prince (an extension of Toraja Cottages) is opening shortly across the road; this will have 100 rooms and will be even more luxurious.

Intermediate ($10-40)

Hotels in this category are family homes with added guestrooms. They are almost always clean and quiet. The important differences are location, view of the surrounding valley, and the warmth of the family in whose compound you stay.

Most *wisma* provide food if you order in advance. If a *wisma* does not have transportation, a car and perhaps an invitation to a death feast can be arranged with the owner's relatives.

It is worth asking whether tax or service is added to the bill; some places add 21%. Prices are flexible in the off-season (i.e. 9 months of the year). If you are staying for more than a couple of days, you may be able to get a 10-20% discount.

Hotel Indra, Jl. Landorundun 63, Rantepao. Tel. 21163. 40 rooms, money changer, supermarket and restaurant, Western and Indonesian menu. $7-15 S, $8.50-20 D, $40 suite. Well-run, conveniently located; good staff.

Wisma Maria II, 2 km out of Rantepao on road to Makale. 20 rooms. $7-12 S, $10-15 D. Clean and well-run. Good breakfast with homemade bread and strong Toraja coffee. 15 minutes' walk from the town center.

Hotel Pison, Jl. Pong Tiku 8, Tel. 21344. $5-14 S, $7-20 D. Small restaurant with white table linen and good Chinese-Indonesian food. The rooms are spacious and spotlessly clean with veranda and private bathroom. All overlook a small lane with a view of the western mountains. The owner, Mr. Luther Pongrekun, is an exceptionally personable man. The hotel is set in a quiet lane less than 5 minutes from town. Warmly recommended.

Pia's Poppies, Jl. Pong Tiku 27A. 7 rooms with a splended view of ricefields and mountains. The restaurant plays rock music until late: a hotel for those who like parties, rising late and breakfasting on fruit salad with Cointreau. $7-10 S, $10-15 D.

Wisma Irama, Jalan Abdul Gani 18, Tel. 21371. 17 rooms, $8-12 S, $13-17 D. Bar and restaurant with Chinese-Indonesian menu. A pleasant hotel set in a quiet lane off Pasar Hewan.

Hebron Inn, Jl. Pembangunan. Tel. 21519. 17 rooms, $19 S, $21 D. An attractive new hotel in an unattractive part of town, facing a sports field.

Hotel Pondok Torsina, Jl. Pao Ruru, 1.5 km (1 mi) south of town on the road to Makale. Tel. 21293. 18 rooms, $18 S, $28 D. Bar, restaurant. Food could be a problem; it's a fair walk into town and the hotel serves only Chinese-Indonesian food.

Rantepao Lodge, Jl. Pao Rura, 1.5 km south of Rantepao on the road to Makale. Tel.21248. 24 rooms, $20-32 S, $30-40 D. Bar and restaurant serving Chinese-Indonesian food. Continue up the muddy path past the Pondok Torsina.

Wisma Tanabua, Jl. J. Diponogoro 43. Tel. 21072. 22 rooms, $6-10 S, $12-17 D. Bar and restaurant, Chinese-Indonesian menu. Centrally located.

Wisma Maria I, Jl. Ratulangi. Tel. 21165. 20 rooms, $5-14. One of the oldest *wisma* in Rantepao, now a bit down at the heels. The guest rooms are set around *tongkonan*, like the classier Wisma Maria II.

Budget (under $10)

Budget accomodation is plentiful, though most of the better *losmen* or homestays are 10 or 15 minutes by *bemo* from the center of town. The cheapest homestays are north of the mini-*tongkonan* on Jl. Mappanyuki, or around the mosque. In July and August the search will take you well out of town into the suburban *kampung* down country lanes.

Wisma Rosa, Jl. Pahlawan. Tel. 21075. 15 rooms, $4-10. The oldest *wisma* in Rantepao. Quiet, with a verandah, trees and a garden. Centrally located, on the road to Sa'dan.

Wisma Irama is a popular budget accommodation charging $4-$5 for pleasant rooms with bathroom.

Hotel Barita, Jl. Londorundun 35. Tel. 21060, 17 rooms, $6-9. A gray cement bunker, centrally located next to the excellent **Irama Restaurant**.

Wisma Nirmala, Jl. Mappanyki. Tel. 21319. 12 rooms, $3-6.

Hotel Indo Grace, Jl. Mappanyuki 72. $3-4. On the main road next to the Liman Express office. Noisy.

Marlin Inn, Jl. Mappanyuki, opposite the Hotel Indo Grace. Bargain hard. 16 rooms, $3-4.

Wisma Flora, Jl. Sesan 25. Tel. 21010. 8 rooms, $3. Next to the mosque and a *bemo* stop. Noisy.

Wisma Nanggala, Jl. Taman Bahagia 81, Tel. 21296. 10 rooms, $4-5.

Hotel Victoria, Jl. Mappanyuki. Tel. 21308. 5 rooms, $5-7.

Wisma Sederhana, Jl. Sulora 110. Tel. 21011. 5 rooms, $5-7. 2 km (1.2 mi) out of town on the road to Tiklala.

FOOD

The specialty of the region is *piong*, food cooked in bamboo sections. Most restaurants serve *piong*, but you have to order at least two hours in advance and specify the kind of meat you want, usually chicken or pork. *ikan bakar* (charcoal-grilled fish) *bistik kerbau* (fried buffalo steak) and black rice are definitely worth trying. Nothing is too spicy for the Western palate, but if you do want to make your meal more authentic, ask for the various condiments (*sambal tomat, sambal asli, sambal lombok*) that traditionally accompany a meal. The menu at most restaurants is a combination of Western, Toraja and Chinese dishes. Most will provide a packed lunch of sandwiches, eggs, chicken, fruit and drinks if you are going walking. Some of the smaller restaurants do not have a refrigerator; meat is best avoided unless you know it is fresh. Listed below are some of the better-known restaurants.

Indra Restaurant (Hotel Indra, Jl. Landorundun 63). Good food and excellent service from friendly staff. One of the best places to sample a Torajan meal; try the *papiong ayam* (chicken in bamboo), black rice and *sayur paku* (delicately cooked fern tips). One order is enough for two persons; total cost $7. Staff will even go out and fetch *tuak* for you; better still, go to the road circle and sample it yourself (bring your own *tuak* container).

Pia's Poppies, see "Accommodation" above. The menu recommends giant *masapi* eel from the depths of the Sa'dan river. Small but elegant portions of delicious fruit salad and *crêpes suzette* with Grand Marnier. Painfully slow service.

Pison Restaurant (Hotel Pison, Jl. Pong Tiku 8). Clean white table linen and pleasant, attentive service. The grilled fish is fresh from their own pond and the enormous fruit salads are attractively presented. Excellent pancakes; one of the few places where you can get chilled Bir Bintang in small bottles. (Refuse all other brands!) Chinese-Indonesian menu, Western breakfast, juices. Toraja specialties on request.

Rahmat Restaurant. Centrally located facing the traffic island, this restaurant caters mainly to tourist groups. Plastic tablecloths, folding metal chairs and a hot, stuffy atmosphere. Indifferent Chinese-Indonesian menu.

Monica Café, Jl. Pasar. Neat little café which serves good charcoal-grilled fish and freshly fried potatoes. Steer clear of meat dishes. Attracts younger travelers. When the rock music is off you can dine to the sound of the *muezzin*'s call to prayer from the mosque opposite.

Kiosk Mambo, Jl. Ratulangi. Standard Chinese-Indonesian menu, Western breakfasts, juices.

Chez Dodeng. One of the oldest cafés in town, it has spawned several offspring establishments of the same name. The original is at the corner of Jl. Monginsidi and Jl. Emisaelan. Classic *warung*-style Chinese-Indonesian food. The open sewer outside the front door does not inspire confidence. Chess players gather here in the late afternoon.

Takumande Opa Restaurant, Misiliana Hotel. Tourist-style European, Chinese and Indonesian cusines and traditional Toraja food. 3 km (1.8 mi) out of town on the road to Makale.

Toraja Cottages Restaurant offers good food and service at reasonable prices (about $4-6 for a main dish) in a nice atmosphere. A drink in the bar and a meal here will set you back $10-15 and make a very pleasant evening out.

NIGHTLIFE

The government of South Sulawesi is resisting attempts to turn Rantepao into another Kuta. As yet there are no discos or pubs, although there are plans for a *karaoke* lounge to be opened shortly on Jl. Mappanyuki. All restaurants serve alcohol, mainly beer (Bintang, Anker, Becks, Carlsberg). The **Misiliana Hotel** stages traditional dance performances, including the *Paranding* war dance. **Toraja Cottages** has a bar and resident band; a noisy, gregarious crowd hangs out here. **Pia's Poppies** plays music till late.

Tuak sellers gather in the town center after dark. Cup your hand and ask for a sample; the taste ranges from a sweetness that makes your teeth sing to a sourness that makes your ears ring. The best solution is to blend a sweet and sour; the sour is more alcoholic and should be drunk with caution.

SHOPPING

Antique baskets, ancient bamboo *tuak* containers, old weavings, stringed musical instruments and ceremonial food containers are still brought down from the mountain villages to Rantepao, where they are sold at reasonable prices. Weavings are expensive, but you may pick up an old Torajan house panel for as little as $25.

Modern handicrafts include carved Toraja trays, boxes and mirrors, and various-sized models of *tongkonan*. Long knives with carved buffalo-horn handles in ornate woodern scabbards hang in shop windows. Bead necklaces and attractively-packed bamboo containers of Toraja coffee make ideal presents.

Most of the souvenir and antique shops are along **Jl. Pahlawan**, north from the traffic island. **Artshop Monika** on Jl. Ahmad Yani is the best place to start: the owner, Monika, is knowledgable and stocks a wide range of sensibly priced antiques and handicrafts. New weavings, as well as weavings from other parts of Indonesia, are sold in the villages of **Sa'dan Sangkombong** and **Sa'dan Tobarana**. You can expect to pay $30 and upwards for hand-woven *kain kipris*, colorful striped local cloth, 8 meters (26 ft) in length, woven on a backstrap loom. It will cost $120 for a weaving from Rongkong, an isolated mountain region to the northwest of Palopo. In the hills behind Rantetayo you may come across an old man selling a Toraja bamboo flute.

MISCELLANEOUS

There are two authorized money changers and a bank close to the town center on Jl. Ahmad Yani.

The Post Office, Jl Ahmad Yani 111, is on the left just before the town center. There is a Poste Restante service here. Next door is the telegraph and telephone office, open 24 hours.

You can get film at **Toko Foto Duta Wisata** on the corner of Jl. Ahmad Yani and Jl. Landorundun; prices are higher than in Ujung Pandang.

The **Hotel Indra** runs a well-stocked little supermarket where you can buy stamps, guide books, canned and bottled drinks, blankets, towels and chocolates. **Toko Remaja**, Jl. Ahmad Yani 181, is the largest department store in Rantepao.

Second-hand paperbacks and travelers' books can be bought from the bookshop up the lane to the right off the Makale-Rantepao road, just before you reach the mini-*tongkonan*.

There are several pharmacies in Rantepao; the **Apotik Delta**, 48 Ahmad Yani, is open from 8:00 to 20:30 Mon-Sat. If closed, knock on the door.

LEAVING RANTEPAO

From Rantepao you can catch coaches south to Makale, Enrekang, Parepare and Ujung Pandang. The **Litha Express**, **Falitah** and **Erlin** bus companies are on Jl. Mappanyuki, near the traffic circle. Departures at 7:00, 13:00 and 19:00. Minibuses to Poso and Palu leave from Jl. Landorundun north through a spectacular mountain pass to Palopo; the trip to Palu (48 hours) and costs $14 (See "Central Sulawesi Practicalities.")

Merpati has flights daily from Rantepao to Ujung Pandang at 10:15. The office is located on the main road south to Makale, 2 km from the town center. (See "Getting There" for flight details.)

Trekking in Tana Toraja

Treks in Tana Toraja can be divided into two types: day treks which you can usually do on your own, and longer, 3-8 day treks for which a guide is exremely useful, unless you speak Indonesian and do not mind getting lost occasionally. The trekking season is from March to November: May to September are the dryest months. In the rainy season (December to the end of February) trails are often impassable and leeches a nuisance.

The best place to hire a guide is the **Himpunan Pramuwisata Indonesia** (HPI), an official association formed two years ago to train and license guides. Among the more experienced guides are Martin Rangan, Exon Tulungallo, Benny Rantelili, Eskel Tulangallo, Nicho Embatau, Daud Tanyongong, Bayo Sampe Rante and Benyamin Parannoan. HPI's offices are at Jl. Landorundun 7.

The official rate for a guide is $20 per day. Like most things in Indonesia, this rate is negotiable, depending on season and the number of people in the group. On top of this you will have to pay for food and lodging for yourself and your guide. This will average between $4-6 per person per day. If you are traveling without a guide, ask for the village head (*kepala desa*) who will help arrange food and accommodation.

Equipment

For a one-day trek you will need good walking shoes, a wide-brimmed sun hat, drinking water, chocolates and biscuits or a packed lunch. A flashlight is advisable in case you return after nightfall. For a trek of two or more days bring a sweater, a light blanket or sleeping bag (blankets can be purchased in Rantepao), a flashlight, a thin foam sleeping mat, and shorts or *sarung* for bathing in the villages. All drinking water should be boiled or sterilized, however clean the stream looks. Water-sterilizing tablets, mosquito repellant and factor 30 sunblock are difficult to find in Rantepao and should be brought with you.

Loose cotton clothes are the most comfortable. For women, a skirt or light baggy trousers and a short-sleeved T-shirt are recommended; for men, long shorts or trousers. A conservative style of dress for both men and women shows respect for local sensibilities. Short shorts are best kept for bathing in.

Lightweight waterproofs are advisable as it can get very cold when it rains in the mountains. A *sarung* is useful for wrapping up in the evenings, warding off the mosquitoes, to sleep in, and as a towel. It's a good idea to tape up your toes with plain zinc strip plaster before you start out; this will help prevent blisters.

—*Ian and Nancy Caldwell*

PART IV

Introducing Central Sulawesi

The province of Central Sulawesi (Sulteng) is a jumble of towering, forest-clad mountains where rain falls almost every afternoon of the year. Yet its most fertile area, the Palu Valley, is also the driest region in all of Indonesia, averaging only 40-80 cm (15-30 in) of rainfall a year. Minutes away from coconut groves and irrigated rice fields are barren, cactus-studded plains riven by empty watercourses, where emaciated oxen and cows wander in search of shrubs.

Religious contrasts abound as well. Scattered in the highlands west of Palu, east of Ampana, and along the ridge of the northern neck, are dozens of relatively isolated ethnic groups practicing shamanic religions. While the Dutch Reformed Church and the Salvation Army have made minor inroads in the area, over 75 percent of the population is Muslim. The proportion is even higher in the densely populated coastal and valley regions, where traders, farmers, and fishermen of Bugis, Mandarese, and Gorontalo origin have settled, bringing Islam with them.

Geologically, too, the province is a stunning mosaic. The volcanic and tectonic activity which created the island left in its wake a network of streams and ravines, along with massive rifts and craters that later became rivers, lakes, and upland plains. Covering 68,033 sq km (26,270 sq mi, roughly the size of Ireland), Sulteng is the largest of Sulawesi's four provinces.

Though classified as a single province for administrative purposes, Central Sulawesi is still at best a tenuous geographic entity. Communication remains difficult in a terrain dominated by mountains. Forests cover 64 percent of the land (over 95 percent of the province's income derives from timber exports, mainly ebony). Between many points along the coasts, travel is still faster by motorized boat than by road, despite the presence of the Trans-Sulawesi Highway.

Even with a population of over 1.5 million and a growth rate approaching 3.5 percent (in part due to the influx of transmigrants), the province still averages only 22 persons per sq km. Furthermore, the vast majority (almost 90 percent) are distributed along the coasts, meaning that the hinterlands are very sparsely inhabited. Many inland settlements are linked only by horse trails or walking tracks. As a result, the social and cultural life of the province is amazingly varied—groups living quite close to one another (as the crow flies) may speak very different languages and follow different customs.

While much of Central Sulawesi remains isolated, a degree of unity has been brought to the area by the Indonesian government and by Islam and Christianity. Even villagers in the most remote settlements have heard and seen something of government development programs. Gradually, the diversity of this hitherto inaccessible area is being eroded by the influx of traders and officials. Crafts such as bark cloth manufacture are on the wane, and baskets and mats are being supplanted by plastic buckets and vinyl floor coverings.

Still, Central Sulawesi remains one of most culturally diverse provinces on an island known for its diversity. Government publications list 12 different ethnic groups and 24 distinct languages for the province, and a trip through Sulteng will give the visitor a chance to witness a sort of microcosm of the multicultural "Indonesian experience" within a small geographical area. This is a rugged province whose natural attractions are best appreciated by the trekker with a sense of adventure and a knowledge of at least a few words of Indonesian. For those with the time and the patience, a trip through Sulteng may be a vastly rewarding experience.

—*Greg Acciaoili*

Overleaf: *The huge megalith known as Palindo, in the Bada Valley.* **Opposite:** *A woman from Tentena, by Lake Poso. Both photos by Kal Muller.*

BARCLOTH

Indigenous Fabric of Sulteng

"It is in this Kingdom where Men and Women are clad in nothing but Paper, and that not being lasting, the Women are always working at it very curiously. It is made of the Rind of a small Tree we saw there, which they beat with a Stone curiously wrought, and make it as they please, either coarse, fine or very fine. They dye it all colours, and twenty paces off it looks like fine Tabby. A great deal of it is carry'd to Manila and Macao, where I have seen excellent bed-hangings made from it; they are the best you could desire in cold Weather. When it rains, Water being the Destruction of Paper those People strip, and carry their Clothes under their arm."

Thus wrote the Spanish friar Domingo Navarette, after a month-long visit to the Palu Valley in 1657. At the turn of this century, when Dutch colonial officials, European explorers, and Western missionaries began to penetrate the mountainous jungles of Central Sulawesi, they found the local inhabitants still wearing clothing made from processed tree bark.

Never having been introduced to the technology of weaving, and having little contact with outside peoples, the interior peoples of the area, largely migratory farming and hunting groups, made use of locally produced barkcloth for all of their clothing needs. Although some groups possessed woven cloths which had been traded from India, Europe, or South Sulawesi, these were not worn, but kept as heirlooms.

A variety of barkcloth fabrics were manufactured by stripping the inner bark of certain trees (mostly wild fig and breadfruit species), then cooking and fermenting or soaking the strips for several days. The softened bark strips were then washed and later pounded together on a wooden board with a set of wooden and grooved stone beaters.

The felted cloth thus produced in one to two weeks' time was treated with a preserva-

tive and dye fluid derived from one of several plant species called *ula'* (meaning "red" in many Austronesian languages). The finished barkcloth was fashioned into tube-shaped blankets or cut and sewn into regionally distinctive clothing styles.

Men's traditional daily wear consisted of simple brown loincloths. Adult women wore full multi-layered, finely pleated skirts and tunic blouses. Black cloth was obtained by soaking the natural reddish-brown material in mud. In some areas, chips of mica stone were added as sequins, or appliqués of differently colored barkcloth were sewn onto the garment with hemp fibers to create geometrical designs. Rough-textured monochromatic daily wear was replaced with finer clothing

LORRAINE V. ARAGON

for important occasions such as feasts and celebrations.

For feasts a thinner, softer, white barkcloth was produced from paper mulberry trees specially cultivated for this purpose. The resulting fabric was intricately painted with plant dyes to create colorful designs for men's headscarfs, sarongs, and women's blouses.

Although today the interior peoples of Central Sulawesi are not generally recognized for their artistry or technical skills, their 19th-century barkcloth manufacture stands out as among the most refined barkcloth production systems ever developed. Prior to the 20th century, Central Sulawesi barkcloth was exported to other islands as clothing material, paper, and even as "canvas" for Balinese calendar paintings.

The period between 1910 and 1940, however, marked the beginning of the end for the barkcloth industry. At this time, the Dutch government and Protestant missions began to assert their presence more aggressively in highland Central Sulawesi. Contact increased with outsiders, including Indonesians from other areas of the country; as a result, woven cotton cloth was quickly adapted in the interior for clothing.

The use of barkcloth for everyday wear had almost vanished by World War II, when manufactured cloth became suddenly unavailable due to the Japanese occupation. From 1941 to 1945 almost no cloth could be obtained in interior Sulawesi, and local women returned to their ancestral technology in order to clothe their families. Today, Western-style cotton or polyester clothing is in general use, but barkcloth for blankets and ceremonial dress is still sometimes produced in the highland regions of Pandere, Kulawi, Pipikoro, Tobaku, Bada, and Besoa.

The production of barkcloth in Sulteng is principally the responsibility of the women, although in some regions male relatives may be enlisted to cut down large trees, strip bark, or make the wood, stone and rattan tools that are used for beating the fermented bark. Only in areas such as Napu, Besoa and Bada were male transvestite priests allowed to practice the art of barkcloth painting for ritual clothing to be used in major ceremonies. Elsewhere, all young girls were taught to beat and decorate barkcloth by their mothers, and girls were expected to produce a full set of feast clothing before their marriage day.

When a Kulawi bride was six months pregnant, she was presented with a white barkcloth blouse, which she donned in another ceremony at the seventh month, and was not allowed to remove the blouse until the baby was born. The fact that barkcloth making had important connections with fertility and womanhood is also shown by a Kulawi ceremony formerly carried out after the birth of a child.

When the child was born, its sex was announced to the village by a set of symbolic objects placed in front of the house. For boys these consisted of a sword, a shield and a brass bell; for girls, a basket of agricultural tools and a set of barkcloth beaters.

The production itself was always regulated by a number of ritual taboos. Women were forbidden to make barkcloth within the agricultural field and settlement areas, or inside the village houses, for fear of disturbing spirits with pounding noises, or even accidentally hitting one.

Nor could cloth be produced after sunset, during the harvest season, during or soon after epidemic illnesses, or during mourning periods following the death of a relative or a noble. Before production began, offerings of betel nut were always put out for the spirits, and in the Poso region elder women would formally appeal to the souls of the ancestral residents of the land. The ancestors were asked not to be angry with the noise, but to wait patiently for the barkcloth that eventually would be shared with them.

LORRAINE V. ARAGON

Prior to the arrival of Christian missionaries, barkcloth was used as a vessel for spiritual power. In some regions, the noble descendants of community founders would bless their community's fields by giving each household a strip of barkcloth. This was to be hung on poles in the fields as a talisman warding off evil spirits and pests. Many of these practices are still followed today, although barkcloth is now produced mostly in Christian areas where the women now also refrain from beating barkcloth on Sundays.

—*Lorraine V. Aragon*

Opposite: *A Bada woman beating barkcloth under the shade of the family granary.* **Above:** *A woman models a barkcloth blouse made by her mother.*

PALU

Postwar Provincial Capital

In his early 18th-century writings on the Indonesian archipelago, the missionary François Valentyn likened the appearance of the area around Palu to the gentle beauty of Holland. With a bit of imagination (block out the coconut palms and mountains which surround the region), it is possible to travel homeward with the writer as he describes "a flat land and its black clay soil ... a gloriously beautiful view upon the fields, pleasant enough by themselves, which are full of all sorts of livestock: fatting cows, buffalo, horses, sheep, goats and all sorts of wild animals. Above all they yield a great abundance of paddy and rice, as the paddy fields are usually worked by these buffalo. It is indeed a blessed land ..." But, adds the priest, "in manner of life, it is an accursed Sodom."

During Valentyn's time, Palu was only one among a number of chiefdoms located in the Palu Valley and the surrounding coasts, inhabited by a people known as the Kaili. The original settlement from which these people spread seems to have been a village on the east shore of Palu Bay.

A century after Valentyn, the Spanish monk Navarette records his shock at the local practice of male transvestite priests or *bajasa* being taken as wives by respected community members. (Was this the source of Valentyn's moral outrage?) Navarette was also impressed, however, by the natural riches of the area—where people subsisted on bananas and produced vast quantities of coconut oil, much of it sent as tribute to Makassar. He also noted the absence of wet-rice cultivation, which is of recent introduction to the area.

Although Palu was not a major town during the colonial period, it is now a rapidly-growing provincial capital (population 150,000), and the starting point for an investigation of the Kaili area. Situated at the foot of Palu Bay, the city is bisected by the Palu River, with downtown and major shopping areas on the west bank and the main government offices and airport to the east.

A general outline of the attractions of the whole province can be obtained by visiting the provincial museum on Jalan Sapiri. Designed on the general plan of a *lobo* or ritual meeting house, the museum includes replicas of the Lore region's megaliths and great stone vats, exhibits of traditional arts and

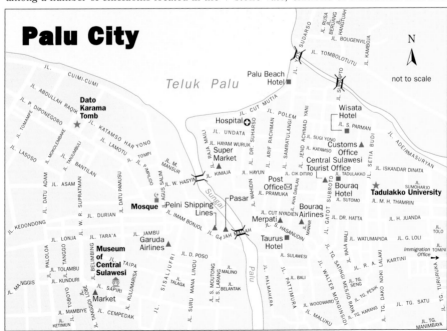

Palu City

crafts, as well as household utensils and weapons. Its collection of heirloom cloths (*mbesa*) is particularly fine.

There are *ikat* cloths from Kalumpang and Rongkong in South Sulawesi, and *patola* cloths from India, still used in marriage exchanges among families of noble descent (and modern wealth). Also to be seen are the locally produced *kain Donggala*—darkly colored silks with supplementary embroidery or *ikat*, sometimes including a tic-tac-toe double *ikat* design, thus making the Kaili region the only one in the archipelago aside from the village of Tengganan in Bali to make use of this difficult technique. Different types of barkcloth—long the primary material for secular and ritual clothing in the highlands of the province—are also on display.

Live performances of local dances are given in the *Gedung Olah Seni* (GONI) on Jalan Professor Muhammed Yamin SH in the eastern half of the city near the immigration office. Inquiries can be made at the helpful Central Sulawesi Tourist Office on Jalan Cik Ditiro. These performances are often held in conjunction with arts festivals where youth groups representing various subdistricts and villages compete in the presentation of newly choreographed adaptations of traditional dances such as the *dero*.

Essentially a city created by the Japanese during World War II, Palu has the feel of a bustling town assiduously asserting its mo-dernity, rather than the elegiac torpor exuded by many former Dutch colonial towns. There is little to remind the traveler that the Dutch once brought their gunships to the banks of the Palu River (now an impossibility due to silting at the river's mouth) to issue demands for taxes and obedience.

What can still be witnessed is the role of Palu in disseminating Islam throughout the region. In Kampung Lere, to the west of the city, can be found the tomb of Dato Karama, the missionary who is said to have come from West Sumatra to propagate Islam in the Palu Valley and northern coasts. The mosque he built in the 17th century, reputed to be the oldest in the province, can be visited on Jalan Kyai Haji Agus Salim.

In the *pasar* on the west bank of Palu, hundreds of hawkers (most of them Bugis) squat in their stalls selling fish, cloth, utensils and a host of other items. This was once the center of the city, just north of the intersection of Jalan Gajah Mada and Jalan Teuku Umar. Although major banks and shops (*toko*) are still located here, the central *pasar* has relocated to Jalan Sapiri just past the provincial museum. Another market has recently been erected for the eastern half of the city on Jalan Walter Monginsidi, the main road leading south out of town.

—*Greg Acciaoili*

Below: *Spinning silk for local* kain Donggala.

KAL MULLER

DONGGALA & THE NORTH

Ancient Port on the Kaili Coast

Forty kilometers (25 mi) north of Palu along a well-surfaced road lies the ancient and picturesque seaport of Donggala. For more than a thousand years, ships from the east coast of Borneo have been calling here to trade, bringing with them Indian textiles and weaving techniques that have inspired the famous silk cloths of the Kaili region. On the opposite side of the huge Bay of Palu stretches Sulawesi's long northern neck. Often considered just an obligatory stretch of territory connecting Central and North Sulawesi, this region is actually quite interesting as a midpoint between Sulawesi's contrasting highland and lowland cultures.

The old port of Donggala

Donggala has been a port of importance for most of its long history, particularly among the traders of South Sulawesi and the east

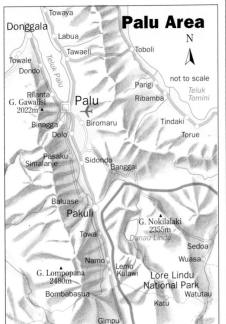

coast of Borneo. The Indian-inspired silk weavings of this area, called *kain Donggala*, are still made at Towale village using silk thread imported from China. Over the centuries, Bugis sailors and traders have settled in Donggala, first integrating with then largely replacing the indigenous Kaili inhabitants. When the Dutch decided it was time to bring Central Sulawesi under their control at the very end of the 19th century, Donggala was chosen as the colonial administrative center.

The seaport lost much of its importance during and after the Second World War, when the capital was shifted to Palu. More recently, new port facilities at Pantoloan across the bay have further eroded the town's importance. Pelni and other larger ships no longer call at Donggala, though Bugis schooners continue to do so, shuttling back and forth to Surabaya. There are at least a half dozen of these vessels in port at any one time, bringing cargoes of foodstuffs, cement and consumer goods which are then transported by small boat or truck to Palu. On the outward journey, these schooners are crammed full of copra, Donggala's main export and primary source of wealth. It is thanks to copra money that the Donggala area has so many *haji*, Muslims who have made the (expensive) pilgrimage to the holy Islamic city of Mecca.

A trip to Donggala provides a pleasant change from the bustle of Palu. It is a sleepy provincial town whose red-tiled roofs (a welcome break from the corrugated zinc of Palu buildings) proclaim its colonial heritage. The harbor still teems with sea craft of all sorts and, invigorated by sea breezes, the town itself is a delight simply to walk through, enjoying views of the harbor and the vegetable gardens in the hills above, with a brief stop to watch fresh fish being brought into its small *pasar* or market.

The town lies on the protected inner shore of Palu Bay, near the very tip of the mountainous peninsula which defines the bay's western shore. The best view onto Donggala's picturesque harbor is from a narrow paved road leading north to Tanjung Karang and Boneage, especially during the late afternoon. From the edge of town, it's a pleasant two-kilometer (1.25 mi) stroll on this road to where it forks; the paved left-hand fork leads to Boneage and the unpaved right branch heads to the water's edge at Tanjung Karang. At Tanjung Karang, the best beach is

Opposite: *View of Donggala harbor from Tanjung Karang, with the "northern neck" behind.*

fenced off and a small entrance fee is charged to swim. The beach is deserted during weekdays.

Off the beach, the bay's transparent waters gradually shift to richer shades of turquoise, abruptly changing to deep blue some distance from the shore and across to verdant hills on the other side. There is usually a variety of sailing craft here, including graceful sailing catamarans, posed for countless photo opportunities.

Further down the coast at Boneage, 7 km (4 mi) from Palu, an incredibly fine sand beach lines a two-kilometer-long, two-house-wide village.

Another paved 12-km (7-mi) road from Donggala cuts across the tip of the peninsula, passing by a golf course to Towale village on the western coast. Nearby, a sunken salt-water pool called Pusenasi provides the setting for an unforgettable swim. Access to the pool is via a notched tree which reaches some 7 meters (22 ft) down to the surface.

From Towale, an unpaved road of sorts runs southward to Suranama village, at the border with Sulsel, 24 km (14 mi) away. From there, bits and pieces of unconnected road head south to Mamuju. However, it's a lot easier to get there by boat.

While the snorkeling off Tanjung Karang is nothing spectacular, there is good diving closer to Donggala as well as off Towale village. During the 1959 Permesta Rebellion, five ships commandeered as troop transports by the Indonesian military were sunk by an American-piloted rebel airplane just off Donggala. One of these ships, the Mutiara, lies on its side, just off the old pier next to the Dutch-built quonset-hut warehouses used to store copra and rattan. While the water tends to be a bit murky here, just a bit further south, close to shore, there are lots of coral species, a fair variety of anemones, purple-veined white and yellow tunicates and some reef fish. An outrigger canoe for snorkeling and exploring the harbor can be rented quite cheaply, complete with paddler.

About 8 km (5 mi) to the south of Donggala on the road to Palu is the Loli Indah recreation park, with swimming pool and children's playground. There is also the smaller port of Wani, whence small boats depart for local destinations along the northern arm up to Tolitoli and down the west coast on the Strait of Makassar and to destinations in South Sulawesi.

The 'northern neck'

The Kaili-speaking regions around Palu and Donggala and along the coasts of the "northern neck"—the long and narrow strip of land connecting Central and North Sulawesi—offer a number of attractions, accessible either by rented car or by any number of minibuses that ply the main roads.

The coasts of the northern neck have

KAL MULLER

long been settled by migrants of Gorontalo, Mandarese, and Bugis origin, who have dominated the fishing villages and established extensive groves of coconuts to produce both oil and copra. The cordillera of mountains is inhabited by scattered tribal groups (*suku terasing*)—including the Tajio, Pendau, Lauje, and others—collectively called "Daya" by coastal dwellers (seemingly a reference to the indigenous Dayak peoples of interior Kalimantan). These highland groups have traditionally subsisted on dry crops, including sweet potatoes, taro, maize and swidden rice, making the descent to the coast occasionally to market forest products and such cash crops as onions, garlic and coffee.

This traditional pattern of highland-lowland relations has changed significantly in recent times. Members of mountain tribes now work alongside Filipino loggers cutting down ebony and other precious woods in the montane forest. The government has resettled whole villages on the coast, providing these local transmigrants with basic housing, implements and seeds to open up wet-rice fields or establish hybrid coconut plantations. As a result, distinctions between the various ethnic groups are no longer easily made according to geography.

The west coast up to Tolitoli

The west coast of the neck still has no surfaced road connecting Palu directly to the town of Tolitoli. Despite its inaccessibility, however, the Tolitoli regency is well worth a trip by local boat from the harbors of Pantoloan or Wani, or by plane from Palu. Approaching by air, the traveler cannot help but be amazed by the endless stands of clove trees below. This region is an ideal one for clove cultivation, as the hills around Tolitoli continuously receive the sea breezes which enable these trees to thrive. Indeed, in the last two decades Tolitoli has been transformed into a veritable boomtown by the income from lucrative cloves.

But there are quiet spots to be found nearby Batu Bangga beach, 12 km (7.5 mi) north of Tolitoli, provides opportunities for swimming or just taking in the scenery, as do the beaches of Lutungan Island, a quick kilometer to the west of Tolitoli and easily reachable by chartered boat.

On the island, the tomb of a former raja of Tolitoli still is a site for pilgrimages. To determine whether their wishes will be fulfilled, the supplicants to the tomb thrust a palm leaf rib into the ground, checking to see whether

upon extracting it the stick is longer (a good sign) or shorter.

At Salumpaga, a village about 70 km (44 mi) north of Tolitoli, you will come across the remnants of another monument to earlier rulers. The towering walls of the crumbling Dutch fort there still evoke the tenuous hold the colonial regime maintained over distant outposts such as Sulawesi.

The east coast

On the east coast of the northern neck, the Trans-Sulawesi highway provides a continuous, if sometimes rugged, link to the provincial border with North Sulawesi, and then on to Gorontalo and Manado. From Palu go north to Tawaeli, then go across the base of the neck to Toboli, just north of Parigi.

This seemingly meandering road, at times a mere track and in stretches often totally washed out, traverses Kebon Kopi, a rolling highland landscape that was a huge coffee plantation in the Dutch era. Now it has mostly been transformed into vast plantations of clove trees, which thrive in the cool, wet montane climate. Farmers sell produce at make-shift stands along the road, while several restaurants reminiscent of American truckstops, and even a *losmen* provide opportunities for refreshment and rest.

Parigi, a Kaili town where the Portuguese first built a fort in 1555 and the Dutch established a gold-trading outpost in 1730, is the starting point for the trip up the northern neck. Proceed north on a partially asphalted road, skirting mangrove swamps and fording streams over which recently washed-away bridges seem always in the first stages of reconstruction.

It is a long, hard journey, often enlivened by the unexpected sight of scampering iguanas or slithering sunbeam snakes that seem to regard the road as a nuisance and an intrusion into their terrain. The road passes mainly through villages of farmers and fishermen, but *losmen* are available in the towns of Tinombo and Tomini for those who would like to remain here for a while to explore the seashore and the interior foothills at a more leisurely pace. Shortly before the border with North Sulawesi, one passes a transmigrant colony of Javanese, Madurese and Balinese settlers. For a brief moment the traveler seems not just to be leaving the province of Central Sulawesi, but to have left this eastern island altogether for the wet-rice fields of inner Indonesia.

—*Greg Acciaoili and Kal Muller*

Palu Practicalities

Includes Donggala. Tel. code: 0451. All prices in US$. S=Single; D=Double. AC=air-conditioned.

Palu is set on the edge of a vast bay ringed by high, grassy hills criss-crossed by small trails. The city has a pleasant, relaxed atmosphere—even the bemo drivers are friendly.

Merpati flies daily to Palu from Ujung Pandang. There are also flights to Palu from Jakarta, Bandung, Denpasar and Surabaya, calling first at Ujung Pandang. (See "Getting to South Sulawesi" in Travel Advisory.) Taxis to and from the airport cost $2.50; you can also catch a *bemo* for the 7-km (4.2 mi) ride into town.

Bemos (also called "Mitsubishi") take you anywhere in town for Rp 200. After dark, more leisurely *dokar* cost Rp300-500, or you can hail passing motorbikes for Rp200.

The **Museum of Central Sulawesi** on Jl. Sapiri, west of the river, houses a large collection of prehistoric stone axes and mortars, pottery burial jars and a wide range of wooden artefacts and basketry. Open 8 to 5 Tues.-Fri., 9 to 2 Sat. and Sun. Closed Mon.

Kain Donggala, the famous *ikat* cloth of Central Sulawesi, is difficult to find in Palu; as yet there are few tourists and the majority of pieces are exported to Jakarta. Ibu Fauzia Hassan, Jl. Jambu 11 (Tel. 22940) has the widest selection of pieces. Prices from $50 for a man's sarong in spun silk, $80 for a woman's *kain* and *selendang*.

ACCOMMODATION

The Hotel Palu Beach, situated on the shore—no beach worth speaking of—looks like a military hospital designed by Le Corbusier on an off day. This formerly first-class hotel offers hefty discounts (currently 30%) to make up for its tatty carpets and empty, cracked swimming pool. The rooms ($20-30 incl. tax and service before discount) have TV, intermittent hot water, a sea-view balcony, real AC and beds with proper sheets and blankets. Service is good and there is a sweeping view of the huge bay from the restaurant.

There are several middle-priced hotels and *wisma*: **Hotel Wisata** on Jl. Sultan Parman 39 has AC rooms from $14; **Buni Nyiur City** on the same road has similarly priced rooms and a restaurant. The **New Dely** Hotel, Jl. Tadulako 17, is clean and efficient with non-AC rooms $7-9; AC $12.50-30. **Hotel Taurus** on Jl. Hasanuddin has small but clean rooms from $3.50-5.

Cheaper accommodations include **Losmen Arafah** on Jl. Sultan Lewara, **Angkasa Raya** on Jl. Danau Poso, **Bukit Indah** on Jl. Maluku, **Losmen Pasific** and **Penginapan Latimojong** on Jl.Gajah Madah. Rooms $2-5.

FOOD

There are several restaurants along Jl. Yos Sudarso, north of Palu Beach Hotel. **Restaurant Meranu Setia Budi** on Jl. Setia Budi 44 serves perhaps the best Chinese-Indonesian food in Palu. The seafood is cheap and delicious. The **Rumah Makan Kembang Joyo** is reputed to be best for chicken dishes. **Padang Raya** on Jl. Iman Bonjol serves spicy Sumatran meat and fish dishes. The **Palu Beach Hotel Restaurant** has a lovely view of the bay and is a good place to linger over a cold beer, though is not noted for its cooking. At night the stalls near the central bridge on Jalan Hasanuddin sell delicious *murtabak* for Rp 250. In the evenings small foodstalls are set up along Jl. Gajah Madah.

LEAVING PALU

From Besusu station on Jl. Dr. Wahidin, minibuses leave north for Gorontalo and Manado, east for Poso and Tentena, and northwest to Donggala.

Merpati (Jl. Hasanuddin 33) flies daily to Luwuk and Tolitoli, to Kendari (Sun. Wed. Fri.), to Manado (Mon. Thur. Sat.) and Poso (Sun. Mon. Thur.). **Bouraq** (Jl. Mawar 5) flies daily to Gorontalo and Manado. Bouraq's number is 21195.

Donggala

Taxis depart for Donggala when full (4 passengers) from Palu's Manonda terminal, near the Pasar Inpres market. It's 55 cents a head, or rent the whole taxi for $2.20 for yourself.

ACCOMMODATION

Wisma Rame, run by Haji Umar, is a small, clean place, $3 a night for a room with attached facilities. Meals can be arranged with prior notice, $1-2. Haji Umar can help you get a local guide (usually one of his relations) as well as a canoe for snorkeling or gliding around the harbor. Guide $3-4 a day, canoe, $3 for a half day with paddler.

Penginapan Anda is cheap at $1.50. There are also the **Penginapan Bruri** ($1.50) and the **Wisma Bakti** ($1.75-2.50).

Horse-drawn *dokar* go anywhere in town for 15 cents. Minibus-taxis leave from the market next to the Wisma Rame, to Towale, 20 cents a head. Or charter one for immediate departure, $2 one-way. Same for Boneage, about 7 km (4.2 mi) away.

SIDE TRIPS

A subdivision of the Kaili ethnic group, called the Da'a, live inland to the south. They are reputed to be quite traditional, some still following their old religion. To reach them, take a regular boat from Donggala to Kasoloan on the west coast (5-7 hours, $1). From there, it's a 20-km (12 mi) climb to Kaluku Nangka village of the Da'a. An English-speaking preacher from Java, married to a local, lives there. Let us know if it was worth it.

—Ian Caldwell

LORE LINDU

Exploring the Western Highlands

Fifty kilometers south of Palu lies the huge Lore Lindu National Park. Covering more than 231,000 hectares (570,570 acres), the park straddles the border between Donggala and Poso districts. This vast and rugged area includes Mt. Nokilalaki and Mt. Tokosa, the entire Lindu Plain with its large lake, the Besoa Valley, and the western sections of the Bada and Napu Valleys. In these three valleys are found the mysterious stone statues and cisterns of a long-vanished culture whose traces continue to intrigue archaeologists.

Most of the park is covered in dense montane forest, inhabited by many of Sulawesi's endemic species—including *babirusa, anoa*, Sulawesi macaques and tarsiers. Though it is often hard to catch a glimpse of these creatures, the avian life of the park is abundant, accessible and very watchable. Whether stalking green imperial pigeons, hornbills, or egrets and herons, the avid bird watcher is not likely to be disappointed. Starting at 300 meters (990 ft) above sea level and rising to 2,610 meters (8500 ft), the park's landscapes are richly varied—dense forests alternate with grassy plains and swampy upland valleys.

While no permits are required to enter Lore Lindu, such projects as climbing Mt. Nokilalaki do require permission from the Nature Preservation (PPA) office on Jalan S. Parman in Palu. There are many points of access to the park. From Palu, minibuses may be taken on a small road through the Palolo Valley to Wuasa (the capital of North Lore, in the Napu Valley), or south through Kulawi as far as Gimpu.

South from Palu

Two roads travel south from the city along either side of the Palu River. Zipping along the main artery on the eastern bank you encounter a succession of Kaili villages, recognizable by the characteristic stilt houses which bear a strong resemblance to Bugis homes, only without the multi-layered gables that denote rank in the South.

At a major intersection near Kalukubula, just south of Palu, you can make a detour to the east to visit Biromaru and Bora, center of the former Sigi rajadom. Here once lived the most powerful *magau*, as Kaili rajas were called—the overlord of the western highlands. Sigi preserved longest the rites per-

GREG ACCIAIOLI

formed by transvestite *bajasa* priests, but unlike the *bissu* of the South, the *bajasa* have now disappeared in this staunchly Islamic area. The mineral waters of the hot springs at Bora are still reputed for their healing properties, and occasional circle dances are performed. (Aficionados of hot springs might also wish to try those at Pesaku in the Dolo subdistrict, some 25 km [16 mi] south of Palu on the main road.)

You can also take the smaller road leading out of Palu along the western banks of the river. This brings you through the Marawola district, with its starkly-eroded mountains towering above sparsely-inhabited savannahs. Farther south towards Binagga, wet-rice fields appear in the midst of ever denser groves of arched coconut trees, now being replaced by dwarf hybrid varieties whose quicker maturation and higher yields, it is hoped, will reinvigorate the local economy. This road then crosses the river to meet up with the main road about 10 km (6 mi) south of Palu, at Dolo.

Continuing south past Sidondo, the main road passes massive irrigation works fed by the Gumbasa River, which drains Lake Lindu. It then begins a gentle ascent into the hills at the village of Pakuli. A steep, winding climb begins in earnest at Tuwa, at the lower end of the Palu Valley. Now the traveler is no longer in the lowland Kaili regions, but has entered the western highlands.

The western highlands

In pre-colonial days the western highlands consisted of a congeries of small chiefdoms paying tribute and performing corvée as warriors for Sigi and other coastal and valley Kaili rajadoms. These upland groups worked swidden fields of rice and tubers cut from the slopes of the mountains and collected sago, supplementing their diet with the plentiful game of the surrounding forests.

Although the Dutch established outposts on the coast as early as the 18th century, it was not until 1903 that colonial forces began to conquer the interior. The fiercest resistance was offered by the people of Kulawi in their fortress on Mt. Momi. Battles raged for 3 months in 1904, until finally an aristocrat of Tuwa was captured and tortured (baked over an open fire at the command of a Dutch officer) to reveal an alternate pathway to Kulawi along the Miu River. After the capture of the Kulawi leader, Toi Torengke, his forces surrendered. The defenders of the neighboring Napu Valley continued to offer resistance, however, until being defeated in a decisive battle at Peore in 1907.

The Dutch set about restructuring local settlements, forcing people down from the hills to open up wet-rice fields in the plain

Opposite: *Bringing vegetables to market by the shores of Lake Lindu, in Kulawi district.* **Above:** *Net fishing in the huge highland lake.*

166   CENTRAL SULAWESI

lands were then divided between the rajas of
Kulawi and of Lore, who ruled under Dutch
supervision and became powerful as a result.

Social changes accelerated once missionaries moved into the area. Soon after establishing a Javanese transmigrant colony in the
Palu Valley in 1913, the Salvation Army began
to convert highland groups from a center in
the southern highlands village of Kentewu.

Today, the peoples of the western high-
lands are overwhelmingly Christian, though
in towns such as Kulawi, Gimpu, Wuasa and
Gintu, numerous Muslim traders of Bugis,
Arab and Pakistani descent are to be found.
Towering wooden church spires—Salvation
Army, Dutch Reformed, and the more recent
Pentecostal and 7th Day Adventist—greet the
traveler on arrival.

There is little of the syncretism that char-
acterizes the Christianity of Tana Toraja here.
Still, local groups are proud of their *hadat*
customs, clothing styles (including ceremonial barkcloth vestments), dances, ways of
greeting and serving guests, as well as forms
of recognition and punishment that continue
to spice marriages, funerals, harvest thanksgiving and other ceremonies that are now
performed under the auspices of the Church.

Visiting Lore Lindu

The village of Wuasa lies on the eastern edge
of Lore Lindu Park, about 100 km (60 mi)
southeast of Palu (a bit over 3 hours by minibus when road conditions are good). Walking
trails lead from here west into the Lindu
Plain or across to Toro, east of Kulawi. These
are infrequently used, however, and hiring a
guide willing to spend two or three nights
traversing the park may be difficult.

The park is more accessible from the
western side from Toro, just southeast of
Kulawi on the main road, about 80 km (50
mi) south of Palu. Local agents at the PPA
office in the village will be able to help
arrange a guide for day-trips or for the trek
across to Wuasa or to the Besoa Valley. The
central part of the reserve accessible from
Toro is its most thickly forested section, with
a watershed of steep ascents and descents.

Another approach to Lore Lindu begins
even before Kulawi at Sidaunta, some 70 km
(42 mi) south of Palu, and there is now a road
adequate for a 4-wheel-drive vehicle from
Sidaunta to Lake Lindu. A bit after noon each
day, horse caravans start out to carry goods
for the four villages around the lake. One can
walk with them, paying a nominal fee to let a

horse carry the bags, or even rent a horse to
ride. Riding can be hazardous, however, as
horses frequently tumble into the ravine
below the trail. The horses and their drivers
usually make the trip in a little over 4 hours,
but the weary walker may require up to 7
hours to traverse the 20 km (12 mi) to the village of Tomado on the lakeshore.

Accommodation in villagers' homes can
be arranged with the headmen of Tomado,
Langko or Anca. Sometimes there is space
available in the Le Petit Soleil research laboratory at the edge of Tomado. (Note: The laboratory was set up to study the schistosome
blood flukes which proliferate in bodies of
standing water in the area—do *not* walk bare-
foot in this region, as schistosomiasis is very
common. Rubber boots are strongly recommended for tramping around the highland
plains of Lindu and Napu.)

Trekking in south Lindu

Three highland valleys around Lore—from
north to south: Napu, Besoa and Bada—are
not only ideal for trekking or horse travel, but
also feature a scattering of megalithic remains of unknown origin. While Wuasa in the
Napu Valley can be reached by minibus,
Besoa or Bada may only be reached on foot
or horseback from Gimpu or Tentena.

From the end of the road at Gimpu, a well-
used trail leads eastward across the southern
stretches of Lore Lindu Park, over the watershed at Ranorano to Hangira in the Besoa
Valley—a hard day's walk. A shelter with roof
and raised floor at Ranorano can be used if
permission has been obtained from the PPA
in Toro.

If instead one proceeds south from Gimpu
on horse or on foot in one of the numerous
horse caravans that periodically leaves with
supplies, one can reach Moa in the southern
Pipikoro region in a good day's journey. After
having spent the night in a villager's house,
another long day of trekking brings you
through a stretch of magnificent forest at the
very southern tip of Lore Lindu Park to the
grassy plains that announce the Bada Valley.
Upon arrival, accommodation can be
arranged in Tuare or Kageroa, or with the
camat of Gintu, capital of Lore Selatan.

You may frequently run into groups of
local people walking up to the highlands, and
it is possible to join up with them. There are
no facilities along the road, so you will have
to depend upon bargaining with local people
for food and accommodation.

—*Greg Acciaioli*

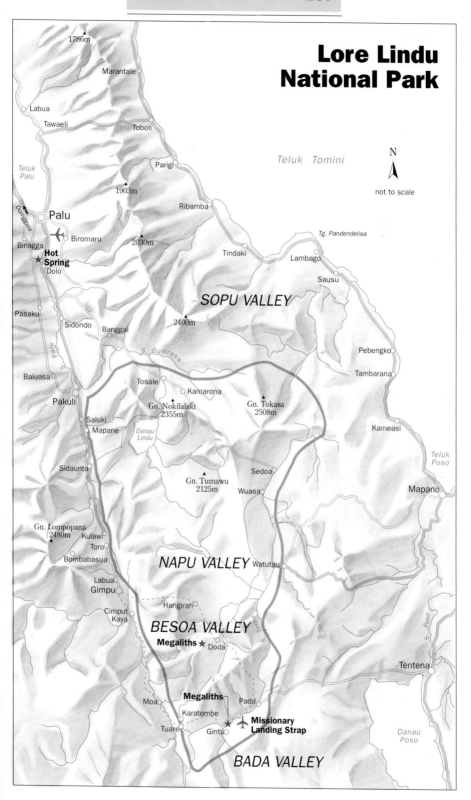

Lore Lindu National Park

1786m

Marantale

Labua

Tawaeli

Toboli

Teluk Palu

Parigi

Teluk Tomini

N

not to scale

1903m

Ribamba

Palu

Biromaru

2030m

Tg. Pandendelisa

Dongasela

Binagga

Hot Spring

Dolo

Tindaki

Lambago

Sausu

SOPU VALLEY

Pasaku

Sidondo

Banggai

2400m

Pebengko

Tambarana

S. njeld

S. Gumrasa

Baluasa

Tosale

Kamarona

Gn. Tokasa
2508m

Pakuli

Gn. Nokilalaki
2355m

Kameasi

Saluki

Mapane

Danau Lindu

Teluk Poso

Sidaunta

Gn. Tumawu
2125m

Sedoa

Wuasa

Mapano

Gn. Lompopana
2480m

Kulawi

Toro

Bombabasua

NAPU VALLEY

Watutau

Labua
Gimpu

Hangirah

S. toille

BESOA VALLEY

Cimput
Kaya

Megaliths ★ Doda

Tentena

Megaliths

Pada

Moa

Karatombe

Missionary Landing Strap

Tuare

Gintu

S. Poso

Danau Poso

BADA VALLEY

BADA VALLEY

Remote and Rugged Land of Megaliths

An imposing phallic figure, minimalistically carved to represent a human form, projects out of the earth at an angle. The face—a few curved lines defining large, round eyes and slightly parted lips—stares westward with a timeless expression as impassive and impenetrable as that of the Sphinx.

This magnificent work of megalithic art—massive, simple and eloquent—retains its awesome, mute power in spite of increasing efforts to develop the area, and even despite the soap scrubs which guardians have recently applied in an attempt to wash away the effects of natural weathering.

Ancient art and modern man

Palindo, as the statue is known locally—along with 13 other statues and many large stone vats—inhabits the Bada Valley which extends 15 kilometers (9mi) south of the Lore Lindu National Park. The Lariang River runs the length of the valley, spanned by three suspension bridges. Along with its tributaries, the Lariang serves to irrigate the valley's rich soils, which are parcelled into neatly terraced rice paddies. Gintu, the capital, is the principal village of the Bada sub-district, with about 1,500 inhabitants. It dominates the area with its handful of government offices, shops and the valley's three TV sets. All in all, some 7,000 Bada people are scattered among 14 villages which dot the valley.

Nothing definite is known either of the origin or the purpose of the megaliths. When the Dutch missionary Dr. Albert C. Kruyt (whose efforts, incidentally, are largely responsible for the high proportion of Protestants in the region) reached Bada in 1908, the megalithic culture had long since disappeared. The inhabitants could provide no clues other than that the statues were already there when their ancestors first arrived in the valley.

The megaliths at Bada draw small numbers of tourists and archaelogists to this remote area. The rugged terrain makes an impressive backdrop for the works of stone: eroded embankments and low-lying mountains two kilometers away complement the rugged grace of the carvings. But for some, this natural setting was not enough.

In 1984 the government persuaded people living in the Bada Valley to construct a huge

carved animals at the edge, very much like the bronze Dong Son drums which made their way to Indonesia from Vietnam in prehistoric times.

Mysteries in stone

No definitive research has yet been done, and estimates of the dates of the statues vary from 3000 BC (most unlikely) to AD 1,300. It is likely that the Bada statues, along with those of the Besoa Valley to the north, are remnants of a megalithic tradition which once spread throughout Indonesia (and continues today in places such as Sumba). In Central Sulawesi, aside from the stone statues and large jars, there is a variety of stone objects which are probably products of the same culture. Walter Kaudern, who lived in the area from 1917 to 1920, gives the best account to date of the megaliths in his *Megalithic Finds in Central Celebes*.

Although the statues of the Bada Valley vary considerably in size—from less than one meter to over four—they are stylistically quite similar. All are roughly oval in shape, with disproportionately large, round faces. The eyes, also round (or slightly oval), are framed by a single curved line which outlines the chin, cheeks and eyebrows. While the faces are carved in high relief, the arms, hands and genitalia (erect penis or parted vagina) are barely raised from the surface of the stone.

wooden house next to the Palindo statue at Sepe, along with a vaguely traditional building which sits behind it. Neither serve any apparent purpose and both are beginning to show signs of shabbiness. For the *coup de grâce*, cement walkways and a number of stone slabs were set up around the statue. There is also a rice barn, with a shaded platform under a raised, rat-proof, but empty storage area. As with the statues themselves, the purpose of the barn remains a mystery, though it provides a good shady spot to sit and look at the back of the statue.

The first Europeans to arrive in the valley, Paul and Fritz Sarasin, trekked through in 1902 but did not notice the megaliths. Dr. Kruyt does mention that propitiatory offerings for abundant harvests were taken to one of the statues; and when rain was lacking, offerings of betel nut were laid in front of the statue known as Tarai Roi. Other early visitors also mention offerings being made to some of the megaliths.

The Besoa Valley, a hard, leech-filled day's walk north from Bada, also has a number of human statues, along with *kalambu*—the large stone jars which are covered with carvings lacking on the ones found in Bada. One of these stone vats has a cover with five

Opposite: *A cistern in the Besoa Valley.*
Above: *The giant Sepe statue known as Palindo.*
Right: *Oba ("the monkey"), squatting in a field.*

It has been suggested that westward-gazing Palindo, the largest of the statues, may be associated with death. For the Toraja, who live some four to five days' walk to the south, west is the direction of death. Linguistic and other cultural similarities between the Toraja and the Bada peoples lend at least partial credence to the theory. The Bada, even after conversion to Christianity, insist on burying their dead facing west, and the Toraja until recently erected megaliths (the stones were roughly shaped but never sculpted) as part of their funerary rituals. The Toraja, like the Bada, sacrifice water buffalo for the souls of the deceased.

Visiting the megaliths

Getting around the Bada Valley to see the megaliths is a wet, muddy affair for nine months of the year. A jeep track links some of the villages; wide footpaths connect the remaining ones. There are frequent stretches of mud, except during the drier part of the year, in June, July and August. Logs span most creeks, but crossing the Malei River's waist-high waters requires some skill or a steadying hand—the bed rocks are slippery. While some of the megaliths can be easily reached from the main tracks or paths, others require navigating through irrigated rice fields and occasional knee-deep mud.

Slogging through the rice fields is in itself a lesson in rice irrigation techniques. You will get a view of water buffalo or teams of oxen churning up the earth to prepare the land. After plowing, the rice shoots which have been raised for 40 days in bamboo-fenced plots are transplanted. A period of alternate three-day floodings and three-day dryings of the fields then takes place, followed by the harvest. The four species of rice planted here require different maturation times: three, four, five or six months. The longest time is for the preferred local variety; the others have been introduced recently into the valley.

Bada economy

Although not overly rich in monetary terms, the Bada Valley's more than 7000 inhabitants enjoy a very comfortable standard of living. The terraced and irrigated rice fields regularly yield a surplus, and coffee is grown as a cash crop. Under government initiatives, cacao and clove trees are being tried out. A recently completed government-funded irrigation scheme added some 1,000 hectares (2,500 acres) of rice paddies to the region. Agricultural experts are trying to convince the people of Bada to sow more than one rice crop per year.

Local gold panners work several of the valley's creeks and rivers, and concentrate on the Malei. According to one local Chinese

Above: *The statue known as Ari Impohi, in Bewa.*
Opposite: *Water buffalo "plow" a rice field.*

shopkeeper, the revenue from gold panning accounts for close to 50 percent of the valley's cash income. It can, however, be a risky occupation: in 1986, 25 men were drowned in a flash flood as they lay sleeping on a small island in the middle of the Malei River.

Even before gold added considerable cash to local incomes, many people were well enough off to prefer taking the MAF plane (service started in 1978) to Tentena, rather than making the two-day hike.

Domestic animals such as water buffalo, cattle, horses, pigs and chickens are plentiful in the valley. Cattle are worth as much as water buffalo (traditionally the most highly valued possessions in many parts of Indonesia) on the barter scale, and prized for their flesh as well as their usefulness as draft animals. Both are used to draw crude plows in the local rice paddies, but water buffaloes are actually more serviceable, as they can plow in areas of deep mud which would be unmanageable for the weaker cattle.

The water buffalo is perfectly adapted to the agricultural conditions of Central Sulawesi. Its reputation as the "tractor of Asia" is well merited. The irrigated rice paddies require extensive aeration before the rice shoots can be planted. Herds of water buffalo, up to two dozen, are driven back and forth in the small, partially flooded paddies, churning the soil with each lumbering step.

The Bada use the water buffalo as a bride price for the traditional marriage ceremonies which usually precede the church ritual. While the aristocracy has lost much of its former privileged status, a noble daughter is still worth a dozen water buffalo, which is quite a sum in real terms. The less blue her blood, the fewer water buffaloes she draws. In deference to "modernization," however the Bada have begun to accept hard cash as part of the bride price if the groom's family and relatives can not come up with enough water buffalo.

If the Bada Valley regularly produces surplus rice and coffee (during the past two decades, the rice crop has failed only once, due to bad weather), getting these items to the market at Tentena is not easy. The twice-weekly MAF flight charges about 14 cents a kilo for freight, and the Cessna's carrying capacity is limited. Men with pack horses levy a fee of about 9 cents per kilo for goods brought to Tentena. So until the road surface improves, the Bada people will receive less for their exports while paying more for essentials such as fuel, matches, tools, soap and clothing. This is typical for the more remote parts of Indonesia.

Funds for construction have been approved but the road work has not yet started. As soon as the roads improve, public transportation will be able to reach the Bada Valley, making it much easier to visit the "Land of the Megaliths."

—*Kal Muller*

BADA MEGALITHS

Mysterious Prehistoric Sculptures

The origin and age of the works of stone that dot the valleys of Bada, Besoa and Napu remain a mystery. Recent excavations of some of the stone cisterns or vats indicate that they probably date back to the first millennium AD (they could be of a later date, but are not likely to be much older than this, as some have speculated). In many areas where they are found, large upright stones (menhirs) are often associated with human sacrifice and with worship of the ancestors. A Swiss explorer Kaudern, who visited the region in 1918-19, made inquiries into the 2-meter (6.5 ft) menhir outside the house temple at Kantewu, southeast of Gimpu.

"When questioned about the stone," wrote Kaudern, "the natives always gave an evasive answer, but for certain reasons I believe it to have been used as a torture pole, to which in olden times, on certain ocasions the victims who were to be killed, were fettered."

Among the major megaliths in the Bada and Besoa area are the following (refer also to the map opposite):

Palindo ("the entertainer"), also known as Raksasa Sepe ("the Sepe giant") or the "Bada Man," located near Sepe, some 1.5 km (1 mi) from Bewa. Over 4 meters (13 ft) in height, this statue is the largest of the subdistrict and certainly the most celebrated of the region. However, it can only be reached by rafting across the Lariang River near Bewa. It is perhaps a representation of Sepe's first mythological inhabitant, Tosaloge. According to local tradition, the Raja of Luwu once ordered 1800 subjects to carry this statue to Palopo as a demonstration that Bada should be considered subject to him, but the effort failed. The statue is said originally to have faced Luwu in the south, but the Bada people turned it around to assert their autonomy. When the Raja of Luwu's followers tried to turn it back, it fell on its side, killing 200 of them. In the past, offerings were brought to this figure before embarking on any new enterprise

such as opening up a new garden.

Tarai Roi ("Banyan Tree") or Pombekadoi, found in the backyard of the former district head of Bada in the village of Gintu. This statue presumably was erected above a buried mass of gold. Its presence symbolized Gintu's pre-eminent position above all other villages of south Lore—the place where all disputes had to be resolved.

Dula Boe or **Baulu** (the "water buffalo") at Badangkai. According to local lore, this statue now rests askew because its owner, irate at having lost a pig, kicked it over.

Tinoe, located about one kilometer from Bakekau. Bearing the likeness of a woman and child, this statue may once have represented a fertility deity. In the past, farmers offered water buffalo to her to insure a good harvest. Even hunters were supposed to request her permission, and after the hunt to hang the skin of their prey upon her head.

Loga ("relieved heart"), in Bada. Standing askew on a hill out in the fields, she is said to be gazing emptily at her husband, now a statue placed some distance away, who was sentenced to death for committing adultery.

Langke Bulawa ("gold anklet"), in Bomba. She was perhaps a patroness of the local *haute coûtume*, through whom the upper-class ladies justified their exclusion from labor in the fields.

Oboka, in Bulili. Now missing its head, this statue was once the protector of the local inhabitants, who gathered around it with fires blazing. In the past it was used as a sacred place to which people brought offerings in order to reach particular goals or fulfill personal desires.

Ari Impohi, in Bewa. This name signifies that the monolith was once the central post of a now vanished ritual meeting house.

There are a number of other works to be seen here, including a stone carved with the motif of banyan tree leaves; the four judgment stones where the raja formerly held court (including the Tohemu stone said to have been Sawerigading's umbrella left behind on his visit to Bada); and the large mortar stone where the first fruits of the harvest were hulled to ensure abundance.

Vast stone cisterns, called *kalamba*, which may have been used as baths or as burial chambers for aristocrats, are found scattered throughout the region. Interestingly—and mysteriously—all of the objects in the area are made from a type of grey stone of which there are no deposits in the near vicinity.

—*Greg Acciaoili*

Bada Valley Megaliths

1. Bada Man/Sepe Giant/Palindo ("Entertainer"); 4.5 m, faces west

2. Mesinga (wearing a scarf); Small, fallen statue with faded features. Wears a bark-cloth headdress. Nearby are 13 stone vats.

3. Maturu ("Sleeping"); Statue is on its back, about 3.5 m long.

4. Oba ("Monkey"); Nice, smallish statue in a sawah.

5. Mpeime; Large megalith, lying down. Plans are afoot to right it.

6. Tarai Roe ("Banyan Tree"); Back of the former raja's house. Small, with faded features

7. Maturu ("Sleeping"); Large statue lying down.

8. Dula Boe/Baulu ("Water-buffalo"); The face is like the other megaliths, but the body, lying down, is like a water-buffalo.

9. Torumpana (a place name meaning, perhaps, "Noble Arrow"); Faded features, hard to get to. Just 1 m high. For archaeologists and masochists only.

10. Tinoe (a place name meaning, perhaps, "Late Woman"); Female, 1.5 m, with nice features.

11. Oboka; In the village, missing its head which lies face-down nearby. The megalith is in a fenced-off area with some stone jars.

12. Ari Impohi ("Main House Pillar"); Small statue, good features. At the intersection of the village's main streets.

13. Loga ("Relieved Heart"); Female, 1.5 m, faces west. Nice view and easy to reach.

14. Langke Bulawa ("Gold Anklet"); Female, 2 m, faces west. Tough mud and thorn path, plus a $1.25 fee from the locals. (No charge for any of the others.) Not really worth it, except for the archaeologists and masochists again.

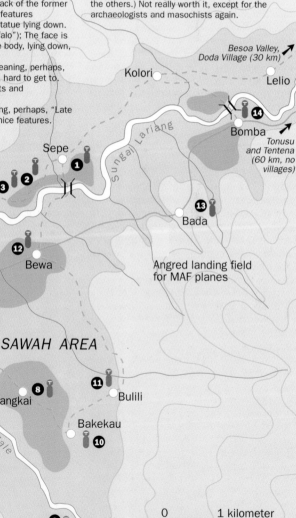

Besoa Valley,
Doda Village (30 km)

Kolori

Lelio

Sungai Lariang

14

Bomba

Tonusu
and Tentena
(60 km, no
villages)

Sepe

1

Kageroa,
Tuare and
Gimpu

5   4

3   2

Lengkeka

13

Bada

12

Bewa

Angred landing field
for MAF planes

6

Gintu

7

SAWAH AREA

Runde

11

8

Bulili

Badangkai

Bakekau

10

Sungai Male

9

0   1 kilometer

POSO AND TENTENA

A Huge and Enchanting Highland Lake

Poised precisely in the center of Sulawesi, Lake Poso appears as the jeweled head of a cosmic pivot about which the pinwheel arms of the island flail as if blown by massive forces. According to local legends, this area is indeed the pivot around which heaven and earth revolve—and long ago a rope connecting the two was located in the vicinity of the huge highland lake.

The inhabitants of the hills and mountains of the Poso area—formerly known as the Bare'e-speaking or East Toraja—were once famous for their inter-tribal raiding and head-hunting expeditions. Though they were at one time united under a powerful raja, when the ruler was captured by Bugis warriors sent by the ruler of mighty Luwu, the people decided to secede. They symbolized their claim for separation by ramming a tremendous stone pillar into the ground on the hill named Pamona above the shores of Lake Poso. This pillar remains here to this day.

The Pamona people of this region, as they are now called, are considered the great success story of Christian missionization in Indonesia. The Dutch Reformed Church missionary Albertus C. Kruyt landed on the southern shores of Tomini Gulf in 1892 from his post in Gorontalo, and began his efforts in the town of Poso. Displaying incredible patience and tolerance—all the while documenting local customs that his missionary work would eventually cause to disappear— Kruyt waited 17 long years before celebrating his first baptism. Within 5 years after that, however, a school for missionaries had been founded at Pendolo at the southern tip of Lake Poso, and in 1947 an independent Church of Central Sulawesi was established. Today most of the highland Pamona are Christians.

Although rarely visited by foreign tourists, the upland region around Lake Poso and the town of Tentena makes a perfect resting spot on the long Trans-Sulawesi Highway, and is a good jumping-off point for visits to the surrounding area, including the Bada Valley and its mysterious megaliths. The road connecting Tentena to the north with Poso and Palu is quite good. However the road leading south from Pendolo to Wotu is still under construction and involves a grueling 4-wheel-drive trip that takes 6-7 hours just to

IAN CALDWELL

KAL MULLER

cover a distance of less than 100 km (60 mi). The road is closed for several hours each day for construction, and is subject to frequent landslides—particularly in the rainy season.

The tidy town of Poso

The modern district capital of Poso is a clean, shady town breathing an air of efficiency, with its Dutch-inspired churches and administrative buildings. Most of the town's main hotels and eating establishments are within a two-block radius of the Poso River, which empties into the Gulf of Tomini. You will find them all on the east side of town, in the vicinity of the harbor (from which you can catch boats across the gulf to Gorontalo). On the west side is the central *pasar*, which can be reached by small outriggers that periodically ply the river.

Sadly, the beaches of Poso have pretty well succumbed to urban pollution. Swimming and snorkeling are still possible, however, at the fishing village of Kayamanya to the northwest of the *pasar,* and at Polande, a two-hour drive to the west.

About 7 km (4 mi) south of Poso along the lilting road to Tentena is the village of Tagolu. This is the place to pick up ebony wood carvings, as works from around the province are on display in stores and shops. Although shops throughout the province (and even the Mutiara Airport in Palu) sell the sets of sprouting coconuts, miniature hornbills, and other mass-produced items worked here, the workshops themselves offer these at far lower prices (bargaining required), and feature a greater and more imaginative variety of carvings—from lamp tables to humorous miniatures.

Tentena

The small church town of Tentena lies 57 km (35 mi) to the south of Poso on the northeastern corner of beautiful Lake Poso, with enchanting views across this huge inland lake, whence cooling breezes waft across the town. There are several very comfortable, if not luxurious, hotels right at the water's edge. Where the Poso River empties the lake, a quaint covered-bridge connects the two sides of Tentena. Most facilities, including the lakeside docks, are on the town's eastern side, although the western side contains the Missionary Aviation Fellowship (MAF) airstrip that provides Cessna service to the Lore highlands in the west and to Kolonodale and Baturibi in the east.

In Tentena itself are several caves full of human remains and roughly carved mini-coffins called *peti mayat.* The most accessible of these lies but five minutes' walk from

Opposite: *The tortuous portion of the Trans-Sulawesi Highway leading from the south up to Lake Poso.* **Above:** *Huge Lake Poso is said to be the "second clearest" in the world.*

behind the Protestant Church's regional headquarters. This is an overhang rather than a true cave—bones and coffins lie scattered about, while the skulls have been neatly stacked in parallel rows on top of each other.

It takes somewhat longer to reach the Latea caves, and the going is a bit more muddy and slippery, involving two crossings of Latea creek (Kuala Latea). There are two caves at this spot. The lower one holds a few clay pots with bones and coffins; the higher one is full of coffins, mostly dilapidated. Don't bother crawling into the caves; there's nothing to see other than the bats that you will find swishing about you.

There are also the well-known Pamona Caves, located at the far side of the Poso River near the Theological School. Nine chambers but no human remains. Nearby there are pleasant places to sit and watch small canoes paddled or poled around the entrance of the Poso River.

Lake Poso

About 37 kilometers (23 mi) long and 13 kilometers (8 mi) at its widest point, Lake Poso covers approximately 32,000 hectares (80,000 acres). It lies at an elevation of 515 meters (1675 ft), bounded by steeply sloping mountains to the west and gentle hills to the east.

A kaleidoscope of greens blanket the surrounding shores—dense, primary rain forest and lush plantations of cloves and coffee, as neatly arranged as 18th-century European armies—are broken only by a dozen villages with neighboring expanses of terraced rice fields whose sensuous, velvety greens turn gradually to a golden yellow when the grain is ready for harvest.

Locals, quoting a foreign expert, proudly proclaim that Lake Poso is the "second clearest" in the world. Be that as it may, the waters are transparent indeed—ranging from a light turquoise color near the shore to a dark blue out in the lake's depths.

Of Lake Poso's five indigenous fish species, two have almost become extinct due to the introduction of carp and catfish (*lele*) from Java. Most impressive of the native species are the huge eels, which reach over two meters (6.5 ft) in length and can weigh up to 20 kg (44 lb). The eels are caught in wide, V-shaped traps just downstream from the covered bridge at Tentena in the waters of the swift-flowing Poso River. It is perhaps these large eels which are at the root of rumors about the sighting of a huge dragon-snake with a body well over 30 meters (98 ft)

long. But then again, perhaps the Loch Ness monster has a cousin in Lake Poso.

You can charter various types of craft for a trip around the lake: outriggers, canoes or motorized boats. The views on the lake are spectacular. Get an early start and bring lunch or snacks. Plan on returning by mid-afternoon, for the waters start to get choppy then and the rough waves can capsize small boats. If things get too rough, you might have to pull into the nearest village and spend the night. There are worse fates.

A trip straight around the lake non-stop takes four to five hours. You might want to stop, however, to watch the fishermen or to take a swim. If you have goggles, take a look at the lake's crabs and exotic shellfish. Lake Poso is quite deep—440 meters (1430 ft).

Landing at Taipa village on the western shore, you can hike 3 kms (1.8 mi) up to a steep promontory which juts a short way over the lake—the perfect spot for photographs. You could also go up the steep hillside directly from the shore to the vantage point, but it's rough and slippery going. And you might miss the occasional wild pig noose-trapped by the roadside.

Further down the western shore, the lakeside Bancea Orchid Reserve offers seven hectares (17 acres) and some 45 species of flowers, which bloom in January, May and August. Along the shore, you might see water buffalo bathing or standing around waiting for something to do.

The main road to the east and south takes you through mountains inhabited by the Mori people. In precolonial times the Mori were constantly warring with Pamona groups and with the sultanate of Bungku on the east coast. The road does not offer any views of the lake, however—you only see it again when approaching Pendolo at the lake's southern tip, as mountains cut off the view. There is, however, a short 12-km (7 mi) road south along the eastern lakeshore leading from Tentena down to Peura village, which climbs up to reveal spectacular panoramas then cuts through a stretch of rice fields.

Along the western side of the lake, a track to Pendolo hugs the shore, climbing a hill just beyond Taipa village. But the road is unspeakable, with bridges often washed out entirely, although work is proceeding slowly to improve things. It is rumored that some day this trail may even be covered with asphalt, which would make it one of the most lovely roads in the world.

—*Kal Muller and Greg Acciaoili*

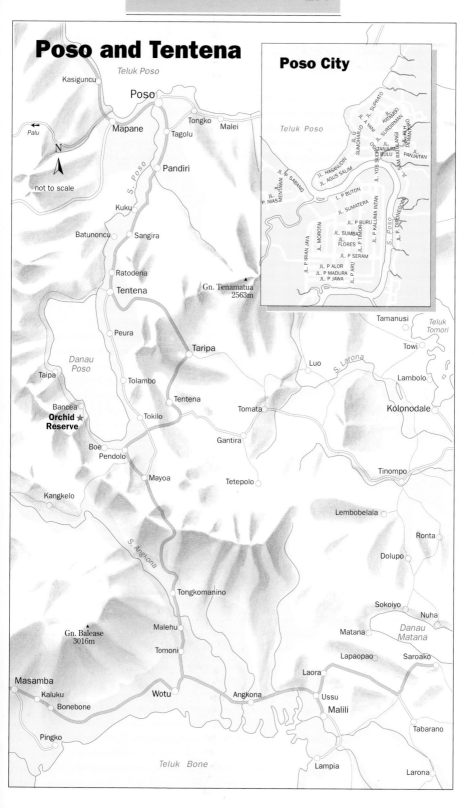

Poso and Tentena

Teluk Poso

Kasiguncu

Poso

← Palu

Mapane

N

not to scale

Tongko

Malei

Tagolu

S. POSO

Pandiri

Kuku

Batunoncu

Sangira

Ratodena

Tentena

Gn. Tenamatua
2563m

Peura

Taripa

Danau
Poso

Luo

S. Larona

Towi

Lambolo

Taipa

Tolambo

Tentena

Bancea

Orchid ★
Reserve

Tokilo

Tomata

Kolonodale

Boe
Pendolo

Gantira

Mayoa

Tetepolo

Tinompo

Kangkelo

Lembobelala

Ronta

Dolupo

S. Angkona

Tongkomanino

Sokoiyo

Nuha

Gn. Balease
3016m

Malehu

Matana

Danau
Matana

Tomoni

Lapaopao

Saroako

Laora

Masamba

Kaluku

Wotu

Angkona

Ussu

Malili

Bonebone

Tabarano

Pingko

Teluk Bone

Lampia

Larona

Poso City

Teluk Poso

JL. U SUMOHARJO
JL. A YANI
JL. SUPRATO
JL. KATAMSO
JL. SURDIRMAN
JL. TANJUNG BULU
JL. RATULANGI
SAM
JL. DEMANTORO
H. PANJAITAN

JL. HASANUDIN
JL. AGUS SALIM
JL. P SABANG
JL. MEN TAWAI
JL. P. NIAS
JL. OSCAR SUDKE

JL. YOS SUDKE
JL. P TIMORDI

L. P BUTON

JL. SUMATERA

JL. MOROTAI

JL. P BURU

JL. SUMBA

JL. P FLORES

JL. KALIMA INTAN

JL. P DIPONEGORO

S. POSO

JL. P IRIAN JAYA

JL. P SERAM

JL. P ARU

JL. P ALOR

JL. P MADURA

JL. P JAWA

Tamanusi

Teluk Tomori

EASTERN PENINSULA

'Fire Cape' and Other Rarities

The eastern arm of Central Sulawesi, including the Banggai archipelago nestling below the head of this peninsula, is the province's least-known region. Many ethnic groups inhabit this isolated area—several of the small groups living in the rugged interior were once coastal dwellers who fled to escape the exactions of the Sultan of Ternate and the Raja of Banggai, who acted as his local representative. These peoples subsist on sago and shifting tuber agriculture in infertile mountain terrain, living in scattered groups of two to ten families. The other major ethnic group in this region are the Bajau, the so-called boat dwellers (though many of them are now found in houses on land near the sea).

The majority of peoples along the coasts and in the foothills were Christianized in the early 20th century, and like the Mori and Pamona to the west now have their own independent church. The coasts are full as well of Muslim fishermen and traders. As a vassal of the Sultan of Ternate, the Islamic raja of the Banggai Islands is of reputed Javanese descent and has maintained Islam as the dominant religion of these small islands.

Ampana

The small port of Ampana, 150 km (90 mi) and 6 hours by jeep or motorcycle from Poso (the condition of unbridged rivers permitting), is a town of some 15,000 souls that serves as a focal point of land communications between Poso and Luwuk, as well as providing a sea link between Poso, the Togian Islands in the Gulf of Tomini, and Gorontalo in the north. The area's chief exports are rattan and copra, followed by damar resin, candlenuts and cloves.

Ampana has seen just enough foreigners that you will be deluged with cries of "hello-meester" along with "where you from" and "wasurnem" (What's your name?). Comic relief comes in the form of unusual phrases such as "bad man"—somehow learned by cute little girls—along with the occasional "I love you" from their older sister. Don't get excited, they don't mean it.

While the town lines a wide bay for a kilometer or so, all the action focuses on a small market by a dock and bus terminal. Just in front of the market are local horse-drawn car-

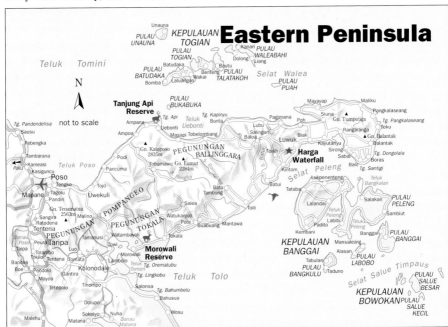

riages or *bendi*, some quite colorful. Drivers tend to zoom out of the lot with Ben-Hur racing spirit. They charge Rp 100-200for a ride, depending on distance.

A visit to 'Fire Cape'

The Tanjung Api Reserve lies on the coast a few kilometers east of Ampana, less than an hour's ride by motorized outrigger. The ride there and back can be beautiful, except during December and January, when the seas become rough. As you pull away from shore,

Ampana falls rapidly into relief: a cluster of nondescript buildings lined by a sea of coconut trees along the bay ʼ7ith steep hills behind. Fishing boats with colorful sails ply the waters, which are incredibly clear. Steep, vegetation-clad slopes plunge directly into the sea, and around each promontory a new cove is revealed. Schools of dolphins are often sighted along the way.

The name Tanjung Api literally means "Fire Cape" and natural gas seeps up at several points offshore, gurgling to the surface through sand and coral formations. Gas also escapes through cracks in a small cliff next to the shore, and is said to ignite spontaneously upon contact with the air, though a match helps. Strangely, the gas does ignite if water is thrown on the rocks or the earth nearby. Best to see this unique phenomenon during a shower or at night. There is a small shelter here but all supplies must be brought along.

In the immediate vicinity, a small crocodile or two may scurry away but that is all the game you will see. A well-trodden path through the sparse underbrush of the forest gives the opportunity for pleasant walks across the cape. It may be possible here to catch a glimpse of the larger endemic species that inhabit the reserve—including Sulawesi macaques, cuscus, tarsiers, *babirusa,* pythons, wild boars and deer.

While the swimming in this area is fine, the snorkeling tends to be disappointing as

much of the coral has been destroyed by dynamite fishing. The government has now forbidden this, but it's too late. Reef fish are few, but they are around: clown fish defending their anemone homes, angelfish, colorful sea trout and a few other species. Near the gas seepages there is less dynamite damage, but the sea floor sprouts only reed-like seaweed. Small coral formations are draped with the occasional blue starfish and shelter small clams which reveal intricate, multicolored swirls when open for feeding.

A bit over an hour northeast of Tanjung Api, the tiny island of Bukabuka harbors a small fishing village known for its delicious coconut crabs—huge animals feeding exclusively on coconuts, which fetch $3 or more apiece at Ampana's market.

The Togian Islands

To get really off the beaten track, hop on one of the small boats running between Ampana and Gorontalo (in North Sulawesi), with stops along the way at the Togian Islands in the middle of the gulf. Several mixed cargo/passenger boats crisscross Tomini Gulf on relatively fixed schedules. The boats usually stop at Wakai, Ketupat and Dolong—villages which look better from a distance than up close. The waters under the picturesque stilt-houses serve as sewers and garbage dumps, and are only partially cleaned by the tides. Houses further inland are nondescript, covered with rusting sheet metal roofs. Foreigners in these parts are few and far between, but the locals have all learned the dreaded "hello meester."

The islands' forests are one of the main habitats of the *babirusa*, while the beaches along the coast function as hatcheries for sea turtles and frigate birds. The Togian Islands

Above, left: *Fisherman spread their haul of trepang near Pagimana.* **Above, right:** *Coasting off Batudaka in the Togian Islands.*

are also unusual in being surrounded by all major coral reef environments, having 115 species drawn from 59 genera.

While the islands may be a naturalist's delight, they also possess latent powers of destruction. The eruption of Mt. Colo, which blew apart Unauna Island in 1983, was one of the most devastating in recent history. A cloud of ash 15,000 meters (9 miles) high covered 90 percent of the island, destroying all houses, crops, animals, coral and shore fish except in a sheltered narrow eastern strip. Miraculously, all the island's inhabitants were safely evacuated.

The Togian islanders are a diverse bunch. Indigenous ethnic groups include the Kaili (on Unauna), the Pamona (on Togian and Batudaka, the two large, westernmost islands) and the Saluan (on the other islands; they also occupy parts of the eastern peninsula). Also present are Bugis and Bajau immigrants. The Bajau language has become a kind of *lingua franca* in these parts, and Islam has been well established here since the 17th century, having arrived from Gorontalo.

Fishing is the primary way of life, so you see scores of tiny boats with striped, triangular sails, sometimes supported by spidery outriggers, cruising to and from fishing grounds that are often quite far out to sea. On the open sea, flying fish scurry along, their beating tails forming overlapping circles on the surface until they gain enough altitude to swoop amazingly long distances.

Most of the commerce is controlled by the local Chinese who own the larger stores, importing foodstuffs and household items while purchasing and exporting sea products that include dried and salted fish, trochus shells, trepang, sharks' fins and mother-of-pearl. Pearls, including the occasional rare black one, are taken to Gorontalo for sale.

As the islands hold a fair potential for pearling, a local Chinese-Indonesian at the village of Wakai, Edi Jusuf, has equipped a boat with a hookah rig for diving. He is also planning to purchase scuba gear, both for pearling operations and to rent to tourists. Edi knows the good dive spots where coral formations are intact and reef fish abound.

Several boats also connect the islands with the town of Pagimana, about 160 km (100 mi) further east of Ampana on the mainland. A church on a rise just in back of the port area here gives a panoramic view of the bay and Tongkabu village just across the bay, dominated by a mosque and settled by Bajau people. At Pagimana you are within 62 km (38 mi) of Luwuk, often hard to reach by road from Ampana as rains and rushing rivers tend to make the minibus passage a long, masochistic endeavor.

Luwuk and the Banggai Islands

Luwuk is the capital of Sulawesi Tengah's easternmost district, controlling commerce

KAL MULLER

and communications to the Banggai Islands, formerly under the sway of the powerful Sultan of Banggai. Like Palu, it was transformed into a government center during World War II by the Japanese.

Nearby Kilo Lima, a white sandy beach 5 km (3 mi) away, offers good diving and swimming. A road southwest along the coast brings the traveler to 75-meter-high (230 ft) Hanga Hanga Waterfall, 3 km (1.8 mi) from the city. Farther down the road is Batui, a maleo bird hatchery supervised by PPA officials. In the other direction, 96 kilometers (60 mi) east of Luwuk, is the Bangkiriang Reserve hatchery. Three hours away by boat lie the Banggai Islands.

Up to half a century ago, the authority of the Islamic Raja of Banggai on Peleng Island even extended to supervising the gathering of maleo bird eggs from the hatchery at Bakiriang, about 100 km (60 mi) away. Besides receiving a tax on all eggs collected, the raja personally received the first 100 eggs and approved the harvest, after which others were allowed to consume the remainder.

Though recognizing the depredations that the "piratical" Banggai raja allowed his subjects and the sea rovers from Ternate, some ecologists have dubbed him one of Indonesia's first resource managers because of his role in the maleo egg harvest. Today such protection is exercised by the Nature Preservation (PPA) department. A permit to visit the maleo hatcheries must be obtained from the PPA agents stationed at Batui, or from the guard post at Bakiriang Reserve.

In contrast to the strict monitoring of the maleo hatcheries, the population of dugongs that range the waters of the Banggai archipelago have long received insufficient protection. These sea cows have been hunted at a level that has not allowed them to maintain their numbers. Despite the frequency with which they continue to feed in the reefs and seagrass meadows surrounding the islands, their shyness and the turbid water around their feeding grounds makes them difficult to view, though the determined or fortunate traveler with a knowledgeable boat guide (preferably not a hunter) may catch a glimpse of them in these waters.

The raja's house on the large island of Peleng is still well preserved, though the raja no longer functions as the ruler of this backwater region. Nearby Banggai Island offers abundant beaches, with corals and brightly-colored fish making for good snorkeling. On the western coast of Banggai pearl fishers can be seen plying their trade.

Kolonodale and surroundings

Some 180 km (110 mi) east of Tentena, Kolonodale lies on the southern shore of Tomori Bay, a westward protrusion of the Gulf of Tolo. Formerly a minor trading town within the Bungku rajadom, Kolonodale has a history of contact with incoming Bugis traders, as well as with the Bajau sea people who have long plied the shores of east Sulawesi, fishing and hunting trepang.

Today Kolonodale is best known as the gateway for the Morowali Nature Reserve, a 160,000-hectare (395,200 acre) wilderness area of unspoiled rain forest, containing three substantial mountains (Tokala, Tambusisi and Morowali), five major rivers (the name Morowali means "rumbling" or "growling" in the Wana language, referring to the sound of the rivers streaming across their stony beds), and the eerily quiet Ranu Lakes where the exhalation of marsh gases keeps birds and beasts away.

In 1980, the British expedition Operation Drake conducted a four-month survey of endangered species to celebrate the quadricentennial of Sir Francis Drake's running aground on a reef off Morowali. (He was only able to free the Golden Hind by jettisoning eight tons of spices and eight heavy pieces of ordnance). As a result, the area was declared a reserve rather than being developed as a transmigration site. The reserve hosts hundreds of unique butterflies and beetles in addition to *anoa, babirusa* and maleo birds.

Morowali can be approached from Kolonodale across Tomori Bay or directly from Baturubi on the bay's eastern edge, where the MAF maintains a landing strip. Although Kolonodale does have a hotel, the reserve itself has no formal accommodation for travelers. Arrangements may be made to stay with coastal Bajau people around Baturubi, or among the Wana people who practice shifting agriculture and hunt and gather forest products in the mountainous interior.

The Wana are also said to make excellent guides for treks into the reserve. Care should be taken during the rainy season (from March to September, especially in May), as heavy rainfall (3500 mm to 4500 mm) can transform the low-lying areas into seasonal swamps and suddenly change the courses of the major rivers.

— Kal Muller and Greg Acciaoili

Left: *A dramatic sunset at Ampana.*

Central Practicalities

All prices in US$. S=Single, D=Double. AC=air-conditioned.

Central Sulawesi is a vast, mountainous province of virgin forests and rugged scenery. Until recently, few Westerners visited Central Sulawesi, which is cut off from the south by a natural wall of jungle and mountain. But recent improvements to the Trans-Sulawesi Highway between Palopo and Poso, as well as a regular Toyota Land Cruiser service between Mangkutana and Pendolo (the worst stretch of the crossing) now bring in some 200 visitors a month. Yet the province is so large that for several months of the year you can travel for days without meeting another foreigner.

The main attractions of Central Sulawesi are Lake Poso and the megaliths of the Bada, Besoa and Napu valleys. The Lore Lindu National Park, which offers magnificent trekking across wild savannahs and deep river gorges, can be entered either from the east via Tentena on the Trans-Sulawesi Highway, or by hiking in from the west via Gimpu, on the southern end of the Palu valley. The crossing takes about a week on foot if you want to see most of the megaliths.

GETTING THERE

The easiest way to reach the hinterlands of Central Sulawesi is by flying directly into either Palu or Poso (see "Practicalities" for Palu and Poso). From these spots you will have a relatively painless ride/hike connection into the valleys.

Those making the overland trip up from the south are bound for adventure. It takes 36 hours (including an overnight rest in Pendolo) to get to Poso from Palopo, via Wotu, Pendolo and Tentena using a combination of 4WD Land Cruisers, boats and minibuses. The road from Tongkomanino to Pendolo is still under construction and is closed for several hours each day. The starting point for the journey is Mangkutana, a few kilometers north from Wotu on the Palopo-Malili highway. Buses to Mangkutana leave from Palopo until about 16:00 each day; the fare is $1.20 and the journey takes three hours. At Mangkutana, 4WD vehicles take you to Pendolo, at the foot of Lake Poso.

It's best to stay overnight in Pendolo and leave the next morning for Tentena at around 06:00 on the ferry *Pamona*, arriving around 11:00, fare $1. There are also smaller motorized *prahu*. From Tentena, a minibus takes you into Poso along a good road for a further $1. Alternatively, you could travel straight through from Mangkutana to Poso by Land Cruiser: with minor hold-ups, the journey should take under 20 hours. From Rantepao there are also coaches which attempt the crossing to Poso. These are strictly for the foolhardy.

The fare of $8.50 from Mangkutana to Pendolo (less than 100 km/60 mi) or $11.50 to Poso gives an idea of the difficulty of the journey. The scenery is wild and the jungle comes down to the edge of the road. Anything other than a front seat means an uncomfortable journey with 8 or 9 other passengers along what is simply the worst road in Sulawesi. From time to time you are thrown violently as the vehicle heaves and pitches its way up an almost impossible track. Landslides—some of them involving several tons of boulders and earth—are an almost daily occurence and the road is virtually impassible in the wet season. Several people die each year when their vehicles slide off the edge of the ravine. Yet despite all this, coaches and even trucks—some without tire chains—attempt the crossing every day, bogging down and holding up traffic at regular intervals. Allowing for the occasional landslide, the journey to Pendolo takes 6-7 hours. In the wet season it may take several days. The Land Cruisers leave Mangkutana only when they have enough passengers; be prepared for long delays. The road is closed periodically for construction work and will take several years to surface.

Jawa Indah is the first travel agent on the left as you enter Mangkutana. Presently, as many as 30 privately owned Toyota Land Cruisers ply the route between Mangkutana and Pendolo, depending on the demand. There are several *losmen* in Mangkutana; the **Penginapan Sumber Urip**, next door to Jawah Indah, has presentable rooms with bathroom for $2.30.

Penginapan Melati Mekar, just up the road, has rooms for $2.30-8.50. Alternatively, you can sleep at the Jawa Indah *warung* for nothing if you are traveling through them. If there are no clear signs of departure when you arrive, it is best to walk up the road and book at the other agencies and take the first vehicle that leaves.

Poso

Poso is a small port town on the shores of Tomini Bay, and the gateway to the rarely visited eastern regions of Central Sulawesi. There is little to see or do in Poso; for most travelers it is simply a stopoff point en route to Palu. The large market on the western side of the Poso River is worth an early-morning visit by *sampan* (a small wooden boat). There is a reasonable beach at Kanawo, 8 km (5 mi) to the west. If you leave early from Tentena, it is possible to avoid staying in Poso: you can eat lunch there and catch the afternoon coach to Palu, arriving late in the evening.

Bemos will take you anywhere in Poso for Rp200, though most places are easily reached by foot.

ACCOMMODATION

The **Hotel Bambu Jaya** on Jl. Agus Salim 105, right on the seashore, is the perfect place to recover from the overland journey. Clean and breezy, rooms with own bathroom from $7 non-AC,

$11-22 AC. Next door is the Bambu Jaya restaurant: the only possible drawback is the proposed Karaoke lounge. There is little competition at the price. The waterfront **Hotel Wisata** on Jalan Patimura 19 has large, gloomy rooms with mosquitoes for $6-12, depending on whether the AC is working. The **Anugrah Inn** on Jl. Pulau Samosir is better ($4 non-AC, $8 AC with simple breakfast) but away from the beach. The **Hotel Nels** has rooms with bathroom for $4.50-8.50. Cheaper, *losmen*-style accommodations include the **Penginapan Poso** and the **Penginapan Beringin** ($2-3), both on Jl. Pulau Sumatera, and **Penginapan Sulawesi** on the corner of Jl. Imam Bonjol and Jl. Agus Salim.

Money can be changed at **Bank Negara Indonesia 1946** on Jl. Yos Sudarso.

FOOD

The **Bambu Jaya Restaurant** serves decent Chinese-Indonesian food, but the **Rumah Makan Jawa Timur** on Jl. Pulau Sumatra is cheaper and better. Further along the same road is the **Rumah Makan Padang Raya** serving spicy Sumatran cuisine. The **Rumah Makan Mekar** on Jl. Imam Bonjol and **Warung Lumayan** on Jl. Teluk Umar offer cheaper Indonesian food.

LEAVING POSO

Merpati flies to Palu on Mondays, Fridays and Sundays and to Luwuk on Sundays, Mondays and Thursdays. Public transport to the airport is difficult: **Merpati** will collect you at your hotel for $1.80. The **Merpati** office on Jl. Pulau Sumatra 69A (Tel. 94619) also houses the **Bina Wiasta** bus company, which runs AC and non-AC coaches to Palu leaving at 13:00, 14:00 and 22:00. The fare is $4 AC, $3 non-AC and the journey takes about 6 hours. Most of the road is now surfaced. Boats for Gorontalo in North Sulawesi leave every two or three days: fares from $11. The journey takes two days, calling at Dolong in the Togian Islands, where there are unspoiled coral reefs. To the east, Ampana can be reached in about 6 hours by minibus for $5. Tanjung Api can be reached in 45 minutes by boat from Ampana. At Ampana, the road continues 10-12 hours east along the coast to Luwuk.

Tentena

Tentena is a little Christian town set on the northeastern edge of Lake Poso, with white sand beaches and high, forested mountains. The town is the headquarters of the Central Sulawesi Christian Church, which operates a twice-weekly flight into Lore Lindu National Park (see below). The weather here is cool (the lake is 575 meters/1870 ft above sea level), and coffee, cloves and vegetables grow on the surrounding hills. The two halves of the town are connected by a covered bridge.

The Pamona people who live around Lake Poso are distantly related to the southern Toraja. But the old Central Sulawesi culture is now extinct: Dutch missionaries arrived in the 1880s and conversion was more rapid and complete than in Toraja.

From Palu, the capital of Central Sulawesi province, 10 hours by bus via Poso, about $5. Or the once-a-week MAF flight in their 5-passenger Cessna, $43. From South Sulawesi and Toraja-land, via Wotu, Mangkutana then a horrible stretch to Pendolo on the south shore of Lake Poso, whence by boat to Tentena. Much easier from Palu, which has regular air links with Ujung Pandang, Manado and Balikpapan.

ACCOMMODATION

The best view in town is from the VIP rooms on the second floor of the **Wasantara Hotel**. The second-floor balcony also overlooks the Poso River. There are 2 VIP rooms at $11, 6 standard rooms at $7.50, 2 bungalows ($9) and 2 economy rooms at $2 a head. No restaurant but meals can be arranged. Satellite reception from Malaysia, Thailand, and the Philippines.

The **Penginapan Wisata Remaja** is a clean and convenient place to stay, close to the boat landing, $2-3 for a room with bathroom.

Pamona Indah. Good view also, right on the lakeshore where the larger boats start and stop their run to Pendolo. 9 rooms, all with AC, WC and bath, $7.50. Restaurant serves genuine cold beer, and has a fair variety of Chinese and Indonesian dishes, 75 cents to $2.50. Try the *sugili*, a local specialty: chunks of large eel either fried or prepared in a hot sauce.

Sintuwu Maroso. Five rooms, $1.50. There are 2 toilets and you bathe in the lake. Government-run, almost always deserted.

Penginapan Rio. Next to the bus station. Small boat landing, 12 rooms $1.50, 2 toilets, 1 bath.

Wisata Remaja. Next to the Rio, run by the village government. 4 rooms, $1.75, basic toilet/bath.

Wisma Tiberias. Church-run, 2 VIP rooms, $5.50 with attached facilities, 6 other rooms with shared facilities, $1.50.

Panorama Hotel. Inconveniently located, but has a good view of ricefields, town and a small corner of the lake. 5 rooms, $1.50 per person. VIP room for up to three $9, not worth it; the only difference is a tiled floor. Meals can be arranged if requested at least a couple of hours ahead.

TRANSPORTATION

At either the **Pomona** or the **Wasantara** hotels in Tentena, you can arrange for a ride on the back of a motorcycle to see a part of the lake from the road. To Peura village, about $5 round-trip (12 km/7 mi each way). To Taipa (on the west side of the lake) and the best panoramic view, it's highly negotiable, perhaps $15-25 for the round trip. Getting through depends on the state of the road, bridges and river levels. When regular buses go from Tentena to Pendolo ($1.60), you could ask the driver to stop for a few minutes at the viewing spot, to take a few quick pictures.

From Tentena a decent surfaced road runs 58 km (35 mi) north to Poso. The fare is $1.50 and the journey takes 2.5 hours. You can also travel 180 km (110 mi) east by minibus to Kolonodale, where you can catch a boat to the Morowali Nature Reserve.

Boat

From Pendolo to Tentena, dep. 06:00, arr. 09:00; the other way, 16:00 to 22:00, 85 cents one way. Charter prices for jaunts around the lake are highly variable, subject to bargaining, and depend on the size of the boat and its engine. The "official" base price is $9/hour but you can arrange for a round trip to the Bancea Orchid Reserve for about $20 in a boat big enough for 2 or 3 large Westerners. The owner of the Pamona Hotel, Pak Yavet Satigi, who has a 40HP speedboat (4-5 passengers), charges $42 for a 5-8 hour tour of the lake.

GUIDES

At the Pamona Hotel ask for Pak Melindo, who speaks English and Dutch, or contact Herman, a Bugis who speaks passable English. Herman has taken several groups on treks to the Bada Valley to see the megaliths. He charges $8 a day plus his expenses for up to 2 people. His fees for larger groups are negotiable.

Bada

It is best to fly into and out of Tentena by MAF, scheduled twice a week on Tuesday and Thursday, for $14. But you might have to wait for a seat—or the plane might be in Tarakan for an overhaul. Or the pilot might be sick. Or he might be out of fuel. Generally, though, it's reliable. If you know your date of arrival, telegram ahead to book: MAF Pilot, Airfield, Tentena, Kab. Poso, Sulawesi Tengah.

There are frequent buses from Tentena to Tonusu, 10 km (6 mi) away. At Tonusu the fun begins. Could be a five-day nightmare, with the jeeps (they travel in convoys of three or more) getting continuously stuck in the mud. Bring food. During the dry season, June to August, it could be as little as 8 hours. The jeeps which make the Tonusu-Bada passenger run charge $8.50 a head, or $85 for a one-way charter. Jeeps seat 6 or 7 in relative comfort along with gear. On the normal run, 10 or more passengers are squeezed in, somehow. If stuck in the mud, you are expected to help push, knee-deep in the ooze. A truck convoy recently took 18 days for the 50-odd-km run.

During the rainy season, it's probably faster to walk, sleeping under any of the six bridges. Some 20 km (12 mi) out, there's a great view back over Lake Poso. You will need about two days of steady trekking to cover the 53 hilly kilometers (32 mi) to Bomba, the first village in the Bada Valley. A porter/guide, if you can find one, will charge $4-5 a day. If you backpack, it's possible to do it alone, as there is only one road and you will not get lost. Bring food.

The other way to get to the Bada Valley is by trail from Gimpu, located 99 km (60 mi) south of Palu along a surfaced ($3 by public minibus-taxi). From here it's an easier two days for the 50 km (30 mi) to Gintu. Same price for porter-guides. If you want a horse, it's $15 for the two days. No muddy feet, but slower. A good, level footpath connects Gimpu to Gintu. The 2-day hike is relieved with an overnight stay at Moa village, just about halfway along. Mostly forest trekking with a few panoramic views. Several long suspension bridges for crossing the Lariang River whose course you follow. Frequent sightings of anoa.

You can see the principal megaliths in one tough day or two more leisurely ones. Expect mud and river crossings where sand fills footwear. Wear long pants for the thorns, and bring along a hat, long-sleeved apparel and a canteen. Remember to be careful about the parasites in this area (see "Lore Lindu" section).

GUIDES

Unless you have an English-speaking guide from Palu or elsewhere, it's essential to know at least very basic Indonesian to get to and around the Bada Valley. For a guide from the valley (none speak English) it's about $3 a day. It's almost impossible to find the megaliths alone.

FOOD/ACCOMMODATION

There are no villages between Tonusu and Bomba, the first Bada village. On the trail from Gimpu, you spend the first and only night on the road with the kepala desa (village chief). Overnight and meals for yourself and porters, $5-10 negotiable. At Gintu there is an unregistered little hotel with no name, 6 rooms, 1 bath, 4 toilets, $5.50 w/meals. Or ask the kepala desa of any village for a place to stay and pay about $5 room and board per person.

MEGALITH HIKES

One-day trek. Starting from Gintu, first visit the statue known as Tinoe, near the village of Bakekau. This statue faces north, the only one of the major megaliths which does not gaze west. Thus afternoon is the best time to photograph the other stone carvings, if there is sunshine. From Tinoe, walk back along the main road to Badangkai, then through rice fields to nearby Baula, the "water buffalo." Although it may look faster on the map to proceed directly to Ari Impohi in Bewa village, walking through rice fields is a time-consuming business. It's faster to return to the main road, then trek through Runde and Gintu to Bewa. From there, head past the landing field to Pada village and the Loga statue, close to the road on a hill with a good view of the valley. Then backtrack to Bewa, walk north to the Lariang River, cross it on a poled bamboo raft and follow the clean, sandy creek to a short climb and the path to Palindo, the largest and best statue, located at a former village site called Sepe.

Two-day trek. First day, walk to the suspension bridge near Lenkeka village, then head back up the valley to the Oba or "monkey" statue, proceed to **Sepe** and Palindo, raft across the river, walk to **Pada** and back to **Gintu**. On the second day, start as on the suggested one-day walk, but after the Loga megalith, go through **Bomba** village and on to the Langke Bulawa statue.

POLICE

You are expected to report with your passport to the main police station at Gintu. Plus, perhaps, to another policeman at the office of the *camat*.

Pendolo

Pendolo, on the southern shore of Lake Poso, is a welcome break in the overland journey. There are several small *warung* along Jl. Pelabuhan, or you can eat at the **Rumah Makan Cahaya**. Most travelers stay at the **Losmen Masamba**, which is right on the lakeside. The rate is $1.50 per person. The more expensive **Danau Poso Hotel** is further from the lake. Early the next morning you can leave for Tentena by boat; the 4-hour journey across Lake Poso with its views of the surrounding mountain ranges of Central Sulawesi is infinitely preferable to the bone-shaking 6-hour ride through them. The large motorized canoes leave before 08:00 to avoid the dangerous cross-winds that blow up later in the day. The fare is $3.

Ampana

To Ampana from Poso by bus, about 5 to 7 hours, $3.50. Includes a simple meal of fish and rice taken at a roadside restaurant, at the tiny fishing village of Padapu. The ride could take as long as a week if the road is washed out. For the foreseeable future, the Bangka River will have to be crossed with the minibus on a raft made up of three canoes lashed together. Impossible for a day or two after a heavy rain. Three different contractors have tried to construct bridges across this river; each has collapsed.

There are passenger boats a couple of times a week from Poso, taking about 8 hours to reach Ampana. Passage, $4, includes a simple meal. Check at the Poso harbor for departure days.

To get to Tanjung Api just stroll around the Ampana docks, and you will be besieged by offers to take you there. No official price, so bargain. An outriggered canoe with a 15HP engine should be around $8-14 round-trip. Bring water and a hat.

ACCOMMODATIONS

There are 4 small 10-room hotels in town, charging similar prices: $2 for just the room (with shared toilet/bath), $5.50 with private facilities and meals. The **Mekar** and the **Irama** are both on Jalan Kartini, conveniently close to the dock, bus depot and market. The **Plaza** is 0.5 km inland while the **Rejeki** is located an inconvenient kilometer away. Try to get rooms away from the afternoon sun, or you are in for sweat-soaked siestas.

Horse-drawn carriages or *bendi* will take you around town for 5-10 cents.

Togian Islands

Boats of 60 to 100 tons frequently ply the Tomini Gulf among these islands. The most convenient places to board are Poso (Central Sulawesi) or Gorontalo (North Sulawesi). Passage, which includes basic rice-and-fish meals and foam rubber sleeping mat, is cheap: $11 for the 3-day trip between Poso and Gorontalo. The crew might offer you one of their cabin bunks ($2-5, depending on your bargaining ability in Indonesian) but the beds tend to be too short for Westerners. Unless the boats are crowded, it's best to sleep in the large passenger compartments, piling up two mattresses for extra cushioning. By all means have your valuables locked up in one of the ship's officers' cabins.

It helps to be friendly with the crew. They will invite you to join them for meals, their fare being somewhat better than the passengers'. Bottled water is usually sold on board while boiled drinking water is freely dispensed. Unless you can survive on a rice-and-fish diet (hard-boiled eggs might be sold by an enterprising youth), bring your own victuals, or purchase them in little stores near the village docking areas. The fish, or whatever is prepared on board, is spiced for Indonesian palates.

Toilet facilities are few and basic. There are no sit-downs: it's the squat, water-and-left-hand universal variety, so bring toilet paper unless used to the Indonesian way of doing things.

The boat's roof is the best spot for sightseeing and photography. Bring sunscreen. If you want to get off the ship for a couple of days and wait for the next boat, the villages where you stop have simple accommodations called *penginapan*. About $4 for room and board. Don't expect too much.

—*Ian Caldwell and Kal Muller*

PART V

Introducing North Sulawesi

"The little town of Manado," wrote the great English naturalist Alfred Russel Wallace after visiting the area in 1859, "is one of the prettiest in the East. It has the appearance of a large garden containing rows of rustic villas, with broad paths between, forming streets generally at right angles with each other. Good roads branch off in several directions towards the interior, with a succession of pretty cottages, neat gardens, and thriving plantations, interspersed with wildernesses of fruit trees. To the west and south the country is mountainous, with groups of fine volcanic peaks 6,000 or 7,000 feet high, forming grand and picturesque backgrounds to the landscape ... I had heard much of the beauty of this country, but the reality far surpassed my expectations."

A land of plenty

Wallace's description is still holds true today, and this is indeed one of the most prosperous and spectacularly scenic areas in Indonesia. Made up of three large districts (Minahasa, Bolaang Mongondow and Gorontalo) and one smaller one (the Sangihe-Talaud Islands), the province of North Sulawesi (Sulawesi Utara or Sulut) occupies the long (600 km/360 mi) and narrow (average width is only 50 km/30 mi) northern arm of the island.

Much of the beauty and fertility of the region derives from its towering volcanoes. Many are extinct or dormant, but Mt. Lokon near Tomohon erupted in 1986, and Mt. Soputan in central Minahasa in 1989. Earth tremors are not at all uncommon. Wallace experienced an earthquake in the hills overlooking Tondano, at Rurukan, that shook the earth at frequent intervals for an entire week.

"We feel ourselves," he wrote, "in the grasp of a power to which the wildest fury of the winds and waves are as nothing; yet the effect is more a thrill of awe than the terror which the more boisterous war of the elements produces."

Volcanoes are only one aspect of a geologically active complex that includes fumaroles and hot springs in the Minahasa district. Studies have been carried out to ascertain the feasibility of generating electricity from geothermal energy here. More importantly, the volcanoes are responsible for the exceptionally fertile soils that are the province's major economic asset. North Sulawesi indeed possesses some of the most fertile land in Indonesia outside Java and Bali. Agriculture, in the form of coconut, clove and nutmeg tree cultivation, forms the basis for great wealth in many parts of the province.

The northernmost district comprises the thinly populated volcanic islands of the Sangihe and Talaud groups, which depend on fishing and coconut production. These islanders frequently travel to the mainland to work as coconut harvesters, among other occupations.

Minahasa, the hinterland of Manado, is the most heavily populated and highly developed district. Only 20 percent of its land remains under forest cover, and the population density has soared to over 300 persons per square km (750 per square mile)—less than half that of Java but still very high.

The Minahasa area is extremely mountainous (Mt. Klabat, the highest peak, stands at 1995 m/6,000 ft), but has a narrow coastal fringe where coconuts thrive, and an interior plateau around Lake Tondano (altitude 600 m/1820 ft; surface area 46 sq km/18 sq mi) where irrigated rice fields provide abundant harvests. The upland hills are covered in clove trees, while in the cool highland areas to the south, near the border with Bolaang Mongondow, vegetables such as potatoes, carrots and cabbages are grown.

Overleaf: *The clear waters around Manado are rich with marine life.* **Opposite:** *Coral reefs and volcanoes provide the North with major scenic attractions. Both photos by Jill Gocher.*

To the west of Minahasa lie the districts of Bolaang Mongondow and Gorontalo. Both are very mountainous also, with an even narrower coastal plain and only a few small, inland valleys, where agriculture is less intensively practiced than in Minahasa. Both districts contain small village settlements created through government-sponsored transmigration from Java and Bali.

The Dumoga Valley to the west of Kotamobagu, for example, supports two prosperous Balinese farming villages (and several Javanese settlements) that have benefitted from the area's fertile soils, extensive irrigation system and good road network. Transmigration settlements have been remarkably successful in North Sulawesi, but local population pressures and a shortage of arable land have led to a virtual cessation of sponsored transmigration into the province.

North Sulawesi is also blessed by abundant rainfall, more or less evenly spread throughout the year, and by a richness of marine life in the surrounding seas. Serious ecological problems do exist, however: deforestation and consequent erosion and silting of waterways can be seen in both Minahasa and Gorontalo.

Rice and coconuts

Products of the soil (and a quest for souls) first drew Europeans to North Sulawesi in the 16th century, and agriculture still underpins the wealth of the province today. North Sulawesi is indeed relatively wealthy, ranking in the top ten of Indonesia's 27 provinces in terms of per capita GNP, with a growth rate well above the national average. In the areas of education and health care, North Sulawesi also outstrips most Indonesian provinces.

Rice was the first crop to interest outsiders. The Dutch, based in the food-poor Moluccan "Spice Islands," looked to nearby Minahasa for their provisions. Ironically, the province now imports rice. Coffee was important during the 19th century, but copra, coconut oil and their by-products are the major revenue earners today. Many of the province's more than 25 million coconut trees are old and less than optimally managed, however, and now need replacement.

Coconuts, like all other agricultural crops in North Sulawesi, are with few exceptions grown not on large estates but by individual smallholders, providing many villagers with a good income. Visiting rural areas, travelers will notice coconut meat being dried in the sun or smoked in cribs to produce copra—a big money-earner.

'Clove fever'

More recently, fortunes large and small have also been made from cloves (*cengkeh*). Native to the neighboring Moluccan Islands, cloves have long been grown in North Sulawesi, but in recent decades this crop has caught on in

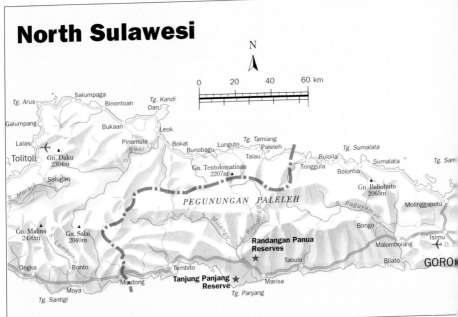

North Sulawesi

a big way. The phrase "clove fever" well describes the atmosphere of the 1970s, when everyone seemed to be planting, growing, harvesting or trading cloves. Prior to the "great harvests" (which occur periodically between more normal annual harvests), consumer goods flood into the villages, supplied by traders as advance payment for specified quantities of dried cloves.

At peak harvest times work in offices and schools grinds to a halt, since the labor-intensive picking of cloves has to be carried out in a very short time. The unmistakable fragrance of the spice then perfumes the air. Picked when still greenish-yellow in color, clove buds are spread on mats to dry in the sun, and quickly turn a dark brown. They are then stored against future price rises, or more often delivered immediately to middlemen as repayment for advances.

Cloves are mainly grown on the slopes of the Minahasa region. Even the possession of a few trees can mean important cash income for a family. The cloves are exported to Java, largely to be used in scented *kretek* cigarettes, which provide the visitor with a distinctive sensory memory of the country. (*Kreteks* contain as much as 50 percent clove powder by weight, but beware—the World Health Organization has recently rated these the world's most harmful cigarettes.) Clove oil is also pressed from the leaves of the tall clove trees; the oil is used for relief from tooth-

aches, among other things. The relative prosperity one notices in parts of Minahasa is largely due to this wonderful tree.

Another important tree crop in North Sulawesi is nutmeg. A sourish fruit that grows on tall trees, the hard kernel produces nutmeg spice while the beautiful lacey vermilion covering surrounding it is dried and ground to become mace. Candien, the nutmeg fruit is a pleasant treat. Besides nutmeg, vanilla is enjoying some popularity now, too, though production is still limited.

Aside from corn, cassava and rice agriculture, the sea is also of substantial importance to the province, whose waters are rich in various species of tuna. A fishing port with modern processing facilities has been developed at Aer Tembaga on the northeastern coast near Bitung, but much fishing is still carried out by small craft instead of by the large seagoing vessels once envisaged. Significant quantities of freshwater fish are also taken from Lake Tondano or raised in fishponds.

A bit of manufacturing, largely the processing of agricultural products such as coconut, is found throughout the province, mainly in the Manado-Bitung region. There is also some mining, including widespread panning for gold in Bolaang Mongondow. Gorontalo has sizeable reserves of copper. Like the rest of Sulawesi, however, the North is still primarily an agrarian region.

—Tim Babcock

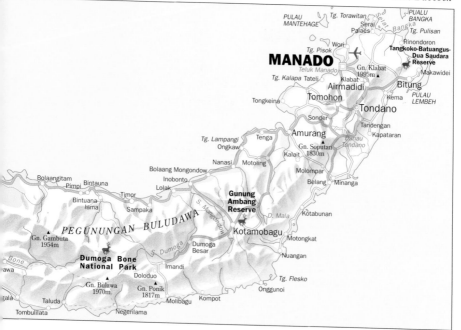

HISTORY

Colonial Stronghold in the North

Legends, archaeological remains and linguistic analyses are the only evidence we have of northern Sulawesi's history prior to the 16th century. No "high" civilization such as was known on Java and Bali ever developed here, and the pre-colonial peoples of the region left behind no written records.

The languages of North Sulawesi are closely related to languages spoken in the Philippines. On the basis of this and other evidence, scholars have suggested that the area was settled from the north, though this no doubt involved a complex and millennia-long process of migrations and adaptation.

Minahasans and other peoples of the province have a different sort of origin story: the myth of Toar and Lumimuut. The primal ancestress Lumimuut was born out of foam from a coral rock thrown up from the sea and impregnated by the wind. She and her son Toar set out in different directions to search for mates. Years later they met but did not recognize one another and so married, giving birth to many children. It is said that Lumimuut gathered her offspring at a sacred stone called Watu Pinabetengan and allocated different parts of the realm to them. This stone, with its undeciphered pictographic carvings, is still *in situ* near the town of Langowan.

At the time of Europeans' first contact with the area, North Sulawesi was inhabited largely by inland and upland peoples who practiced shifting cultivation. The Minahasans were not organized into states, though unions of villages did exist. Petty coastal kingdoms had been established in Gorontalo, as a result of Islamic influence emanating from Bugis kingdoms to the south and from the sultanate of Ternate to the east.

Ternate, a mighty maritime power which then controlled the world's supply of valuable cloves, wielded considerable influence over northern Sulawesi. The language of Manado contains numerous words originating from the non-Austronesian languages of the Moluccas, and some traditional titles in Bolaang Mongondow and Gorontalo derive from the Ternatean language.

The first Westerners to visit the area were the Portuguese; in the mid-1500s they sent a priest to spread the faith. During the next century, the Spanish arrived via the Philippines; though they never settled in large

numbers, their influence is still visible. They introduced corn, tomatoes, chili peppers and horses. Indigenous words for horse are variations on the Spanish *caballo*, and other Spanish and Portuguese words not found in Indonesian are preserved in the regional *lingua franca*, Manado Malay (*Bahasa Manado*). Two other cultural peculiarities of rural Minahasa which appear to be inherited from the Iberians are Christmas mumming—a tradition once widespread throughout western Europe—and, oddly enough, square-dancing (locally called *katrili*, presumably from the French *quadrille*).

In the 1650s the Dutch, under the aegis of the United East Indies Company (VOC), supplanted the Spanish and established a post at the site of present-day Manado. In 1673 the Dutch constructed Fort Amsterdam here (which was bombed during the Second World War and, unfortunately, later razed to the ground). Not until the early 1800s, however, did they penetrate the interior. The Minahasa highlands were subjugated in 1808-1809, and rapid and massive conversions to Protestantism, along with the forced cultivation of coffee, began to take place soon after.

Christianity became an emblem of Minahasan culture and identity and helped reinforce a local attachment to European culture, as well as in some cases an identification with Dutch interests. The Church and the Dutch administration were instrumental in spreading education and basic health services throughout the district. By the turn of the century, there was a school for every 1,000 people in Minahasa, whereas in Java the ratio was one to 50,000. Thus by 1930, Minahasa registered the highest literacy rate (in Malay as well as Dutch) in the country. Minahasans made up a significant portion of the colonial bureaucracy as well as the army; needless to say, their status as colonial "Tories" did not greatly endear them to other Indonesians.

The Japanese occupation was followed by Dutch reoccupation, and by revolutionary activity that eventually brought independence in 1949. Not everyone in North Sulawesi initially supported the revolution; for a long time, in fact, pro-Dutch sentiments among Minahasans earned the region the nickname of the "twelfth province" of Holland. On the eve of independence many Minahasans emigrated to Holland. Today, however, such things have long been forgotten and most of the talk is of economic development. Government policies in the New Order era have focused mainly on this, and have been remarkably successful in bringing progress to even remote areas of the province.

—*Tim Babcock*

Opposite: *Fort Amsterdam in Manado as it appeared in the 19th century.* **Above:** *The regalia of the kingdom of Sekoyo in North Sulawesi, guarded by a nobleman and female exorcists.*

PEOPLES OF THE NORTH

Lively, Fun-Loving and Extroverted

Over the centuries four main ethnic groups have coalesced out of the dozens of interrelated peoples that formerly inhabited North Sulawesi. Their names parallel the names of the province's four districts: Minahasa, Gorontalo, Sangihe and Mongondow. In practice, people still recognize and identify many local subgroups, distinguished mainly by language or dialect.

Outside the province they are often all referred to as *orang Manado,* though in other contexts this term refers more specifically to (Christian) Minahasans, the outgoing group who make up half of the province's 2.5 million inhabitants. Although Minahasans were once the educated and professional elite, in recent decades other groups have been catching up. Gorontalo people in particular are known as successful petty traders.

The North also contains significant immigrant populations, of whom the most noticeable are the Chinese, concentrated in the towns and engaging in wholesale and retail trading. Over the years there has been much intermarriage between Chinese and Minahasans, and inter-ethnic tensions here are less pronounced than in other areas.

Small Arab communities (primarily in Manado and Gorontalo City) engage in commercial and professional occupations. Bugis and Makassarese from the South are found in small numbers; about one percent of the population is made up of Javanese or Balinese transmigrants. Coastal settlements of Bajau also exist, though not in the numbers found in Central or Southeast Sulawesi.

In Minahasa, 95 percent of the population is Christian—mostly Protestant with a small Catholic minority. While there is an established, dominant Protestant Church (descended from the Dutch Reformed Church), perhaps 50 other sects exist. Gorontalo and Mongondow people are almost entirely Muslim, the latter group having undergone conversion in the 19th century. In Manado and Bitung, the Christian and Muslim populations are more evenly balanced.

In spite of the impact of Christianity, Islam and the West, traces of indigenous culture remain. Today among Minahasans (and presumably other groups as well) there is still a lively (though often covert) belief in a supernatural world populated with *opo-opo*—gods,

KAL MULLER

JILL GOCHER

culture heroes, or similar helpful or harmful beings. These can be contacted either directly or with the assistance of ritual specialists (who may be devout Christians or Muslims). Offerings and spirit-possession are common; the sacred ancestor stone, Watu Pinawetengan, is especially favored for such activities. Also popular are the pre-Christian stone burial chambers (*waruga*) found at many locations. Coconut shells left as offerings here are said to be a modern substitute for the human skulls left in earlier times.

Today, what is generally propounded as "traditional culture" by the Department of Education and Culture and the national television network, TVRI, is limited to the visual and performing arts and devoid of much of its original ritual significance. Alas, North Sulawesi is no Bali, nor even a Tana Toraja, though a number of interesting forms of dance, for example, do exist and with some effort may be seen by the visitor.

Perhaps the most accessible of the local performing arts is Minahasan singing. The fun-loving Minahasans are famed throughout the country for their vocal skills, displayed to best advantage during their huge ritual celebrations, when wine and song flow in equally copious quantities. Songs are often accompanied by a *kolintang* orchestra consisting of several wooden xylophones. *Kolintangs* are found in almost every village and occasionally at popular seafood restaurants in the

Manado area. Cassettes are also sold locally.

A variety of modernized and secularized dance forms are often performed to greet important visitors, or in competitions, rather than in their original community-rooted context. *Maengket* and *marambak* are forms of Minahasan group dancing, often with verses sung as accompaniment, that once had connections with harvest ceremonies and inaugurations of new houses. The *cakalele* war dance, known throughout the province and in the Moluccas (from where it may have originated), is danced by men dressed in red, waving swords and shields and uttering ferocious cries to frighten the "enemy."

Of sculpture, painting, and other plastic arts there is little today, though there is a tradition of ebony carving in North Sulawesi, most notably in the Sangihe-Talaud Islands. Weaving died out in Minahasa some time during the last century, but an attractive form of pulled-thread embroidery called *krawang* is made in the Gorontalo City area, and is widely available in the form of ready-made clothing (shirts, dresses), tablecloths, sheets and pillowcases. One can also buy the material as dress- and shirt-length pieces of cloth ready for custom tailoring.

—*Tim Babcock*

Opposite: *A* cakalele *war dance.* **Above:** *A group of kids outside Manado screaming the inevitable "Hello Meester" at our female photographer.*

MANADO AND BUNAKEN

Thriving City and World-Class Diving

The city of Manado, bustling capital of North Sulawesi, spreads across low, coconut-clad hills around a wide bay, with three volcanoes providing a spectacular backdrop. Its splendid setting is an attraction in itself; with only a limited number of other attractions, the city's main interest to the traveler will most likely be its location, its relatively high standard of living and its convenience as a base from which to explore the surrounding region.

The city (population 250,000) is predominantly Christian—a legacy of several centuries of Portuguese and Dutch domination. There are 349 places of worship, including 266 churches, and more are still being built. The church plays a key role in society here; the streets are filled on Sundays with smartly-dressed churchgoers.

Manado was a major seaport until the early 1960s, but the harbor has silted up and now most of the shipping has now been rerouted to the nearby harbor of Bitung. It is still possible, however, to travel by boat from Manado to Tahuna (on Sangihe) and to other local ports.

City sights

Manado has a wide variety of shops, hotels, and restaurants. As a service and administrative center for the entire province, it is also the site of numerous educational institutions, banks and government offices. Since the Indonesian government recently named the area an official tourist destination, several major development proposals have come under consideration: extension of the Trans-Sulawesi Highway to the airport, construction of a seaside boulevard and several international-class hotels, and so on.

Much of the surrounding area has been designated a nature reserve, including the crystal-blue seas around Bunaken Island just to the north, with their extraordinary coral-reef sea gardens. The local beach at Tasik Ria to the south of the city offers good swimming and dramatic tropical sunsets.

The city center contains bustling shops filled to capacity with goods of every imaginable description, at bargain prices. Pasar Bersehati, the largest food market in town, displays an overwhelming quantity and variety of fresh produce, meat, fish and chicken, sold amidst a splendid chaos of noises, aromas and crowds of shoppers. One section of the market is devoted to freshly butchered dog, a local delicacy. Watch for signs proclaiming "RW," a euphemism for dog meat, either to avoid or to sample the local canine cuisine. Foreigners are seldom seen here, and are often stared at or even followed. The market is situated on the northern side of the harbor close to the Jumbo Supermarket.

The Ban Hian Kiong Buddhist-Confucian Temple (on Jl. Panjaitan in the center of the city) was built in the early 19th century and rebuilt in 1974 after being partially destroyed by vandals. Two weeks after the Chinese Lunar New Year, the large Cap Go Mei (15th of the first lunar month) celebration held in Chinese communities throughout Southeast Asia is held at this temple. You may see local residents practicing various forms of divination and geomancy. Ascend to the top floor of the temple to get an excellent view of downtown Manado. Oddly, the temple also has a display of Portuguese artifacts.

The North Sulawesi Provincial Museum on Jl. W.R. Supratman has interesting displays of historical and cultural relics from all around the province. It is not officially open yet, but tourists are welcome anyway. Guides are well-informed, though their English may be far from fluent.

If the midday heat and humidity become too much for you, the Kawanua City Hotel pool offers a quiet respite. It is virtually deserted until the late afternoon, and food and drinks can be ordered at the poolside.

Trying out the wide variety of Indonesian cuisines available, choosing strategic locations from which to absorb the city's magnificent natural scenery (and its sunsets, in season), will profitably occupy time not devoted to exploring the Bunaken coral gardens and the upcountry areas.

Bunaken sea gardens

The prime tourist attraction in North Sulawesi is the spectacular sea garden located off Bunaken Island, less than an hour by boat from Manado. It contains an unbelievable abundance of marine life, in one of the world's most impressive diving spots.

Four companies just outside Manado specialize in organizing tours to this lovely spot, and also offer scuba diving instruction. Snorkeling and diving equipment can be rented from all of them, though some divers may prefer to bring their own equipment and rent only tanks and weightbelts. Surface water temperatures are usually between 25 and 28 degrees C (77 to 83 degrees F).

A day-tour starts off with morning coffee or tea at a beachside restaurant. A motorboat takes visitors to two of the five islands—Bunaken and Manado Tua—which make up the goverment-protected, 75,265-hectare (186,000-acre) marine reserve. The latter is a dormant volcano that rises majestically out of the ocean.

A submarine trench reaching to depths of 1200 meters (4,000 feet) separates these islands from the mainland, shielding them from the pollution and silt generated in Manado and nearby coastal villages. The reserve is protected by law from spearfishing and coral or fish-collecting, as well as from dynamite fishing. The development of tourist facilities is banned on the islands for environmental reasons, so most people stay in Manado or with their tour company in one of several diving resorts that have sprung up around the city (see "Manado Practicalities" for details).

The safest and most popular dive site is the sheltered south cove of Bunaken Island, where the coral reef starts just below the surface and plunges vertically to 3,000 feet, with downward visibility of up to 100 feet. Here, it is said, is the best wall and drop-off diving in the world. The density of the fish and coral population, the dazzling colors and the sheer coral walls with their numerous caverns combine to make this a breathtaking experience for experienced and novice divers alike.

Snorkelers may also like to explore areas off the southern side of the island, where the fish density is not so great, but where numerous species of soft coral can be seen. For those who do not want to enter the water, glass-bottom boats are available, but be sure to arrange this ahead of time.

According to the Nusantara Diving Centre (NDC), Manado's oldest diving tour operator, the coral formations begin with a flat reef reaching down to about 15 feet, then sloping downward to form underwater valleys or vertical drops plunging several hundred meters. There are fantastic "underwater greatwalls" cut by crevices and large caves with hanging masses of coral. On these unique coral reefs, a tremendous collection of marine life thrives: red and orange encrusting sponges, Christmas tree worms, basket and tube sponges, anemones stocked with clown fish, brightly colored crinoids, giant tunicates, sea-

Above: *A view of the green hills surrounding Manado Bay.*

whips, nudibranches (Spanich dancers), transparent and red-striped coral shrimp, lobsters, crabs, molluscs, thousands of ornamental coral fish and the larger pelagics.

Often seen also are giant Napoleon wrasse, angelfish, turtles, blue ribbon eels, morays, stingrays and eaglerays, snappers, groupers, tuna, sharks, sea-snakes, barracudas and dolphins. Bomba sponges so large that two men have trouble encircling them with their arms have been found. At 20 to 25 meters (70 to 80 ft) you may be lucky enough to spot a rare Gloria Maris. On night dives you can see sleeping fish, mating shells and invertebrates, the swinging lantern fish and colorful feeding corals.

Completing the diving experience are several exciting World War II wrecks in 90 to 120 ft of water, encrusted with marine life such as colored sponges, soft and hard corals, deepwater gorgonians and large schools of lionfish, batfish, stonefish, upside-down shrimpfish, trumpet fish, jacks, giant groupers and mother-of-pearl.

After an hour or two of whatever aquatic activity you prefer, a delicious lunch is available at a *warung* on the white sand beach of Bunaken Island, or on board the boat. You can spend time exploring the beach, collecting sea shells (remember that live shells and coral from the water are off limits, but you may pick up empty ones from the beach), or just relaxing—the boat will take you out again for more time in the warm waters of the Sulawesi Sea.

Two of the five islands, Siladen and Nain, are known for their abundance of shells. If you have time, you might want to ask the boatmen to make a stop there. On the return trip back to Manado, you will get a beautiful view of Manado Bay. With a little luck, you might also catch a glimpse of a school of diving pilot whales or dolphins.

You can ask any of the tour companies to arrange customized fishing, sailing, windsurfing or camping trips for you to destinations all around the Manado area; just be sure to make your requests known well in advance, and avoid the period from December to February, when heavy monsoon winds and rain cause frequent cancellations.

The Murex Diving Centre, for example, will take visitors on a delightful 2.5-hour boat trip along the coast to the northernmost tip of Sulawesi, where you can snorkel or dive off Banka and Talise Islands. Again, lots of unique coral and fish to see here, and you get a scenic one-hour drive back from the village of Likupang in the afternoon.

—*Sheridan Angerilli and Mary Thorne*

Below: *Diving off the coast of Bunaken, just an hour north of Manado by boat. The reefs here feature a dramatic, 3,000-ft vertical drop and lots of exciting tropical marine life, all of which adds up to some of the best diving in the world.*

LOKY HERLAMBANG

Manado Practicalities

Telephone code 0431. All prices are in US$. S=Single; D=Double. AC=air-conditioned.

The main point of entry to North Sulawesi is Manado, which is well served by air routes. **Merpati/Garuda** has a daily early-morning flight—economy class $200 one way—from Jakarta via Ujung Pandang, arriving in Manado around 11:30. **Bouraq** operates two early-morning daily flights from Jakarta which are cheaper but take longer. One is via Banjarmasin, Balikpapan, Palu and Gorontalo, arriving in Manado 16:00, and one via Balikpapan, which is a shorter journey arriving at 12:30. Both cost $180 one way. **Sempati**, flies Fokker 100s from Singapore., Jakarta and Surabaya. Dr. Sam Ratulangi Airport is 7 km (4.2 mi) out of Manado, and a taxi ride from there to anywhere in the city costs about $3. Buy a coupon at the taxi counter. A better price is possible by chartering an *oplet* or minibus.

For those with more time, **Pelni** has two ships, KM Umsini and KM Kabuna, sailing from Jakarta to Bitung (about 40 min./$12 taxi fare from Manado). First-class adult fare is $145, including all meals on the five-night trip. The fare for children under 11 years of age and babies is less. These large, well-appointed German-built ships also call in at Surabaya and Ujung Pandang. on the way. Smaller ships sail between Manado's small harbor and other Indonesian ports.

A third and much more challenging way to reach Manado is to travel the whole length of Sulawesi by road from Ujung Pandang to Manado along the Trans-Sulawesi Highway. The road is not up to "highway" standard along the whole route, so a sturdy four-wheel drive vehicle with a winch is recommended. Allow at least two weeks for this adventure, which is best attempted in the dry season from April to October. You can also make the journey by bus, with lots of transfers.

GETTING AROUND MANADO

The ubiquitous *oplet* has a Rp150 (8 cents) flat-rate fare which is paid at the end of your journey; have correct change ready. The destination is shown on the front of the vehicle, and they will pick you up anywhere along the route: just raise your arm slightly. To alight, ring the bell on the ceiling. If the bell is broken lightly tap the window behind the driver.

The *mikrolet* operates on the same principle but carries more passengers and is entered at the side. Two passengers can sit beside the driver. For short city journeys the fare is Rp150, but if your journey is to the city outskirts offer Rp200. Some are fitted with internal bells as in *oplets* but you can also alert the driver by shouting "stop," which he will do with alarming alacrity.

All manner of things are carried on board, so be prepared to step over live, trussed chickens and sacks of coconuts. Most routes converge at the terminal at Pasar 45, outside Jumbo Supermarket. *Oplets* and *mikrolets* are not allowed to stop near main traffic junctions or directly in front of the Kawanua City Hotel. People will request the driver to make short diversions to their destination, so don't be alarmed if the *oplet* suddenly leaves the main road down a narrow side street; enjoy the change of scenery. It is also possible to charter an empty *oplet* for around $1.60/hour (no minimum) which makes a cheap alternative to a taxi.

There are two types of taxi operating in Manado. One looks like an ordinary car and has no meter. They will take you anywhere in the city but you have to negotiate a price. Or you can hire them by the hour at $2.75/hour with a three-hour minimum. If you wish to travel outside the city, the hourly rate is the same but there is a five-hour minimum. You can pick up a taxi at the Kawanua City Hotel, the Garden Hotel, or on the south side of the city center square (Taman Kesatuan Bangsa). You can also telephone **Indra Kelana Taxi Company**, Tel. 52033. The other recently introduced taxis are metered white sedans with a large sign on the roof. These are run by a company called **Dian Taksi**, Tel. 62421, which currently has 20 cars that tour the city looking for customers. The first km is Rp600 (35 cents) and every subsequent km Rp300. There are no car rentals in Manado yet.

Like the other towns in North Sulawesi, Manado has horse-drawn carts called *bendi*, but they are restricted in where they can operate. *Bendis* tend to congregate at the markets and near the harbor. They will take up to two adults, and a short journey should cost around Rp300. It is possible to hire a *bendi* for a limited city tour at around $2.50/hour.

ACCOMMODATION

There is a good range of hotels in Manado in most price brackets. Nothing as yet in the five-star category, but some may be ready in the near future. Rates listed below include 21% service charge and government tax unless stated otherwise. For lengthy stays, discounts are often available.

Diving/Snorkeling

The following companies can be contacted to make reservations or provide current rates for package tours:
Murex, Jl. Jend. Sudirman 28, P.O. Box 236, Manado 95123, Tel. 66280 Fax/phone 52116. Owned and operated by a friendly couple, Dr. and Mrs. Hanny Batuna. Boats and equipment are well maintained, and knowledgeable, attentive guides are provided. Sightseeing is $25 per day, snorkeling is $30 and diving $60 plus a 20% service tax. Prices include equipment, food, and 2 dives per day. Package rates, which can also include scuba

certification lessons, can be negotiated. Seven modern and local-style fan-cooled cottages w/hot water and private bathrooms are available if you plan to stay longer. These are situated in a pretty, peaceful setting along the shore, on the road south to Tanawangko at Kalasay. Costs with meals range from $15-25. Credit cards accepted, Excellent food and serene atmosphere.

Nusantara Diving Center (NDC), Molas Beach (mangrove and mud), Dusun III (Batusaiki), 20 min. north of Monado. 25 fan-cooled rooms w/hot water, private bathrooms. $7.50-30.00. meals $10/day. P.O. Box 1015, Manado 95001, Tel. (0431) 63988, 60638 Telex 74100 Fax 60368, 63688 BCA MO/74228 BCA MO. A fully equipped diving center which has been in operation since 1975. The owner, Loky Herlambang, who speaks excellent English, was among the first to discover and develop this area; in 1985 he received an award from the Indonesian government for his efforts in preserving the marine environment. Daily tour rates are about the same as for Murex. Package rates $70-80.Caters to tour groups. Reservations recommended for July, August. Travelers' checks and major Credit cards.

Barracuda (12 or more rooms) at Molas beyond NDC. Best views. S $20, D$25. Restaurant.; Dive master, 56 tanks, guides, boats, one large glass-bottom sight-seeing and dive boat, dive locations map, catamaran to Bangka Island dives. Manado office: Jl. Sam Ratulangi 61, Tel 62033, 66249 Fax 6484;. German office: Michael Smith, Geibelstr. 43, 3000 Hannover 1, Tel. (0511) 888836, 6476129, Fax 6476120.

For info on a new dive center 10 km north of Bitung with deep caves and sharks contact Billy Matindas at Tarsius Restaurant, in Manado, Tel.65164-5.

To go to **Bunaken** on your own, Willy Bansaleng at the harbor behind **Pasar Bersehati** will arrange a *prahu* ($20), not including equipment, a guide or food. You can eat at the *warungs* on Bunaken Island. One, run by the congenial Ibu Jet Tamparutu, has two rooms in which 2 people can sleep on the floor for $6 a day with three meals.

Luxury ($30 and above)

Kawanua City Hotel, Jl. Sam Ratulangi 1, Tel. 52222, Fax: 52220. Swimming pool, dry cleaning service; rooms are dark and dingy. Good restaurant, and a travel agent in the lobby. $30-40 S, $35-50 D, plus tax. Credit cards accepted.

New Queen Hotel, Jl. Wakeke 12-14, Tel. 52979, Telex: 74212 QUEEN IA, Fax: 52748. $14-26 S, $15-33 D, plus tax. Credit cards.

Sahid Manado Hotel (formerly New Garden Hotel), Jl. Babe Palar, 50 rooms. Tel. 51688, 52688, Telex: 74236 SMH IA. Fax: 63326. Rooms are clean and bright, some with a great view. $20-50 S, $24-63 D. Restaurant .

Manado Beach Hotel, 250 rooms, Tasik Ria Beach 18 km from Manado City, Tel. 67001/5, Fax: 67007. $70-80 S, $80-90 D, $100-500 Suite. Up to 2 childrent free in parents' room.

Coffee shop, supper club, 2 bars, beach restaurant. Two swimming pools. Free airport-hotel transfers.

Intermediate ($10-30)

Kawanua (Kecil) Hotel, Jl. Sudirman 40, Tel. 63842, 51923. Great value for the money. Prices including breakfast from $6-12 S, $8-12 D. Highly recommended.

Hotel Minahasa, Jl. Sam Ratulangi 199, Tel. 62059, 62559. Family-run hotel in an old Dutch mansion with a friendly, homey atmosphere. $8-13 S, $11-17 D. Highly recommended.

Panorama Ridge, Jl. Tomohon Raya, Tel. 51158, 63447. Fantastic view of the bay. Clean and quiet. $10-15 S, $13-18 D. Highly recommended.

Manado Seaside Cottages, Malalayang. 10 min. south of Manado; 8 Minahasan-style cottages. Excellent restaurant. $12 S, $15 D w/breakfast.

Wisma Tokambene, Jl. Sam Ratulangi VII, 12/A, Tel. 63753. Charming, small, well-run. Prices including breakfast $7 S, $9 D. Quiet location. Recommended.

Mini Cakalele, Jl. Korengkeng 40, Tel. 52942. $9-38 S or D.

Yepindra, Jl. Sam Ratulangi 33, Tel. 64049. Lobby and eating area are nice but the rooms are drab. Prices including breakfast $11 S, $13 D.

Manado Inn, Jl. 14 Februari, Tel. 51129. Good food. Rooms are spartan. $15 S, $18 D.

Tountembuan, Jl. Sam Ratulangi, Tel. 51117. Lobby and eating area are nice but rooms are dingy. $8-16 S, $8-19 D. Credit cards.

Mitisyla, Jl. Sarapung 11, Tel. 63445. Basic but clean. $6-8 S, $8-10 D.

Budget (under $10)

Jakarta Jaya, Jl. Hasanudin 25, Tel. 64330. $2.50/person including breakfast. Rooms are minuscule but clean. Good value.

FOOD

There are many restaurants in Manado, serving most of the popular Indonesian cuisines from Padang to Javanese. Particular effort should be made to enjoy at least one meal at a restaurant specializing in the hot and spicy Minahasan dishes. A large selection is brought to your table and you pay only for what you eat. Two such restaurants, highly recommended if you can get to them, are **Inspirasi**, about 15 minutes out of town in Tinoor, and **Kasuang Indah**, which is a 45-minute drive on the road to Remboken. In town, try **Tinoor Jaya** on Jl. Sam Ratulangi near the Minahasa Hotel, or the **Selera**, which is rather unprepossessing but conveniently located in the city center. If you wish to sample, or avoid sampling, some of the more exotic local dishes, you will need to know the following words: *tikus* (field rat), *paniki* (fruit-bat) and of course, Man's Best Friend, RW (pronounced "airway").

Because seafood is plentiful and cheap it is eaten daily in the home but is not usually considered worthy of being served at parties or in restaurants. However, the **Manado Seaside Cottages Restaurant**, 10 minutes out of town in Malalayang, is one which specializes in seafood that is consistently delicious, although a little expensive. **Klabat Indah**, which opened recently, is a good second choice. Large shrimp (*udang besar*) and squid (*cumi-cumi*) are available in many of the carp (*ikan mas*) restaurants. The nicest of these in Manado is the **New Bamboo Den**. Other carp restaurants are found outside the city, on the road to the airport and elsewhere.

Your best choices for Javanese fare are the **Surabaya** or **Kalasan**. For Chinese food try the popular **Dua Raya**, **Fiesta Ria** or the **Manado Hilltop Restaurant**, which also offers a spectacular view of the city. Padang cooking can be sampled at **Singgalang Sago**.

The following list of dining establishments includes some of the more popular eateries, but is by no means exhaustive. Ask for advice at your hotel or *losmen* and it's unlikely that you'll be disappointed. The Manadonese love to eat.

Cakalang, Kawanua City Hotel, Jl. Sam Ratulangi 1, Tel. 52222. Indonesian, Chinese, American and European dishes. Food is good but expensive.

California Spicy Chicken, one floor above Jumbo Supermarket, Jl. Let. Jend. Soeprapto No. 1, Tel. 51465, 51455. Fried chicken, burgers, chips, etc. The only American-style fast-food joint in town.

Dua Raya, Jl. Walanda Maramis 84, Tel. 62236. Good Chinese food; nice interior. Popular with the local Chinese community. Sit upstairs on the second floor where it is quieter if a wedding reception isn't in progress.

Fiesta Ria, Jl. Sam Ratulangi. Next door to Fiesta Ria Supermarket. Chinese and some European food available in a pleasant interior. Try the shrimp hotplate (*udang besi panas*). Expensive.

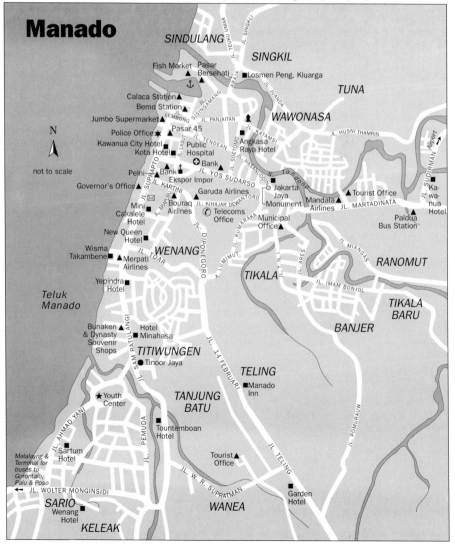

Jawa Timur, Jl. Diponegoro No. 73, Tel. 51085. Good Javanese food. There is a branch on Jl. Sarapung, but the interior of this one is nicer.

Kalasan, Jl. Sudirman 9, Tel. 3253. Javanese fried chicken. Fixed menu of flavorful chicken (Kalasan-style), vegetables in a spicy broth (*sayur asam*) and rice. Very good, cheap food.

Klabat Indah, Jl. Sam Ratulangi 211, Tel. 62405. Serves seafood including *baronang*, *oci* (a small fish, good barbequed), *cumi-cumi* and *ikan mas*.

Manado Inn, Jl. 14 Februari, Tel. 51129. Cheap and tasty Indonesian food.

Manado Hilltop Restaurant, up the hill from the Tourist Office, located on a sidestreet off Jl. 17 Agustus; watch for the large sign. Average Chinese food but the view is great.

Mentari, Jl. Sam Ratulangi. Freshwater carp, squid, and prawns (*udang*) available with rice and a spinach-like vegetable (*kangkung*) to go with it. Interior is basic but you can sit outside to eat. The food is good and cheap.

Mie Medan 99, Jl. Sam Ratulangi. Chinese food.

Minahasa Hotel, Jl. Sam Ratulangi 199. Good, fresh European and Indonesian food. It's better to order in advance. Cheap.

New Bamboo Den, Jl. Tumatenden 5, Tel. 52459. The best *ikan mas* restaurant in the city; basically the same menu as the Mentari.

President Fried Chicken, President Shopping Centre, 3rd floor, Jl. Dotu Lolong Lasut. Tel. 51999. Besides fried chicken, Indonesian dishes. Cafeteria-style.

Rumah Makan Kartini, Jl. Kartini 5 (side street off Jl. Sam Ratulangi between Kawanua City Hotel and the Post Office). Tel. 51970. Javanese food served in a pleasant interior.

Selera Minahasa, Jl. Dotu Lolong Lasut on the main square—center of town, a convenient place to try Minahasan food. Cafeteria style. A popular place for business lunches. Cheap.

Singgalang Sago, Jl. Sam Ratulangi 164, Tel. 52573. Cheap Padang food. You can buy good box lunches to go. Inside is spartan. Closes early.

Surabaya, Jl. Sam Ratulangi, Tel. 52317. A large selection of Javanese dishes. Good food served in a pleasant interior.

Tinoor Jaya, Jl. Sam Ratulangi. Minahasan cuisine. Clean and bright inside.

Turin Italian Restaurant and Bakery, Jl. Sam Ratulangi 50, Tel. 51611. A very limited selection of Indonesian dishes, but this place does have decent ice cream. A new branch has opened opposite Fiesta Ria Supermarket.

There are also a number of good restaurants within a half-hour of Manado. These might be good stops on sightseeing trips outside the city. A few in the immediate vicinity of Manado are:

Inspirasi, on the road to Tomohon in Tinoor. A lovely interior, combined with a spectacular view of coconut and clove plantations, with Manado and the ocean in the background, make this place a must. Excellent spicy food, reasonable prices.

Kelapa Gading, on the road to Tomohon in Pineleng. A nice, spacious interior. Serves *ikan mas*. Food is good but expensive.

Manado Seaside Cottages, on the road to Tasik Ria in Malalayang. This open-air restaurant, built in the traditional Minahasan style, absolutely should not be missed. Best to go before sunset, as it is located just across the street from the ocean, and has a beautiful sea view. Before dark you can order coconut punch (a delicious combination of young coconut, coconut water and palm sugar) and watch a man climb a nearby palm tree to gather the ingredients. This place serves excellent fresh seafood. If you want them to pick you up and return you to your hotel, phone the Manado Inn (Tel. 51129). If possible, speak to the owner of both places, Bapak Max, to make arrangements.

Pondok Bambu, on the road to the airport in Paniki Bawah. *Ikan mas* and fried chicken served in a nice, peaceful setting.

Pongkor, just before Airmadidi in Suwaan. *Ikan mas* is available as you prefer—baked, fried or in a tangy soup. On Saturday evenings you can listen to a live *kolintang* band while you eat.

Tindoor Indah, on the road to Tomohon in Tinoor. The menu and prices are the same as Inspirasi.

Tinoor Jaya, also on the road to Tomohon in Tinoor. Menu and prices the same as Inspirasi. Has a branch in Manado.

In addition to the above, there is an endless range of small *warungs* which usually provide good value for the money. There are also many night food stalls which offer food-to-go including fried bananas, noodle dishes, *murtabak* and *malabar* (omelette-like concoctions; the former is sweet, the latter savory) and fried, filled *tahu* (tofu). These can be found on the road leading to Kalabat Stadium or on Jl. Sudirman near the city center.

MONEY

All of the national banks have branches in Manado, mostly located in the city center. Banks are open Monday to Saturday from 07:00 to 17:00 and are shut for lunch from 12:30 to 14:30. There is very little difference between their respective rates of exchange.

There is one money changer, the **Authorized Money Changer**, Jl. Dr. Sam Ratulangi 136. Open from 06:00 to 22:00 and sometimes open on Sunday. The exchange rate is equivalent to the bank rates and there is no service charge.

Bank Negara Indonesia (B.N.I.) 1946, Jl. M.T. Haryono, Tel. 62977.

Bank Bumi Daya (B.B.D.), Jl. Dotu Lolong Lasut, Tel. 61017.

Bank Ekspor Impor (Bank EXIM), Jl. Yos. Sudarso, Tel. 64177.

Bank Central Asia (B.C.A), Jl. Dotu Lolong Lasut, Tel. 52778.

Bank Dagang Negara (B.D.N), Jl. Dotu Lolong Lasut, Tel. 63278.

ACTIVITIES

There is a 9-hole golf course 7 km (4.2 mi) from Manado on the way to the airport. Fees are $2.50 on Sunday and $1.70 during the week. Two sets of clubs are available for rental.

Tennis is quite popular in Manado and there are several courts. Those at Sario Sports Complex on Jl. Ahmad Yani in the south part of the city are modern and well-maintained.

Horse and bull races are held on major holidays at the Maesa Race Track in the east of town.

There are four movie theaters which often show fairly recent North American movies about the same time as they come out in video.

There are several discothèques in Manado: the **Hotel Angkasa Raya**, the **Manado Plaza,** the **Garden Hotel**, and **Hot Gossip** in Malalayong.

TOURIST INFORMATION

The **North Sulawesi Provincial Tourism Office** is very difficult to find, tucked away on a little side street down the hill off Jl. 17 Agustus. They are open government hours: 07:00-14:00 Monday to Thursday, to 11:00 Friday, and to 12:30 Saturday. They can also be reached by telephone at 64299.

More conveniently located is the **Tourist Information and Booking Center** at Bunaken Souvenir Shop on Jl. Sam Ratulangi 178, open every day except Sunday, from 08:00 to 20:00.

There is a Visitor Information Office at the airport but it is not always open.

COMMUNICATIONS

The main Post Office (*kantor pos*) is located on Jl. Sam Ratulangi 23, a 5-minute walk south from the Kawanua City Hotel. Open 08:00 to 20:00 Monday-Friday; 08:00-18:00 Saturday and Sunday.

For long-distance phone calls within Indonesia, go to the **Perumtel** office on Jl. Sam Ratulangi between the Kawanua City Hotel and the Post Office on the other side of the road. It is open 24 hours a day. Only the larger hotels have international telephone facilities.

SHOPPING

Minahasa has a limited range of native arts and crafts, but it is possible to buy *krawang*, the fine embroidery from Gorontolo, and carved ebony wood from the Sangihe-Talaud Islands in several Manado stores. There are a number of local specialties, especially sweets. These include candied nutmeg fruit (*pala manis*), an unusual candy made from candle nuts cooked in brown sugar (*halua kenari*), coconut cookies (*kue kelapa*) and a cookie made from sago flower baked in leaves (*bagea*). You can find these at the following shops:
Bunaken Souvenir Shop, Jl. Sam Ratulangi 178. Has a good selection of souvenirs as well as a tourist information service.
Dynasty Art Shop, Jl. Sam Ratulangi 187 has a good selection of antiques. Flexible prices.
Krawang, Jl. Walanda Maramis. Large selection of *krawang* goods.
U.D. Kawanua, Jl. Balai Kota 1/30, Tel. 63601. Carries only *krawang*; reputed to sell the best cloth for the lowest prices. It is in a private home which is difficult to find, but most taxi drivers know where it is. Tell them it's near Lapangan Tikala.

Warung Ventje I, Jl. Panjaitan 65 (near the Chinese temple), Tel. 65105. This shop and Ventje II are the hot spots to buy cookies.
Warung Ventje II, Jl. Sam Ratulangi 184. Larger and newer.

For Western-style baked goods, try **President Bakery**, President Shopping Center, 2nd floor. Good cakes, pastries and ice cream. Nice place for a snack with fresh fruit juice or coffee.

Clothing

The **Ramayana** and the **Makmur** department stores, both on Jl. Walanda Maramis, sell mainly clothing, very cheap and usually of good quality. Another place to stroll around, either to buy or just to enjoy the variety, is **Pasar 45**, across from Jumbo Supermarket. A maze of small shops that sell clothing and many other goods.

Tailoring in Manado is quick and inexpensive. Bring a picture or a garment to be copied and have yourself measured. Fabric is between $1.75-3.50 per meter. There are many shops selling textiles along Jl. Dotu Lolong Lasut near the **President Shopping Center**. North down this street and left around the corner at Jl. Lembong 11. is **Toko Esa Genangku,** a fabric store with a large selection of good-quality material. Throughout the city there are numerous tailors and seamstresses. Some of the better ones are:
Kalvin Tailor, President Shopping Center, 3rd floor, Jl. Dotu Lolong Lasut.
Paris Menswear Tailoring, Jl. Babe Palar 7, Tel. 52183. Good quality and accordingly high prices.
Aneka Darma, Jl. Walanda Maramis. Women's clothing only.

PHOTO SUPPLIES

There are many photo shops of all kinds throughout the city but two are highly recommended for their reliable, fast service.
P.T. Modern Photo Film Co. (Fuji Color Plaza), Jl. M.T. Haryono, between Jumbo Supermarket and city center square, Tel. 51556.
Angkasa-Color Photo Service, Jl. Yos Sudarso 20, Tel. 62467. Color slide processing facilities; provides developing and mounting. 24-hour service.

HEALTH FACILITIES

The **Rumah Sakit Umum** on Jl. Yos Sudarso is the best, Manado hospital, but if you have time to make the 30-minute drive to Tomohon, the **Rumah Sakit Bethesda**, run by the Seventh-Day Adventists, is reputed to be the best in the region. A new hospital to be the biggest in Sulawesi is being built just outside of Manado.

Dr. Batuna, who also operates the Murex dive resort (and speaks excellent English), has an office across from the Rumah Sakit Umum, open in the late afternoon and evening. Next door to Dr. Batuna, is a very good English-speaking dentist, **Dr. Liman**, using modern equipment.

Drugstores are plentiful and cheap; prescriptions are not usually necessary.

—*Sheridan Angerilli and Mary Thorne*

EXPLORING MINAHASA

Extraordinary Day Trips from Manado

Roads radiate outward from Manado in several directions, all of them, it seems, leading somewhere interesting. Since the best hotels and travel facilities are in the city, and since most of the surrounding sights can easily be reached in a series of day-long excursions, your best bet is to base yourself in Manado and make a number of trips into the hinterland by rented car, minibus or public transport. This can actually be done in any number of ways, and the itineraries given below are merely intended as suggestions that neatly encompass many of the major sights.

Tomohon via Tasik Ria

This round-trip excursion follows the coast south out of Manado to Tasik Ria beach and on to Tanawangko, then cuts inland via Taratara to the highland town of Tomohon, offering a delightful combination of a visit to the beach, a taste of delicious Minahasan cuisine, and spectacular views of coastal coconut groves and highland clove plantations, all the while passing through picturesque rural villages. Start out early to fully enjoy the sights.

Tasik Ria is about 30 minutes from Manado, and is worth a stop to collect seashells, have a swim in the warm Sulawesi Sea and watch the local fishermen. There are tennis courts here, a children's playground and several cottages for rent by the beach. On Sundays it gets very crowded. Manado Seaside Cottages, on the road from Manado before Tasik Ria, offers excellent fresh seafood.

The village of Tanawangko, further south along the coast, has a deserted beach which fits perfectly most peoples' image of a tropical island paradise. At the southern end of the village, just after the Pentacostal Church and a bridge, turn right along a small, rough road that leads 2 kilometers (1.25 mi) to a long, sandy beach bordering on a wide bay. The swimming here is excellent; gentle waves lap the shore and there are plenty of seashells. Look out for falling coconuts, however, and be aware of unconfirmed rumors of small crocodiles said to inhabit the rivers flowing into the ocean at this spot.

Back at the north end of Tanawangko, turn inland to the mountains and follow a road that winds up through coconut plantations to the highland town of Tomohon

KAL MULLER

JILL GOCHER

(some 45 minutes away) via Taratara. Along the way the magnificent active volcano, Mt. Lokon (1595 m/5181 feet), looms into view.

The village of Tara-Tara at the southern foot of the volcano is a regional center for traditional music and dance. Performances of the *kolintang* (wooden xylophone) orchestra, the *cakalele* war dance, the *maengket* song and dance group, and the *lancier* dance group are held here at the Kemer open-air auditorium by prior arrangement.

The hilltop town of Tomohon, known locally as the "City of Flowers," sits in a saddle between two volcanoes, Lokon and Mahawu. The climate is delightfully temperate; fruits and a wide range of flowers—hibiscus, angel trumpets, bougainvillea, lilies, gladiolas, carnations and irises—are grown commercially to supply markets in Manado. The town's main road is lined with flower stalls, every yard seems to overflow with lush foliage, and the roadsides are planted with deep red croton plants. Well-proportioned ponies pull beautifully-decorated horsecarts, known as *bendi*, often leaving little room for motorized traffic. On Tuesday, Thursday and Saturday mornings a local market sells rats, bats and dogs (ingredients in the notorious local cuisine). Tomohon is famed as an educational center, and there is a large auditorium atop Bukit Inspirasi, a hill that gives a striking view of the town with Mt. Lokon in the background.

If you wish to climb Lokon, head back on the main road north toward Manado and obtain permission first from the village head (*lurah*) of Kakaskasan, a small village just to the north of Tomohon. The ascent begins just behind the village; any of the small lanes leading up the volcano will eventually bring you to a large stone quarry. From here, follow the lava flow up to a large side vent in the crater. At this point the landscape takes on the appearance of a charred moonscape. To reach the top takes a total of about 2 hours; be sure to bring sturdy footwear.

The half-hour journey back to Manado along a winding mountain road affords spectacular views. Excellent Minahasan food is available at restaurants in the town of Tinoor, from where you also have a panoramic view of Manado Bay. *Durian, langsat* and other locally-grown tropical fruits are also sold from stands along the wayside, as is *dodol*—a sticky-sweet concoction of dried palm sugar, coconut milk and nuts wrapped in bamboo leaves.

Further along, a turn-off to the right at the distinctly Sumatran-style gate at Pineling leads after about a kilometer to the Mausoleum of Imam Bonjol, the Islamic cleric who led Minangkabau resistance against the Dutch in West Sumatra. Bonjol was captured

Opposite: *View inside Mt. Lokon before the 1986 eruption.* **Above:** *Tropical sunset at Tasik Ria.*

Manado Region

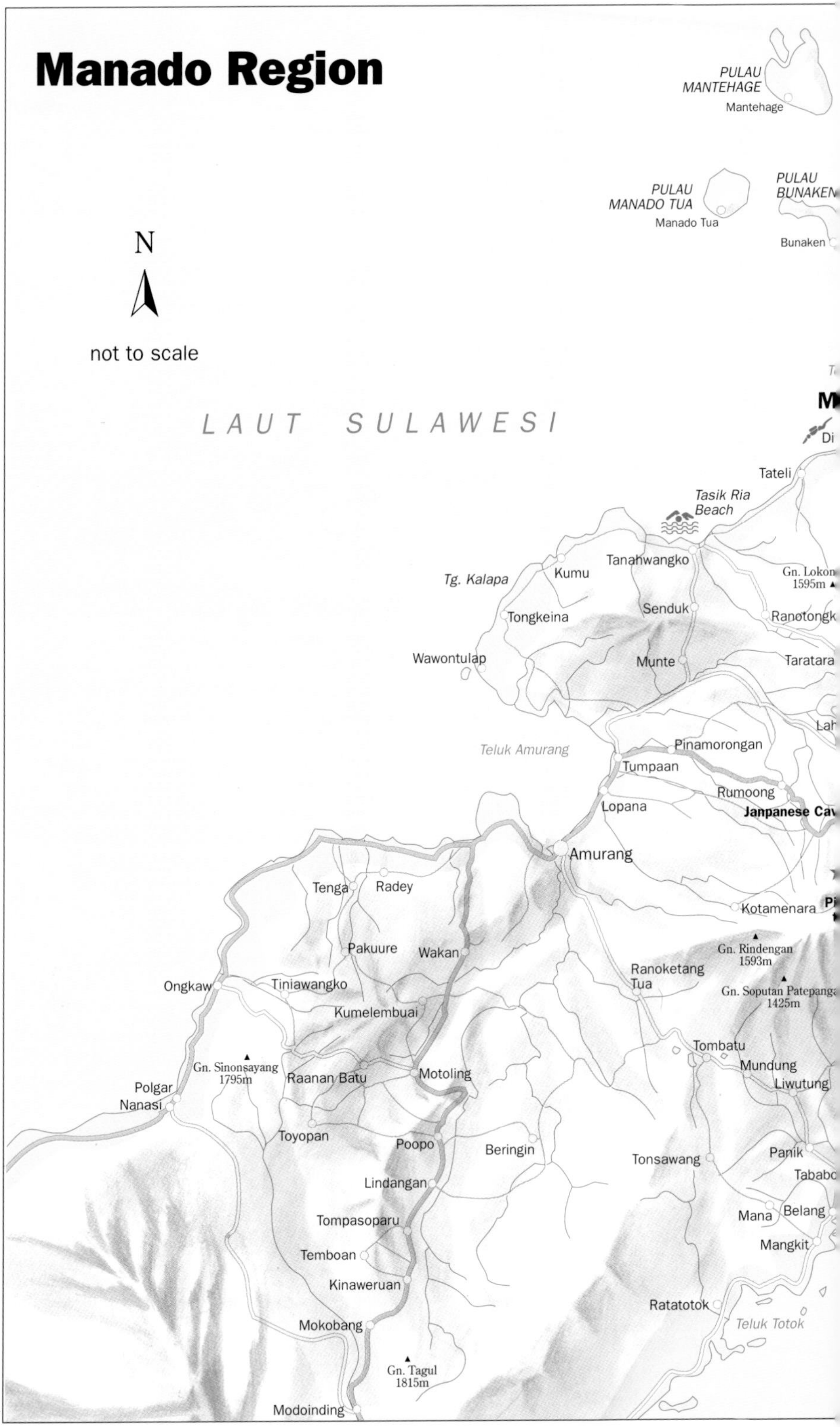

PULAU MANTEHAGE
Mantehage

PULAU MANADO TUA
Manado Tua

PULAU BUNAKEN
Bunaken

N

not to scale

L A U T   S U L A W E S I

M
Di

Tateli

Tasik Ria Beach

Tg. Kalapa   Kumu   Tanahwangko

Gn. Lokon 1595m ▲

Senduk

Tongkeina

Ranotongk

Wawontulap   Munte

Taratara

Lah

Pinamorongan

Teluk Amurang   Tumpaan

Lopana   Rumoong

Janpanese Cav

Amurang

Tenga   Radey

Kotamenara   **Pi**

▲ Gn. Rindengan 1593m

Pakuure   Wakan

Ranoketang Tua

Gn. Soputan Patepanga 1425m

Ongkaw   Tiniawangko

Kumelembuai

Gn. Sinonsayang 1795m ▲

Tombatu

Polgar
Nanasi

Raanan Batu   Motoling

Mundung
Liwutung

Toyopan

Poopo   Beringin

Tonsawang

Panik
Tababo

Lindangan

Mana   Belang

Tompasoparu

Mangkit

Temboan

Kinaweruan

Mokobang

Ratatotok   *Teluk Totok*

▲ Gn. Tagul 1815m

Modoinding

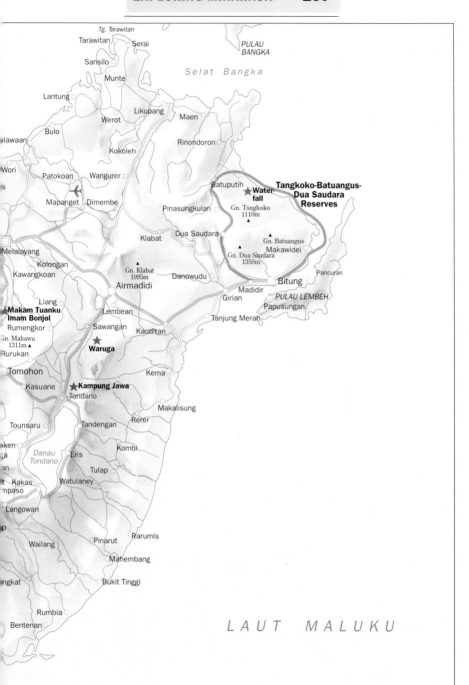

Tg. Tarawitan
Tarawitan
Serai
PULAU BANGKA
Sansilo
Munte
Selat Bangka
Lantung
Likupang
Maen
Werot
Bulo
lawaan
Kokoleh
Rinondoron
Wori
Patokoan
Wangurer
Batuputih
Water-fall
Tangkoko-Batuangus-Dua Saudara Reserves
s
Mapanget
Dimembe
Pinasungkulan
Gn. Tsngkoko 1110m
Klabat
Dua Saudara
Melalayang
Gn. Batuangus
Makawidei
Kolongan
Gn. Dua Saudara 1350m
Kawangkoan
Gn. Klabat 1995m
Danowudu
Pancuran
Airmadidi
Bitung
Liang
Lembean
Madidir
Girian
PULAU LEMBEH
Makam Tuanku Imam Bonjol
Sawangan
Kauditan
Papusungan
Rumengkor
Tanjung Merah
Gn. Mahawu 1311m
Rurukan
★ **Waruga**
Tomohon
Kema
Kasuane
★**Kampung Jawa**
Tondano
Tounsaru
Makalisung
Tandengan
Rerer
ken
à
Kombi
an
Eris
t Kakas
Tulap
mpaso
Watulaney
Langowan
p
Rarumls
Wailang
Pinarut
ngkat
Mahembang
Bukit Tinggi
Rumbia
Bentenan
LAUT MALUKU
Danau Tondano

in 1837 and exiled to Ambon, then later to North Sulawesi. He died in 1864 near the site of the grave.

Lake Tondano

The main road out of Manado to the east to Airmadidi and Bitung leads through coconut groves past a large factory, P.T. United Coconut Tina Indonesia, which is a good place to see the ubiquitous nuts being processed. Every part of the coconut is used—to produce oil, charcoal, animal fodder, coconut

milk and mountains of copra or dessicated coconut meat. If phoned ahead of time, Bapak Dengah (Tel: 52108) can arrange a tour if the factory is currently in production.

Also on this road is Taman Anggrek, an orchid garden containing more than 80 varieties of orchids from the different parts of North Sulawasi. Over 10,000 specimens, including 2,000 hybrids, are on display in gardens and greenhouses. All varieties bloom only part of the year, at different times. If you are lucky you may see the rare Anggrek Hitam, a black orchid which usually blooms in November and is found only here and in Kalimantan. Hours are 08:00 to 17:00. There is a children's amusement park next door.

Just beyond Airmadidi (30 minutes from Manado) a road to the right leads south to Tondano. The village of Sawangan, five minutes further on, is the site of the largest collection of ancient sarcophagi or *waruga* in the province. A small sign (on the right) indicates a narrow road to the left. The cemetery contains 144 *waruga* and a small museum.

Dating from as early as the 9th century, the *waruga* are rectangular stone burial chambers with holes in the middle and prism-shaped lids. According to legend, people knew of their death shortly before it occurred in pre-Christian days. Endowed with supernatural powers, they singlehandedly carried a mammoth stone tomb to a chosen site, with the top balanced on their head.

The sarcophagus was placed above the ground and the deceased was later arranged inside, sitting upright on a porcelain bowl. Tradition decreed that valuable jewelry adorn the body, but no clothing was permitted. The lid was placed over a layer of sealing material. However, the temptation offered by the jewelry was often too great, and many *waruga* have been opened and plundered.

In 1828 an epidemic in Sawangan forced the colonial government to ban the practice of above-ground burials. In 1977, most *waruga* in the area were moved to Sawangan, and the cemetery and museum were officially opened in 1978. The location downwind from the village is thought to provide protection from evil smells or anything untoward (of a spiritual nature) emanating from the graves.

Each *waruga* is decorated with carvings denoting the occupation, cause of death or characteristics of the owner. One shows a woman giving birth and women with fertility problems come here to pray for a child. The oldest resident of Sawangan conducts a ceremony beside this *waruga* on the night of the full moon. All *waruga* face the rising sun.

The museum displays salvaged contents of some of the *waruga*. There is a traditional belief that ancient Minahasans were of large physical stature, and the rings and bracelets on display do nothing to disprove this.

Beyond Sawangan, the narrow, winding road continues on up into the hills, arriving at the town of Tondano after half an hour. It follows the course of the Tondano River, with spectacular views of the gorge, skirting a recently expanded hydro-electric power station at Tanggari which supplies electricity to the region. Shortly before Tondano, caves used by the Japanese during World War II to store ammunition can be seen on the left.

Above, left and right: *The scenic highland town of Tomohon.* **Opposite:** *Ancient stone sarcophagi (waruga) at Sawangan, south of Manado.*

Just before Tondano town, a sharp turn to the left (at a point where the main road turns sharply to the right) takes one through the historically and culturally unique village of Kampung Jawa. Its name ("Java Village") indicates that some of the population descend from fighters captured in the Java War of 1825-1830, and exiled here by the Dutch.

Visit the unique Javanese-style Alfalah Mosque, which has been reconstructed several times on this site. It features old pillars inside as well as an intricately carved pulpit dating from 1868. The culture of the inhabitants of the village is a fascinating blend of elements. The language they speak is Tondanese (with a sprinkling of Javanese words), but many of the rituals and art forms derive from Java and Sumatra.

The road through Kampung Jawa and on past nearby Wulauan leads to a Muslim cemetery containing the recently renovated mausoleum of Kyai Modjo, the leader of the exiles. The hillock on which the mausoleum stands offers a dramatic view of Lake Tondano and the surrounding area (as do points further along the road should you wish to continue on up the mountain).

Tondano town, the administrative center of the Minahasa region, lies on the northern shores of Lake Tondano. It is a small town laid out with straight streets crisscrossing at right angles. Dr. Sam Ratulangi, an early Swiss-educated nationalist leader and the first post-war governor of Sulawesi, was born here, and there is an impressive monument to his memory in the north of the town.

Smaller roads from Tondano skirt both shores of the lake, and a trip all the way around it provides ever-changing vistas of the nearby mountains, rice fields and the lake itself. At the town of Remboken on the lake's western shore there is a government-operated tourist development which includes a small park, a hot spring-fed pool (open Thursdays, Saturday afternoons and Sundays) and a restaurant with a view of the lake. Boats may be hired for a spin around the lake, and there are cottages for rent. It is quiet and peaceful, except on Sundays.

Not far from Remboken, past the village of Kaima, is the small village of Pulutan where pottery is made. Just inside the village gates is a small factory where you can watch pots, vases and the like being made on a kick-wheel. You can buy the finished products for a few thousand rupiah.

Backtracking to Remboken and continuing on south around the lake, the road eventually brings you to Kasuang. Here a number of restaurants serve traditional Minahasan cuisine, which you can watch being baked in bamboo tubes over a large, open barbecue. The Tondano Indah Restaurant, on the eastern shore of the lake between Eris and Tondano, is also a good place to stop for food.

Once back at Tondano town, instead of

returning directly to Manado along the main road via Tomohon, you might want to take a scenic detour. Follow the narrow little road from Tondano up to the mountain village of Rurukan, half an hour away. This is a lovely excursion through small coffee stands and vegetable gardens. Once in Rurukan, turn left up a hill to a small area known as Temboan ("lookout"). It is only about 100 m away, but the road is so bad that you might as well walk. At the top of this hill you will find one of the most spectacular vistas in Minahasa—high-altitude, terraced vegetable gardens spread out before you in every direction, with Bitung, the Molucca Sea and Lake Tondano visible in the distance. From here a road leads down to Tomohon and thence to Manado.

Sonder to Watu Pinabetengan

The beautiful and varied scenery on this day-long trip beyond Tomohon to the south makes it well worth the effort. Added bonuses are visits to a natural hot spring and to the most sacred spot in all of Minahasa.

The road south of Tomohon to Sonder passes first through Lahendong, where seething energy just below the earth's surface is dramatically apparent. A hut and a green sign on the right mark the head of the well-marked trail to the springs. These are interspersed with ominously hissing fissures and gurgling pools of mud. There is a primeval feel about the site, and the sulphuric odors are powerful. The largest hot spring provides a place for bathing, and there is a small changing hut.

Past Leilem, a village known for its handsome handmade furniture, you come to the village of Sonder, which in the 1970s had the highest per capita income of any village in Indonesia. Many of the people here got rich when clove prices were high. Unlike many other Minahasans, however, they diversified their investments and survived the subsequent drop in prices relatively unscathed. The people of Sonder are known throughout the region as energetic businessmen; indeed, they are involved in everything from selling cookies in small villages to running large businesses in the city.

The nearby Toar-Lumimuut tourist resort has a lovely swimming pool and park, and is a good place to relax and cool off after the drive from Manado.

About 15 minutes south of Sonder, and shortly before Kawangkoan, are the Japanese Caves—large tunnels built with forced labor where the Japanese hid ammunition and supplies during World War II. Enter this extensive cave system if you don't mind the pitch blackness and the bats flying around you. A guide from the restaurant across from the biggest cave will escort you with a flashlight.

Continue south from Kawangkoan toward Langowan, turning right just after the Minaesa Institute of Technology. A pretty drive through terraced rice paddies then brings you to Watu Pinabetengan—a stone believed to be the most spiritually powerful site in Minahasa. Through the ages, this has also proved to be a politically potent gathering spot for Minahasan leaders.

According to legend, Lumimuut, the primal ancestress from whom all Minahasans are decended, divided up her people at this stone and drew maps on it denoting the territory of each group. Later, seven Minahasan chieftains negotiated a unification of the area here. In 1642 a meeting was held to devise a defense against the invading Spaniards. Later in the 17th century, the Minahasan chiefs met at the stone to plan strategy during a war with neighboring Bolaang Mongondow. Dr. Sam Ratulangi, subsequently the first governor of the province, gathered here with other notables in 1939 to pray for success in the struggle for independence from the Dutch, and when this was achieved in 1949 another large meeting was held here to bless the newly-formed republic.

Pictographic carvings on the stone have never been deciphered, and most had unfortunately already been encased in concrete along with much of the stone before the government declared it a public monument. Ceremonies involving chicken and pig sacrifices are still held during the full moon, and people come here to consult with the spirits of their deceased ancestors. A local elder acts as medium.

Back on the main road, shortly before Langowan, a left-hand turn at the village of Toraget leads to another small village by the name of Karumenga, where you will find baths fed from a clear, sulphurous hot spring. Villagers boil eggs in the main pool, cooking them from the inside out to produce a firm yolk and soft, wobbly white. A five-minute walk through the jungle from here leads to bubbling mud pools. The return trip to Manado from Langowan can then be made via the scenic shores of Lake Tondano.

Opposite: *Dense, tropical rainforest inside the Tangkoko-Batuangus-Dua Saudara Reserve.*

Climbing Mount Klabat

Those with the agility of a mountain goat will welcome the opportunity to climb Mt. Klabat. Located directly to the east of Manado, this dormant volcano is the highest peak in Minahasa at 1,995 meters (6,500 ft)—offering fine views from the summit across the entire northern end of the peninsula.

A well developed trail begins just behind the police station in Airmadidi (see above under "Lake Tondano" for sights along the road leading here from Manado). You will need to stop here first to register. They will be somewhat concerned if you plan to make the climb without a guide, and local children will be appointed to lead you to the trailhead. Here, you'll have to pay a small "tax" on all cameras. Receipts are issued, and the children can be dispatched with a small tip.

Follow the trail to the first sign, marked "Pos 1," and take the left-hand trail up the hill. There are shelters midway up where you can spend the night if you get caught in a sudden storm. It takes most people 7 to 8 hours to reach the summit—but you had best plan an overnight excursion, climbing up the first day and spending the night on top to wake up early to catch the sunrise. Be sure to bring along warm clothing, a good sleeping bag and plenty of food and water.

Climbing or descending after dark can be risky along stretches of the trail because of the severe erosion, and should only be attempted with headlamps, as both hands are sometimes needed to negotiate the trail. The vegetation is quite dense, and moonlight would not be adequate. Water is only available at a few spots. On a Saturday night, expect to have company at the summit as this is a popular weekend outing for university students.

Into the tropical rainforest

The entire tip of the peninsula to the north and east of Mt. Klabat is covered in lush, tropical rainforests which have been declared a nature reserve. The Tangkoko-Batuangus-Dua Saudara Reserve, as it is known (the name refers to three peaks in the reserve) encompasses 9,000 hectares (22,230 acres) ranging from sea level up to 1,100 meters (3,400 ft). This is a spectacular area which offers you the possibility to see not only some of Sulawesi's unique animals and plants, but also a wealth of corals and fishes.

The most notable species in the reserve is the endemic maleo bird (see below). Alfred Russel Wallace visited the area in 1859 to collect specimens along the black sand beach. Sadly, the maleos have disappeared from this site, largely because of over-exploitation of their eggs after the village of Batuputih was established here in 1913. The few remaining maleos now lay their eggs at two open spots inside the reserve.

ALAIN COMPOST

The reserve also offers excellent opportunities to see the bear cuscus. This arboreal marsupial is fully dependent on a few species of trees; usually the guards know where to look. Tarsiers, macaques and wild pigs are also common. The anoa is rare and usually found at higher altitudes, but the *babirusa* is thought to be extinct here.

A wide variety of birds can be seen, notably the lilac kingfisher and a relative of the maleo—the much smaller Phillipine scrubfowl. The latter deposits its eggs between the decaying roots of trees, where heat generated by the decomposition of the wood incubates them. Flying lizards, gliding from tree to tree, are more numerous than in Dumoga-Bone. Mudskippers are common on the stones and rocks along the shore. Frigate-birds, white-bellied sea-eagles and other marine birds are often seen soaring overhead or fishing offshore.

Though it is only 60 km (38 mi) from Manado, access to the reserve is difficult and several days are required to see it properly. If you don't have the time, you can also simply hike into the rainforest from Danowudu along short, well-maintained trails. Danowudu is reached by taking a turn-off to the left (north) at Girian, just before Bitung.

After Danowudu, a narrow and dangerous track composed of loose volcanic scree runs north through the village of Dua Saudara to Batuputih, at the northern end of the reserve near the coast. Jeeps can make the trip in the dry season, but during the rainy season (November to March) you will have to hike three hours from Dua Saudara. You can also get to Batuputih by hiring a boat from Bitung—only an hour's journey.

There are two guesthouses near Batuputih, though accommodations are poor. However, several good trails give access to the forest, to the maleo nesting grounds, and to the summit of Mt. Tangkoko, which is covered in moss forest. Bring snorkling equipment, a sleeping bag and food along. There are a few shops in Batuputih which may be of use in obtaining fresh food. Sometimes villagers show up at the guesthouse offering fruit, fish or other seafood. During the hottest hours of the day, you can swim and relax on the black sand beach nearby.

Bitung

The port of Bitung is the other main point of interest in this area. Neatly laid out with wide boulevards, it boast two bizarre replicas of the Eiffel Tower and a striking church. Bitung is the main port of North Sulawesi, and has a fine natural harbor protected by the island of Lembeh. This is also the center for commercial fishing in the region. There are several excellent restaurants in Bitung serving Chinese-style seafood.

—*Sheridan Angerilli, Mary Thorne and RenéDekker*

MALEO BIRD

Sulawesi's Endangered Megapode

The unique flora and fauna of Sulawesi are characterized by both Asian and Australian features. One of the island's most spectacular birds, the maleo or *Macrocephalon maleo,* is of Australian origin. This endemic megapode does not lay its eggs in a nest or incubate them with body heat, but buries them on beaches or in volcanic regions where they are hatched by the sun or geothermal heat.

The unmistakeable long and rolling call of the male, one of the characteristic sounds of Sulawesi's tropical rainforest, betrays the presence of the maleo. Male and female are always seen together, looking for snails, insects and fruit on the forest floor or resting in trees. They are the most colorful of all megapodes (mound-building, large-footed birds native to Australia and eastern Indonesia), with their black-and-salmon plumage and strange, featherless helmet.

During egg-laying season, the maleo (which is abut the size of a chicken) digs a deep hole in which they bury their enormous egg (200-250 grams or 7-9 ounces). After the egg has been hidden away, the birds disappear into the forest and do not take any further care of it. The large size of the egg is an adaptation to the maleo's strange reptilian-like incubation process. It contains a large yolk, guaranteeing adequate nourishment during incubation.

The maleo chick can fly immediately after hatching and is completely independent, surviving without any form of parental nurturing. However, before it can fly away, it has to free itself from the burrow in which the egg was laid. This often requires struggling through more than 50 cm (20 in) of sand; it can take several days and is fraught with danger. Monitor-lizards, feral dogs and ants are never far away, ready to prey upon the chickling.

Maleos are found nowhere but on Sulawesi; there are approximately 50 communal nesting sites known on the island, most of which are situated on the northern peninsu-

la. The national parks offer excellent opportunities to watch the birds closely. You can even see the chicks raised, as part of a conservation project, under semi-captive conditions in hatcheries at the Tambun and Tumokang nesting grounds in Dumoga-Bone.

An endangered species, the maleo has a tenuous claim on its future survival. A considerable number of nesting grounds have been abandoned by the birds because of deforestation and the island's ever-expanding urban population. At other nesting sites, maleo eggs are heavily over-exploited for human consumption. Until recently, egg-collecting was traditionally supervised by local authorities, and enough eggs were left behind to guarantee viable populations. Despite regulations in force since 1970 which prohibit collection, nearly all eggs are harvested by human predators. Some of the eggs even find their way to markets as far away as Jakarta.

Hopefully, increased attention on the international scene will stimulate greater awareness among the local population as to the precarious existence of the maleo. Its preservation is important from a conservational point of view, and also simply because it is a unique part of the life of Sulawesi.

—*René Dekker*

Opposite: *A newly-born maleo chick burrows its way to the surface.* **Above:** *The author examines a maleo egg for signs of activity.*

BEYOND MINAHASA

Magnificent Land and Seascapes

The three districts of North Sulawesi beyond Minahasa are not prime tourist destinations, and facilities are more limited than in Manado. However, the magnificent land and seascapes, and the Dumoga-Bone National Park are ample reward for the extra effort required to visit the area.

Bolaang Mongondow

With at least two days to accomplish it, a "figure-eight" trip from Manado to the national park at Dumoga offers some of the most majestic scenery in the entire province.

Just south of Amurang, take the right fork onto the Trans-Sulawesi Highway, bordered by "wall-to-wall" coconut palms. Traffic consists of bullock carts laden with coconuts, and people carrying water to their homes. There are small roadside restaurants where you can have a meal and take in the seaview.

At Inobonto, the road turns inland to Kotamobagu, but a smaller road also continues down the coast to the subdistrict town of Lolak, where you can stay at the comfortable beachside cottages of the Molosing Beach Motel. The hotel is quiet and often empty—an excellent place to relax.

Kotamobagu, the district capital, is set in a lush valley of irrigated rice fields. Beyond it, the road leads down into the Dumoga River valley. Following the eruption of Gunung Agung in Bali in 1963, hundreds of Balinese families were resettled in the Dumoga area under a government transmigration program which has also brought numbers of Javanese to the area. A sidetrip off the main road to the village of Werdhi Agung offers a little bit of Bali, Sulawesi-style.

Dumoga-Bone National Park

The jewel of the valley is the Dumoga-Bone National Park, a large and fascinating reserve unlike any other, which merits at least several days' exploration. Naturalists from Indonesia and elsewhere often conduct research at the

park, and you may make some interesting acquaintances in addition to enjoying the region's natural wonders.

Dumoga-Bone Park consists of 300,000 hectares (741,000 acres) of virgin rainforest lying between Gorontalo and Kotamobagu. Its primary function is to protect the water-catchment area for the new irrigation project. It was set aside as a national park in 1984, following severe deforestation of the surrounding hills that resulted in erosion and flooding, upsetting the irrigation plans. As a bonus, the unique flora and fauna of this large primary rainforest has been preserved as well.

Parts of the park ascend to 2,000 meters (6,600 ft). Most of it is impenetrable because of dense vegetation and steep hills. Several forest types, each with its own characteristic vegetation, can be recognized. Visibility in the lowland rainforest, with its undergrowth of rattan and giant livistona leaves, is often less than 10 meters. At 800-1,000 meters the lowland rainforest gradually changes into a more open montane rainforest with pandanus trees. At approximately 1,500 meters, the montane rainforest gives way to cloud-covered upper montane forest, and thick bright-green moss covers the ground. Trees are covered with beard-moss, which gives the forest a fairy-tale air of enchantment.

Only a few trails and rivers give access to the interior of the park, which is extremely rich in animal and plant life. Most of the island's 80 endemic bird species are found here. The best place for bird-watching is the forest edge, where magnificent hornbills, beautifully colored kingfishers, parrots, pigeons and birds of prey are common.

Wild pigs, Celebes macaques and the tiny, night-dwelling spectral tarsier, which produces high-pitched, insect-like sounds, are all around. *Anoa* and *babirusa* can be seen, but they are shy and normally inhabit higher altitudes. Insect life is abundant and fascinating. Butterflies (especially common on sandy riverbanks), moths and dragonflies are present in an unbelievable rainbow of colors. The humming of cicadas fills the air and beetles of all sizes seem to be everywhere.

Although there is little to fear from ferocious fauna inside the park, some animals and plants can be a nuisance. Leeches are common at higher altitudes, and are always eager to tag along. Shrub-mites, practically invisible, will dig under your skin and cause incredible itching. A mixture of dibuthylphtalate (5%) and benzylbenzoate (5%) in soapy water, splashed on your socks and clothes, is

sufficient protection from these pests, even after wading through rivers. Fortunately, mosquitoes are not much of a problem.

Snakes are common, but seldom seen. Pythons grow up to seven meters (22 ft) or more. Poisonous pit vipers and kraits will not cause you any harm unless you disturb them. Rattan, a natural resource with high economic value for the furniture industry, is covered with sharp spines which can rip your clothes. Good boots and proper clothing are therefore *de rigueur*. If you want to spend the night in the forest, you are advised to bring a hammock and basher instead of a tent. At higher altitudes you will definitely need a sleeping bag, for the nights can get cold.

Park headquarters are at the eastern entrance near the village of Doloduo, 50 km (30 mi) west of Kotamobagu (an hour by car or minibus). Over 200 scientists participated in Project Wallace in 1985—the largest international entomological expedition ever mounted—and their basecamp and a newly constructed laboratory at Toraut close to the headquarters may now be used by tourists and students. Accommodation and hospitality are assured, and the park guards will act as your guides. Near the entrance are several small restaurants offering excellent food.

Several day-long excursions can be made. Ask at the office for the best routes to follow. Tambun and Tumokang, two major maleo nesting grounds heated by hot springs are in the vicinity and offer you the opportunity to watch the birds and their chicks closely. The Kosinggolan floodland—an artificial wetland resulting from the irrigation project—harbors darters, woolly-necked storks, herons, whistling-ducks, rails and eagles. Mt. Mogogonipa, an isolated peak rising 1008 meters (3,325 ft), has a beautiful forest with pandanus trees and tree ferns; the top of the peak itself is covered with moss. If you'd prefer to just relax, you can sit on the veranda of the guesthouse and read, or go for shorter strolls in the forest just behind the headquarters. September and October, when rainfall is the lowest, are the best months of the year to visit this side of the park.

Return to Manado

Returning past Kotomobagu, travel up the valley through the coffee plantations toward Modoinding, near the border with Minahasa. Another smaller national park, Gunung Ambang, may be visited with a guide from the PPA office at Mongkudai Baru. A bit

more than three hours of walking leads through highland agricultural fields and into montane rainforest with tropical birds and *anoa*. The latter, it should be remembered, are aggressive and are to be treated with respect. Smoking sulphur fumaroles overlook the valleys here, and it can be cool and wet, so bring suitable clothing, water and food.

Coming out of Gunung Ambang, the road skirts two highland lakes, Moat and Bunong. The lakes are apparently very deep, and are even said to harbor monsters. Once again, spectacular views. The road leads through neat little mountain villages which provide an interesting contrast to the coast. Vegetable gardening is the mainstay of the local economy, providing the wide variety of vegetables available in the markets of Manado.

Having descended along the winding forest road, you rejoin the Trans-Sulawesi Highway before Amurang. The trip back to Manado can then be made either through the mountains and Tomohon, or via Tanawangko and Tasik Ria along the coast.

Gorontolo

Gorontalo, the second-largest city in North Sulawesi with a population of some 110,000, is located at the eastern end of Lake Limboto, at a point where the lake and three rivers

Above, left: *The tiny tarsier.* **Above, right:** *The colorful maleo bird, with its featherless "helmet."*

drain into the sea. There are daily flights from Manado, as well as a rather lengthy bus connection. This attractive little city has wide, tree-lined avenues and some interesting examples of Dutch colonial architecture.

The main form of transportation here is the horse-drawn *bendi*, and an interesting hour or two can be spent touring the city and the harbor area for around $1 per hour. There is an impressive range of shops, and several on Jl. Jendral Suprapto specialize in the local *krawang* embroidery for which Gorontalo is famous. At *warungs* you can sample a local delicacy known as *milu siram*, a tasty fish stock with corn (*milu*), lemon and grated fresh coconut.

The coast to the east of Gorontalo is picturesque, and you will find good beaches along the road. Charter *mikrolets* at the central terminal for around $1.75 an hour to make a trip past the harbor along the coast. The ruins of an old fort can also be seen in the vicinity, overlooking Lake Limboto.

Tahuna on Sangihe Besar

Tahuna is the capital of the Sangihe-Talaud group, which includes some 77 islands strewn to the north of Sulawesi, 47 of them inhabited. The area is known for its fertile soil, its high-quality nutmeg and its palm trees. There are many active volcanoes here, including Mt. Awu on Sangir Island, which has claimed over 7,000 lives in recent years.

The early-morning Merpati flight from Manado to Tahuna ($40) gives you magnificent views of Bunaken and other small islands fringed by coral. Naha Airport is a thin swath cut into the coconut plantations; from here minibuses pass along the coast road and then up into the mountains through clove and nutmeg plantations.

Explore the morning market at the old harbor, to see tuna being landed from small fishing boats. The market is a five-minute walk from the New Victory Hotel along Jl. Raramenusa past the post office. Spare some time to examine the craft shops selling the carved ebony for which the area is famous.

The Pan Marine boat, which offers the fastest service back to Manado, leaves in the afternoon. Dolphins often follow you out of the harbor, and you are likely to see flying fish as well. During the remaining daylight hours, the passing island scenery mirrors all the most romantic images of the tropics. During the hours of darkness, distant volcanoes emit a red glow from lava pouring down their sides. The boat calls at Siau around midnight and arrives in Manado at 04:00. This boat trip is best avoided during September and October, when prevailing southerly winds make for a rough voyage.

—*Sheridan Angerilli, Mary Thorne, and René Dekker*

Above: *An old fortress overlooking Lake Limboto.*

North Practicalities

Includes all areas outside of Manado. City code: Gorontalo 0435. All prices in US$

For transportation details, see "Manado Practicalities." The most efficient way of traveling around Minahasa and on to Bolaang Mongondow is by rented vehicle, though armadas of minibuses ply many of the routes mentioned. In towns like Gorontalo and Sangihe, small local public transport (*oplet*, *mikrolet*, etc.) can be chartered by the hour for modest amounts. Hotels can usually help in making arrangements. The overnight bus trip from Manado to Gorontalo takes around 12 hours.

By air, Gorontalo is an hour from Manado, and both **Bouraq** and **Merpati** operate daily flights. The local airport, Jalaluddin, is about an hour's drive from the town, and minibuses provide good connections to your hotel for about $1.75.

Merpati flies early in the morning from Manado to Naha on Sangihe Besar ($40 one way). The plane is a small 20-seater Casa and the flight takes one hour. Views are superb.

By sea to or from Sangihe, the best service is **Pan Marine** boats. There are both VIP and first-class cabins; only the former provide any privacy. Snacks and meals are included in the price of the ticket, and are served in the cabin. It is advisable, however, to take additional food and drink along.

Sonder

Stay at the **Toar-Lumimuut** tourist resort. New, lovely swimming pool and park. Can be booked through **Indra Kelana** travel agent in Manado, $12-17 D with breakfast. On the road out of Sonder towards Kawangkoan, **Yehovani's** is open 24 hours, serving Minahasan dishes for a fixed price of 80 cents; *sate* is extra.

Bitung

Good places to eat seafood and Chinese food include: **Hawaii**. Jalan Pertamina, Tel. 21712; and **Virgo**. Jln. Jos Soedarso (the latter is on the main road from Manado as it enters Bitung).

Bolaang Mongondow

A relaxing and quiet place to stay is the **Molosing Beach Motel and Cottages** in Lolak, just past Inobonto. Manado office: Tel. 62162. 8 chalets on the beach, AC, small refrigerator; 3 basic chalets on nearby Molosing Island. All meals must be taken on the mainland. Electricity and water available for part of the day on the island.

In the **Dumoga-Bone Park**, stay in the government chalets at Toraut. Must book in advance through the PPA (Nature Conservation Bureau) office near the New Garden Hotel in Manado. Failing this, try *losmens* at Imandi.

Gorontalo

Hotel Indah Ria, Jl. Ahmad Yani 29, Tel. 21296, is a basic but comfortable hotel. Some rooms have AC and video; $8 includes all meals. Great bargain. **Mini Saronde** at Jl. Walanda Maramis 17, Tel. 21735, 22677, is Gorontalo's top hotel; AC, fridge, hot water and balcony for $23 D. **Wisata Hotel**, Jl. 23 Januari 19, Tel. 21736 or 21737, is comfortable with good food and AC for $10.

Eat at **Milado**, in the center of town for good Chinese food, or at the **Brantas** *warung* opposite the central mosque.

Tahuna (Sangihe Island)

The place to stay is the **New Victory Veronica** on Jl. Raramenusa 16, Tahuna, Tel. Tahuna 79 or 111, the best hotel in town. VIP or standard rooms with or without AC. The food is good and plentiful.

Tangkoko-Batuangus-Dua Saudara Reserve

Try to spend at least one day in this beautiful nature reserve and enjoy some jungle hiking. You have a good chance of encountering some interesting species of wildlife here.

Get a permit from the PPA Office at Jl. Babe Palar 67, P.O. Box 80, Manado, Tel. 62680; a permit costs 60 cents. The head of PPA (Ir. Mulyadi Susanto) will provide a 4WD vehicle to take you to Batuputih, the village at the northern entrance to the reserve, $45 each way. Or go by public transport at a fraction of the cost, which does not take much longer. Catch a *mikrolet* bound for Bitung and get out at Girian. From there a jeep or Chevrolet will go to Batuputih, leaving at 07:00, 10:00 and 12:00. During the wet season, jeeps can only go as far as Dua Saudara village. From here you can walk to Batuputih in 3 hours.

There is a guesthouse at the edge of the park for $2.50 a night with breakfast ($3 with lunch or dinner). Prices negotiable. There is another guesthouse 30 min. inside the park entrance. Similar rates though less well-equipped, but it has the advantage of being inside the park itself. You must hire a guide at $6 per day. They are invaluable for taking you to the best places and for spotting the animals once you get there. They will even carry your pack, but you should tip for this.

There is a good walk up to the top of Mt. Tangkoko (1109 m/3400 ft). You may encounter cuscus, tarsiers, hornbills, flying lizards, maleo birds and Sulawesi macaques.

If you have the time to stay overnight. Get up at 05:00 for a walk with the Ranger; this is the best time of day to view wildlife.

To return to Manado you can charter a boat to Bitung for $18, stopping to snorkel along the way, or you can drive or walk out. There is a nice trail back to Dua Saudara which takes roughly 6 hours, enjoyable but tiring.

—Sheridan Angerilli and Mary Thorne

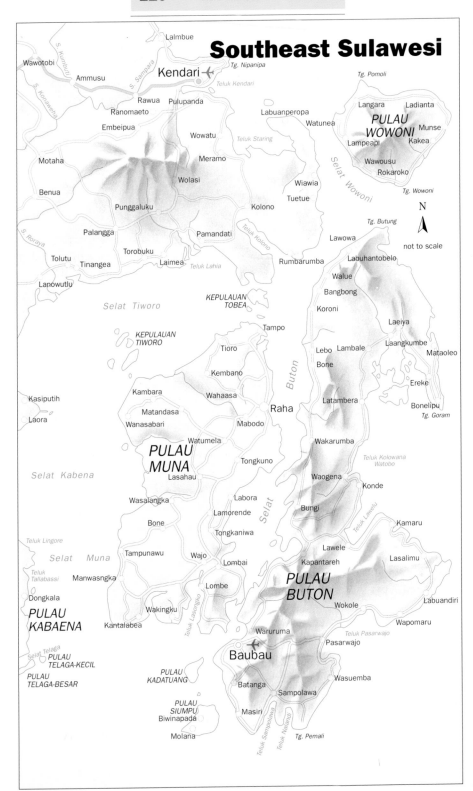

Southeast Sulawesi

Southeast Sulawesi

The province of Southeast Sulawesi (Sulawesi Tenggara, or Sultra) covers a total area of 38,000 sq km (23,750 sq mi, or slightly smaller than Ireland). Much of the peninsula is mountainous. Menkongga, the highest peak, is 2790 meters (9070 ft) high.

The southern plains are covered in the west with forest, and in the drier east with swaying fields of *lalang* elephant grass, while the low-lying area around Aopa, probably once an inland sea, is mostly swampland. Southeast Sulawesi has the feel of a largely undiscovered wilderness.

During the 17th century, the island of Buton off Sultra's east coast was an important stop for VOC ships en route from their headquarters at Batavia (Jakarta) and Makassar (Ujung Pandang) to the Moluccan "Spice Islands" in the east. The peninsula itself, however, was virtually unknown to the West until the early 19th century.

While Southeast Sulawesi is still the remotest, least developed and least-traveled area of the entire island, links with the outside are fairly good. There are daily flights from Ujung Pandang and Palu to Kendari. A well-paved road with a regular bus service connects Kendari with Kolaka on the west coast (140 km/85 mi away) in under four hours. Ferries link the peninsula with Bone in South Sulawesi, with Buton, Muna and Kabaena to the south, and the remote Tukang Besi Islands to the southeast. Smaller interior settlements are joined by unpaved roads and footpaths, which are often impassable in the wet season.

The province is sparsely populated by Indonesian standards. Its 1,220,000 inhabitants comprise several ethnic and linguistic groups. The Tolaki and the Tomekongga number 250,000; some 40,000 Tomoronene, who speak languages akin to those of Central Sulawesi, inhabit the Rumbia Poleang district and the island of Kabaena. On the islands of Buton, Muna and Kabaena there are 25,000 speakers of Wolio—the language of the former sultanate of Buton. Munanese is spoken on the northwest coast of Buton.

Bugis and Makassarese immigrants have settled along the coasts, as have groups of Bajau. More recent arrivals include transmigrants from Java, Bali and Lombok. In some parts of Southeast Sulawesi, new settlers actually outnumber natives. While there are occasional flare-ups between native inhabitants and the transmigrants, inter-ethnic relations in the province are generally smooth.

Rice and maize are the main crops on the islands, supplemented by cashews, cacao and teak. The sea yields trepang, tuna, shellfish and mother-of-pearl. The agricultural staple on the mainland is dry rice, though sago and various tubers are also planted. Fruits, soya, coconuts, cacao (especially in the area north of Kolaka), cashews, coffee, kapok and pepper provide additional income as cash crops. Forests yield valuable ebony and rattan.

In former times, the peoples of the interior bred water buffalo, which they traded as far away as the Toraja highlands. During the civil conflicts of the 1950s and 1960s, however, the buffalo population of Southeast Sulawesi was virtually decimated—plundered for food by rebel and government armies alike. Today goats, poultry and a bovine species imported from Bali are the most common domestic animals in the region.

On the west coast of the peninsula, where annual rainfall is as high as 3,000 mm (120 in), several thousand Bugis from Bone on South Sulawesi have planted more than 10,000 hectares (24,700 acres) of cacao gardens. Every weekend, a small flotilla of Bugis vessels makes the six-hour sea crossing over the Bone Bay into the Southeast, where the commuter-farmers tend their crop.

—*Dinah Bergink*

Overleaf: *Canoers in Napabale lagoon on Muna Island. Photo by Kal Muller.*

KENDARI AND KOLAKA

Major Towns of the Southeast

When a Dutch seaman named Vosmaer sailed into Kendari Bay in 1830, he "discovered" a tiny trading village made up of some 30 houses. Situated on a natural harbor in a narrow passage between steep cliffs, its entrance hidden from storms and invaders by a small island, Kendari was little known even to most local seafarers. The town was populated by various Bajau, Bugis and Makassarese merchants, who traded with the native Tolaki for forest and agricultural products.

The Tolaki trace their origins to the highlands north of Kolaka, near Andolaki at the source of the Konaweha River. As the "Brave People" (*to laki*) moved gradually southward, they pushed the peninsula's original inhabitants, the Tomoronene, down to Rumbia Poleang and onto Kabaena Island.

Kendari today is a growing town of 115,000. The provincial capital of Southeast Sulawesi and its largest city, Kendari is the key point of entry for travelers to Sultra, most of whom fly in from Ujung Pandang or Palu. The city consists of a long main road running along the north bank of the bay. On this road you will pass every building of importance in the city—government offices, hotels, restaurants and shops—as you head toward the rather shabby business district around the ferry terminal. As the administrative center for the province, Kendari is home to all major government agencies, along with entities such as oil-exploration companies.

The morning flight from Ujung Pandang gets in at about 10:00. The time between your arrival and the next afternoon's ferry to Buton and Muna should be just right to see what the area has to offer. While most visitors hit Kendari as a stopover on their quest for the thrills of Southeast Sulawesi's rugged, unspoilt natural charms, the town does offer a few incentives of its own.

Silversmithing, introduced by the Chinese about 150 years ago, is still practiced here, and there are high-quality works of gold and silver filagree for sale. There is also an 18-hole golf course, Kendari's main attraction, with well-kept greens and friendly caddies.

The area around Kendari offers some of Sulawesi's most scenic wilderness. The spectacular seven-level terraced waterfalls at Moramo, 75 km (45 mi) south of Kendari, are not to be missed. The trip by minibus takes

KAL MULLER

KAL MULLER

edge of thinly-forested hills, then crossing a rickety cantilevered bridge before moving into the grasslands which precede Raterate.

Here the vegetation is richer. Low hills covered with bright green *lalang* grass stand out sharply against the darker trees and bushes. Fruit trees line the road, and women gather firewood from the hills. After passing through Raterate, the road makes a gentle ascent before reaching a wide plateau. Roadside stalls along the way offer local produce: wild honey, pomelos, jackfruit, guava and *ubi-*

about two hours. The area near the waterfalls is home to a goodly number of West Javanese transmigrant families.

The fresh, cool water at the falls makes for excellent swimming, and enterprising locals there sell all kinds of drinks, including beer. The falls are best visited after heavy rains which swell the Kali Osena River, on which the falls occur. The river's source is two large mountain lakes 7 km (4.2 mi) distant. You can hike up to the lakes, a leechy business as there are no trails.

You can water-ski in nearby Moramo Bay (get there by speedboat from Kendari), which offers white sandy beaches and unpolluted waters. For more white sand beaches along with secluded rocky coves, head for Pulau Hari, half an hour by boat from Kendari harbor. The translucent green water and virgin coral gardens are ideal for snorkeling.

From the town itself, you can take a short 2-km stroll to an area with waterfalls and mature rainforest. Start out from the huts and Javanese-run shops (which cater to the hordes of local weekenders) at one end of the town's road. Some of the roadside trees have labels, though none in English except for those of the handsome ebony.

The road to Kolaka

Starting out from the Wawotobi bus terminal 8 km (4.8 mi) outside of Kendari, the minibus to Kolaka follows a reasonably good road through scenic countryside, albeit relatively unspectacular by South Sulawesi standards. About 40 km (24 mi) out of Kendari, after passing through a stretch of broad, marshy plains, the bus may stop at the town of Ammusu. Here you can enjoy a delicious meal of grilled river fish, spicy soup, rice and freshly squeezed lime juice.

Continuing on across the wide, muddy Kumbuti River (where you will see canoers poling their craft slowly by), the bus twists up through a hairpin-bend pass, skirting the

KAL MULLER

ubi, a tuber which many people in this region prefer to rice.

The view across the plateau, just before reaching Mowewe, is splendid—fields and houses quilt the broad expanses of the plain. The road cuts a long curve through more hills before winding down to Kolaka. Here the road follows a sparkling, rust-brown band of river through lush greenery. Flocks of goats slow the bus, and a large lizard occasionally scampers across the road.

Kolaka is a small, dusty town lying on a vast, sweeping bay set against a background of jungle-clad hills rising from the shore. Horse-drawn carts and stray goats saunter down the narrow back lanes of the town. In front of the decaying bus terminal, *bemos* and minibuses vie for passengers for the four-hour westward journey back to Kendari.

There is little to see or do in Kolaka, which is primarily a transit point between Kendari and Bone. Kolaka is, in addition to Kendari, the only practical port of access to Southeast Sulawesi. Travelers in South Sulawesi may wish to take the ferry from Watampone to Kolaka, then make the above overland voyage to Kendari in reverse (see "Southeast Practicalities" for details).

—Dinah Bergink, Ian Caldwell, Kal Muller

Opposite: *Southeast Sulawesi boat-builder.*
Above, left: *View of Kendari from the water.*
Above, right: *The steps of the Moramo waterfall.*

BUTON

Palace of a Powerful Sultanate

The little town of Baubau is set on the water's edge at the southern entrance of the Buton Strait. Including the nearby district of Wolio, Baubau has a population of some 52,000 inhabitants. From the hill above you can see the narrow strait stretching far to the northwest. On this hill sits the former fortress and palace of the rulers of Buton, an Islamic sultanate which traces its roots back over 30 generations to a goddess.

The kingdom of Buton

Legend tells of four immigrants from Johore who settled on the island of Buton. Moving inland, they founded a village on the site of the present-day palace of Wolio. The village became four separate districts, ruled over by the sons of the original settlers.

One day, one of the rulers chanced upon a bamboo stalk, inside of which he found the goddess Wakaakaa. She became the first queen of the territory, and even married a prince of the famous Javanese Majapahit kingdom. Their descendants became the royal line of the Wolio kingdom, whose influence extended throughout the region.

In 1540, the sixth ruler of Buton converted to Islam, becoming the first sultan. The sultan of Wolio was seen by his people as God's representative on earth, and was held responsible for the welfare of his country. If disaster struck the realm, the sultan could be forced to abdicate.

In its heyday, the sultanate of Buton included four vassal states: Muna, Tiworo (northern Muna and some small islands); Kalingsusu (northern Buton) and Kaledupa, one of the Tukang Besi Islands. The sultanate is mentioned in records of the Dutch East India Company as early as 1613. Buton sought support for its struggle for independence against the expanding kingdom of Makassar and the Ternate sultanate, of which it had been a vassal state in former days. After the Makassar kingdom was defeated by the Dutch in 1669, Buton became part of the territory administered under the Pax Neerlandica. This provided some protection for Butonese traders, but the Dutch monopoly excluded them from the spice trade.

In 1906, the sultanate was incorporated by the Dutch colonial government as a self-governing state. After independence, Buton was

integrated into the Republic of Indonesia. The last sultan, the 38th of the royal line, died in 1960, though his descendants still live in the *kraton*, or palace, of the ruler.

The palace of Wolio

The Wolio *kraton* is a large and relatively modern building built of teak in the traditional style. For a small fee (plus an official contribution) local children will show you inside; the palace is still inhabited, and is full of memorabilia. Of particular interest is the

cloth money once used in Buton—a hand-woven forerunner of the modern banknote.

Inside the *kraton* grounds is the *mesjid agung*, "great mosque," a rusting, tin-roofed affair claiming to be the oldest (16th century) mosque in eastern Indonesia. Inside the mosque is a sacred stone with two footprints, on which the newly elected sultan had to place his feet upon his enthronement.

The walls of the fort, built of white coral, stretch for nearly three kilometers (1.8 mi) round the summit of the hill. The walls were built in 1613 following clashes with the Dutch East India Company. In 1637, the Dutch general Anthony van Diemen (who gave his name to what is now Tasmania) tried to take the *kraton* with 700 soldiers, but was forced to relent because of the "terrible steepness" of the mountain, on top of which lay the city. Today the walls are in ruin, though restoration is beginning. Rusty cannon, many bearing the blazon of the VOC, lie at the walls pointing out to sea, or half-buried and forgotten in groves of banana plants.

The hilltop area encircled by the walls of the fort contains a number of wooden houses as well as several smaller *kratons,* the residences of former sultans (each new sultan built his own palace). Next to the mosque is an interesting creation—an ancient, weathered, teak flagpole-looking structure.

There is also an enclosed area in front of the mosque which appears to have had some

sort of ritual function. The *"yoni"* (female genitalia) half of a *yoni-linggam* stone altar is kept in here. Unfortunately, the male part is broken off and reportedly lost.

Next to the mosque lies the combined grave of Buton's first sultan and its last raja. Also in the vicinity of the mosque-grave complex are a few craftsmen turning out fine brass items. With the dissolution of the sultanate, most of the court arts have disappeared. However, the brass works (known as *kerajinan kuningan*) are still around, along with some pottery and silver. Traditional Butonese weaving, a dark blue or black cloth with silver stripes, is also still worn here as sarongs, shirts and jackets.

If you are planning to spend more than half a day in Baubau, you could hire an English-speaking guide. Expect to pay about $10-12 a day; you can ask your hotel to contact the office of the *camat*, or district head (tel. 318), to make arrangements.

A good white-sand beach called Nirwana is located about 10 km (6 mi) outside of Baubau. On Thursday and Sunday mornings from around 5:30 to 8:00, fishermen from the area sell their fresh catch here. You can buy a large fish for less than $1, and grill it for a picnic at the beach. The place gets pretty crowded with locals on Sunday.

For more beach activity, the Tukang Besi Islands can be reached in about 11 hours by freighter (usually daily) from Baubau, or in 6-7 hours from the port of Pasar Wajo down the road from Baubau. At the town of Ambuea on Kaledupa Island, you will find some magnificent coral gardens. There is no scuba equpment available in the area, so it's swimming and snorkeling only.

—*Dinah Bergink and Kal Muller*

Opposite: *Morning mists hang over Baubau.*
Above, left: *A "Mongol" helmet at the Wolio fort; said to be a momento of Genghis Khan's army.*
Above, right: *Dutch cannon at Wolio.*

MUNA

Horsefights and Cave Paintings

Red horses of all sizes and shapes, some mounted by stick-figure riders, cover the off-white walls of a large chambered cave near the town of Raha on Southeast Sulawesi's Muna Island. Other tableaux vie for space and the visitor's attention, but the horses run away with the show.

Barely a couple of dozen kilometers away from the caves and their stylized equines, the ancient practice of horse-fighting remains an integral part of local rituals, even though most of the inhabitants of Muna converted to Islam long ago.

Heady stuff, cave paintings and horse-fighting, complemented by one of the most beautiful turquoise-colored lagoons anywhere in the world. Raha, the capital of Muna district, is the undisputed highlight for travelers with the initiative to make it to these rather remote parts.

This would not necessarily be evident to the traveler who has just disembarked at Muna. While the docks, located at the end of a long jetty, have a touch of the picturesque at night when the ferries from Baubau or Kendari call into port, the town itself is one of those many places in Indonesia which seem to exist quite happily with no redeeming features. Rusting tin roofs, "hallo, meesters" and stares at foreigners.

Like many nondescript towns in Indonesia, however, Raha is the gateway to a fascinating hinterland. Accommodations here are inexpensive and quite passable, if far from international-class. In addition, Muna has a surprisingly decent network of paved roads, part of Indonesia's unheralded but rapidly improving infrastructure.

As in most parts of Indonesia, seeing the hidden virtues of Muna requires some initiative and a few words of *Bahasa Indonesia*. The owner of your hotel can arrange for you to find an English-speaking guide, or you can try to find Pak Suarnadi, who speaks English, at the office of the local *bupati*. You can also pick up an English-speaking guide in Kendari. If you really want to play it safe, you could also join a tour out of Jakarta, Ujung Pandang or Kendari.

A minimum of two days is suggested for the vicinity of Raha, and at least double that if you want to explore other parts of Muna Island. First thing after arrival is to send

KAL MULLER

word to Latugo village if you want to see horsefighting. It will take a day for the villagers to get the horses and their act together. Also send word to Bolo village that you will need a guide early the following morning to visit the caves with the prehistoric paintings. It's 9 kilometers (5.5 mi) by paved road from Raha to Bolo.

Visiting the caves

You want to get an early start to see the paintings, starting no later than 7:00, as there's a good hour's brisk walk to get to the main cave, and the sun can make life a bit too warm for comfort. You will be hot enough on the way back. Also, you might want lots of time to see other caves. Eighteen of the caves here have paintings, but only dedicated archaeologists will want to visit them all. Nine are readily accessible, and visiting these will be enough for a full day.

Leaving Bolo village, you pass through groves of cashew trees whose nuts are by far the most important cash crop for the locals. While you may be able to arrange for a motorcycle to take you most of the distance (around 6 km/3.6 mi) to the main cave, we suggest walking to simplify things. Taking short cuts, it's about a 4-km walk (2.5 mi), a bit over an hour at a brisk pace.

As you head out of Bolo village, the road takes you through fields of corn and cassava, staples in the local diet. Walls of coral block surround the fields to keep out wild pigs as well as the native *babirusa,* who would otherwise gorge themselves on the fruits, so to speak, of man's labors. (To further "enhance the region," as they say, police teams from Java have been coming on a yearly basis to have fun and practice their marksmanship on the animals. In 1989, a group of 150 military police bagged over 5,000 of them. The bodies were buried, as Islam forbids the consumption of pork. Though *babirusa* do look like pigs, technically they are ruminants, and *halal* or "kosher" under Islamic law.) Huts set on tall stilts serve as watchtowers to keep monkeys out of the fields—another pest against which crops must be guarded.

Taking shortcuts means clambering over the stone walls, but there are crude notched-log ladders to facilitate passage. Otherwise, the walk is an easy one, encompassing a series of low, rolling hills. The landscape around the caves is actually created from raised coral bumps and ridges, some with bare sides but most covered with vegetation.

Less than a half hour out of Bolo, just off the trail, you pass a large block of coral vaguely resembling a dugout cave. A few minutes further, you come to the first "cave," Liang Lasabo, which is only an overhang protecting the paintings—all red here as in the

Opposite: *Horsefighting at Latugo.*
Below: *Coin-divers in the Buton Strait*

KAL MULLER

KAL MULLER

other caves—of horses, people and (perhaps) deer. There used to be an impressive store of human bones and carved coffins here, as well as at other caves, but all the goodies were removed in a series of raids by Jakartan archaeologists between 1984 and 1986. The locals were not very happy with this plundering, but appear resigned to the wisdom of the central government.

Don't linger too long at this first cave—a better one, Liang Toko, is just over half an hour away. This is the most important of all the caves, with the most and the best paintings. A huge chamber cave, some 15 to 20 meters (50-65 ft) deep, it is filled with rounded stalagtites and stalagmites, covered with a layer of (clothes-staining) green. The ceiling drips and there is a trickling stream in the back. One of the rounded walls is covered with paintings, mostly large horse-like creatures, the biggest one of which has two riders. The other paintings, whose themes include suns and insect-like figures, vie for the white space. A magical place.

Evidently, the locals also think that there is some magic going on here. There are three permanent cave-keepers living close by, and offerings of food (topped by a white flag to attract spirits' attention) are made here at regular intervals. Every year in mid- to late January, during the lull in the rainy season when the planting of the corn takes place, a week-long ritual is held here, with dances, carousing and discreet drinking by the nominally Muslim villagers. The ceremony is called *tolak bala*, literally meaning "warding off disaster."

The village head, after consultation with the people, decides on the exact date every year. Aside from averting disasters such as epidemics and boats overturning at sea, the ritual also proposes to ensure abundant harvests. During one part of the festivities, groups of young people, boys on one side and girls on the other, recite formulaic quatrains

made up on the spur of the moment (*pantun*) to each other as a way of showing off their wit. Kick-fights between the young men are also held.

At harvest time, in late August and early September, many places on Muna hold festivals. There are dances where guests must participate, pulled out of the ranks of spectators by a pair of comely maidens. Food is cooked overnight on hot stones in a covered pit. Bamboo tubes filled with cassava paste and red sugar are a local speciality which is always served here. The harvest festival is held at or close to the time of the full moon, and lasts anywhere from one to three days.

Near Liang Toko, there is another similar—if somewhat smaller—cave, Liang Kobori, with but a few small paintings. These are primarily interesting because of their motif—they represent men in tiny ships. If you still have the stamina, there are other caves nearby to explore. Or you can head back for something completely different.

The emerald lagoon

About 16 kilometers (10 mi) south of Raha is the Napabale lagoon, a local recreation spot. Crowded on weekends. Low but steep coral walls surround this breath-taking natural gem. You can rent canoes here; one of the outriggered or double-hulled jobs with a connecting plank platform helps prevent heart attack for those carrying cameras.

KAL MULLER

KAL MULLER

You can paddle your own canoe or rent one with one or two paddlers. At one end of the lagoon, a low cave allows passage to the next lagoon at low tide. This second lagoon is connected to the sea through the Strait of Buton. A small island, easy to circumnavigate, protects the entrance into the lagoon. There's a white-sand beach there and clean waters with seaweed.

The swimming is great everywhere, but the snorkeling is mediocre, as there are few fish around. In the inner lagoon you might see some long, thick, worm-like beasts feeding on the bottom. This is a wonderful place to spend a couple of hours but, especially on weekends, you are the main attraction for the crowd of locals.

Mustang machismo

Horsefighting goes on everywhere on Muna, but it's easiest to arrange and see at Latugo village, 24 kilometers (15 mi) outside of Raha. While it was—and still is—primarily a ritual practice, locals are willing to stage the event for visitors, provided they are given at least a day's notice.

A wide field is used for the event. Two troops of mares are "shown" to each stallion to "put them in the mood," as the villagers say. Then, with ropes around their necks, the two contestant stallions are introduced to each other, with obvious results. Rearing up and looking for a likely hold for their power-ful teeth, the stallions fight savagely for supremacy of the passive mares, with the crowd cheering for their favorite.

Eventually, one of the stallions decides that flight is the better part of valor, and gallops off the field to the jeers of the audience, which bother him not at all. Another challenger is brought in to dispute the hard-won victory. Although they do bite and kick each other quite enthusiastically, the damage is seldom serious. If it looks like the fight is getting too rough, the horses are pulled apart. It's a magnificent spectacle, much appreciated by the villagers, but somewhat unsettling to faint-hearted foreigners.

Horsefighting appears to be a remnant of the island's heathen days before the advent of Islam. Apparently, it was once performed to celebrate the return of victorious war parties and their booty of human head trophies. Stallions also fought at various festivals held among the aristocracy—weddings, first haircuts, 40 days after birth, etc. Then, as now, the spectacle was enlivened by lady jockeys riding astride piles of pillows and men with *parangs* (local machetes) demonstrating the art of horseback deer-hunting.

—*Kal Muller*

Opposite, above: *Ancient art at Liang Toko cave.*
Opposite, below: *An Islamic Muna boy during the celebration of his circumcision.*
Above: *A quiet corner of the Napabale lagoon.*

Southeast Practicalities

Includes Kendari, Kolaka, Baubau (Buton) and Raha (Muna). Telephone code: 0401. All prices in US$. S=Single; D=Double. AC=air-conditioned.

The main attraction of Southeast Sulawesi is its scenery—wild and grand. Very few tourists visit this province, and you should expect to be the center of attention for much of your stay. This is "Hello Mister!" country, but people are friendly and helpful. A smile and a "Hello Mister" in return work wonders, as do a few words of Indonesian. People are naturally curious to know more about their foreign visitors, and what life is like in the remote, outside world.

Kendari

It is impossible to get lost in Kendari: the town consists essentially of a single main road 8 kilometers long: its name changes several times along the way. Most hotels, restaurants and government offices are located on this road.

There are daily morning flights and four afternoon flights a week from Ujung Pandang ($39); there are also daily flights from Palu. There are 2 twin Otter flights a week from Pomala (mine and ferro-nickel processing plant, 25 km/14mi south of Kolaka). You can charter planes to Baubau.

Kendari's airport is 35 km (21 mi) north of town: both **Merpati** (Jl. Konggoasa 29, Tel. 21729) and **Garuda** operate a taxi service for $2.50. You can also hop on one of the crowded minibuses at the airport, which take about half an hour and charge $2 a head for a dropoff anywhere in town.

Minibuses to and from Kolaka run regularly from the Wawotobi bus terminal. The journey takes four hours and costs $2.

A passenger ship, due to begin service in 1991, will make the following run twice a month: Surabaya—Ujung Pandang—Kendari—Kolonodale—Poso—Gorontolo—Bitung—Tahuna; return the same way.

GETTING AROUND

Bemos run constantly along the main road from Wawotobi to the shipping offices at the mouth of the bay. The fare for any distance is Rp150. Minibuses, or *mikrolet*, zip all over town. It's Rp200 to anywhere. There are four bus stations:
1) **Sentral Kota** for in-town minibuses
2) **Powatu** for transportation to Kolaka.
3) **Madonga** to waterfalls and villages near Kendari.
4) **Wawa** to **Tampo** (about 2 hours), the ferry terminal on the "mainland" opposite Muna Island.

ACCOMMODATION

Unless stated otherwise, the hotels below are all on the main road. The **Kendari Beach Hotel**, Jl. Sultan Hasanuddin 44, (Tel. 21988) is the only really good hotel. Set up on a hill a few minutes from the town center, it offers a sweeping view of the bay. At the rear is a landscaped garden and tennis court. Rates are $30-80 S, $35-85 D. Also has the best restaurant in Kendari.

Armins Hotel has recently opened a new extension at Jl. Diponegoro 75. This is the second best hotel in Kendari. The older **Armins Hotel** at Jl. Diponegoro 55 is small, hot and dimly lit: $8-12 S, $10-15 D, some rooms AC. **Sultra Hotel**, Jl. Sultan Hasanuddin 62, and **Resink Hotel**, Sultan Hasanuddin 54, are comparable: rooms range from $8-20.

Wisma Dua on Jl. Drs. Abdullah Silondae (just off the main road) is set on a hill with a view. **Wisma Cendrawasih** on Jl. Diponegoro is reputed to be the best budget hotel, but the family-owned **Wisma Nirmala**, Jl. Ir. Sukarno 115, a rambling wooden building up on a small hill close to the Merpati offices, is definitely worth a try.

FOOD

Eating in Kendari is more a challenge than a pleasure. Only the **Kendari Beach Hotel** can be positively recommended. Its restaurant serves a wide range of Chinese seafood for around $3 a dish, plus ice-cold beer and fresh lime juice. At the back of the menu are the cheaper, but tasty, Indonesian dishes: *nasi cap cai* (rice with vegetables and meat) and *nasi udang* (rice with shrimp) for just $1.50. The kitchen is spotless and the cooking good.

The dingy, dimly-lit **Restaurant Hillman** and the marginally more inspiring **Restaurant Royal**, opposite the old Armins Hotel, offer little competition, although the food at the **Rumah Makan Pekalongan** on Jl. Sultan Hasanuddin is said to be tasty. At night, the food stalls outside the cinema serve *bakso*, *mie* and other cheap dishes.

SIGHTSEEING

To see the wild and lovely scenery around Kendari it is best to hire a car or minibus. Contact the *Badan Pekerjaan Umum* (Department of Public Works) at Jl. Konggoasa 48 (Tel. 21019), which functions as a sort of travel agent and is delighted to show visitors around the area. The BPU (pronounced Bay-Pay-Ooo) has its own boats and vehicles and its rates are reasonable (a minibus costs $25 for the day). Basic diving equipment and water skis are available.

The BPU also has a glass-bottomed boat for visiting the coral gardens. To contact the BPU, call at the tourist information office on the hill above the shipping offices in the center of town; the staff are keen to help visitors.

The month before Ramadan, the Muslim month of fasting, is the usual time for marriages, which you may observe if you are decently dressed. Bring a small gift.

Muslim circumcisions (*sunat*) are frequent

occurences. These are festive occasions to which many guests may be invited, depending on the family's resources.

TOURS

P.T. Alam Jaya, Jln. Kongoasa 50, Tel. 21729 and 21019. Telex: 71447. The owner, Pak Suroso, and some of his staff, speak English. 5-7 day all-inclusive tours of Kendari and vicinity, Raha and Baubau, about $270 per person for 2, slightly less for larger groups.

Tourism Office

Kantor Parawisata Diparda, on the hill just behind the harbor, Tel. 21764. The head of this office, Pak Abdul Galib, speaks some English. His home phone is 21421.

SHOPPING

A good place to buy silver jewelry, carved ironwood and other items is the **Handicraft Exhibition Center** run by the Association of Government Wives, on Jl. Abdullah Silonda, across from the *Badan Pekerjaan Umum.*

If you have the time, we suggest checking out the government-run craft center **Pusat Kerajinan,** Jl. A. Yani, about 5 minutes from the center of town towards the airport. There are usually a half dozen men busy making filagree jewelry and other objects while the ladies do *ikat* dyeing and weaving. The center is open 08:00-13:30 except Sundays. A shop on the premises sells silver jewelry. Fine scale model sailing ships go for under $100—and a large boat, weighing 1 kg, for around $800. There are also woven cloths for around $20, and beautiful (but heavy) teak tables from $50-500.

Money Exchange

None for travelers' cheques. Bank Indonesia might accept US$ in mint condition.

Kolaka

There are more than a dozen *wisma* and *losmen* in Kolaka, but as yet no hotel. Few visitors stay here; most simply pass through en route to Kendari or Watampone. The main attraction is the hot springs 15 km (9 mi) north of Kolaka.

Kolaka is small enough to walk around by foot. The best places to stay are the **Losmen Rahmat**, Jl. Kadue 6, (10 rooms with bathroom at $4 per person) and the **Losmen Alkaosar**, Jl. Jendral Sudirman 20, which has rooms from $3-5.

Cheaper *wisma* include the **Losmen Aloha**, Jl. Kewanangan 19, also spacious and clean, for $3.50 per person; **Losmen Pelita**, Jl Repelita 56 ($3 per room); **Losmen Family**, Jl. Jendral Sudirman 6, $3 per room; and **Wisma Mustika**, also $3.

Ten minutes from town in the countryside is **Losmen Monalisa** with 9 rooms w/bathroom at $4 per person.

There are few good eating places in Kolaka; the **Rumah Makan Santana**, Jl. Kadue 17 and the **Restaurant Cita Rasa** on Jl. Repelita are okay. There are several more places alongside the bus terminal, the external appearances of which do not inspire confidence. There are an *apotik* (pharmacy) and a doctor on Jl. Rahma Farma: consultation hours are from 16:00-19:00.

A well-paved road connects Kolaka with Kendari in the west. Minibuses leave regularly from the main terminal; the fare is $2 and the journey takes 4 hours. The ferry to Bajowe near Watampone leaves nightly at 21:00. A number of unpaved roads connect Kolaka with the north and south of the peninsula.

Baubau (Buton Island)

Baubau is an attractive little town stretching along the foot of the steep hills along the southern entrance to the strait. The commercial district is around the river mouth; to the north are pleasant suburbs with old, Dutch-style bungalows and leafy gardens.

At the harbor entrance, take a *becak* to the *Pasar Sentral*. When you get off at the minibus terminal there, charter a *mikrolet* for the half-day ($2.50 to $4 depending on your Indonesian).

Baubau is small enough to walk around. To get to the old fort (called the *kraton*) catch a *bemo* up the hill for Rp150. You could also wait for a mikrolet marked "Kraton" to pass by, but they are crowded and you may have to wait quite a while to get one with an empty seat. If you decide to walk up to the fort, get an early start to avoid the heat.

KENDARI/MUNA/BUTON FERRY

If you want to visit Muna and Buton, there is no choice out of Kendari—it's ferries or nothing. When you disembark, purchase your return ticket as soon as possible upon arrival—the ticket offices can get crowded around departure times.

While some of the trip takes place at night, there is enough scenery in the daytime to make the trip memorable. The best views are in the late afternoon leaving Kendari. There are several idyllic islands on the left, and you will get a close-up view of Pulau Hari Island. On the right, steep vegetation-clad mountains tumble directly into the sea, interrupted only by an occasional sliver of deserted white sand beach. You will pass the odd sailing craft, as well as Campada, a Bajau village located on an island of the same name. Night falls much too soon for the rest of the ride to Raha. During the east monsoon, from June through August, the seas can get quite rough between Kendari and Raha, before reaching the shelter privided by Buton Island.

For the return trip from Baubau, you can take in the scenery missed during the night on the way there. The Straits of Buton narrows in a couple of places, but the low terrain on either side does not make for spectacular scenery. About 45 minutes out of Baubau, naked kids in canoes line the ferry's passage, begging for coins to be thrown into the water. Their eager, anxious expressions and shouts will part you with any spare change. A bit further, more canoes wait in "ambush" in case you have any coins left.

We recommend that you take one of the ferries with the two-passenger VIP cabins, where you can safely lock away your gear while wandering around the ferry—or even for a half day while you check out Baubau before taking the return trip on the same ship to Raha.

Ferry schedule

Departs		Arrives	
Kendari	(14:00)	Raha	(21:00)
Raha	(22:00)	Baubau	(05:00)
Baubau	(13:00)	Raha	(17:00)
Raha	(23:00)	Kendari	(05:00)

If you are fortunate, you may connect up with Pelni's **Rinjani** (see "Leaving Baubau" below).

FOOD AND ACCOMMODATION

Lodgings in Baubau are neither good nor cheap. The **Losmen Debora** on Jl. Kartini has dingy, box-like rooms for $6-10 non-AC, $25 AC. Across the street, the older but more spacious **Losmen Liliyana** has rooms for $6-10, plus a lounge and TV. **Losmen Pelangi** down at the waterfront has rooms for $1.50. There are several small restaurants; if you are there during *puasa* (the fasting month) many will be closed. The small, unnamed restaurant on the corner of Jl. Mohd. Husni Thamrin and Jl. Jos Sudarso serves decent if overpriced Chinese-Indonesian food. Portions are large: one is enough for 2 people.

The **Pelni** office is "up the hill a little way"—the local children will lead you there for a fee. The Post Office is to the right of the harbor entrance. Further into town there are a bank and a number of well-stocked shops, some selling film.

LEAVING BAUBAU

From Baubau you must return to Kendari by the same ferry, or—if you time it right—to Ujung Pandang (and Surabaya and Jakarta) on the **K.M. Rinjani**. A first-class ticket to Ujung Pandang, sharing a private cabin with AC and shower, TV and meals, costs just $30, versus $45 for the **Merpati** flight from Kendari (not including the return ferry to Kendari and airport taxi). The **Rinjani** sails once a month—any **Pelni** office will have the schedule—departing in the late afternoon and arriving in Ujung Pandang around 07:00. Book in Ujung Pandang, or in Baubau; the agent in Kendari deals only with freight and has little useful information. If there is any difficulty in booking your ticket, ask someone to 'arrange' it for you, for a small fee.

Raha (Muna Island)

For ferry connections, see "Kendari/Muna/Buton Ferry" under "Baubau" above. You can also take a bus (*bis Artur*) from Kendari to Raha. It's about a 2-hour ride to the port-village of Torobulu, then 2 more hours on the ferry and another hour from Tampo to Raha. It's $3.25 for the ride all the way; we suggest paying for 2 seats as things get mighty crowded. Not much to see along the way; the ferry ride is much better. At Torobulu, check out the barge, a simple outriggered canoe.

FOOD/ACCOMMODATION

There are 8 hotels/losmen on Muna Island, all in Raha. The **Andalas Hotel** ($8S, $14D) is the best—they even provide toilet paper with the sit-down johns, attached to the rooms. Three other hotels are more or less suitable: the **Rauda**, the **Alia** and the **Uham** ($7S, $12D), followed by the **Berlian**, the **Wuna**, the **Tani** and the **Karmia** (all $3S, $6D, with shared facilities).

The hotels provide a light breakfast as part of the price. Other meals must be ordered ahead, at $1.75, drinks extra. The **Andalas Hotel** will provide more Western-style meals for $3. There are 3 restaurants in town: the **Pacific**, the **Hawaii** and the **Nikmat**, all serving Chinese and Indonesian dishes, $1.50-2.50 per meal, plus drinks.

TRANSPORTATION

Public minibuses charge 20 cents to $2, depending on distance. The leave when fully crowded. The **Andalas Hotel** has an AC minibus for charter at $30 for a day.

The ferries from Kendari arrive around 21:00, the ones from Baubau in the late afternoon. Eager hands will vie to carry your luggage about 50 meters to *becaks* just outside the dock area. The *becak* drivers know where all the hotels are. It's Rp200 to anywhere in town.

For a guide, have your hotel contact Pak Siddo Thamin, who charges $20 a half-day, $30 for the full day. His English is quite good and he knows heaps about the history and culture of Muna. He can tailor a program to your schedule, interests and budget.

You can also get a guide through the *bupati* office (cheaper but not as good as Pak Siddo). Contact Pak Suarnadi there. Indonesian-speaking guides, who can also carry your gear, will take you to see the cave paintings for $3-4 a day.

MISCELLANEOUS

Stallion fights cost $140. Traditional dances, with full costumes and musicians, run about $100. Ask to see a *sunat* or a wedding. If you are lucky, one of might coincide with your stay in Muna.

There are excellent swimming and snorkeling off southwest Muna, at an island called Pasi Kuta, which in the Bajau language means "squid reef." Another island, Tapitapi, offers probably the best snorkeling anywhere in the vicinity of Muna. Bajau/Bugis villages on stilts are located at Pulau Bangko and Pulau Renda islands, along with Lakarama village.

—Ian Caldwell and Kal Muller

Travel Advisory

VISA FORMALITIES

Nationals of the following countries are granted entry into Indonesia without a visa for 60 days. For other nationals tourist visas are required and can be obtained from any Indonesian embassy or consulate.

Argentina	Italy	Switzerland
Australia	Japan	Thailand
Austria	Liechtenstein	United Kingdom
Belgium	Luxembourg	United States
Brazil	Malaysia	Venezuela
Brunei	Malta	Yugoslavia
Canada	Mexico	
Chile	Netherlands	
Denmark	New Zealand	
Finland	Norway	
France	Philippines	
Germany	Singapore	
Greece	South Korea	
Iceland	Spain	
Ireland	Sweden	

To avoid any unpleasantness on arrival, check your passport before leaving for Indonesia. You need at least one empty page for your passport to be stamped. Make sure it will be valid for at least six months after arrival. You must also have proof of onward passage, whether return or through tickets, and suffcient money. Employment is forbidden on a tourist visa or visa-free entry.

Visa-free entry is not extendable, and is only possible when entering via the following airports: Medan,Batam, Padang, Jakarta, Bali, Manado, Ambon, Biak, Kupang, Palembang, Pontianak, Balikpapan and Surabaya, or the seaports of Medan, Batam, Jakarta, Surabaya, Semarang, Riau, Bali, Manado and Ambon.

GETTING THERE

There are no international flights to Sulawesi. Most international flights to Indonesia arrive at Jakarta's international airport, where travelers must transfer to a domestic flight on **Merpati**, to reach Ujung Pandang, Sulawesi's major city. There are direct flights to Ujung Pandang from Jakarta, Surabaya (East Java) and Denpasar (Bali). Schedules and prices given below were correct in July 1990.

Merpati flights to Ujung Pandang

	Departs	Arrives	Fare
Jakarta	05:00	08:20	$210
(daily)	07:35	10:55	
	13:25	16:55	

Merpati flights to Ujung Pandang (cont'd)

	Departs	Arrives	Fare
Surabaya	06:00	08:30	$145
(daily)	09:20	11:50	
	10:45	13:15	
Denpasar	07:05	08:25	$105
(daily)	16:10	17:35	

During peak season, flights to Ujung Pandang are heavily booked. To complicate matters, Garuda and Merpati are in the process of rationalizing their operations, with Garuda handling international flights and Merpati all domestic flights. In theory, the above schedule will apply to Merpati flights. But don't be surprised if you book on a Merpati flight and a Garuda aircraft appears instead!

Garuda now offers a flight from Los Angeles to Biak, in Irian Jaya, via Honolulu. This flight either continues on to Bali, or there is a connecting flight. (Waiting passengers are sometimes entertained by local dancers—at four o'clock in the morning!) It may be possible to connect up with the daily Merpati flight from Bali to Ujung Pandang, which leaves Ngurah Rai airport at 07:05 am., though few people will wish to bypass Bali.

Airfares to Indonesia vary greatly, depending on the carrier, the season, and the type of ticket purchased. Generally speaking, a round–trip discount ticket from the States costs $800-1000, while a one-way ticket costs half that. From Europe it should be possible to fly for $1000 return to Jakarta.

Another way of getting to Sulawesi is by boat. Indonesia's biggest passenger shipping company, **Pelni,** calls frequently at Ujung Pandang from Jakarta and Surabaya. If you have three or four days to spare, it is possible to travel by luxury liner, the Rinjani, to Ujung Pandang, which departs from Tanjung Pinang (a three-hour ferry ride from Singapore) once a month. Write or enquire at Pelni's offices in Singapore at 50 Telok Blangah Road, 02–02 Cityport Centre, Singapore 0409 Tel. 2726811. A first-class cabin with private shower and meals costs less than the airfare from Singapore to Ujung Pandang, and you get to stop off en route in Jakarta and Surabaya.

CUSTOMS

The entry into Indonesia of narcotics, arms and ammunition, TV sets, pornographic materials, printed matter in Chinese characters and Chinese medicines is strictly prohibited. Advance approval is necessary to bring transceivers or large movie equipment. All films and video cassettes must be reviewed by the Indonesian Film Censor Board.

On entry into the country, 2 liters of alcoholic beverages, 200 cigarettes, 50 cigars or 100 grams of tobacco are allowed. Perfume in reasonable amounts is also permitted. There is no restriction on the import and export of foreign currencies in cash or travelers cheques, but there is a limit on the export of Indonesian rupiahs—no more than Rp50,000.

TRAVELING IN SULAWESI

Ujung Pandang's airport is located some 25 km (14 mi) north of the city. There is a taxi service from the airport, with fixed one-way fares of $6 and $8 (AC) to anywhere in town. Pay the cashier at the desk and receive a coupon which you will give to your driver. If you don't have much luggage, you can also walk out of the airport to the main road and catch a public *bemo* minibus into town for just $0.30 (Rp500).

Taxis and minibuses with an English-speaking driver/guide can be hired at good hotels in Ujung Pandang. Rates are about $3 per hour (two hours minimum) or $30-40 per day, a bit more for air-conditioning, newer vehicles and longer journeys. Families or small groups can charter a private mini-bus with driver at about $25 per day plus fuel. Stopovers and side trips can be planned, and this is an ideal way to see South Sulawesi.

The local pick-up minibuses (known as *bemo*, derived from *becak-mobil*) and inter-island buses are convenient and inexpensive. You can travel from Ujung Pandang to Manado in the distant north for less than $50, though a straight–through journey is not recommended. Self–hire vehicles without drivers are difficult and expensive to obtain. Unless you are used to Indonesian driving conditions—a complete absence of rules and a sixth sense as to what the other person is about to do—it is better let a local driver take the strain.

There is one *bemo* station (Sentral) and one main bus terminal (Panaikan) in Ujung Pandang. *Bemo* routes radiate outward from Sentral, as far north as Maros and as far south as Sungguminasa. Fares for any distance in town are Rp200; to Sungguminasa the fare is Rp250. *Bemos* can be flagged down in most parts of town, or along any main road, though the government is trying to regulate routes and stops.

To travel to more distant places, you must catch a coach or minibus from Panaikan terminal. The terminal is 15 minutes from the center of town (as much as 30 minutes if traffic is bad). The taxi fare is $3, though you may be asked for $5. There are regular *bemos* to Panaikan from Sentral.

From Panaikan, coaches and minibuses leave frequently to all large towns in South Sulawesi. The last coaches to Rantepao leave at 19:00, though it is sometimes possible to catch a coach to Bone or Singkang as late as 20:00.

Bus

Below is a guide to the fares and times to the major towns of South Sulawesi from Ujung Pandang:

Palopo	$4	8 hours
Polmas	$3	5 hours
Mamuju	$5	10 hours
Malili	$6	12 hours
Bone	$2	4 hours
Soppeng	$2	4 hours
Singkang	$3	5 hours

Companies in Ujung Pandang (to Tana Toraja):

Litha, Jl. Gunung Merapi 160
Liman Express, Jl. Laiya 25
Usaha Baru, Jl Lembe 28
Flora, Jl. Cendrawasih 218
Damri, Jl. Gunung Latimojong 21

Air

Merpati operates an extensive air network around Sulawesi and neighboring islands. Daily flights connect Ujung Pandang with Rantepao, Palu, Manado, Kendari and Rantepao. There are no flights to Buton in Southeast Sulawesi; service was cancelled owing to a lack of passengers.

Departure and arrival times given below were correct in July 1990.

U.P. to Rantepao: dep. 09:00 arr. 09:55.
U.P. to Palu: dep 12:30 arr. 13:40.
U.P. to Manado: dep. 09:20 arr. 10:55.
U.P. to Kendari: dep. 09:10 arr. 10:00.

From Palu there are flights to Tolitoli (daily) and Buol (Sat); to Poso (Sun, Mon, Thur), Luwuk (daily) and Kendari (Sun Tues, Fri, Sat). **Garuda** also flies to Manado daily (dep. 09:20 arr. 10:55).

Internal schedules are liable to change frequently, and you should check at Merpati's offices in Ujung Pandang. **Bouraq** also operates an extensive service, though finding a Bouraq office can be a problem outside Ujung Pandang.

ACCOMMODATION

There are two international-standard hotels in Ujung Pandang, and several good intermediate hotels. Rantepao has two international hotels (Makale has one) and a wealth of clean and attractive intermediate accommodation.

Outside of Ujung Pandang and the Makale-Rantepao area, accommodation is basic, although most towns have at least one passable hotel. But don't let this put you off traveling outside of the usual tourist areas, as many of the smaller hotels and *losmen* (the name comes from the French *logement*) are family–run and very pleasant. Many hotels, even in the smaller towns, are air–conditioned. Check the "Practicalities" section for each of the areas before deciding.

CURRENCY

Indonesia's currency, the rupiah, is remarkably stable against the US dollar, barring the occasional, and often drastic, devaluation. There are coins of Rp5, 10, 25, 50 and 100, and bills of 100, 500, 1000, 5000 and 10.000. The exchange rate as of August 1990 was about Rp1850 to US$1.

Change is often difficult to come by, even in government offices, and it is worth asking for small bills when changing your money. (Be prepared to carry large wads of money around if you do.) Exchange currencies only at leading hotels and banks, or with authorized money changers. Credit cards are accepted by many hotels, shops and restaurants in Ujung Pandang and Manado, but travelers' cheques are usually difficult to cash in out-of-the-way places.

Tax and service charges of 21% are charged in the larger hotels and tourist establishments.

Tipping is not a general practice in Sulawesi. In the larger hotels a service charge is already included; in the smaller restaurants tips are not expected. However, if the service has been good, a token sum (Rp500-1000) would be appreciated. At the airport, porters expect Rp500-1000 per bag (depending on the size). Tour guides expect about a $3 tip per person per day.

COMMUNICATION

Indonesian (*Bahasa Indonesia*, a modern dialect of Malay) is the official language of the republic, though local languages are spoken at home and at informal gatherings. Familiarity with a few common phrases, like 'thank you' (*terima kasih*) guarantees you contact with Sulawesi's prime attraction—its people.

English and Dutch are spoken in the cities (the latter mostly by older people). A good language book is *Practical Indonesian* by John Barker; another is *Speak Indonesian* by Sylvia Tiwon.

HEALTH

Proof of smallpox and cholera vaccinations is no longer required, only valid yellow fever vaccinations when you come from infected areas. Typhoid and para-typhoid shots are recommended. Remember to avoid drinking unboiled water and using ice in your drinks, or eating fruit that has been cut in wayside stalls. Bottled water (Aqua, and the unfortunately–named Ades) is readily available but be sure that the seal is intact. Try not even to brush your teeth with unboiled water.

There is a slight risk of malaria in the South (especially on the south coast) and the Southeast. Fortunately, the parasite is still sensitive to chloroquine–based drugs such as Maloprim. Visitors are recommended to use one of these drugs as a prophylactic—your doctor will write a prescription. The drugs have to be taken for one week before arrival and continued for six weeks after departure.

The best defense is not to get bitten. Use mosquito coils, those green, twisted spirals of incense that are so hard to separate and were recently banned in the States. Light one before sleeping—they work for about 8 hours. A mosquito net offers the best protection and can be bought cheaply in Singapore, Jakarta or Ujung Pandang.

Do bring a small, basic medical-kit with bandages, antiseptic cream, scissors and water tablets (and any other tablets) especially if you are thinking of trekking. In this climate a mosquito bite can become a major infection. Any cut or abrasion must be treated immediately with iodine and a protective bandage. Bactrian is an excellent broadspectrum antiseptic ointment available at any drugstore (*apotik*). Tiger Balm and other camphorated salves relieve itching.

Diarrhea is a frequent problem. Most cases are due to a combination of climate, fatigue, food, and culture shock. Treat with Lomotil, which is available over the counter in *apotiks*. DO NOT GIVE LOMOTIL TO CHILDREN UNDER 16–it can be fatal, though it is remarkably safe for adults. Drink plenty of water or tea with a bit of sugar and salt, or rehydration tablets, such as Servidrat. Stick to dry biscuits and bananas (high in potassium) until it has cleared up. Go easy on the antibiotics: chloramphenicol—a cheap and potentially dangerous treatment for typhoid—is widely used in Indonesia and should be avoided at all cost. For constipation, eat a lot of fruit.

In the event of an emergency, call your consulate or a leading hotel for the name of a good doctor. Each large village in Sulawesi ha a government clinic called Pukesmas, but few have medical supplies, such as bandages or penicillin. Any serious illness is best treated in Ujung Pandang or in your home country. For a list of recommended hospitals and doctors, see "Ujung Pandang Practicalities." In case of life-threatening emergency, your best bet is to try to get to Singapore. Your embassy in Jakarta may help arrange this.

CLIMATE

The Indonesian climate is composed of two elements: a bright, intermittently burning sun and high humidity. Average temperature is between 25° and 30° C, or the mid-80s F. The dry season extends from April to October and is the best time to visit Sulawesi. Lightweight, loose clothes are both comfortable and sufficiently formal in the country's tropical setting.

Caution is required when sunbathing, especially if you have recently arrived. Always use a good sunscreen and start slowly; even on a cloudy day the ultraviolet is strong enough to burn unprotected skin. Sudden downpours should be expected the year round (especially from November to May). A collapsable umbrella should provide ample protection against afternoon showers. Warm clothing, such as a light sweater, is a must in the mountains and for rainy nights.

TOUR AND TRAVEL AGENTS

There are many tour and travel agents in Ujung Pandang, catering both to domestic and international visitors. The largest of these is **Pacto** (Jl. Jend. Sudirman 56, Ujujng Pandang, Tel. 83208), an Indonesia-wide agency. Unfortunately, the Ujung Pandang branch has a reputation for inefficiency, a reputation confirmed by the present writer, who was told by the manager that he was "too busy dealing with complaints" to provide any information on Pacto's tours in Sulawesi.

An up-and-coming agency is **P.T. Ceria Nugraha**, owned by a well-educated and helpful Torajan aristocrat. This agency offers a wide range of tours within Sulawesi as well as to other parts of Indonesia. The staff is pleasant and efficient. One of their tour leaders and consultants is Dr. Darmawan Masud, a well-regarded local scholar who has studied in the United States and speaks excellent English.

Reputable agents

Ceria Nugraha, Jl. Usman Jafar 9, Ujung Pandang. Tel: (0411) 22482, 311846, 311847, Fax: (0411) 311848. Conveniently located behind Marannu Hotel in the center of town.

Indonesia Safari, Jl. Somba Opu 111, Ujung Pandang. Tel: (0411) 21757, 28757. Cable: INSANTRA UPG Telex: 71172–INSANTRA UPG

Irama Suka, Jl. Amanagappa 3, Ujung Pandang. Tel: (0411) 6643, 71503 Cable: IRAMA SUKA

Limbunan, Jl. Gunung Bawakaraeng 16 (P.O. Box 97), Ujung Pandang. Tel: (0411) 21710, 5010 Cable: LIMCO Telex: 71185–LIMTOUUP

Matapa, Jl. Patimura 38, Ujung Pandang. Tel: (0411) 3932, 3993

Makmur Travel Service, Jl. Bau Massepe. Parepare. Tel: (Parepare) 21991, 21071

Maktour, Jl. Kakatua 38, Ujung Pandang. Tel: (0411) 84678 Cable: MARAYATOUR

Nitour, Jl. Lamadukelleng 2, Ujung Pandang. Tel: (0411) 5082, 7723 Cable: NITOUR UJUNGPAN-DANG. One of Indonesia's oldest and most experienced travel companies.

Pantravel, Airport Building, Soroako. Tel: (Soroako) 28545 Ext. 119. If you are ever stuck in this small nickel-mining town and need a ticket out, try here.

Pantravel, Jl. Somba Opu 223, Ujung Pandang. Tel: (0411) 3272, 22864. They might be worth trying if you want to arrange a flight from Soroako to Kendari or back to Ujung Pandang.

Ramayana Internasional, Jl Bawakaraeng 121 (P.O.Box 107), Ujung Pandang. Tel: (0411) 22165 Cable: RAINT.

Tunas Indonesia, Jl. Nusantara 41, Ujung Pandang. Tel: (0411) 84181. Cable: TUNAS UPG.

ETIQUETTE

Personal conduct is largely a matter of sensibility to another's feelings and "face," that subtle but important quality of personal dignity in Asian countries. The ideal demeanor is friendly and open, ever ready to answer questions: where one is going, how much one's purchases cost, how long one has been in Indonesia, how rich one is (all foreigners are rich by Indonesian standards) and dozens of other questions which in Western society are considered personal matters. Few of us are likely to be able to maintain an open and friendly personality for long, especially when the sun is high, the bus is two hours overdue, and you have just answered the same question for the fifteenth time that morning. In short, the local people's ebullient enthusiasm, curiosity and eagerness to speak English often antagonizes visitors.

In return, the local people often find Westerners "standoffish" and cold. Different attitudes towards privacy may also cause misunderstandings. Indonesians show intense interest in books, writing or photographs which the Westerner considers "private property." Concepts of ownership, privacy and individualism are very different for the rural Indonesian, who is accustomed to living and sharing with a community.

The tourist who wishes to travel independently will have a happier and more successful stay if he keeps as calm, cheerful and friendly as humanly possible. Everything takes a bit longer here. Patience and courtesy are virtues that open many doors. Dressing right has definite advantages, both for men and women. Shorts (with the exception of elegantly cut long shorts) are best kept for sitting around in at your hotel. Skirts and loose trousers for women, and trousers (not sarongs) for men, are the correct dress for adults. Foreigners, especially young ones, are often the worst-dressed people in Sulawesi, and Indonesians judge by appearances.

Handshaking is customary, both on introduction and greeting, for both sexes. In rural areas, women will sometimes cover their hand with a cloth according to Islamic custom when offering it to a man. The use of the left hand to give or receive is taboo, and crooking your finger to call somebody is considered extremely impolite. In a crowd that gathers, an appeal to a responsible older member will usually win his protection and ensure a hospitable welcome. Similarly, with officials, a patient, pleasant manner will achieve more than an angry outburst.

PRICES

Prices quoted in this book are in US dollars and were noted in April 1990. The reason for this is that the Indonesian Rupiah is being allowed to slowly devalue, and prices stated in US dollars are more likely to remain accurate.

PHOTOGRAPHY

Never to take new equipment on a trip. Bring plenty of film—at least twice as much as you think you'll need. 35 mm color negative film is usually available in the bigger towns but the stock may be old and the color balance ruined by heat and humidity. Slide film and black-and-white film are difficult to get.

Most professionals use Kodachrome. Its slowish speed is compensated for by its stability (it is essentially a black-and-white film to which color dyes are added during processing) and its natural color balance. Fujichrome 100's faster speed gives you a useful edge in low lighting and is simpler to process (Kodachrome has to be sent away to a Kodak Lab) but its colors are a little warm.

Don't load yourself down with equipment. Handled properly, it is possible to shoot an entire article for *National Geographic* with just two lenses: a wide-angle for scenics (24-35 mm) and a zoom for details and flattering portraits (85-105 mm). A flash is useful for photographing inside caves. Carry your camera with you everywhere: most pictures are lost by simply not having it handy.

Slow film is generally safe from airport X-ray machines, but in general its better have the airport official hand-check the film. Keep it in a separate bag ready for inspection. Resist the urge to

port official hand-check the film. Keep it in a separate bag ready for inspection. Resist the urge to have film developed in Indonesia. Bad processing has ruined more film than X-ray machines

Heat and humidity are a problem in Indonesia. Try to keep your camera and film out of direct sunlight and use film as quickly as possible. If you are staying any length of time, equipment can be stored in a plastic supermarket bag with an opened jar of Silica Jel.

Indonesians generally enjoy being photographed, and will even ask you to take their picture, but if you are in any doubt it is polite to ask. Cockfighting (now officially banned) and eating (a private activity) are sensitive subjects.

TRAVELING WITH CHILDREN

Luckily for those with children, Indonesians of all ethnic groups love to have children around and are very gentle. But you should organize beforehand: sunhats, creams, medicines, disposable diapers if needed, special foods and a separate water container for babies, so as to be sure of having sterile water always. Nights can be cool, so remember to bring some warm clothing for your tot. Fresh or UHT milk, eggs, fruit which you can peel and porridges are available in the supermarkets in Ujung Pandang and other large towns. Babysitters are available for a moderate charge in good hotels. See local "Practicalities" sections for specific practitioners and clinics.

LOSING YOUR PASSPORT

Always keep a photocopy of your passport and driver's license separate from the originals. This way you can prove who you are to your consul in Ujung Pandang or Jakarta in case of theft or loss. When theft occurs, you have to report to the police, who will furnish a report for your consulate. Verification of your identity and citizenship takes two or three weeks and involves going to the immigration office in Ujung Pandang.

DRUGS

All narcotics are illegal in Indonesia. The use, sale or purchase of narcotics results in long prison terms and/or huge fines. Best advice is: Don't. Laws in Indonesia are extremely strict and apply to all foreigners as well as to Indonesians. Once caught, you are placed in detention, sometimes for months, until trial. Sentences are very stiff.

TOURIST SEASON

The best time to visit Sulawesi is during the dry and cooler season which usually runs from April to October. Thousands of Europeans, mostly French and Germans, visit Sulawesi in July, August and September (the peak month is August). During these months, book well in advance to ensure cheap flights and good accommodation. Tana Toraja especially is very popular these days.

BUSINESSS HOURS

Government offices open at 8:00 every day except Sunday. Monday to Thursday they are open to around 15:00, Fridays to 11:30 and Saturdays to 13:00. Shops in Ujung Pandang and other towns close in the afternoon for a siesta (usually 13:00 to 18:00) and re-open for business in the evening until 21:00. In the tourist areas, they generally stay open through the afternoon. Banks are open from 8:00 to 12:00, Monday to Friday, and 8:00 to 11:00 on Saturdays.

TIME

Sulawesi is on Central Indonesian Time, the same as Singapore, 6 hours ahead of GMT and 4 hours behind Australian Eastern Standard Time. This means that when it is 12:00 in London, 20:00 in Sydney, 7:00 in New York and 4:00 in Los Angeles, it is 18:00 in Sulawesi.

TRAVEL INSURANCE

Look over your health insurance policy before you take off. It is very important to be able to cover the cost of emergency air transport back home or to Singapore. Emergency medical facilities are available only in major cities, and these are not very good. For information on facilities in Ujung Pandang, see "Ujung Pandang Practicalities."

LEAVING SULAWESI

Always reconfirm your flight 1 to 3 days in advance of departure, or your reservation may be automatically cancelled. Garuda is notorious for this, as they are routinely overbooked. This is especially true during peak tourist seasons. Trying to get a flight out at these times can be something of a nightmare. Keep some spare cash in case your ticket doesn't include airport departure tax: Rp2,000 on domestic flights and Rp9,000 on international flights.

Airline offices - Ujung Pandang

Bouraq, Jl. Veteran Selatan 1.Tel: 83039, 851906
Garuda, Jl. Slamat Riyadi 6. Tel: 315405, 315719
Merpati, Jl. Bawakaraeng 109. Tel: 24114, 24155

MISCELLANEOUS

Shipping goods home can be a bit of a problem. ETH International (pronounced Eh–Tay–Hah) on Jl. Baumasseppe 5, will airfreight goods door to door to the USA for $17 a kilo (6–45 kg); to Sydney airport $6 and to Amsterdam $11. P.T Jakarta Lloyd (whose manager speaks fluent English) on Jl. Sawerigading 16A, can ship a container to Europe or the States for about $1,300. If you don't need 26 cubic meters, it may be possible to ship smaller amounts to Europe for $180 per cubic meter.

A final tip: if you do not enjoy the raucous Indonesian (or Western) pop music which usually blares from the sound system on bus trips, why not bring your own classical cassettes? Indonesians are far too polite to tell you how awful Mahler or Stravinski sound, and will soon turn the cassette player off!

Further Readings

A number of books and monographs on Sulawesi's history and culture have appeared in recent years:

Andaya, Leonard Y. *The Heritage of Arung Palakka: A History of South Sulawesi (Celebes) in the Seventeenth Century*. Martinus Nijhoff, The Hague, 1981.
A dull but solidly researched study of the 17th-century Bugis warlord who allied himself with Admiral Speelman to overthrow the Makassarese kingdom of Gowa.

Errington, Shelly. *Meaning and Power in a Southeast Asian Realm*. Princeton University Press, 1989.
A rather speculative reconstruction of state and society in pre-colonial Luwu.

Hamonic, Gilbert. *Le Langage des Dieux; Cultes et Pouvoirs pré-Islamiques en Pays Bugis Célèbes-sud, Indonésie*. Paris, CNRS, 1987.
A study of the *bissu* transvestite ritual priests of South Sulawesi and their sacred texts.

Horridge, Adrian G. *The Konjo Boat Builders and the Bugis prahus of South Sulawesi*. London, National Maritime Museum, 1979.
Detailed, well-illustrated account of the construction and launching of a Konjo *prahu*, describing the various types of Bugis *prahus*. A simpler and very readable account of Bugis ships is found in the same author's book *The Prahu: Traditional Sailing Boat of Indonesia*. Singapore, OUP, 1985.

Koubi, Jeannine. *Rambu Solo': "La Fumée Descend"—le Culte des Morts chez les Toradja du Sud*. Paris, CNRS, 1982.
An outstanding study of Torajan death rituals.

Macknight, C.C. *The Voyage to Marege*. Melbourne, Melbourne University Press, 1976.
An informative, readable account of the Makassar traders who sailed to the north coast of Australia to collect trepang (sea cucumber) for the Chinese market—bringing with them smallpox.

Millar, Susan B. *Bugis Weddings; Rituals of Social Location in Modern Indonesia*. Berkeley, Center for South and Southeast Asian Studies, University of California, 1989.
The best study of the Bugis yet published. To know what makes Bugis society tick, read this one.

Nooy-Palm, C.H.M. *The Sa'dan Toraja; A Study of Their Social Life and Religion*. 2 vols., Dordrecht, Foris Publications, 1979, 1986.
The standard work on the subject in English.

Robinson, Kathryn M. *Stepchildren of Progress: The Political Economy of Development in an Indonesian Mining Town*. Albany, State University of New York Press, 1986.
On the impact of PT Inco's nickel mine on the village of Soroako, Luwu.

Volkman, Toby Alice. *Feasts of Honor; Ritual and Change in the Toraja Highlands*. Urbana; University of Illinois Press, 1985.
Based on the author's PhD thesis, which has the intriguing title *The Pig Has Eaten the Vegetables*. A good introduction to modern Torajan society and its rituals.

Waterson, Roxana. *The Living House: An Anthropology of Architecture in Southeast Asia*. Singapore, OUP, 1990.
A fascinating and beautifully illustrated study with many examples from Tana Toraja.

Whitten, Anthony J., Muslimin Mustafa, Gregory S. Henderson. *The Ecology of Sulawesi*. Yogyakarta Gajah Madah University Press, 1988. (P.O.Box 14, Bulaksumur, Yogyakarta, Indonesia).
A magnificent 777-page study of the flora and fauna of Sulawesi. Copiously illustrated with drawings and color plates. Written in a clear, straightforward style.

Some of the best reading on Sulawesi is to be found in older travel accounts. Many have been reprinted in recent years:

Beekman, E.M. *The Poison Tree; Selected Writings of Rumphius on the Natural History of the Indies*. Amherst, University of Massachusetts Press, 1981.
"U for the Upas tree, which casts a blight/On those who pull their sisters' hair, and fight." Belloc's legendary Upas tree—the source of a valuable poison—was vividly described by the blind 17th-century Dutch naturalist Rumphius, who located it in Tana Toraja. "The tree grows there on bald mountains. The soil beneath it is barren and singed. The only thing that lives under it is a horned snake that cackles like a hen and by night has fiery eyes." By the early 19th century the tree had become a grotesque vision in the European mind. The valley in which the tree stood was dreary and desolate, and suffused with a sickening and suffocating smell. Criminals sentenced to death were given one alternative—to go to the land of Upas and collect its deadly poison.

Blok, R. *History of the island of Celebes*. Calcutta, 1817.
Written in Dutch in 1759, Blok's history is a valuable source of information on 15th- and 16th-century South Sulawesi. His sources included Bugis and Makassarese histories, Speelman's unpublished writings, and later Dutch records.

Gervaise, Nicolas. *An Historical Description of the Kingdom of Makasar*. London, 1701.
Recently republished in facsimile, this is an absorbing and entertaining account of the customs and manners of 17th-century Makasar: "They pick out two Cocks, the ftrongeft and the moft coragious they can find, and after they have half fuddl'd 'em with Rice-Wine, they tye to the places where the Spurrs grow, little pieces of Iron, flender and very fharp pointed, and then setting 'em down together, provoke 'em to fight. This is a great Diverfion for 'em, to fee with what fury thofe Creatures tear and mangle one another.".

Holt, Claire. *Dance quest in Celebes*. Paris; Archives Internationales de la Danse, 1939.
Standard work on the subject, recently reprinted.

Kaudern, Walter. *Megalithic Finds in Central Celebes*. Göteborg, Elanders Boktryckeri Aktiebolag, 1938.
The standard work in English on the megalithic culture of Central Sulawesi by a Swiss scientist who visited the region in 1918-19. Illustrated with drawings, maps and photographs.

Mundy, R. *Narrative of Events in Borneo and Celebes Down to the Occupation of Labuan. From the Journals of James Brooke, Esq. Rajah of Sarawak*. London, 1848.
Before becoming Raja of Sarawak, Brooke visited South Sulawesi, where he climbed Lompobatang, was received by the ruler of Bone, and searched "in high spirits, but doubtful expectation" for the lost kingdom of Mampu.

Sarasin, P. and F. *Reisen in Celebes, Ausgefuhrt in den Jahren 1893-96 und 1902-03*. Wiesbaden, 2 vols., 1905.
The Swiss cousins Sarasin traveled extensively throughout Sulawesi studying and photographing its people, artefacts and flora and fauna.

Stavorinus, Jan Splinter. *Voyages to the East*. Indies 2 vols., London; 1798, facsimile reprint 1969.

Wallace, Alfred Russel. *The Malay Archipelago*. London, 1869; reprint New York 1962.
A 19th-century classic; one of the greatest books written on Indonesia.

Westerling, Raymond 'Turk'. *Challenge to Terror*. London, Kimber, 1952.
The notorious Captain Westerling's account of his suppression of 'terrorists' during the Indonesian revolution. "I was only six when I began to attack detective stories, preferably bloody. At seven I was already a good shot. By the age of eight I began to really worry my mother, my father and my older sister."

Wilcox, Harry. *White Stranger: Six Moons in Celebes*. London, Collins, 1949.

Toraja before the tourists: "Like millions of others I wanted to escape for a while from the post-war world and the twentieth century; unlike those others, I did escape." Recently reprinted in paperback by OUP, Singapore.

Woodard, D. *The narrative of Captain David Woodard and four seamen, who lost their ship while in a boat at sea, and surrendered themselves up to the Malays in the island of Celebes*. London, 1805 (2nd edition), facsimile reprint 1969.
Captain Woodard spent over two years in captivity in Palu ("a fine town, containing perhaps five hundred houses at the head of a bay") and Donggala, its rival, which was surrounded by a wooden fence. Donggala's refusal to surrender Woodard led to war: "The engagement took place between the two tribes; there were about two hundred men on each side. The people from Parlow killed eight of the men of Dungally, and wounded a number of others. They immediately cut the heads off those who were killed."

Most writings on Sulawesi are in the form of journals and papers. The French journal *Archipel* often publishes articles about Sulawesi in French and English. Number 10 (1975) is a special issue devoted to South Sulawesi, with more than a dozen articles by well-known scholars on subjects ranging from architecture to transvestite priests. Below is a short list of interesting articles:

Andi Zainal Abidin. *The I La Galigo Epic Cycle of South Celebes and its Diffusion*. Indonesia, 17, 1974.

Crystal, Eric. *Mountain Ikats and coastal silks; Traditional textiles in South Sulawesi*. Fischer, J. (ed.) *Threads of tradition: Textiles of Indonesia and Sarawak*. Berkeley, Lowie Museum of Anthropology, 1979.

Errington, Shelly. *The Cosmic House of the Buginese*. Asia, 1(5), 1979.

Macknight, C.C. *The Rise of Agriculture in South Sulawesi Before 1600*. Review of Malaysian and Indonesian Affairs, 17, 1983.

Reid, Anthony, *The Rise of Makasar*. Review of Malaysian and Indonesian Affairs, 17, 1983

Volkman, Toby Alice. *The Arts of Dying in Sulawesi*. Asia, 2(2), 1979.

Welsch, Robert. *Traditional Silk Sarongs of Mandar, South Sulawesi*. Indonesia. Field Museum of Natural History Bulletin 59(4), 1988.

Zerner, Charles. *Silk from Southern Sulawesi*. Orientations, 13(2), 1982.

About the Authors

Greg Acciaioli is a Lecturer at the University of Western Australia. He has spent over three years in Indonesia, and has written on ritual change in Central Sulawesi, stressing the effect of national culture on indigenous ceremonies.

Kathleen M. Adams is an Assistant Professor of Anthropology at Beloit College in Wisconsin and a Research Associate in Asian Ethnology at the Logan Museum of Anthropology. She spent two years in Sulawesi conducting research on ethnic and artistic change in Tana Toraja.

Sheridan Angerilli spent two years exploring Manado and the surrounding area. She now lives in Jakarta.

Lorraine Aragon is a doctoral candidate in anthropology at the University of Illinois. Her dissertation concerns cosmology and social change in Christian regions of highland Central Sulawesi. She is currently working at the Smithsonian Museum of Natural History, preparing an exhibit and catalog entitled "Beyond the Java Sea: Art of Indonesia's Outer Islands."

Tim Babcock is an anthropologist and author of the book *Religion and Culture in Kampung Jawa Tondano*. He has worked on regional development projects in Sulawesi, and has also worked in Malaysia, Sumatra, and Peru. He lives in Jakarta and is a faculty member of the School of Rural Planning, University of Guelph, Canada.

Peter Bellwood is a Reader in Prehistory at the Australian National University, specializing in Southeast Asian and Pacific prehistory. His books include *Man's Conquest of the Pacific*, *Prehistory of the Indo-Malaysian Archipelago* and *The Polynesians*.

Dinah Bergink, a cultural anthropologist (Free University of Amsterdam), is a researcher at the Faculty of Social Science, University of Leiden, and works for Pelita Foundation, an organization supporting Dutch Indies victims of World War II.

Ian Caldwell was educated in London at the School of Oriental and African Studies, and holds a doctorate from Australian National University. He is a lecturer at the Singapore National University.

Nancy Caldwell was born in India and grew up in Singapore. She has traveled widely in Asia and Europe and worked as a freelance writer and editor. She has a degree in modern and primitive Indonesian art.

René W.R.J. Dekker is an ornithologist who worked for a year and a half in the Dumoga-Bone National Park in North Sulawesi, on the conservation of the maleo, Sulawesi's endemic megapode. He is currently employed as a biologist, specializing in megapode biology and conservation at the Institute of Taxonomic Zoology of the University of Amsterdam.

Horst Liebner conducted research among the Ara boatbuilders and sailors of South Sulawesi from 1987 to 1989. As part of his research he and a crew from Ara circumnavigated Sulawesi on a two-masted, five-sailed *prahu*.

Kal Muller is a veteran photographer whose travels have taken him to over 80 countries. For the last 16 years he has explored, photographed and reported on the Indonesian archipelago. He has a PhD in French literature, and has authored several travel guides on some of Indonesia's more remote areas.

Anthony Reid Tony Reid is a professor of Southeast Asian history at the Australian National University in Canberra. He has published numerous articles on the history of South Sulawesi. His most recent book is *Southeast Asia in the Age of Commerce, 1450-1680: The Lands Below the Winds*.

Mary Thorne, a town planner, worked in Manado in 1988-90 as a senior planner in the provincial government, and has toured North Sulawesi extensively. She now works in Glasgow, Scotland.

Roger Tol is a lecturer at the State University of Leiden, where he received a doctorate for his work on Bugis-language texts. He is presently working in Jakarta at the National Language Center for the Indonesian Linguistics Development Project.

Toby Alice Volkman, an anthropologist, is the author of *Feasts of Honor: Ritual and Change in the Toraja Highlands*, as well as several articles on Toraja cultural identity, social and religious change, and tourism. She is a staff associate at the Social Science Research Council in New York.

Roxana Waterson studied anthropology at Cambridge University, and wrote her thesis on the Sa'dan Toraja people. She is the author of *The Living House: An Anthropology of Architecture in South-East Asia*, and presently lectures in anthropology at the Department of Sociology, National University of Singapore.

Tony Whitten is an ecologist who has lived in Indonesia for nearly nine years, working with the State Ministry for Population and Environment. He is the author of *The Ecology of Sulawesi* in English and Indonesian language editions.

Charles Zerner, a lawyer and environmental consultant, conducted research in 1989 in Mandar, on fishing and conceptions of the marine environment. He has also researched tourism in Tana Toraja, and has published articles on Toraja iron forging, oratory, agrarian ritual, ephemeral architecture, and Bugis silk.

Index

Bold numerals indicate the beginning of an article on the subject. Cursive numerals indicate an illustration.

Notes

Following pages: A fisherman throws his net against the background of a spectacular sunset.